I0641512

# At Home and Abroad: Prize-Winning Stories

2007 Joyous Publishing Writing Contests

Joyous Publishing
Columbia, Maryland, USA

Copyright 2007 by Joyous Publishing
Columbia, Maryland, USA
www.joyouspub.com

ISBN: 978-0-9722740-9-8

Cover design by Jenna Pempek

Edited by Barbara J. Olexer

# TABLE OF CONTENTS

## FOREWORD

This anthology contains the best of the stories, memoirs, and essays that were submitted to the Joyous Publishing quarterly writing contests from December 2006 through June 2007. It was no easy task to select the top two entries each quarter. Our judges try very hard to keep their personal preferences out of the process and, on the whole, succeed quite well. A couple of the stories would not have been selected if the judges' taste were the deciding factor but the quality of the writing earned them a place in the book. Other stories were so appealing that inclusion was almost automatic.

Overall, we have been pleasantly surprised at the high quality of the pieces entered in our contests. Some betray the uncertainties of beginning writers but most appear to flow from the keyboards of confident writers who know they have a good story to tell. Some of these writers are seasoned professionals, some write mostly for their own satisfaction, some are hopeful beginners. One thing is certain, we'll hear more from some of these writers as their careers unfold.

Enter within, then, and allow these writers to take you places you've never been to consort with some very interesting characters.

# CLAWING AT THUNDER

**Frederic Rohner**

*Frederic Rohner is a recent graduate of St. Mary's College of Maryland with a Bachelor's Degree in English. He is originally from Silver Spring but recently moved to Boonsboro. He works full time at Vegas Radio WTRI 1520 AM in Brunswick, Maryland.*

The other night a magnificent storm rolled through our little southern Maryland town and brought with it outstanding violence—a barrage of quarter-sized raindrops, lightning bolts that traveled from the clouds and stabbed themselves into the earth, thunder that shook the walls of the house and made the ground tremble beneath our feet. Truly a fantastic storm to have the good fortune of being able to sit and watch.

I think my tomcat Calypso would partially disagree with me on that last point, though. He is a year and a half old and although I was sure he'd seen a thunderstorm before, he was terrified and spent much of the night beneath the bed, where it was safe. As afraid as he was, Calypso couldn't help being mesmerized over and over again by the lightning. He would sit on the window sill watching the flashes, only to be sent running for cover when the subsequent rumbles of thunder struck.

And strike the thunder did, with a ferocity that reminded me of a thunderstorm I camped through in the Rockies (where thunderstorms are less frequent but, from my experience, more intense). From the loud, brief claps to the wobbly extended rumbles that sounded like a ten-year-old shaking a saw around to the low, long roars that sounded like freight trains careening recklessly through the sky—there were even mixes and combinations—thunder that began with a loud clap as if the sky were being torn apart and then dissolved into a growl that went on for seconds and shook the floor and walls (these were the ones which Calypso hated most).

Little else excites the senses like a fierce spring thunderstorm—the smell of the wet soil mixed with the blooming flowers, the sight of lightning flashes and bolts that strike the ground we stand on, the taste of drops of rain on the tongue and lips, the soothing pitter patter of small raindrops tapping the rooftops or the alarming noise of large ones sounding as if they will smash through the ceiling at any moment, the vibrations of the thunder making the very air around us throb. It's extraordinary what the right mixture of moisture and static electricity as well as the collision of hot and cold air are capable of creating.

Again and again, Calypso would find himself drawn as I was to watch the power of the storm. Bravely, calmly, coolly he would climb back to the window sill, determined, just like he was fixing broken levees or reconstructing oceanfront resorts. He even tried to fight the thunder at one point, clawing at the windows until realizing the fruitlessness of his labors. It didn't take him long at all to realize that nature cannot be beaten with claws or teeth—*or* manpower or intelligence. Nature is just too powerful, but I did admire the little guy for doing anything in his power to fight the violent presence. Calypso has always been tough; he's not the type of cat to back down from anything. But he backed down from this.

As the storm passed and the thunder rolled off slowly into the distance, Calypso began nipping and clawing at my feet as I tried to sleep. I think he was eager to show how tough he was, eager to show that he wasn't really afraid of a little thunderstorm.

Strange isn't it, how I, how all of us see human emotions in our animal friends, fear and pride and humiliation? But these are our emotions, our faults and our shortcomings. Calypso had no idea what was going on when the thunderstorm struck; all he knew for sure was that it was loud. I understand what a thunderstorm is because I learned it in school, just like I learned the difference between a cat and a dog, or an animal and a human. Humanity is the top of the food chain, separated from all other creatures by our reason and our societies. We are unnatural. We've made ourselves unnatural through our intelligence, our logic, and our hubris. Ever since humanity discovered fire, tools and shelter we have set about distancing ourselves as far as possible from our natural surroundings. We try to keep the outside world from invading our homes when the reality is that the outside world *is* our home.

We put cities where they don't belong. We cause problems for ourselves and then revel in our ability to solve those problems. A city below sea level? No problem; we'll just build dikes and levees to keep the water out, and should the water pour over the levees, should the dikes collapse, we'll come in with water pumps and make the city livable again—even if it takes years—because we're the most intelligent beings on the planet. That's why we choose to live in areas where hurricanes, mudslides, and wildfires are annual threats. A category five hurricane has enough power to send a two by four through the trunk of a tree and yet year after year there is video of people up and down the mid-Atlantic coast in North Carolina or Florida or Georgia or Virginia covering their windows and doors with quarter inch plywood in preparation for the arrival of the latest hurricane. We're drawn by nature's beauty to volatile, dangerous places and then we spend our time clawing at our chosen environment when it scares us.

There is a reason Calypso gave up clawing at the thunder, there is a reason we claw at hurricanes every summer in Florida, at mudslides and wildfires out west. We think we know better, we think we can solve any problem set in front of us. Failure is not an option, we can't be quitters. But there is a difference between tenacity and stubbornness. We can't "beat" nature, and why would we want to? How can we keep fighting against the very places we live? Our animal friends are better than we are because they realize the futility of trying to contend with and fight the land around them. Calypso realized so quickly that he couldn't fight this awesome power that confronted him, he gave up clawing at the thunder, he never rebuilt his levee bigger and stronger than it had been before, he never put the pieces of his destroyed oceanfront resort back together again, he just found a safe place to ride out the storm and watch the lightning bolts, a safe place to hide from the thunder until the storm passed.

I think Calypso knows more than I do, more than any of us. He didn't surrender to nature, he realized the power against him, he realized there was nothing he could do but wait out the storm. He stopped clawing at the thunder, and instead he just sat and watched—maybe we all should follow his example and just stop clawing and start watching—from a distance.

# HELLENISTIC ZEITGEIST: 335-146 BCE

## Conrad Jalowski

*Conrad Jalowski is a sixteen-year-old student of Hellenic Studies with a voracious thirst for Macedonian history from 335-146 B.C. He has written multifarious conjectural emendations on the tragedy of autarchies – from apotheosis to its nadir. At its apogee, eudemonia is achieved, yet through hubris it is followed by anagnorisis.*

How is it verisimilitude that leviathanesque, brobdingnagian, antediluvic behemoths were not sempiternal but a vicissitude of the nugacious, feliginous and fugacious; from protopalatial to neopalatial in which the pugnacious and invidious ecumene ascended to its plenipotentiary, apogee and apotheosis of scintillating hubris to a valetudinarian of the multitudinous and multifarious pusillanimous. From Alexander III's demise to the failed rebellion of Diaeus, Critolaus, Damocritus and Andriscus to the tetrarchotomous of Macedonian symmachias of Pella, Pelagonia, Thessalonica and Amphipolis from 149-148 BCE and Aristonicus of Pergamus from 133-130 BCE; of the Diadochoi/Epigonoi from 322-320, 319-315, 314-311 and 308-281 BCE of Paraitacene, Gabiene ,Gaza, Salamis, Rhodes, Ipsus and Corupedium. This somniferous dissertation will be circumforaneous and phantasmagorical. From Alexander III's death on 323 BCE, a ditrichotomous agglomeration of autarchies and stratocracies were castrametated: the Antigonid: 323-146 BCE being eponymous of Antigonus I 'Monopthalmus' with the propitious debellation and pessundation of the Grecians led by Demosthenes and Hyperides at Crannon on 322 BCE of the opprobrium of the Grecian lucripetous and concupiscible of apocolocyntosis and ultramontane at such a velitation and obstrigillation. Pyrrhus of the Epirotic stratocracy through his usual prestidigitations, subjected the Grecian ecumene under his hegemony and suzerainty of Illyria, Tymphaea, Ambracia, Amphilochia, Acarnania and Paravaea from 306-302 BCE and 297-272 BCE. He next exeunted in the Pyrrhic peregrinations from 280-275 BCE in Heraclea: 280 BCE, Ausculum: 279 BCE,

Lilybaeum: 278 BCE and Beneventum: 275 BCE, and though he surreptitiously absquatulated from Italy, he spread Hellenistic cultural syncretism and synoecism throughout Italy as seen in the future Roman comitatenses and limitanei phalangiarchies and quincunciali. The eastern autarchies were divided amongst the Seleucidae from 312-65 BCE, with its cleruchies and peripherals stretching from Anatolia though Syria-Cilicia Phoenice being north of the Himyarite Despotate and Nabataeans with the palatinate at Greater Armenia to the Jaxartes and Hydaspes. After a fugacious obstrigillation with Sandracottus, Seleucus I 'Nicator' was furnished with 500 cataphracted pachyderms . At Ipsus on 301 BCE and Corupedium on 281 BCE, he debellated and pessundated Antigonus I 'Monopthalmus', Demetrius I 'Poliorcetes". He would have reunited the ecumene to one amelioration and contesseration as his hercotectonics and thalassocracy were well established in the Phoenician autarchies including the famed Sidonian and Egyptian harbors, until he was slain in Chalcidia by Ptolemy Ceraunus. Under the porphyrogene of Antiochus Theos on 250 BCE, multitudinous 'heresiarchs' promulgated in order to become autocephalous or autonomous from heterochthonous influence. This hegemon insatiated in the salacious and meretricious, with flosculative and dispendious bacchanalias. Those that revolted were Attalid Pergamus, Pontus, Bithynia, Cappadocia, Paphlagonia, Graeco-Bactria from 250-125 BCE and the Indo-Greek Despotate from 180 BCE-10 CE. The peripherals consisted of Ectabana, Ferghana, Sogdiana, Tapurai, Traxiane, Hyrcania, Hecatompylus, Arachosia, Paropamisadae, Gandhara, the Punjab, and from Mathura to Pataliputra. Such were these internecine, kleptocratic, truculent, acrimonius, facinorous events. However, most of the peripherals were subjugated by the Yuezhi on 162 BCE, Xiongu on 126 BCE, Scythians on 140 BCE, Chionites, Hepthalites, Kidarite, Indo-Scythians and eventually the Indo-Parthians and the Indo-Sassanians. The last spark of Hellenistic autonomy was subjugated on the velitation of Actium on 31 BCE with the losses of Alexander Helios, Cleopatra Selenia and Ptolemy Philadelphus who were to be the next generation of 'Successors'. Such a demise was due to military expenditure, over-extension of manpower and the resultant economic exhaustion of the once belliferous Hellenistic autarchies.

# AN AMAZING JOURNEY

## Melanie Hubbard

*Melanie Hubbard was raised in Virginia's Shenandoah Valley and now enjoys a quiet life in rural Oklahoma. She's been married to a wonderful man for nearly 30 years; they have three children. She writes for fun, her only training being in the "school of hard knocks."*

The slam of that heavy, metal cell door behind me will forever echo in my mind. Suddenly I found myself completely alone for the first time in my life. Because I was a woman, I was placed in an enclosed cell. I could only hear what was around me but could see nothing outside that box. I was the only woman in the county jail, surrounded by twenty-five men. It seemed like the end of the road but in reality it was the beginning of an amazing journey.

Earlier that day I had prepared meals for hundreds of homeless people at the tornado shelter. Two weeks earlier half of our small Oklahoma town was leveled by a tornado. Luckily, our house was unharmed and I needed to keep busy as my sentencing date was approaching. After lunch I cleaned up and went to the courthouse to hear my fate. The judge sentenced me to six years in prison, followed by three years probation, 500 hours of community service and a $10,000 fine. I was now a convicted felon. My crime was embezzlement of $27,000 from my employer over a period of several years. The money I stole was repaid that day by my husband's family and my retirement fund proceeds. The judge gave me two hours to say goodbye to my family and report to the jail. I went home and packed a few things, enjoyed my final glass of wine and reported to jail. Once there I was photographed, fingerprinted and given an orange jumpsuit to put on. At this point I was given the first of many strip searches and asked to "squat and cough" before a female officer. I was so naïve and would've never thought to hide something in a body cavity to sneak it into jail, but it is a common practice. This was my first contact with the law. I was a wife of twenty-four years with children ages 20, 17 and 10.

7

I had to be scared to death. I lay on a thin, green mat on a concrete slab, realizing that all hope was gone. In the darkness I listened to the deafening noise and the vilest language I had ever heard. Wondering all the while who these men were and what they had done. Were they as violent and angry as they sounded? I was somehow unable to pray. I knew how but I was somehow numb and frozen with fear; the fear of the unknown life ahead. I simply cried, for the first time in many years, and trembled for the first three days and nights. The men cried out to me but I did not utter a single word. The guards brought me food and drinks and checked on me periodically. They treated me well for the most part.

By the third night, I was missing my family badly and coming to know the feeling of true loneliness. Late that night I made friends with a young man in the cell next to mine. He was only 20 years old and was in there for drugs and the failure to pay fines. He had gone to school with my oldest daughter. I soon learned all of their names and weaknesses. I found them all to be people, just like me, who had made mistakes. Most were there for drug and alcohol crimes, a few for weapon charges or money crimes. In the endless days I began to shame myself for thinking I was better than others and somehow above the law. I never once considered that there would be consequences for my actions.

I was truly in a place where no one could reach me except God. As I began settling into my new surroundings I was able to think, pray, read and sort things out. I read tons of inspirational materials and my Bible and practiced yoga. It was at this time that I received an indescribable sense of peace. It was like a warm hug from a good friend that gave me assurance that it was all going to be okay. It was a peace that remained with me through my whole journey and is still present today. I believe it to be the result of a "real" personal relationship with God. This peace allowed me to walk on through some really hard days. It was not long after I arrived in the county jail that other women began to arrive. At first it was hard to make friends with them. I had been alone for a long time and actually enjoyed the peace and time to heal myself on the inside. It was a preparation time for what was ahead when I would never be alone. There were several women I was with for months and I learned to love them like sisters. One in particular I am still in touch with over five years later.

I spent five months in the county jail. I was transported to prison at 5:00 a.m. on a rainy March morning. I will forever remember the evil laugh of the officer who woke me that day. That morning I cried for the first time in months. I wanted to hug my family once more

8

before I left and I had been assured that would be allowed. I should've known they were not that compassionate. Was I still so naïve? I was taken to a receiving facility about three hours away. I had only my fashionable orange jumpsuit, a Victoria's Secret bra, white socks and panties, my legal papers and my Bible. I was not allowed to keep the bra or the Bible and returned them with the officer who had transported me. She was a real jewel. She informed me that she had seen grown men cry when they saw the razor wire. I had read my Bible the entire trip and was completely at peace with what was ahead.

Once there, we were sorted into groups and crammed into holding cells. They gave us sack lunches to eat, into which the inmates who prepared them had strategically placed roaches. Needless to say we chose to fast that day. We were stripped and inspected for tattoos and scars. They issued us some new clothes and locked us into two-bunk cells. My roommate was a real nice American Indian girl and we were instant friends. I spent a week at the receiving facility in a pod with about sixty women. We were allowed to shower during recreation time in the evenings but only had hot water every fourth day. I learned a lot there. The girls would flash the male inmates walking by, in exchange for tobacco, which was smuggled in every day. The trustees passed the lighters from cell to cell. Blank pages of the Bibles were used to roll cigarettes. Smoking in the facility was not allowed. While we were there we were weighed and measured. Our vision and teeth were checked. They woke about ten of us in the middle of the night one night to have blood drawn down at the lab. It was no big deal for me. But I had to wait and watch as they poked and prodded some of the girls, trying to find a vein they had not blown out while doing IV drugs. I prayed and ached for them, wondering what their lives had been like. I continue to thank God that I was blessed with two good Christian parents. Too many times I have had to call on those verses and songs I learned growing up to keep my sanity.

We were allowed to purchase items from the canteen on about the fifth day. I had $7.46 on the books and chose to buy a brush, conditioner, pencils and stamps. I had been using a small plastic comb on my foot long hair. Nothing felt as good as that conditioner and brush that night. I guess it was at this time I realized the difference between needs and wants. It was a lesson I wished I had learned a few decades earlier. I'd spent years keeping up appearances for my family and myself. I learned finally that it's just "stuff"; we can live so simply and be just as happy.

After a week there about sixteen of us were sorted out to be shipped to a minimum security facility about three hours away. My roommate went with me so I did not feel so alone. Our few belongings were packed in a clear plastic bag and we were shackled and cuffed for transit. When my roommate saw me in shackles she died laughing, citing how I never should be in them. It was interesting and uncomfortable but safe for the drivers. They stopped for pizza on the way and they enjoyed every bite. We enjoyed the aroma, while dreaming of better days. We arrived at our new home at about 9:00 p.m., were searched and briefed, then issued a mattress, sheets and a pillow to go along with our neat, clear plastic bag. These items were to be carried in one trip about a quarter mile up hill to the dorms. I was the only one assigned to Dorm #6 and entered in the dark at about midnight. There were 400 watching eyes as I made my bunk and collapsed. I was too tired to care; it had been a very trying day.

There were over 900 women at this facility. Not only were they women but also wives, mothers, daughters and grandmothers. Mothers' Day was unbelievable there; bittersweet. That is another story in itself. It was great to be able to walk around and see the sunrise and sunset and let your hair dry in the wind. It had been so long since I had even seen day light. Simple things I had been unable to enjoy for months. I received a good, but hard job in the maintenance department. I had a great supervisor who served as counselor, father and friend to all of the girls under his care. He was never afraid to ask vital questions; the kinds that make you think about your life. He made a positive impact on every person he met. I mowed grass all day, every day, all summer; with a push mower.

I was too tired to get into any trouble. I slept all night every night, luckily. There was lots of sexual and violent activity at night and I wanted no part of it. I learned to be still and take my mind a million miles away. I spent much time in prayer and in the Word. It provided so much strength and hope for me. There were religious services of all kinds and I attended many. I made several friends who were on the right track and I remain in touch with some of them still. I was allowed to participate in several group recovery programs that helped me restore my self-image. I began to believe that life would be okay again. I was at that facility for nine months. I actually was content to finish my time there, but that was not an option. On the day after Christmas I was moved in the late evening to a work release facility closer to home. All I could think was each step was one step closer to home. I prayed the entire way that I would be blessed with good roommates. This time I had a duffel bag of books and toiletries I had purchased with my $20 per month wages and money my husband sent each month.

We arrived at about 9:00 p.m., were searched, were issued different clothes and allowed to go to our rooms at about 11:00 p.m. My roommates were incredibly nice; a real blessing. This was the first place I had been able to watch TV in almost two years. I still stayed in the Word and chose to keep to myself. I received a good job cleaning offices and mowing lawns at the Department of Corrections headquarters. They discovered my computer skills and kept me busy in the office organizing things in the maintenance department. I was befriended by a male inmate there who talked to me one-on-one every day about the past, present, future and eternity. He knew the Word inside and out and spent his entire life sharing his knowledge with other inmates. He encouraged change and was an example of what happens when people refuse to change. He had been in prison 32 calendar years. He was the most hopeful person I ever met. He taught me to never give up, to continue to trust in God and walk on through whatever trials might be ahead. He is the one person I wish I had not lost contact with. I believe he was placed in my path at a time when I needed to be reminded of the things I already knew but had become too busy to practice.

One day at work I was sick with allergies and, without thinking, took an allergy pill from the first aid kit. That night we had an institutional shake where everything is searched. We were ordered into the courtyard in the dark and ordered to put our hands on our heads. We were placed in rows and drug dogs sniffed us. The dog sat down behind me, indicating drug use. I had never used drugs in my life and informed the officer at that time. I was cuffed and taken to "lock". They strip searched me and did a urinalysis which indicated I was using Meth. and Amphetamines. I was placed in a cell with three other women. I was devastated, as I knew I was not guilty of the misconduct I had been charged with. I remained calm in an attempt to show the guards that I was not using drugs. I repeatedly asked for a Bible to be brought to my cell and my request was repeatedly denied. I was lucky to be able to call upon verses and songs in my past to sustain me. The guards continually checked my well being because I was so quiet compared to their usual "lock" inmates. I prayed and planned my defense statement. It took five days and the help of my supervisors at work to beat it. If I had not beaten this misconduct, I would've been sent back to minimum security for an additional year. I was scared to death but never lost my faith that God would walk me through this as well.

Following my release from lock, I was relocated to another room with some really trying roommates. I was also allowed to return to my former job. I was determined to finish my time and return home.

I spent my final six months working for Panera Bread and I began to sparkle there. I was encouraged by a preacher I met on the bus to abandon worry and fear, and to trust God completely. These final lessons were the most valuable. Now I walk by faith and completely rest on those everlasting arms.

One month after my third Christmas away from my family, I was released. My husband who had stood by me through thick and thin picked me up. We began to make up for lost time. I returned to our small town and was received with open arms by most. I was blessed with a great job in a bakery.

I wish everyone who is faced with a loved one in jail or prison could know ahead of time that they may be right where they need to be at that time in their life.

# MEMORIES OF INCARCERATED MOTHERS

## Melanie Hubbard

*Melanie Hubbard was raised in Virginia's Shenandoah Valley and now enjoys a quiet life in rural Oklahoma. She's been married to a wonderful man for nearly 30 years; they have three children. She writes for fun, her only training being in the "school of hard knocks."*

Because of senseless actions and years of trying to be the perfect mother, I found myself in a women's correctional facility. It was overall a good experience for me. I have been free for over three years now and am able to clearly reflect on the experience.

One particular day stands out in my mind above all others. It was the Friday before Mother's Day 2002. In the small mail building, mail was placed in boxes by 4:00 p.m. The line to check our mail began forming before 3:00 p.m. It was a long and winding line where the majority of 900 women waited quietly for the chance to check their box, many resting on curbs and talking to their neighbors in line.

I can remember no other particular day in my nine months there where so many women were gathered in one place at one time. The sight was beyond belief and bittersweet. How many mothers were there, not to mention grandmothers? Each woman hoping and praying that someone cared enough to remember her on this day. Most viewing themselves as failures for making such a horrible mess of their lives; not to mention the mess they had left their families in.

Finally the door to the mail room was opened and the inmates were allowed in three or four at a time. Some emerged empty handed and slowly returned to their dorm, hopeful that Monday's mail would be better. Others emerged with a letter or card or two. Some contained a photo or small child drawing. These were shown with pride to friends still waiting in line. The whole yard was abuzz with activity and chatter that evening. For the most part it was a joyous day.

It is hard to not hurt for the ones who were left out. I guess God gives female inmates a special measure of comfort and a treasured friend or two to get them through those days when they miss special events like: graduations, weddings, holidays and birthdays.

Visitation was allowed on Saturday and Sunday as usual for Mother's Day and the women prepared themselves as best they could. They would often finish early, in anticipation of their family's arrival.

In typical prison fashion extra guards and drug dogs were brought in for visitation on Sunday. There were more searches than normal of visitors coming in. Would husbands or kids actually bring mom drugs or other contraband for Mother's Day? I am afraid so. Several were not allowed in and some were even arrested that day. I was not an illegal drug user so actions like this are foreign to my thinking. Looking back at my own life I see many occasions when my judgment was poor and my choices were on the verge of insanity.

Visitation was always crowded, especially on Mother's Day. There were lots of kids playing in the sandbox or on the playground. Parents visiting and holding hands, catching up on the events since they last spoke. Many families planning for their future once their release was granted. Some families played dominos or cards and ate strawberries or other special treats purchased from the vending machines. Some mothers braided their children's hair. Simply troubled families within the confines of a tall metal fence doing normal, everyday family activities.

Of course the ultimate form of degradation would be done following that special Mother's Day visit. Before the inmates were allowed to return to their dorms there was a strip search. This was done twenty at a time with a female guard present. Inmates were instructed to form a large circle and remove each article of clothing, shake it and place it in a pile. Once all were standing naked, inmates were instructed to lift their breasts and run their fingers through their hair, turn their backs to the guard, squat and cough, one by one. Once this ritual was completed inmates were allowed to redress and go back to their respective dorms.

It was not uncommon to see an inmate staring out beyond the fence, wondering how she could ever have enough courage to walk out that gate when the time came. So today let's stop and say a little prayer for those troubled families of the incarcerated.

# THE CITY OF ENLIGHTENMENT

## M. Carole Wyatt

*Carole Wyatt lives with her husband and children between soybean fields and a cemetery. In addition to writing, she works in an organic market and dairy. Her stories have won many prizes and been included in several anthologies. Her latest novel is called* Weather Swans.

The Paris Train Station bustled with people moving swiftly on silent feet to their destinations. Vendors' voices shouting their wares at the hurrying passengers carried over the screech of train brakes. An occasional baby cry pierced the air thick with smoke from the arriving engines. I sat on my suitcase and pondered the scene while waiting for the train to the coast. Goodbye, Paris, time to move on.

Paris, the City of Lights, the city of dreams and the city of romance was not the Paris I found. It was like stepping back into the past, touring places up to now only seen on the History Channel. The monks, who maintained Notre Dame, urged me to the top with a smile never imagining I could make it all the way up. American tourists seldom did. It was a matter of pride, besides the three flights of stairs at work prepared me. Once up, the spectacular view left me amazed. The Eiffel Tower stood in the distance, a serpentine line stretched around it, which discouraged me from visiting. Instead, I imagined the view to be almost as good as the one from the top of Notre Dame.

Located on the picturesque Left Bank, squeezed in between two taller buildings, sat my quaint bed and breakfast. Only a striped canopy that extended out to the sidewalk announced its presence. The proprietor chatted away to me in rapid French while I seemed to encourage her gregariousness with my Miss Piggy French monosyllabic replies. The abrupt, rude Frenchmen featured in almost every travel horror story didn't show on my trip. Friendly natives smiled and spoke emphatically with much animation; unfortunately, I didn't understand most of it. Hand gestures, a beseeching look, or artfully displayed merchandise got the message across. Miscommunication usually involved sizes. The European sizes seemed so large, it was hard for me reconcile that a single digit size in the U.S., could mushroom into a double-digit size abroad. The shoe sizes were a killer too, professional basketball players back home didn't rate shoe sizes as large as my size eight feet required. The only way to deal with this culture shock was to try everything on. International travel wasn't as hard as I thought it would be.

Some things were so different while other things remained the same, well almost the same. In a large shopping mall in the middle of Paris, a two story Burger King dominated, complete with white tablecloths and red candles. Parisians and tourists alike sat drinking red wine with their Whoppers. This blending of cultures I observed from my sidewalk café seat and wondered why anyone would come to Paris and eat fast food. The French have a love affair with food that included everyone from the chef to the consumer. My waiter described every entree in such sensual detail, for a moment I thought it was an invitation to partake in a torrid affair, instead of the various daily specials. Paying attention in French class might have helped me to discern that the waiter was in love with his job, not me.

Despite the rulings of the French culture minister, American movies reigned supreme at the cinema. A touch of homesickness prompted me into the cinema only to indulge in the surreal experience of listening to Eddie Murphy speak French. My ears still ringing with Eddie's perfect Parisian accent, my other senses encounter the bidet, a urinal gone mad that sprayed water up instead of down. The bidet was a definite culture shock that earned my respect. Still the general attitude about public restrooms was an even bigger shock.

While touring Versailles, the search for a restroom found me in line with a few hundred other women. The attendant motioned the willing into the men's restroom, which did not have a line. Hurrying in with the other women, I vigorously grabbed the opportunity to bypass dozens of women waiting for toilet facilities. Men crowded around urinals joked and called out greetings at our entry. Mumbling an apology, I locked myself in a stall waiting for an appropriate moment to escape.

While that was an exciting moment, the best was the Louvre. The Louvre; intellectual sorts had bandied about the name as long as I could remember.

"Pickpockets are in the Louvre, please secure your purses and wallets," the announcement played continuously in five languages as I examined the exhibits. "Winged Victory" stood not more than eight feet from me, something before I had only seen as a small black and white photograph in my art history book. A velvet rope kept the gawkers away from the Dutch Masters display. A nearby Brit nodded at the exhibit and explained a terrorist had attacked it the year before.

Terrorists attacking old dark paintings by Dutchmen; what possible statement could they have made? My ponderings on art vandalism soon ended as I drifted over to view the *Mona Lisa*. It was much smaller than I imagined, still perfect in its climate-controlled case. My newfound museum buddy informed me I was lucky to see the *Mona Lisa,* because usually the crowds around her were extreme. Slipping away to the Rodin exhibit, I managed to lose my self-appointed guide. Art was something to reflect on in silence. Still avoiding my guide, I slipped out the side door which I wasn't sure was an official exit.

Numerous street peddlers hawking various wares dispelled me of the idea that I found a secret exit. Shaking my head *no*, I darted around their outstretched hands displaying perfume, postcards, purses with famous paintings duplicated on their sides and scarves with the Rose window imprinted on them. The main boulevard sighted, I surged ahead unaware that I had one last hanger-on trailing me.

His beautiful precise English alerted me that this was not a Parisian. Where had I heard that accent before? Startled by the accent, I stopped, which only encouraged him. His smile was wide in his burnished face as he held out a bangle bracelet. "No money, no francs," I explained.

"American dollars will do," he assured me, pegging me easily as an American by my soft, rounded syllables.

My hesitation noted, he launched into a tragic story about his whole family immigrating and how he was their sole source of income. Handing over a five-dollar bill, I knew it was a scam, but it was such a convincing story and he told it so well. Overall, it was not a bad bracelet about an inch wide and ivory in color. Turning it, I looked for the mold line or the Made in China imprint without any luck. Just at the edge of my mind, I wondered if it could be ivory, but rejected the thought.

Rubbing my fingers over the bracelet, I re-examined it as I waited for the train that would soon take me to my ferry that would start the British Isles part of my tour. The Chunnel would have been much quicker, but considerably more expensive for a person on a budget. Besides, the ferry wasn't bad. Last time I was on the ferry they had excellent food, the equivalent of being in a three star restaurant. My stomach growled at the thought of eating. The vendors at the perimeter of the station sold food. I noticed the woman while I scanned the food stalls for some tasty comestibles.

She was a tall, long-legged beauty, moving with an athletic stride. Perhaps I noticed her because she stood out with her long mass of tiny black braids and ebony skin surrounded by slight winter-white people clutching purses and luggage. For a moment, I admired her confidence and attitude and wished I could be similar. Behind her slithered a small white female who was gaining rapidly. Maybe they're friends, yet the smaller woman was moving in such a furtive fashion that other people were stepping away from her.

Eyes glued to the unfolding drama, I wasn't ready when the furtive woman pulled out a knife and plunged it into the striding woman. The woman fell immediately, like a sparrow shot out of the sky. The furtive female who was so noticeable before had disappeared. The crowd simply flowed around the fallen beauty, no screams of horror were uttered, no everyday hero was running down the felon, instead everyone was busy looking for their train platforms. Seconds later paramedics arrived. They carefully placed the woman on an inflatable stretcher and bore her away. *Was she dead? How could she be otherwise with the large knife handle sticking out of her back? How could the people be so apathetic?*

My train arrived and I grabbed my bag, looking back at the scene of the crime one last time. What could cause a person to act in such a way? Jealousy perhaps. She was a beautiful woman; she probably could have stolen anyone's man. Or did I just witness a terrorist attack? I didn't know, maybe this happened everyday, so no one was surprised.

Thinking back, I realized the people started moving away when they spotted the slinking woman. Maybe on some instinctual level they felt threatened. It was a hard lesson to accept that reality is so different from the manufactured fantasy. My trip to Paris was unforgettable to be sure. Would I hold that one incident against the city? In truth, I couldn't because it could have as easily happened in LA, Athens, Rome, New York, or even my own hometown. Would I act like the Parisians and assorted tourists hurrying off to my train? How did I act? Frozen in silent horror, I watched the whole episode play out without speaking a word of warning, or taking a step forward to help. What a hard truth; the City of Lights had become the City of Enlightenment.

# DEATH OF A PATRIARCH

### Betty Kreier-Lubinski

*First Prize – contest of December 2006*

*Betty Kreier-Lubinski is a great-grandmother from Washington State. She writes non-fiction, mysteries, romance, and flash fiction. Her book of short stories,* Other People's Lives *was published in 2004 by Epress-online.*

When the phone rang at 3:15 a.m. that morning, I grabbed it before it could wake up my husband.

"He's dead, Betty. Daddy's gone." My sister, calling from the nursing home. Her voice cracked, threatening to erupt, out of control.

"How's Mom?"

"We haven't told her yet. She's asleep outside in Jan's camper in the parking lot. Jan just went out to wake her up."

I took a deep breath. "I'll be there as fast as I can."

I sat on the edge of the bed, breathing hard, numb, exhausted. I'd come home from the nursing home only two hours ago. This vigil had been going on for four months, and I'd stayed late every night, first at the hospital and later at the nursing home, but I had to go to work each morning.

Relief swept through me--I was glad Dad was gone--but that was followed by searing pain. How could I be glad?

"Daddy," I whispered, "What will we ever do without you?"

In movie death scenes, the dying person says heart-wrenching, beautiful things to loved ones. No one warned me about the gasping for air, the shudders, the little hurt whimpers of pain, the long drawn-out moans, the incessant diarrhea and the angry red bedsores that wouldn't heal. No one ever told me a time would come when I'd beg for Dad to let go.

On the drive to the nursing home, I left the car window open so that the crisp night air brushed my hair from my face and cooled my forehead.

Now, I could go to work and not jump every time the phone rang. Now I wouldn't have to spend my lunch hours running to the hospital to spell my sisters or my mother.

We took turns sitting with Dad and holding his hands so he wouldn't pull out his IV tubes, so the nurses wouldn't have to tie his hands to the bed rail. He cried when they tied his hands. He couldn't understand.

My dad was not religious, but he was a good man. My lifelong uncertainties about God raced through my mind. Was there really a life after death? Would I see my beloved father again?

Tears cascaded down my face, and the road was a blur. I pulled over to the curb. "Thank you, God, thank you for taking Daddy home, but why did he have to suffer for so long?"

For the moment, I wasn't sure there really was a God. It hadn't felt like it, the past few months.

But maybe the drawn-out death was part of God's plan. I didn't think my family could have handled Dad's death four months ago when Dad was first hospitalized. He was only seventy-one. None of us could bear to think about losing him. Maybe the long illness had been God's way of preparing the family for his loss. Now we were ready to see him go.

* * *

When I got to the nursing home, my mother was weeping in the lobby.

"I should've been with him. I was sleeping in the camper," Mom wailed. "We've been married for fifty-one years, and I couldn't even go without a little sleep to hold his hand. Oh, Betty, how can he ever forgive me?"

I put my arms around my mother, holding her tight. "Mom, there was nothing you could do."

"I could've been there. He would've known I loved him."

"He knew you loved him. Doris was there, Janet was there."

"But I'm his wife. I should've been there."

The nurse beckoned. "If your family wants to spend a few minutes with your dad, you'd better do it now. The doctor will be coming in to sign the death certificate. And then the people from the funeral home will be here."

A sudden fury washed over me. Darn! I thought. Why are you hurrying us? Do you have to rush to empty his bed so you can put someone else in it? Can't you give us five darned minutes?" Keep a lid on, I told myself. It's not their fault. But the anger kept me from crying.

Each of us wanted a few minutes alone with Daddy. Doris went first, then Janet, then me. Daddy's body was still warm, his whimpers quieted. He looked as if he had just relaxed into a deep, comfortable sleep. I laid my cheek on his, and his whiskers pricked my skin.

"I love you, Daddy," I sobbed.

In a very short time, the nurse came in. "It's time to leave, sweetie. Your mom wants to come in."

I wiped the tears on my coat sleeve. It was Mom's turn.

"Goodbye, Daddy," I whispered as I smoothed his white hair with my fingers. "Goodbye."

* * *

The family gathered in the hall, standing quietly, looking awkward, not saying anything. Finally, I said, "We should call people and announce the good news." My morbid sense of black humor.

"Dixie said she'd call everybody," my sister said.

Dixie was my daughter, the oldest female grandchild, a mother-of-the-world type who always took care of everyone. I was disappointed. It would've been something for me to do, something safe to think about.

I noticed the nurses continuing on their rounds, laughing together, telling jokes, unconcerned that someone had died. It made me furious.

One nurse asked if the family would like coffee. "Yes," I said. "That's very kind." Why couldn't they all be like that?"

But a minute later, the nice nurse who brought the coffee laughed with the orderly down the hall.

I'm being unreasonable to expect everyone to care, I thought. But how can I be reasonable when my father just died? I felt like a little lost, abandoned baby.

* * *

By 6:30 a.m., the grandchildren began to arrive. Dave, oldest grandchild, named after his grandfather, was first. He stood in the hall, his eyes red, nose running, bundled against the cold in his plaid hunting jacket. "Did he hurt?" he asked. "Was it quick?"

"You know it wasn't quick. He's been in the hospital off and on for four months. That's the stupidest question I ever heard." My sister glared at David, and I moved closer to take a protective stance by my first-born.

"Cut it out, Doris, he was only asking."

"It was a stupid question," Dave said, "I just don't know what to say. I've never lost anyone before." He hauled a large red-checked handkerchief out of his pocket and blew his nose. "I remember when he taught me to play the guitar. And when he took me down in the pasture and showed me how to pee in the woods when there wasn't a bathroom around. And how he told me to get an education because he only got through the fourth grade."

I reached over and hugged my son.

Danny, my younger son, came with his small daughter at seven o'clock, and then Doris's kids arrived. By the time the funeral director arrived, the hallway was full of family members standing around, nothing to do, not sure how to grieve, how to fill the time, how to face the empty days and years ahead.

The funeral director whispered to me, "We're going to remove the body. Would you take your mother out to the car so she doesn't have to watch?"

My sister snapped, "It's not a body. It's our father."

When I tried to coax Mom outside, she whimpered, "They're going to take him away, aren't they? They want me out of here so I can't watch."

I didn't answer. A heavy fog had settled in my brain, and words wouldn't, couldn't push through.

The family went outside, milling around in the parking lot, still not knowing what to do. What do you do when your heart is gone? Mom, three daughters and their  husbands, eleven grandchildren, fourteen great-grandchildren--for years Dad Kreier had been our core, the heart and soul of our family.

"Let's go to North's Chuck Wagon for breakfast."

"I'm not hungry."

"I'm not either, but I don't want to go home."

North's Chuck Wagon was a buffet restaurant, down the road a mile, that opened early for breakfast.

Family members congregated in one corner of the restaurant, fifteen of us. Coffee and toast. No one could think of anything to say, but no one wanted to leave.

I grasped my sister's hand. "Thanks for staying the night with Daddy. I'm so glad you were there."

"Mom was there most of the time," Janet said. "We encouraged her to take a nap 'cause she was dead on her feet. I don't want to lose her, too. She's almost as old as Dad, and her health isn't much better than his."

We stared in panic at each other, and then I said quickly, "Don't say that!" Don't think the unthinkable! Losing one parent is enough!

Someone called out. "What are you guys whispering about down there? Secrets?"

I smiled. "No secrets. Just girl stuff. I'm telling all my secrets about my husband."

"Better be careful. He just came in."

My husband, Myles, pulled up a chair beside me. "Doing okay?" he asked softly.

"Yeah, I'm okay. Thanks for coming. I needed you." I reached over and tucked my hand in his pocket.

"You should've woke me up when you left."

"At 3:30 in the morning? No way. No sense in both of us being wasted. How'd you find us?"

"Dixie left a message at the nursing home. How's Mom?" he asked.

Mom, seventy years old, gray-haired, wore a sad, small smile. Her eyes stared vacantly.

"She needs to get home and get some rest," Myles said. "It's been a long haul for her, all these months."

"If she goes home, she'll start blaming herself for not being there when Daddy died."

"Did they ever decide what was wrong with him?"

"No," I answered.

* * *

Dad had gotten sick at Thanksgiving, running a high fever. Mom planned to cook dinner but she'd cancelled because Daddy didn't feel up to company.

At Christmas, he still had a fever. He and Mom came in from the farm to open their presents but didn't stay for dinner because he felt so badly.

In January, his fever skyrocketed. He was hospitalized, and they lowered the fever with massive doses of antibiotics and aspirin. Extensive tests showed nothing so they sent him back home.

"Boy, when you call it the practice of medicine, you really mean it. You're just practicing. None of you quacks know what you're doing." Dad said that with a smile on his face, and his doctor laughed.

A week later, Dad went back to the hospital, with convulsions from the high fever. He couldn't keep food down, he had diarrhea, he was losing weight, and they still couldn't identify a cause for the fever. The hospital kept him a few days and sent him home again.

Trips to the emergency room and the hospital went on while he got weaker and weaker. He finally became so weak that he couldn't go home.

Each time he'd been hospitalized, he said, "I don't want to go to the hospital. I'll never come back." He would say, "If I'm going to die, let me die at home. Don't take me to a nursing home, whatever you do. Take me home to die." He was so tired by then.

During the last hospitalization, his condition worsened as they did a whole range of tests but still couldn't find out what was wrong.

My family was gradually accepting that Dad would die, and we might never know why.

* * *

I'll never forget the family conference with the doctor the day we voted not to tube-feed Dad.

The doctor offered no hope. "Mr. Kreier can't eat, or even swallow liquids anymore. He's losing weight steadily, and his electrolytes are not good." The doctor stopped speaking, and then sighed. "Mr. Kreier's body seems to be giving up. His vital signs are not good, his liver is failing, he can't urinate without a catheter. I don't think there's a lot of hope, Mrs. Kreier. You and the family need to help me decide what to do at this point. Mr. Kreier has always said he didn't want to be kept alive by artificial methods, but if we don't start tube-feeding your husband right away, he'll die."

"He's going to die soon anyhow, isn't he?" Mom said.

The doctor wouldn't answer.

Daddy hated the idea of being tube-fed. He always said he didn't want to be kept alive that way.

"I vote that we let him go. No tube feeding," someone said.

I jumped up and ran to the bathroom, feeling as if all the meals I'd eaten for the past six months were sitting right behind my lips, ready to explode.

But all of us agreed. If there was no hope, let him go. The doctor said he'd mark the chart, "No heroic measures."

The next morning when I got to the hospital, Dad was connected to feeding tubes.

My mom explained. "Daddy sat up in the middle of the night and started talking. He said you guys are trying to starve me."

My heart leaped. "Is he better?"

Mom said, "I think so. He has to be, doesn't he?"

The doctor told us, "At that point, all our agreements had to be cancelled. We *had* to feed him."

Those words were the last words Daddy ever said.

* * *

The hospital staff discharged Dad to the nursing home when there was nothing more they could do for him. There was no real treatment, it was just a matter of waiting for him to die. The family objected. Dad had begged not to be taken to a nursing home. But the hospital was firm. Mom couldn't take him home so he had to go to a nursing home.

The family still didn't know why he was dying.

"People don't just die for no reason," Janet said.

The doctor answered, "People die of old age. Your father is

seventy-one, he is not a young man."

Tell us why, we wailed, but there was no answer.

We had felt the nurses in the hospital isolated themselves from my Dad when they decided he was dying. We didn't get that feeling at the nursing home.

The nursing home attendants knew what to do. Every fifteen to thirty minutes, Dad pooped his bed, and the orderly came in, cleaned him up, changed the bed, said soothing words. I will always be grateful for their attitude.

For some reason---no one could ever explain why---we three sisters bought a sturdy recliner for Dad's room. Mom could sit in it, we said, while visiting Dad. Later, when Dad got better, he could sit in the chair, we told ourselves.

The chair cost $350, plus an extra $50 to have it delivered. We gathered up the cash to pay for it. The chair sat in the corner of the tiny room, and no one ever used it. Two nights later, Daddy died. We couldn't remember why we had bought it.

* * *

I glanced quickly around the restaurant. "What are you guys going to do? I'm sure the restaurant would like us out of here before lunch."

Mom said, "I have to go to the funeral home. I have to pick out the casket."

"You don't have to do it today."

Mom squeezed her eyes shut tightly, and her voice came out in a whisper. "It's the last thing I can do for your Dad, and I have to do it today."

My sisters and I went with mother to the funeral home to arrange the funeral.

As we sat in the stark, cold office of the funeral director, I felt a giggle start to erupt. This was all so serious, and my father had never been a serious man. He was always joking, always laughing, always alive.

Mr. Stiler said in a low soothing voice, "How are we going to dress Mr. Kreier for the funeral? We'll want to pick out something comfortable, perhaps a favorite suit." His use of the pronoun "we" made me giggle louder.

"Overalls." I said, "We want to bury him in overalls."

Mr. Stiler said, "I don't think . . ."

"That's what he was most comfortable in. That's what he always wore, bib overalls and a flannel shirt. Do we want him to look like himself, or do we want him to look like a phony? People who come to his funeral won't even recognize him without his overalls."

25

Strong emotions always made me kind of crazy. My gallows jokes irritated everyone, but I couldn't seem to help it.

"Betty," my mother said reprovingly. "Dad can wear his leisure suit."

"Leisure suits went out of style years ago, Mom. And besides, Daddy only wore his once. He wore bib overalls and a plaid flannel shirt all the time."

"He did, too, wear it more than once." my mother insisted. "He got all dressed up for Doris's wedding and Janet's wedding, and . . ."

"That was years ago, Mom. He . . ."

Janet leaned over and said in my ear, not unkindly, "Shut up!"

I shut up.

"Now, music. Did he have a favorite song?"

"Tonight We're Setting the Woods on Fire!" I answered. That old country western song had been a favorite of Daddy's for years.

Mr. Stiler said, "I hardly think . . ."

My mom said, "I Come to The Garden Alone and The Old Rugged Cross."

"He liked Settin' the Woods on Fire, Mom." My emotions were running away with me. I felt like giggling, and crying, and hitting people. "If ever a person ought to have the music he likes, it should be at his own funeral," I said through gritted teeth.

My mom started crying. Doris said firmly, "Betty, Dad picked the hymns he wanted years ago. Will you shut up?"

I shut up, again.

Finally the arrangements were complete, and the casket selected. We all agreed the cheapest casket, the least pretentious, was the one Dad would've liked. The funeral director said it was very plain and asked if we wouldn't like something a little more special for our father. But we knew what our Dad would've wanted.

"That casket won't look too bad when you get it away from the rest of those cheap ones," I said.

When we left the funeral home, Mom went to Doris' house to rest. Janet and I drove out to the farm to get Dad's clothes for the funeral home, and a change of clothes for Mom. The mechanics of who would do what when occupied our thoughts. We knew we all wanted to get together somewhere that evening.

Dave, my son, had a gig to play with his band that night. "Can he get someone to play for him?"

"No, the band can't get along without him. They'd have to cancel their gig." We couldn't leave Dave out, but he couldn't come to be with the family. It suddenly seemed like an impossible hurdle.

"So, let's all go to the dance." Janet said.

"Someone would have to stay with Mom."

But Mom wanted to go, too. Dixie phoned children and grandchildren, and we agreed to meet at the dance that night.

* * *

The dance hall was a rowdy place, but popular. David's band, "River City," played a wide variety of music--western, bluegrass, top 40's. The band started playing at 9:00 p.m. and Dave saved a large group of tables for the family.

"Good thing you got here," Dave said. "I don't know how much longer I could have defended these tables."    The room filled up quickly, more single females than couples. The guys in the band attracted a number of young groupies who hung close to the edge of the stage and smiled at band members.

"My son, the sex symbol," I whispered to my sister. "Off stage, Dave is so shy, but when he gets up there in front of all those admiring girls, he struts around the stage as if he owned it. I've seen that transformation a dozen times, and I'll never understand it."

The house was serving a specialty for the night, Singapore Slings, and Dave ordered one for each person in the family.

Everyone got up and danced. Even Mom danced with her grandsons. When the band played a western set, we called to each other about how Dad loved western music. The family whooped and hollered their way through the songs, just like Dad would have done.

At intermission, Dave came over, high from the exuberance and energy of the music, and walked around the table, hugging his grandma, hugging me, visiting with his younger cousins. Many of them hadn't heard him play for years, and they were all properly impressed. "Hey, guy, you're good."

Dave's eyes shone with pleasure. "Grandpa taught me how to play guitar years ago," Dave said. "I'm so glad you all came out tonight. I sure didn't want to be here alone."

When intermission was over, Dave took the microphone and announced in a husky voice, "I want to dedicate the next song to one of the greatest men who ever lived, my grandfather. It's an oldie, and a lot of you may not remember it, but it was one of his favorites, and I want to play it for him one last time. 'Tonight We're Setting the Woods on Fire.'"

I gasped. I was amazed that Dave even knew it was his Grandpa's favorite or knew the words to the song. As the wild raunchy music rang out over the room, I laughed in delight.

"It's a shame Grandpa couldn't be here to hear this," someone said.

"I'll bet he is here," someone else answered. And I knew it was true.

The music seemed to spin higher and louder as the night wore on. Some of our family danced, stomping our feet wildly on the floor, whirling around like tops, out of control, spinning, turning, falling breathlessly into our chairs. We danced as though the devils were after us.

Some of us got drunk. Some of us cried. Some of us smoked cigarettes and made eyes at the bartender or the pretty young girls who were parading back and forth to the ladies' restroom.

Diana, my youngest daughter, was pregnant, and late in the evening, I found her sobbing in the restroom. "Grandpa will never see this baby, and all her life, she is going to miss knowing him."

Someone asked Mom if she was tired and wanted to go home. She grinned and said, "No, I'd better stay. This may be the last dance I ever get invited to."

"Grandpa would have loved this music." We all agreed. "He would have enjoyed every minute."

The celebration continued.

As the night wore on, we danced wildly, courting oblivion, celebrating the fact that this man had lived and spawned this great, loud group of people who loved him and loved each other.

We remembered all the years he had been our patriarch, our teacher, our wise one, our beloved, our heartbeat. We were a family, and we would never be the same for his loss.

My dad had been loud. My dad had been larger than life. My dad had been the center of the universe. My dad had been alive. Oh, God, how alive my dad had been!

That night, we celebrated his life in a way he would have loved, and we tried to forget for a little while that he was dead -- before we wiped our tears and went on with our lives.

28

# FLIGHT FROM FLOYD: A TRUE STORY

David P. Andersen

*David P. Andersen is a retired computer design engineer. His first book,* At The Field, *is online at www.mnbigbirds.com.* The Cello Maker and Other Stories *is nearing completion.*

September 16, 1999:

I was trapped in a hotel room in Newport News, Virginia, as hurricane Floyd raged around me. I feared that the rain and debris striking my third floor window would break it, so I closed the curtain and sat in the opposite side of the room. Days of downpour brought the city to a halt. I had no place to go and nothing to do but plan my escape.

I called Northwest Airlines reservation number in an attempt to change my departure to the next day, but only all-circuits-busy signals were returned. People with Internet access to NWA's reservations would gobble up tomorrow's flights before I could get through, so I gave up on that approach. Even if successful, I didn't want to deal with the dreadful thirty-mile traffic snarl that would surely develop when evacuated folks returned to the flooded streets.

And so I monitored the storm's progress by television and telephone calls to the Virginia highway department's automated road condition reports. TV was interrupted by power glitches and satellite "searching for synch." It appeared that the storm would be over by late afternoon, giving me enough information to extrapolate the weather data to my flight time of 8:00 p.m. I concluded that airplanes would begin flying by then, so I decided to attempt to drive to Norfolk International Airport at the earliest opportunity.

The major problem was flooding. Interstate 64 was closed. Alternative roads were also blocked by water. With my limited knowledge of the high ground in the area, I calculated an egress

29

on my Hertz road map that avoided known flooded intersections. I also planned several alternatives. Al Capone couldn't have plotted a better escape from Alcatraz.

From my hotel window, I watched the water rise on the road leading out of the complex. Two lakes formed over it. I could not be certain of their depth because no traffic was passing through them. Eventually, an eighteen-wheeler crept through, seeking shelter from the storm. I noted the water level on its tires and the level of the water on the nearby lawn. From this I would later calculate the depth of the water for my car. I decided that if the water level were no higher than the lower door seals, I could safely pass.

Consuming my last TV dinner, I realized that stocking up on food that could be eaten only with the help of a microwave oven was not a good idea. I couldn't expect the hotel's emergency power generator to last much longer—I was lucky to have any electricity at all. Civilization is so fragile.

At 2:00 p.m., the worst of the storm was over. If I left now, I would have five hours to drive what normally would require 45 minutes. This should be enough time to meander the maze. As a first step, I would test the local roads before checking out of my room.

I successfully forded the local flooding. The interstate entrance was closed as expected and a yellow highway department truck blocked its ramp. I stopped and talked to the driver and asked him to 'critique' my escape route. He knew of more blocked roads so some revisions were made. This was a most fortunate break. I felt confident in my plan.

I returned to the hotel, packed my bag, called Northwest once again to confirm my flight and tested the BAT-ROAM-SYNC of my cell phone. All was ready.

I tuned my car radio to the local high school station because it provided weather reports and road conditions. And it played great classical music. Wagner's Ride of the Valkyries would have been appropriate.

The drive was eerie, like a post nuclear war movie. The road was all mine, driving virtually alone. Only a rare SUV splashed in the street. Shopping centers, businesses and homes were dark, many boarded with plywood and duct tape. No people were to be seen. Stoplights were out or blinking. I was nearly alone on the road that was littered with debris, branches and big water puddles. Even the massive Newport News shipyard was ghostly still in the rainy mist.

So far, my route worked as planned. The last challenge in my odyssey would be crossing the mouth of the James River at Chesapeake Bay. Only two of the four bridges remained open. My plan included one of the bridges plus a diversion to the other as a back-up. Reluctantly, I entered the freeway entrance to the Hampton Roads Bridge/Tunnel, knowing that if it were blocked, it would be perilous to go back. Alone on a 6-lane freeway, no traffic in either direction, I launched the over water segment of my adventure.

Seven feet of storm surge, combined with high tide and swells, formed waves that nipped at the base of the roadway. I rolled down the window to smell the salt spray. The radio played Tchaikovsky's "Fifth Piano Concerto" like a movie score to my action flick, while a salty mist wetted my face. It was glorious.

But it was also scary. As a Midwesterner, I am not accustomed to crossing a stormy ocean alone--in a car!

Now the road ahead disappeared—only ocean lay before me. I was about to dive under the water as I entered the tunnel entrance. There was no going back now. I slowed and checked the road for water and I examined the ceiling for leaks. To my relief, no giant squid had commandeered the tunnel to devour me, car and all. Yet I marveled at my situation—silently alone, under the ocean, in the remnants of a hurricane.

Eventually my car emerged from the ocean and glided into Norfolk, another city darkened and silenced by the storm. Approaching the airport, I looked for air traffic. None. The control tower looked lifeless, the parking lots were empty. The only moving creature was the rotating antenna of the ASR-9 radar, hungry for airplanes.

I surrendered my faithful car to a lone Hertz employee who was well covered in a yellow poncho. His handheld computer spit out a receipt from its protective baggy.

Three of the four entrances to the terminal were sandbagged, but the ultrasonic ear of the fourth heard my approach and opened the door. The ticketing area was dark and devoid of people. Even the overhead monitors were dark. The flight status boards of US AIR, United and other airlines displayed all flights cancelled. Almost discouraged, I walked the length of the hall to the NWA counter. There, I found a handwritten note that said all flights before 7:00 p.m. were cancelled. Hmmmm--my flight was scheduled for 8:00 p.m. I called Northwest's talking computer once again and entered my flight number on the touch-tone buttons of the pay phone. Not cancelled, the synthetic voice of the mainframe assured me. There was still hope.

I bought a TIME and Scientific American at the newsstand, the only vender open. I found a seat in the passengerless terminal and waited.

Eventually a Northwest employee in a backwards baseball cap appeared at the NWA ticket counter. As he issued my boarding pass, I asked if he was confident that this flight would actually take place.

"That's what I'm told," he replied. Who are we to doubt the word of a mainframe?

I walked to gate 30, the last gate in the concourse. It was dark and lonely. Never before have I experienced an airport concourse completely devoid of life. But there, at gate 30, an Asian couple waited in the gloom. I wondered if they felt reassured by my arrival.

By 7:30, about a dozen other adventurers found their way to the gate. We chatted about the routes we took and pondered the fate of others who tried and failed or never tried at all. Then, as if by magic, a red-tailed airplane materialized, exactly on time. We boarded quietly.

From my window seat (adventurers choose window seats) I looked for other airplanes while we taxied. None. All left to avoid the storm. Mine was the first to return. Imagine a major airport devoid of airplanes. Not even ground support equipment. Could it be that I, a lover of airplanes, had died in the hurricane, and this was God's amusing means of transporting me to heaven?

As we climbed to altitude over the city, lights below were coming on. Traffic was returning to the streets.

Descending into Detroit's congestion and debarking into the busy terminal, I fell into the commotion of concourse E. It was filled with people fussing with baggage, exhausted mothers lugging small children, workaholics tapping on laptops and chatting on cell phones. Like a time traveler, I felt back to normal and back to home.

# HER FIRST SUMMER

## Mary Best

*Mary Best is a lover of life. She is retired and lives in a small town in North Carolina in a hundred year old house that she restored.*

Summer had never been her favorite time of year. For her, autumn had it, hands down. But summer had its joys, and this summer she saw and appreciated its wonders as she never had before. Those eyes to see were one of the blessings of her life. So many gifts she had so often refused, focusing on the negative aspects of every experience instead of embracing the beauty. But she'd learned somewhere along the way that there was value in every experience, and she found the symbolism perfectly represented in the dark summer clouds that once would have taken away her enjoyment of the sun. Now she saw the silver lining that ringed those clouds and she gave thanks for the beauty.

It had taken her years to get here, with constant attention to her own growing consciousness. Even with that, she could not have crossed the threshold into this place of awe and gratitude without the gift of the diagnosis of a disease that threatened to cease her existence in this world. Looking back on it she could remember no time between her wish to die in the depth of the black hole she had fallen into, and the delivery of that diagnosis. The cancer had been a welcome distraction, giving her a new focus and a reason to pull herself out of the darkness, if only to prove that she could. She never had been able to refuse a challenge. And when it came, the acceptance of the fact that she would cease to be, if not now, then later, became the silver lining that ringed the cloud of threat she might have seen. This was the impetus she had hoped for on her spiritual path, the experience that can turn a belief into a knowing when the rubber hits the road. And so she used it up, facing and accepting the inevitable demise of her ego, and embracing her truth that what she really was would never die. She found in this a freedom she could never otherwise have known. Now her life was lived in every moment, with "a peace that surpasses all understanding." Now she could see the beauty and the perfection of the plan. And so summer was to her now more beautiful than it had ever been. Yet it was the same. It was she who had changed, for now her eyes could see all that she had taken for granted.

For her summer was not sunning by the pool, or partying at the beach. It was not baseball games, Fourth-of-July picnics, or outdoor barbecues. Neither was it an excuse for more TV watching due to the incessant heat, as had been the miserable cold of winter. It was in fact none of those things generally associated with summer. For her, summer was appreciated as nature's beauty, as were all the seasons. Each season had its unique gifts to bring and, as with people, she found its beauty in that uniqueness. Summer was nature, and as she grew older she had become more in tune with nature and its beauty and perfect balance. Summer was a part of that balance.

She was blessed to live in the South, the humid and unbearably hot south, so she could not deny the potential misery of those summer days when the temperature hovered near one-hundred, and the humidity pushed the effect beyond the mark. But she found that the towering pecan and oak trees that shaded her yard would also shade her, and the gentle welcome breeze that played in their branches and cooled her body brought with it a symphony she had never taken the time to hear before. Even in the unrelenting heat, she preferred lying in the cool grass beneath the trees to sitting in the air-conditioned house where all the comforts she'd thought she needed deprived her of the gifts of nature. She learned to work before the sun exerted its authority over the day, and after it gave it up. She learned to flow with nature that way, and in many other ways. She finally saw the insanity of how she'd lived her life, always struggling against the tide, resisting the natural flow of things. Nature said to follow its lead, and now that meant that she rested in the heat of the day and paid her respects to it.

She made herself a glass of iced tea and added a spearmint leaf from her herb garden. She sat in the shade and watched the robins find worms and feed their babies. She watched a squirrel work busily to build its nest in the pecan tree. It bit off one twig after another, then carried them and placed them in the fork of the branches. She sipped her tea and knew that she was the most fortunate person in the world for having the eyes to see the beauty all around her. She marveled at the innate wisdom of the squirrel. She wondered about things like whether the squirrel knew what she was doing. Was it thinking, as we think, that this twig must go here, and that one there? That the nest should be on one side of the tree or the other, for shelter from the wind and rain? Or did it just happen? Was all this busyness just a result of basic instincts, or might the squirrel process thoughts to achieve her goal? Wasn't this worth pondering? For her it was. For her, it was more valuable than all the money she might have made in the hour she spent watching this miracle and considering its implications.

When the heat was finally no more bearable, the skies darkened and the clouds burst and threw down to earth the precious gift of wetness, driving her inside. This was the time for a cup of coffee with enough cream to turn it almost white. This was the time to stand by the window in the shelter of comfort and dryness and watch nature throw her tantrum. She heard the thunder and saw the lightning and was again in awe. She wished her lover were there with her, for a storm always awakened something in her, a desire to act out her deepest passions, as nature acted out hers. A storm, she thought, was nature making love to the earth. It went as suddenly as it had come, and when it was over, she ventured outside again to sit in the garden and smell the rain.

The butterfly bush was now in full bloom and its denizens obliged, flitting about for her enjoyment. Her thoughts of them were always of their short life and of their magnificence, and she was reminded of the plaque that hung in her hallway, the one her mother had given her for her birthday. It read: "Life is not measured by the number of breaths we take, but by the moments that take our breath away." She knew that this was how she measured her life now, and that she had had more than her share of those moments. She found it interesting that humans felt the need to measure everything. They measured their age, their weight, time, the temperature, rainfall, the cost of gasoline, as if there were some reason to know these statistics. They needed to gain some measure of control over those things that controlled them, she thought, and this was their way of pretending to do that. She realized that she was excluding herself from these judgments, for though she had been one of them for most of her life, she had allowed herself the gift of freedom in giving up that need to measure and to try to control those things she could not. Now she never wore a watch, nor did she even own a clock or a calendar. Learning to live in the present had become one of the gifts she was most grateful for. She had discovered that her life was so much easier if she emulated nature and just accepted what is. She had once prayed for discernment, and finally she knew where to draw the line between surrender to what is and action to change. She saw her inspiration in the butterflies she now watched, knowing that in their perfect peace they were not concerned that they were just born yesterday and had only days left to live.

They just went about their lives, doing what butterflies came here to do, living in the moment with no care of tomorrow.

The magnolia beside her door bloomed and its fragrance was breathtaking. The wisteria that had climbed and entwined its branches no longer displayed its blossoms. Like so many of the most beautiful things in this life, they had been short-lived. Yet she knew that they would come again next spring. Just as the magnolia blossoms had opened to take the place of the clusters of purple flowers that had hung like grapes, she knew that life would offer new beauty in place of that which was lost, if she opened her eyes to see it and her heart to receive it. She understood that if she longed only for the wisteria that was no more, she would miss the joy of the majestic and fragrant magnolia flowers opening to the sun. She believed that this gift was meant just for her. What other purpose could there be for such simple beauty, but to be seen? And she knew too, that nothing of beauty could ever be lost if she held its memory in her heart.

Outside the fence, the herb garden beckoned with every imaginable herb. She adored the different scents they provided and their willingness to proliferate. The rosemary was there for her hand to brush as she walked past. The scent lingered on her hand and she could not inhale its fragrance deeply enough. She made a mental note that tomorrow she would gather the lavender flowers to make oils. Her tomato plants had been especially productive this year, and their fruits hung from their vines, red and ripe, begging to be plucked.

She could spend the entire day just noticing, paying attention, to the beauty of summer, feeling no need to be productive or to do what society said she should in order to be deemed responsible. And so on this day she did just that.

Late in the day, as the sun was giving up its reign, she and her lover took a boat ride out on the lake. The water was a mirror, perfectly still, disturbed only by their boat as they glided over the surface. Not one detail was missed in the reflection of the trees and the sky in the water. Close to the shoreline, a heron took flight as they approached, its long legs trailing its body, its size diminished by the distance it traveled. The background of the sky it flew against was lit at the horizon as if someone had switched on a lamp behind the curtains. The clouds that were puffs of white earlier in the day were now colored purple and gold as they veiled the setting sun. It was all too beautiful to express. With the waning of the sun came a gentle coolness and she drank it in, as a tall glass of water that slaked her thirst.

Maybe tonight, she thought, she would sleep out under the stars with her lover. She might be bitten by mosquitoes. She might even acquire a tick. Her friends would say that she shouldn't do such things, that she would surely get lyme disease, or be struck by lightning. She wouldn't try to convince them of what she knew. That life is too short and too beautiful to be missed because she was bound to the expectations of society by fear of sickness or death or even of being accepted as "normal." Life was too short, or maybe it was just the right length. And so too was it true of summer.

# PLAYING WITH FIRE

### Lily Iona MacKenzie

*A Canadian by birth, Lily Iona MacKenzie has taught college level writing, the humanities, and English in the San Francisco Bay Area for more than twenty years. Her poetry, essays, articles, and short fiction have appeared in numerous U.S. and Canadian publications.*

My older sister Monica and I were sharing the same bed, drifting to sleep, curled around each other like twins in a womb. I awakened briefly to the dogs' barking and then drifted off again. They were always chasing things in the night, rousing out of their dreams and pursuing shadows.

Then I was awake. Wide awake. Someone pounded on the door, and a man shouted "For Christ's sake woman, don't you know your house is on fire!" Mum shrieked, "Dad, get the girls." I clung to Monica. Heavy boots thumped on the kitchen floor, and the screen door squeaked and slammed shut several times. Another unfamiliar voice shouted, "We need lots of water, Alan, start pumping. Lloyd, start a bucket brigade. Murray, get the goddamn hose!"

By then I could smell smoke. Faintly. Headlights swept across the bedroom wall, chasing away the dark, and tires ground on gravel. Cars pulled into the yard, their doors slamming. More shouts, voices yelling, words indecipherable.

This must be a bad dream; I wanted to go back to sleep. But Monica grabbed my hand and pulled me off the bed. Though only twelve, she suddenly stepped over into the adult world, knowing what to do. I was confused and frightened, looking around for something to take with me. I would never see this room again.

The door opened, and smoke seeped into the bedroom. Grandpa stood there, coughing, a halo of light surrounding him. He was wearing only his dark trousers and white undershirt, black suspenders cutting into his shoulders. His gray hair stood straight up, like our roosters' comb, and his eyes bulged as I've seen them do when he's angry, red crowding out the white. "Get out. We don't have time to waste."

I held back. We always seemed to be leaving. I could see all the rooms I'd lived in since I was born, anonymous places in rooming houses in Edmonton and Calgary. One had no windows and only a grimy skylight. Another had cockroaches that crawled out of every crevice.

Mum, who barely finished high school, had struggled to feed my sister and me, leaving at dawn to work. She picked up any job she could as a chambermaid, cook, waitress, or house cleaner. She even sold her sewing machine so she could buy us food.

Then she married Frank, my stepfather. In the two years we'd been at his farm, I grew to love the place, all of its nooks and crannies—the walk-in pantry, shelves filled with Mason jars of food my sister and I helped Mum can: chickens, beets, dill pickles, beans, peaches. We never needed to worry about going hungry here.

I didn't want to leave again.

I also didn't want to lose anything more. I'd lost too much already. A father I'd never known. Cities we'd lived in briefly and then left.

I dove under my pillow and grabbed a tiny doll. She wore a red plaid kilt and a Tam O'shanter. A Scottish relative, one of our cousins, had sent it from Scotland, reminding me of where Mum was born. The doll seemed like family, representing the relatives I longed for.

The next I recall, someone picked me up and put me in the Mercury with my half-brother Bobbie; he wasn't quite two at the time. I was four years older. We both stared out the car windows, screaming. Smoke hovered over everything, an evil presence. Frank showed up suddenly—he'd been working in a distant field—and disappeared into the blazing house, joining the others, trying to salvage his dead parents' pictures and other family treasures. Mum flickered in and out of view, still wearing her bathrobe and slippers.

In the barn, the cattle kicked against the walls, and the chickens screeched louder than when I rode our horse Smoky into the hen house one time. The dogs crouched at the edge of the yard barking continuously, the flames wild beasts they were trying to subdue.

Neighbor men and women rushed into the house and grabbed clothes, dishes, and furniture, dropping them in the yard and going back for more. Some frenzy took over, and a few people deliberately smashed dishes and other things. When Mum talked of the fire later, she couldn't get over the way her friends attacked our crystal chandelier, an antique that Frank's mother had brought with her from

Chicago when she and her husband homesteaded in Alberta. The neighbors seemed determined to destroy it. And they did.

I was learning fast that humans could be "two-faced," as Mum called it. They could be generous, loving, and kind one minute. The next, they might be the exact opposite, stabbing you in the back with their words or actions. It was a lesson I never forgot. I found myself always waiting for the other shoe to fall with family, friends, or strangers. A Mr. Hyde lurked inside everyone. But sometimes it took being under pressure, internal or external, to release him.

Monica—hysterical because the black ebony upright she spent hours playing was still inside the house—tried to move it herself. Two men carried her out, and she beat on them with her fists, kicking and screaming. "Let me go. I want the piano!"

She wanted the piano, but I wanted the whole house. A two-story, wood-frame structure, it had a wrap-around wooden porch. We sat out there on summer evenings and visited with neighbors passing by. I loved the attic where Monica and I gave tea parties with the doll-size set of real China cups, saucers, and plates that Frank's mother had kept from her own childhood. I also spent hours there going through scrapbooks Frank's mother accumulated of all the greeting cards she'd received during her life. They amazed me. Angels popped out on the end of three-dimensional coils, and girls my age wore picture hats trimmed with ripe cherries and delicate chiffon dresses.

The flames, more visible now, took large bites out of the roof, sparks sending shooting stars into the night sky. It took two men to keep Monica outside, and she didn't stop struggling until she saw the piano wobbling over the doorsill, onto the porch, and then into the yard. It looked terribly out of place there.

The fire hypnotized me. The way the flames changed shape, suggesting multiple images, reminded me of clouds. I found them beautiful. At the same time as I was screeching, tears running down my face, I also was enjoying the excitement, the raw power that was devouring our house.

This fire reminded me of another. Not long before our first Christmas at the farm, we all had returned from the city late. It was a Saturday, the day we went to the farmer's market to get rid of our eggs and whatever vegetables we had to sell. We did our shopping then, too, always a full day.

When we got home, the house was freezing, and we hadn't had dinner yet. We needed a fire, quickly. Frank stuffed the stove with wood and coal, took a can of kerosene, poured it into the interior, and lit a match. It exploded, flames biting into his wool shirt and his hair, searing his face, attacking the wall. We managed to put this fire out before it did more damage, though the walls were blackened with soot and we had to repaint them.

I don't remember how we got Frank to the hospital in Calgary. Grandpa couldn't drive; Mum had just learned. She could manage the country roads, but city streets frightened her.

I do recall how strange that house felt without my stepfather. He was a strong presence, moving quietly from task to task, his whole history embedded in that place. I never knew, though, when he might explode like that stove. It happened when I least expected it.

One night we got home late from a party at a neighbor's place. I was just four then, and I had to pee before going to bed. I sat on the chamber pot (we didn't have an indoor toilet yet), whining a little. Frank stood over me, the veins in his neck bulging, his face red. From that angle, he seemed like an enraged giant. Furious because I was taking too long, he slapped my face so hard I flew off the pot. Its contents showered us both.

Mum screamed at him not to hit one of her girls again. If he did, she would leave him. But the damage was done. One of my eyes was blood red for weeks, and I never lost the memory of that outburst. I always felt wary around him, even when he called me "toots" and patted me affectionately on the head.

After that first fire, we visited Frank in the hospital, and I couldn't get over how different he looked in that setting. He seemed much smaller wearing a hospital nightshirt and faded blue bathrobe, his face wrapped in bandages. His weathered skin appeared vulnerable surrounded by all that white, and he no longer felt threatening. He had to remain in the hospital until the scab from the burn came off.

Monica and I were appearing in the Christmas concert that year. My brother Bobbie had just been born. I had turned five in October, and Mum and Grandpa were teaching me to play "Good King Wenceslas" on the piano. Grandpa had been a schoolmaster in the highlands of Scotland till he moved to Canada, seeking a better life. He never found it. His rigid, authoritarian teaching style never caught on in the new setting. He had to resort to blue-collar work, difficult for a man who spoke several languages, read 18th and 19th Century novels, and always wore suits and a fedora.

Frank promised to be home for the performance, so everyday he worked at removing the scab. The night of the concert, a full moon hung in the sky like a cameo, its light causing the new snow on the ground to glow from within. Monica and I walked to the Oddfellow's Hall, leaving early so we could do one more rehearsal, our feet disappearing in a foot of fresh snow. Mum and Grandpa were coming later.

Since I was one of the youngest performers, I appeared early in the program. I walked out onto the stage and found my mum's face in the crowd before taking my seat on the piano stool. Seeing her there reassured me. I wore a dress she made me from an old one of hers and white cotton stockings held up with garters. I had practiced the piece so many times, my fingers played it automatically.

After I finished, I stood in front of the piano and took a bow. That's when I noticed him at the back of the hall. My stepfather had caught a ride with someone and made it to the concert just in time.

And then the fire was over, though smoke still billowed into the sky, its smell everywhere. It followed us for months, everything we'd rescued permeated by its odor. I'm not sure I ever lost the stench. It penetrated to the core of my being, lurking there to remind me of how little control I had over anything.

I felt like something that had been roasted over a grill, the outside burnt to a crisp, my interior raw, still registering the shock of seeing our home destroyed—how quickly things can change. It set up an underlying terror in me. Life seemed too unpredictable, like Frank's mood swings—a nice guy one minute, but who knows what the next.

Luckily, before the fire, he'd picked up another piece of land just four miles out of town that had a house on it. But it needed painting and fixing up, so we camped out at the Watsons' place for a few nights, some neighbors of ours. Then we moved everything we'd rescued into the one-story, three-bedroom bungalow. Though it was good to have a home again, we felt more isolated, our nearest neighbor at least a mile away. We'd been used to living in town, and though it was not more than a hamlet, at least we had others nearby.

Monica and I shared one bedroom. So did Grandpa and Bobbie. Mum and Frank had the other. One winter night I awakened after a few hours, needing to pee. I inched out of bed, the linoleum floor cold under my bare feet, grabbed the chamber pot, pulled it out, and sat on it, staring out the bedroom window, curtains parted as in a theatre. Chartreuse veiled the night sky, whispers of smoke falling from the heavens, a waterfall of light and color.

I sat there for a long time, enchanted, forgetting the cold. I thought I was dreaming. Here was a very different kind of fire—soft, haunting, mysterious. Not destructive.

In the morning, I overheard Mum and Frank talking about Northern Lights. They sat at the breakfast table, elbows resting on the frayed, flowered oilcloth cover, each smoking a cigarette rolled from the blue can of Players' tobacco. He wore a red wool plaid shirt with gray wool trousers; Mum was still in her green chenille bathrobe. "They put on a great show last night, eh?" Mother said. Then she looked at me: "You should have seen them. It looked like the sky was on fire."

I only nodded, standing close to our woodstove so my body could soak up the warmth, wanting to protect the image I saw in the night and hold it inside—not let it evaporate.

I held other things close to me in that house. The runts of the litter found a home in our kitchen, kept in a box by the stove. They replaced dolls for Monica and me. We cradled them in our arms, baby lambs bleating, their mouths dripping the milk we fed them from baby bottles. Piglets, pink and hairless, squirmed and oinked, dribbling all over us, pushing wet snouts into our hair.

We had a collie, Lassie, and another dog that waited at the corner for us to come home, sensing us miles away and running to meet us. Monica, Bobbie, and I rode both dogs. There were always cats as well, living in the barn, sitting outside the kitchen window and watching us.

The radio was our main connection to the world, a magical box that we all gathered around most evenings. Mum would sew or work on the huge stuffed dolls and animals she made us for Christmas gifts. Grandpa sucked on a pipe. Frank wheezed, suffering another asthma attack. Monica did her homework.

I lived for the radio dramas: "Fibber Magee and Molly"; "The Green Hornet"; "Boston Blackie"; "Amos and Andy." And "Frankenstein." I can still hear his footsteps echoing throughout the house, terrifying and terribly real. So real that for years I swore he was following me if I was outside at night.

We didn't just listen to dramas on the radio. Some of the stations played popular music—hits by Cole Porter, Lerner and Loewe, Rodgers and Hammerstein. Monica had a gift for improvising on the piano and was able to imitate what she heard on the radio. Mum and I sang along: "Santa Lucia," "Whispering Hope," "Galway Bay." Music flooded the house.

At Halloween, the harvest over, we had a party, kids and adults. We filled our metal bathtub with water that we usually only hauled out on Saturday nights. Everyone took turns bobbing for apples, blindfolded. While we younger children were with the adults inside, the older kids roamed the countryside, looking for mischief.

After we went to bed, an insistent bawling awakened us. We all went outside to see what was wrong and found one of our calves in the back seat of our car. Panicked, it had shit all over the seat and floor. When we got up the next morning, we found the outhouse on its side, knocked over by pranksters.

And then it was Christmas again, and Mum made us identical dresses out of scraps she found, gold with red trim, to wear at the Christmas concert. Mum and Grandpa helped me memorize "I had a little doggy. He used to sit and beg. But doggy tumbled down the stairs and broke his little leg. Oh, doggy, I will nurse you, and try to make you well. And you shall have a collar, too, and little silver bell." Of course, I didn't just memorize the words, but I had to know all the inflections as well—when to emphasize a phrase and when to pause.

No one seemed to realize how painful it was for me to sing this song. A car had run over Ginger, my first dog. Ginger's face swam in front of me every time I uttered the words, and I often stumbled at the part "Oh, doggy, I will nurse you and try to make you well."

The night of the performance, I was so nervous my teeth chattered. I waited back stage with the other kids, lined up by age. Finally my name was called. I walked out on stage and froze. Bears stared at me from the audience, brown bears just like I'd seen in the picture book, *Goldie Locks and the Three Bears*.

The woman accompanying me on the piano hissed, "Hurry up, you're on." Terrified, my legs almost crumpling under me, I managed to walk to the piano. During the whole performance, I stood with my head turned to the side so I couldn't see the bears while I sang. And then I ran off stage, wondering how bears could make such loud clapping sounds with their furry paws.

I liked it best when we visited the Wilsons, a family of thirteen kids who lived just a few miles away. Inez and Howard had produced this brood, and they always seemed somewhat stunned that they'd done it. They lived in a ramshackle two-story house, the exterior just bare wood, any paint having worn off years earlier. The harsh winters and driving summer sun took their toll on the place.

Inez, a big sturdy woman, as tall as Howard and white haired though she was only in her forties, wore ill-fitting flowered housedresses, but she appeared queenly even in rags. The Wilson kids didn't seem to mind wearing clothes that had seen better days. The elbows, knees, and sometimes rear-ends were worn out of the fabric, their skin showing through.

Whatever the Wilson house lacked in beauty it made up for in warmth, human hospitality, and caring. During the coldest winter nights when their furnace had barely enough fuel to heat the drafty rooms, the number of bodies in the place managed to make it seem balmy.

Whenever I could, I slept over with my best friend Annabelle, one of the younger girls. All thirteen children crowded into two or three big beds, the smell of urine and unwashed sheets overpowering. But it grew on me, like the strong-smelling blue cheese Grandpa taught me to love, feeding me Roquefort from his fingers.

We stayed awake at the Wilsons for hours telling ghost stories, screeching and laughing, eventually falling asleep when our eyelids could no longer stay open.

They also had a large barn with a hay loft, and when the kids took a break from their chores, we swung on a rope from one end of the barn to the other, letting go and landing in piles of sweet-smelling hay that scratched our legs and arms; it also smelled of the mice that scurried around under its surface. Work and play: we wove them together like the rope we swung from. If we hadn't embellished on cleaning the stalls or weeding the garden, life would have seemed too grim.

Tired of swinging in the hayloft, we rode calves around the corral, our feet grazing the ground. Or we cut the tails off salamanders, wanting to see if they'd grow back. It was all for science, all an experiment. Life was an experiment. How far could we push the boundaries? How high could we fly in the hayloft and drop without breaking bones or getting lost in the rafters?

I was getting used to our new house; it began to feel like home to me. One night I woke to the smell of smoke again. This time I didn't wait for someone else to get me. I jumped out of bed and yelled at Monica. "Fire." We both rushed into the living room, coughing.

Frank flew out of the other bedroom, zipping up his trousers, naked from the waist up. Mum followed, hair in rags, wrapping her chenille robe around herself. We swooped into the kitchen. Smoke billowed out of the oven, jabs of flame feeding it. Frank opened the oven door and cursed. "Christ, who put the leftover grease in here?" We always put drippings from bacon or other fatty foods in a jar and left it on the counter so we didn't clog the drain.

Grandpa wandered into the room, his hair tousled, still half asleep. "What's going on?" he asked, looking first at Mum and then at Frank.

"Did you put grease in the oven?" Frank asked.

Grandpa nodded.

"Where's your head, man!"

Grandpa hadn't started this fire intentionally, of course, just as he hadn't deliberately started the other fire. Trying to be helpful, he'd taken ashes outside after dinner and dumped them under the wooden porch.

Unfortunately, the embers were still alive.

Luckily, we were, too. But Frank refused to take any more chances and ordered Grandpa to move out. This time, Mum didn't resist, but I hated to see him go. Grandpa got work as a hired hand someplace else, and, as far as I know, he never started fires again.

# YOU CAN'T HATE ME FOR LONG

## Annie Neal

*Second Prize – contest of June 2007*

*Annie Neal is from rural North Carolina, currently working on her BFA at Goddard College. She loves and is loved devoutly, and that makes the only difference – in writing and life.*

When my friends meet Roy he always wants to know if they, on that particular day, are sober. They inevitably raise their eyebrows in surprise and ask, "Do I look drunk?"

"He just wants to know how you're doing," I whisper and they nod and smile and are grateful to get away from my crazy grandfather who has his own lingo and is proud that he's scared them. When we make our escape I can see their mental wheels hard at work. They're trying to figure him out. They want to pin him down, but I have no advice.

I've been working on the same thing for twenty-one years. It's taken six of those for me to accept how incomprehensible he can be. The last six years without my grandma have taught me two concrete things about my grandpa. He is capable of anything, and if I am infuriated by his actions then he will probably enjoy them all the more, just as he enjoyed annoying his wife.

She had been dead two weeks when I found him ripping a bush from the corner of her flowerbed. "What in the hell are you doing?" I screamed at him, but he didn't even look up. "They're not your bushes. What are you doing?" I tried again. I hated him, because I knew he wasn't going to answer me. All my spring memories include this same scene. Roy picks one living thing out of the yard, and he wages war with it. We've lost two cherry trees, a peach tree, a red tip, and a cactus. Now my grandma was gone, and it seemed like this poor box wood was just the opening act for his reign of terror.

As he's cutting the limbs from the stump, one by one, I know I can't stop him. You can never stop him. Still I don't have to help him

47

either. I sit on the porch, my grandma's porch, and watch the carnage. It's always like this with him. He's a movie I can't pause, and sometimes the subtitles disappear but the sound keeps going.

He cuts another branch. The subtitles are nonexistent now. I am without translation, my interpretation of the plot is shot to hell, and all I can do is infuse the scene with my own meaning. He's taking over.

He finishes his destruction of the bush and hauls all its parts to the brush pile. I never move to help, and he doesn't ask. Usually he would tell me how lazy I am, or at least point at the limbs and mime laborious action. Now, as if to confirm my worst fear, he ignores me completely. I have no control.

As the weeks go by he checks off more of his list. He goes looking for all her secret hiding spots for everything from twenty dollar bills to candy she kept for her low blood sugar. He gets down her Bible and pulls money from between the pages like he had put it there himself. I catch him wearing her coat to the mail box one evening, and even though her injured back had forced them into different beds before I was born the light is on in her bedroom every night when I look across the yard from our trailer. I spend most of my time cursing him under my breath while I spy on his every move. At least no more bushes have been sacrificed to his insanity.

"Pauline is going to come back and haunt him if he doesn't stop," I tell Mama. "Maybe he wants her to," she says. This hurts. I think about Roy opening the two twenty dollar bills that my grandma had folded in her Bible, and I become newly enraged that he was undoing what she had done and could never do again. Only then I think about his fingers working so slowly, smoothing the creases back, so carefully, tracing her invisible fingerprints. We're in the same world of hurt with two different maps.

The first week after the last frost I find Roy out in the flower bed again. His back is to me, and I sneak up on him slowly, afraid of what I'll see. There's a tiny green stalk encompassed in earth, its skinny body the replacement for the murdered shrub. "Where'd you get that?" I want to know.

"Somebody up at the church." He doesn't tell me the whole story, so I don't ask. "It needs some water," I offer.

"Done gave it some."

He pulls himself to his feet and goes in the house. I'm left staring at this plant wondering how the same man who conveniently forgot to water my grandma's violets and who is systematically ridding our yard of all things leafy has purposefully sustained life. The months turn my disbelief to amazement when the plant doesn't die but instead gets taller and finally becomes recognizable as a flower with actual honest-to-God blooms clinging to its stem.

We're half asleep one morning when Roy bangs on the trailer door and comes in.

"Well did you see it?" he asks Mama without specification. She looks at me blankly. "The flower," I tell her.

"It's got five blooms," Roy says without skipping a beat. "Bet you can't get one like that." He's proud. So am I. I'm learning his language.

# THE CURSE OF THE GIFTED

## Carol Ryals

*Carol Ryals currently resides in Brownsburg, Indiana, with her husband and their two children.*

*The opinions expressed in this essay are my own personal observations and theories. I have not done extensive research, and I do not consider myself to be an expert on this subject.*

Based on some standardized testing at his school, my son's IQ is considered to be genius level. He has also been called "intellectually gifted" and "high ability." My son has been labeled, and people have made many misconceptions about him based on that label.

People assume that, because he has a high IQ, my son will do well in school. When I was first told of his test results and that his IQ was at genius level, I was somewhat bewildered because he does not excel in school. In fact, he frequently and repeatedly underachieves. I have since often exclaimed, "I don't understand it! You could be getting straight A's if you would just get your act together and apply yourself." Apparently, "getting his act together," is not something he, as a gifted person, is likely to do. In his "gifted" eyes, getting his act together also means conforming to someone else's half-baked notion of the way things should be. He marches to the beat of his own drummer, and sometimes that means not conforming to what is expected by educators and, therefore, also means not always getting high grades.

People sometimes also assume that, because he has a high IQ, he learns quickly. However, sometimes I feel like he is being taught the same concept over and over again, and he just doesn't get it. It may not be that my son doesn't understand what's going on. It may be that he understands too well. I believe that, when he sees that others lack the patience and understanding to see his vision, intelligence and courage to do what he knows is correct (rather than what the status quo expects), he may very well give up. Another theory I sometimes entertain on this issue is that his brain has already gone on to something else before whoever is teaching him is finished. Therefore, he has long stopped listening and misses whatever point the teacher is trying to make.

Another misconception people make about my son is that, because he has a high IQ, he should be more mature than other kids his age. I have found this to be quite the opposite. He is considerably less mature than his peers of average intelligence. In fact, some people have assumed he is mentally disabled because they witness extremely immature behavior coming from a boy who is obviously too old to behave like a three year old. My theory on this issue is that his brain is working at a higher level than those around him and, when those around him don't see things the way he sees them, he gets frustrated. As stated above, although he has been taught time and again the appropriate way to handle frustration, he hasn't grasped the concept yet. Therefore, he is prone to meltdowns.

People also assume that, because he has a high IQ, he can communicate well. Once again, I have found the opposite to be true. Even though his test score shows his language arts skills should be superior, he does not communicate well, either orally or in writing. Again, people who do not know him think he has a disability when they see his written work, listen to him read aloud, or even try to carry on a polite conversation with him.

One more assumption people make is that, because he has a high IQ, my son will be accepted and well liked. Society does not accept those who don't conform. Being a nonconformist, he argues frequently, which doesn't earn him points with anyone. People find it hard to accept those who are different. Therefore, he is quite often alienated by his peers. Children can be very cruel. As a mother, I find this to be exceptionally heart wrenching.

People assume that the intellectually gifted know who they are at a very young age. However, I believe my son has had a difficult time finding his identity. People usually find their identity, in part, by trying out and testing various things to see what they enjoy and what they are good at. I find that gifted people are better than average at many things. Therefore, they are not always given the opportunity to try something they might enjoy because they are already considered to be intellectually past it.

People believe that those born with a gift are lucky. A gifted child may think he has been cursed. My son is considered brilliant. Others rarely see beyond that. They might admire him. They might resent him. They might think he is strange. They very well might not include him in the simple pleasures of life because they think whatever they are doing is beneath him.

People also assume that, because my son has a high IQ, I also have one. I do not. However, although my son doesn't conform and tends to argue every step of the way, he rarely points out the fact that he is much smarter than me. My genius child does not expect me to teach him things he will learn from those who have been trained to teach the intellectually gifted. He does not expect me to be smarter than him. He does not expect me to be better than him at anything. He only expects me to be his mother. By definition, a mother's role is to love, nourish and protect. It doesn't take a genius to do that.

# Gutenberg's Gift

## Alex Weisler

*Alex Weisler is in his first year at the Schreyer Honors College of Penn State University. Majoring in journalism and international politics, he hopes to pursue a career at a major metropolitan daily.*

Don't scoff at my choice of the printing press, for there exist entire galleries devoted to industrial design. And no Cynthia Wynn scrap-metal rocking chair and no Walter Dorwin Teague camera is as necessary as the book-maker, nor can any other piece of art hope to claim as potent an impact.

Johannes Gensfleisch zur Laden zum Gutenberg. It's a remarkably lengthy name for the man who engineered a silent revolution by breaking words into their smallest, most fluid components. The printing press's deceptively simple design -- dipping small, carved pieces of wood or metal into ink -- belies the magnitude of Gutenberg's impact.

The other night, I visited Gutenberg in the dank, German city of Mainz. Gutenberg brought me into his sanctum, the area of his laboratory where he had first printed his vellum bibles. I brought him news from our time -- tales of *Harry Potter* books selling billions of copies, stories of daily newspapers, of protest novels and of trashy romance tomes. Perhaps I was too eager a raconteur, for Gutenberg began to weep. I asked him what was wrong, and he replied in a voice filled all at once with gladness and bittersweet regret that nothing was wrong; rather, everything was right.

No piece of art is more intrinsically linked to posterity and to the past than the printing press; for no other piece of art is it as necessary that the government fund and nurture it. It is literacy that brings knowledge, literacy that brings toddlers out of the dark ages of board books and into the rich, fulfilling landscapes of Thomas Hardy and the Brontë sisters. And for those who absorb the works of these grand masters in different ways, the government should focus on enhancing their experience, too; catering to students with each of the multiple intelligences imbues a greater number of people with knowledge in a greater number of ways.

True, too, is the need to bring a wider swath of America's social and cultural diversity into its classrooms. It sounds foreign (and it is) but English classes would benefit from studying Vikram Chandra's Indian epic *Red Earth and Pouring Rain* or Uzodinma Iweala's visceral, electrifying *Beasts of No Nation*. Reading foreign books is like tasting a piquant jambalaya or learning about the intricacies of the Baha'i religion; more modalities of thought bring cultural awakening and understanding.

None other than the humble, faithful printing press engineers this innovation in insight. As it stamps our thoughts into thick, leather-bound volumes, it codifies and exalts human diversity. So as I ponder the most influential piece of art I know, I think, why the printing press? Surely the atomic bomb had more awesome force. Certainly Grand Central Terminal possesses more beauty. And there is no denying that the telephone contains more utility. It is the printing press I keep coming back to because it is the fruits of the printing press that have launched wars and lost them, that have deluded and informed, that have been read at baptisms and read at executions. It is through the filter of words that we define our world.

# THE BACKSTREET BOOKSTORE

## Big Jim Williams

*Jim Williams, author of* THE OLD WEST *and* TALL TALES OF THE OLD WEST *audio books, has written for Western Horseman, Shoot!, Texas Livestock Weekly, American West, Orchard Press Mysteries, Radio World, and other magazines. He announces at KZSB, Santa Barbara, California. E-mail:* bigjimwilliams2@cox.net.

Charlie woke in his cluttered bedroom, and decided he'd like to re-read all the wonderful books he'd read as a boy.

Stacks and shelves of paperbacks, hard covers, and classics stuffed his small apartment, confirming his love of books. Rose, his ex-wife, called it an addiction. To Charlie it was "love," a word she never used in their book-littered bedroom she called a "pig sty!"

"I think you'd rather read than talk to me," she complained.

Charlie, on page 237 of Victor Hugo's, *The Hunchback of Notre Dame*, muttered: "Could we talk later, please? I'd like to finish--"

Her expletives startled Charlie, but he didn't stop reading.

Rose threatened divorce many times in their twenty-year marriage. Then one weekend, while Charlie's nose and thick glasses were deep in Shakespeare's "Richard III," she left without a word. She took suitcases, silverware, bankbooks, and her collection of salt-and-pepper shakers. Removing the collection, the latest copy of TV Guide, and their cell phone and charger indicated she wasn't coming back, confirmed hours later after Charlie finished "Richard III" and found Rose's farewell note, in that order.

That was four years ago. Now retired a month, Charlie was no longer head bookkeeper of the town's paper mill. Forty-three years was enough.

It was a beautiful day, clear and warm, the way Charlie liked mornings. His long bout--the doctor said it bordered on pneumonia--was suddenly gone; his cough, too, and his chest no longer hurt, or rattled.

He put on his best suit and tie, and donned his bowler hat, but left his cane by the front door. A hip begged for surgery, "Thank God it doesn't hurt today," he said. "Feels great!"

He wished he still had his old dog to walk. Rose's allergies had long ago sent Hugo, his beloved golden retriever, named after author Victor Hugo, to the pound where he died a week later.

"Of a broken heart," claimed the attendant.

Charlie never forgave Rose.

Charlie decided to walk downtown to the big-chain bookstore. The exercise might reduce his growing paunch. It was only ten blocks. He felt so good he almost bounced. He whistled, too, something Rose hated. In no hurry, he took a shortcut through a side street.

"What's this? I didn't know there was a book store back here."

The small frame building, squeezed between two office buildings, was in a block Charlie hadn't walked in months. He thought he knew where every store was in town-—especially bookstores.

"Good Morning, sir," smiled a short man behind the counter. "How are you?"

"Never felt better. I don't remember seeing your shop before. How long has it been here?"

The man laughed and said, "Years and years. But seems like an eternity."

The sign on the storefront window read:

Books
Old & New
Bought & Sold

A big yellow cat was sleeping in the sun in the book-filled window.

A tiny silver bell above the door announced customers.

"Glad I found you." Charlie's eyes searched the long shelves, then turned to the proprietor. "Been thinking about re-reading all my childhood favorites. Do you have a copy of Mark Twain's *Huckleberry Finn?* I'd love to--?"

Charlie stopped in mid-sentence. "Well, I'll be. It's right in front of me here on the counter. What a coincidence."

"Yes, it is." The squat shopkeeper came with a pixie smile, wire-rimmed glasses, and a round head ringed with white fuzz. He wore a bow tie, multi-pocket vest, and sleeve garters like his grandfather.

"The very book I wanted."

Charlie read it in one day. "Now, I'd like to read *Tom Sawyer*," he told himself. The bell above the shop door signaled his return.

"I'm back, to find a copy of--"

"*Tom Sawyer*," interrupted the bookseller, cleaning his glasses.

"Yes, but..." sputtered Charlie.

"It's on the counter."

"...how did you know?"

"Anyone reading *Huckleberry Finn* and returning a day later, smiling, must want to read *Tom Sawyer*."

Charlie took the book home and laughed and cried with Tom, Huck, Jim, Becky Thatcher and Aunt Polly. A reading hunger always gnawed at his stomach. "Now," he told himself, "I'd like to re-read all the adventure books I had as a kid: *Last of the Mohicans, The Rover Boys, Swiss Family Robinson, Call of The Wild, Kidnapped*, and *Treasure Island*."

"*Last of the Mohicans* is on the shelf behind you," said the shopkeeper when Charlie returned. "It's been waiting *just* for you."

"You must be psychic."

Charlie returned the next day. "What about--?"

The proprietor gestured toward an adjacent shelf containing *The Rover Boys, Swiss Family Robinson, Call of the Wild, Kidnapped*, and *Treasure Island*.

"How did you know?" asked Charlie.

The man patted a thick volume of Sherlock Holms: "Elementary, my dear boy. Elementary." He released a cherubic smile. "See anything else you'd like?"

The overflowing shelves contained Charlie's favorite authors: Shakespeare, De Maupassant, O. Henry, Jack London, John Steinbeck, and more.

"Incredible," chuckled Charlie. "I never knew your bookstore existed until days ago, and I've lived here for years. Your shelves contain every book I've ever read."

He caressed the volumes, and stopped on Daniel Defoe's, *Robinson Crusoe*. "Looks just like the copy I had when I was a kid." He opened it and gasped: "My name and age are on the flyleaf. This was my book! Mom gave it to me on my tenth birthday. How did it get here? Unbelievable."

"Not really, Charlie."

"How...How did you know my name?"

"*We* know you, Charlie. Always have."

Charlie smiled and shook a finger at the bookseller. "Did the guys at the mill put you up to this? Those jokesters would love to--"

The shopkeeper interrupted and gestured toward the rows of bookcases. "These books are yours, Charlie. Every one. Read by you and locked in your 64-year-old memory."

Charlie looked dazed.

"Look behind you," said the shopkeeper.

"What?"

"Turn around."

Charlie did.

The shop's interior had mysteriously expanded with endless shelves of books.

"Where did all these come from? They weren't here minutes ago." Charlie searched the titles. "These are all the books I've ever *wanted* to read."

"You've always said: 'So many books, so little time.'"

Charlie's hand delicately brushed the titles: "The complete works of Ernest Hemingway, Stephen King, John Steinbeck, James Michener, Faulkner, London, Thackeray, Hugo, Dickens, Thoreau, Hawthorne, and Melville...all here; and biographies, philosophers, the great plays, too. And history: the Civil War, the World Wars, Lewis and Clark, the great explorers, and David Lavender's *Bent's Fort*. All his books on the American West I never had time to read."

"Now you've all the time in the world."

"I'm retired," grumbled Charlie. "But still have things to do. Can't just sit around all day and--"

"Remember the first morning you walked in here? Didn't need your cane. Said you'd 'never felt better.'"

"How did you know I used a cane?"

"That was the morning you *left*."

"But I'd just *arrived*. You're talking crazy!" Charlie moved toward the door.

"Wait! Let me explain."

Charlie reluctantly dropped into a chair by the counter.

"This isn't just a bookstore, Charlie."

Charlie stared at the proprietor. "Who are you?"

"Name's there in the corner of the front window."

Charlie looked. "Says 'A. Gabriel, Proprietor.'"

"That's me."

"The 'A' stands for what?"

"*Angel*. I'm an Angel."

Charlie snickered. "You're what?"

"I'm The Angel Gabriel."

"You're The Angel Gabriel?" Charlie shook his head and continued snickering.

"I play a mean trumpet, too."

Charlie stood. "Think I'd better go."

Gabriel touched Charlie's coat sleeve. "I'm here to help you transfer to a mystical world of untold beauty behind a door you've wondered and heard about all your life."

"You're telling me you're the Angel Gabriel. I'm sorry, but I find that—"

"And that you'll now have all eternity to read all the books you've ever wanted to read."

"I must be going crazy." Charlie fell back into his chair.

"And, Charlie. Look outside."

A Golden Retriever dog, tied to a lamppost, quietly sat staring at the shop entrance. Then it saw Charlie, wagged its tail, frantically tugged at its leash, pawed the air, and barked loudly.

"Why...Why..." stuttered Charlie. "That looks just like my old dog, Hugo.

"It is Hugo."

"But Hugo's dead!"

Gabriel smiled his broadest smile. "And so are you, Charlie. You died two weeks ago in your sleep."

# THE BLACK STAG AND HIS MISTRESS

## Monica Eaton

*Monica Eaton lives in a small town in Minnesota and has been writing for about two years. In her spare time she likes to read, write, knit and play with the family dog.*

It was thought that he was a demon and she was an immortal sent to that world to tame him. He was twice the size of the desired White Stag. His antlers were glossy obsidian, his hair as black as a starless sky, his eyes were bright embers and his hooves were as coals. They all called him demon; she called him Lacksteeg.

She, too, was dark and mysterious. Her chestnut brown hair cascaded to her waist and her gray eyes shone like the moon. Some say that her voice was enchanted, that it was soft and melodious, to hold him under her power. The wind carried her name and spread it across the earth, telling everyone that she was called Kadreya.

The Black Stag and Kadreya were inseparable; no one knew how they had met, what exactly they were or what their purpose in that world was. But now, growing older, they feel it was time that the world knew their story. I am here to tell it to you, so gather round and allow me to open the door for you that will take us into the world of the Black Stag and his Mistress.

The story begins when Kadreya was only eleven years old. She lived with her family in a small, broken down hut in a village called Queyance; a small community consisting of many small huts, a merchant shop and a tavern.

Kadreya had two siblings, both older. They were Andreya, who was at the time seventeen, and a brother called Hutton, who was fifteen. Her brother and sister were both kind to her, but she seemed to constantly be in their way. She felt very alone. Her father, Garwood, was often in the village tavern, while her mother, Della, constantly fancied herself ill.

They were farmers, and as such kept great fields of corn, wheat and barley. But this year the crops were not growing well. Something was eating them. Kadreya stayed in the fields for many nights, trying to find out who or what it was. Then, for many days there was no evidence of the culprit ever having been there, it was as if it had disappeared. Finally, one evening the something returned and revealed itself. It was a deer, bigger than any Kadreya had ever seen before. He stood there eating, she squealed with joy and his head shot up. Kadreya quickly put her hands over her mouth, afraid that she might have scared him away. He just looked at her. She timidly took a couple steps toward him. She saw her reflection in his eyes. Suddenly his head turned. Kadreya heard the whir of an arrow, and then the deer was lying motionless on the ground, his expressionless eyes wide open and an arrow in his heart.

Kadreya knelt by the deer's lifeless body and began to silently weep for this lost mystery as Hutton strode toward her and pulled his arrow out of the poor beast.

"Father will be pleased," he said proudly.

Kadreya could only nod. Hutton did not notice his sister's silence and so left her outside and returned to the house to tell the story of his heroism to attentive ears.

Kadreya soon followed Hutton to the house and heard him telling the story as everyone sat around the table. When he finished, the family applauded except Kadreya.

Her father noticed the sad look on her face and was very angry, as he had not had a drink in a long time. His debt to the tavern had grown too large for him and he refused to work off what he owed.

"What is the matter with you?" he demanded.

"Nothing," she answered softly.

"Then congratulate your brother!"

By now, everyone was silent; they all knew better than to interrupt an argument with Garwood. Kadreya looked at the deer still lying outside; her father followed her gaze and realized what was wrong. Picking up his big hunting knife he stomped out the door, they all watched as he marched toward the deer. Their father soon returned with his sleeves pulled up, blood covering his arms. He held something in his fist.

"Make a fire outside." His voice quivered with anger and fear of the thing he held.

Everyone hesitated.

"Now!"

Hutton quickly went outside and built a fire.

Their father followed the boy. Everyone else came also. When the entire family was gathered around the fire, Garwood turned to them, their terror mirrored in his eyes.

"The heart still beats," he held up his fist, and they all gasped as they saw that he held the beating heart of the dead deer.

Garwood turned to the fire and threw the heart into it, then went back to the house, his family following silently. Kadreya quickly wiped away the tears that filled her eyes. She did not know why she mourned for the deer. Perhaps he felt as alone as she did. Another tear ran down her cheek and fell onto the fire, somehow extinguishing it. Kadreya did not notice until she felt something softly nudge her shoulder. It was the deer, reborn from the ashes as the Black Stag. She looked up at him with a fear that soon changed to curiosity and wonderment. He saw her expression change and turned away, galloping off into the night. Kadreya lingered for a little while longer after he disappeared from sight. She looked down at the place where the fire had been and noticed a single glowing ember in the ashes with something around it that sparkled in the dim light. Kadreya picked it up and held it in front of her face. The thing that she held was a silver chain and hanging from it was silver in an elliptical shape circled by a spiral made of the same stuff and in the center of the ellipse was a glowing ember in a perfectly spherical shape.

"*Iyen rae het hoseheno.*" Kadreya heard a strange voice whisper; she looked around for the source but heard nothing, "*Emonmistess.*" She heard the voice again; it was a language she did not know; a language that everyone thought to be dead as well as its people.

She clutched the necklace in her fist and ran into the house. Everyone was already asleep, a good deal shaken by the events of the evening. Kadreya crawled into the bed that she shared with her sister, thinking about what she held. It filled her with a strange mixture of fear, curiosity and excitement, as did the Black Stag. She soon grew tired trying to make sense of the things that had just happened and fell asleep.

When Kadreya woke the next morning she found the house deadly quiet and the room extremely cold. She couldn't stop shivering. As she sleepily looked around the room she quickly sat up, startled. There were people in her room, strange people elegantly dressed in clothes of black, silver and midnight blue. One of the women held something in her hands, as she walked toward Kadreya she let it unfold. It was a cloak of midnight blue satin, the trimming was silver mink fur and the lining was a thick, black fur that she had never seen before. The woman wrapped the cloak around Kadreya's shoulders and she instantly stopped shaking and grew comfortably warm.

"Come." The woman spoke kindly but firmly in a thick accent and took Kadreya's hand.

"Where?" the girl asked as she let the woman lead her through the house.

They stopped just before the woman opened the door; she looked at Kadreya and whispered, "*Iyen rae het hosheno.*" Kadreya had no idea what the words meant, but from the tone with which they were spoken, she decided that these strangers must have thought that she was someone of great importance.

The woman held her gaze for a couple of seconds longer, then turned again and they walked out the door. Kadreya's eye immediately went to the grand carriage that stood on the road near their house. It was all black with silver trimming and the harnesses were midnight blue. There were four horses to pull the carriage, each had a gleaming black coat and their hooves shone like silver.

Kadreya's family was standing in a line next to the door of the house. Her mother embraced her with no tears in her eyes and a blank expression on her face, "Good-bye my darling, you must go with these people."

Her voice was filled with false sadness and regret. Kadreya's father roughly patted her head with one hand and held his morning bottle with the other. Her siblings, Andreya and Hutton just smiled and waved; there was a fleeting expression of sadness and regret on their faces. Kadreya knew that she wouldn't be missed and even though she cared as little for her family as they cared about her, tears stung her eyes just knowing that they truly didn't care.

The woman who had led her outside gently touched her shoulder, so Kadreya wiped her tears away and they stepped into the carriage and drove away.

Kadreya and the woman sat in silence for a while, just looking out the window and observing each other.

Finally the woman touched her hand to her chest and said, "Leila."

Kadreya decided that 'Leila' must be the woman's name, so she did the same to introduce herself, as she concluded by now that they did not speak the same language.

Leila shook her head and took the necklace that Kadreya still held and clasped it around her neck.

"*Emonmistess.*" She said pointing to the necklace, "Kadreya, *Emonmistess.*"

"What is it?" Kadreya asked, "What is *Emonmistess*?"

Leila put a finger to her lips and said, "Sleep."

The last thing Kadreya remembered was someone putting an arm around her shoulders, then she closed her eyes and slept.

When she woke she found herself in a giant mahogany bed with a maroon colored canopy. Kadreya was certain that the bed could have fit at least six girls her size. The mattress was soft and stuffed with goose feathers, except Kadreya didn't know this, as she had never had a mattress of this sort of quality before. The bed linens also were so comfortable and warm, she felt as if she could have stayed there forever. But there was the rest of the room to discover; its size for one thing, seemed to be a good deal larger than the hut that she used to live in.

She climbed out of bed and her feet instantly sank into a large wool rug. The hem of a silk nightgown fell to her feet. Kadreya felt the soft material. She never had anything so fine before. But she quickly drew her attention from the nightgown and back to the room.

The floor was bare and cold beyond the wool rug, but remained mostly covered by an intricately woven aerial rug. There were two large windows on opposite ends of the room and a balcony that had giant glass doors leading out to it. When she walked onto the balcony she could see the moat that surrounded the castle. Beyond the moat was a field of bluets. Inside, all of the walls were covered with tapestries that were filled with scenes of foxhunts, balls and such grand occasions as happen to people of noble bloodlines.

Next to one of these giant tapestries was a door. When Kadreya walked through it she found it was a dressing room filled with all sorts of fine clothes. She walked out again and investigated the rest of her new bedroom. A small mahogany table with a candle on it stood next to the bed. Another larger table and chair of the same wood stood near the center of the room. There were three bookshelves completely filled with leather bound wonders. Kadreya looked longingly at the books; she always wished she could read. The last that she observed were a few chairs and couches, which stood on claws, scattered about the room. Kadreya stood in the center of everything to stare and observe in awe at the wonderful things that she guessed would be hers for the time that she was there, however long that was.

As she was about to go over to the books and try to make sense of the great mysteries that lay in them, the door opened and she jumped at the sudden break in the silence. Leila, followed by two young lady's maids, walked in; they smiled and nodded at Kadreya then went into the dressing room. They stayed there for a few minutes and when they walked out again, Leila had a dress over one arm and with her other arm she pointed at the maid closest to her, "Ahra," then she pointed at the other one, "Aila." They curtsied in unison; Kadreya soon came to discover that they were twins and because of a very close relationship they did nearly everything together. They both had long blonde hair and dark blue eyes, the only difference was that Ahra was slightly taller and Aila's hair was one or two shades darker.

Leila spoke to Ahra in their language, the young lady's maid disappeared into the dressing room for ten minutes and came out again and nodded to Leila. The twins were dismissed and the older woman led Kadreya into the dressing room. Set up in the center of the room was a porcelain tub sitting on golden claws; steam rose above the hot water that was filled with aromatic oils.

"Bath," Leila said to Kadreya. She helped the young girl lift the nightgown over her head and Kadreya climbed into the tub. She never felt anything so good before, she felt as though she could let the water and oils soak into her skin for hours. But it had its end as everything does. Leila held a fluffy white towel out to her and Kadreya let herself be wrapped into it. When her skin was dry Leila slipped the dress over her head. The inside layer was a dark green silk and the outer layer was a spring green gossamer-like material, sprinkled with embroidered bluets at the hem.

When this was done Leila took her out of the dressing room and brought her to the fireplace where the maids had started the flames so they could be welcoming and warm when Kadreya finished with her bath. A chair was set up so that Kadreya faced away from the fire to let her hair dry and a table was in front of it with a breakfast of toast, sausage, eggs and many other things that Kadreya had never even heard of. She turned and looked at Leila, who smiled at the joyous expression covering the young girl's face. They did not know then, but this moment was a turning point in their relationship together, no longer strangers, but instead friends.

Kadreya spent five happy years with these people, who she found out were Ahbrenians, learning their language and customs. She learned that their ways were not dead as everyone had thought, instead they were hidden.

One day, two years after Kadreya was brought to Ahbren, Leila was giving her a lesson in history when she was interrupted by a question that was often asked by the young girl during this part of their day.

"Where is the King of Ahbren now?"

"I don't know," Leila answered.

"Why not?"

"Let's not stray from the subject," Leila evaded.

"Why doesn't anyone tell me why I was brought here?"

"*Miet eil teyell*," Leila answered in Ahbrenian; "Time will tell." Kadreya sighed; she was used to this. Their conversation ended and they got back to the lesson. Although no one would tell her why she was there, Kadreya did enjoy the new opportunities that she received. Here she learned to read, and read as many books as she could, she learned history and how to write and began keeping a journal. She was taught Elfin, Ahbrenian and some of the dead languages of the world. Sometimes she and Leila would venture to the shore of the Sapphire Sea or some such far off place.

Though it always bothered her to be left in the dark she got past this and learned that someday she would solve this mystery as the Ahbrenians considered her very important. She knew this when they said "*Iyen rae het hosheno*," which she was taught meant, "You are the chosen one," then they would call her, "*Emonmistess*," "Demon Mistress." Then one day she came one step closer to getting her questions answered. She was in the field of bluets just a week after her sixteenth birthday when she saw the Black Stag once again.

Now, it must be explained that in these five years the ember of Emonmistess had not glowed, but now as she watched the Black Stag it glowed brighter than it ever had before.

"*Lacksteeg*," Kadreya whispered his name in the Ahbrenian language. He looked up and their eyes met, his ember eyes glowed as brightly as the one that she wore around her neck. They locked gazes for a second and he ran away again. In that short time she was told what to do, "*Ahces amin*," a voice whispered in her ear, "Chase him." Kadreya ran to the castle and hurriedly searched for Leila who she found in her room.

"Leila," Kadreya spoke hastily in Ahbrenian, "I must go."

"Yes," the woman answered and gave a haversack to Kadreya, "Your things are ready, go and find him."

Leila gave Kadreya a pair of sturdy leather boots that the young woman quickly put on.

"Pick as many bluets from the meadow as you can, then when you need food, sprinkle a pinch of this onto one," Leila opened a sack the size of two fists, Kadreya looked at what was inside; the sack contained a gray powder that looked like cold, dead ashes. The women hugged and said their good-byes, and then Kadreya turned and began her search for the Black Stag.

She went through the meadow, in the direction that she had seen him go, picking armfuls of bluets along the way. She found the trail that he had left. It wasn't very hard to find, his hooves singed whatever he touched; Kadreya had only to follow the trail of blackened flowers.

For days she traveled this dark trail, never knowing where it may lead, but following it nonetheless. She did as Leila told her and sprinkled the gray powder on a bluet whenever she was hungry; each time a meal fit for a wealthy traveler was produced. Kadreya did eventually grow tired of her journey. She felt as if it was pointless to be chasing a demon-like stag. She wondered if perhaps it was a dream and that sometime she would wake up and it would all be over. Finally, however, the day came that her journey neared its end. In a forest Kadreya walked on one of the many trails and a clearing came into sight. There in the center of it stood the Black Stag.

"Lacksteeg," Kadreya whispered his name; he looked up. She walked closer, step by step until she entered the clearing Then he walked the rest of the way to her and put his nose in her hands, she touched him gently and realized that he was no demon. There was, however, some mystery about him, something that she didn't know but was determined to find out.

She moved her hands along his neck and down his shoulder, he looked back at her, knowing what she had in mind, he knelt down and she climbed onto his back. Suddenly the world passed by in a blur. He moved so fast, so gracefully, she could feel the power with which he moved and had to shut her eyes to keep the wind out of them.

They spent a year together, roaming from village to village, country to country. Whenever they were spotted a look of fear was seen in the eyes of the viewer, especially when he was alone. But the fear was usually set to rest when Kadreya was seen with the Black Stag because it was thought that she could keep him tame.

It was true too; Kadreya was able to keep him tame and quiet. She had gotten used to his different moods and habits during the year that they had been together. She began to wonder what he would be like if he were human. She wondered how she would feel about him; even now as the Black Stag she questioned her feelings for him. There was something about him, the look in his eyes seemed to tell her an unspoken secret that at one time he was indeed human.

"Who are you?" Kadreya would ask him.

"Lacksteeg," she would hear his voice in her head, it was the only way that they could talk.

"But you weren't always the Black Stag," she said jokingly as she had become used to his evasive answers. "Who were you before you became the Black Stag?"

"A deer."

"How did your heart continue beating after you were killed?"

"Fate," he said this word quietly and his voice would sound relieved.

"Why are you so evasive about your past?"

"Why are you so nosy?"

She would then smile; he sounded so human-like and boyish when he said this. She loved the sound of his voice. When she first began hearing him in her head it was an odd feeling, but later she began to appreciate this. It would be an even odder thing to see the words come from his mouth.

They spoke often to each other, like any two friends would. Kadreya would tell him of her past, bitter memories of her family and her dreams of the future. But he told little of his past and even less of the future; when these two subjects were brought up his eyes seemed to become a little darker and he would become angry and upset though he tried not to show it. But there was always sadness in his eyes. Kadreya got the impression that he was not much older than she was, but the human side of him was like a downhearted youth. He showed his emotions so clearly and involuntarily and they talked like they were old friends so often that Kadreya sometimes forgot that he wasn't a human.

Kadreya's questions, not only about her feelings for him, but also about his identity grew more and more insistent, but little did she know that her questions would soon be answered in the most unexpected way.

She rode him near a village on a bright sunny day. They were both happy and their spirits seemed to fly. Kadreya was sure that they weren't too close to the village, that they were a safe distance away. But she found that she was wrong, she heard the soft whir of an arrow and before she realized what it was the Black Stag fell beneath her and she had to jump. She hit her head on a rock, then there was nothing.

When she finally came to, she did not at first recognize where she was, but as her vision became clearer she recognized her room in the Ahbrenian castle. Her head hurt with confusion and the bump that had steadily grown since she hit her head. Then suddenly Kadreya remembered the Black Stag. She flew out of bed and put a robe on over her nightgown and ran out the door and through the never-ending corridors of the castle, trying to find him. As she turned one corner she bumped into somebody. She looked up into the face of the good witch, Atalina.

Kadreya had heard stories of her goodness and beauty from Leila, but had never believed they were true as she had grown up in a home where magic and miracles were empty dreams. Lady Atalina was one of the few good witches left in the world and many people sought advice and help from her if they had a problem. It was said that she was more powerful than the fairies.

Kadreya stared at the long golden hair, the sparkling blue eyes, and her white staff filled with intricate carvings and her silk gown.

"Excuse me ma'am, I'm sorry," Kadreya stuttered.

The Lady Atalina smiled, "Do not be sorry," she said in a soft, musical voice, "The one whom you seek is just in that room," she pointed to a door with her long finger.

Kadreya looked at the witch; her expression was that of confusion.

"Go to him," was all that Atalina said to her.

Kadreya went to the door, her courage slowly fading; she quietly turned the handle and walked in.

There on a small bed he lay, the room that he was in was reserved for sick or wounded people. Because of its purpose, the room consisted only of a bed, a small table, a window and a few chairs.

He was almost exactly as she had imagined him, his hair was black and a little long, his complexion was dark though a shade or two lighter due to his current state of health. Kadreya stared at the man whom she had known so long as Lacksteeg, and suddenly became shy in his presence. What should she say to him when he finally woke? What would he think of her? Would they still share that bond that they had when he was the Black Stag? Would he care for her the way she cared about him?

She sat on a chair next to his bed and looked at his face; she got a funny feeling in her stomach as he opened his clear blue eyes and looked at her. He smiled and she smiled back. What else was there to do?

He slowly sat up; there was an awkward silence, both were unsure of what to say.

"Kadreya," he finally said quietly; she looked up.

"Yes," she answered.

They were silent again, he continued to look at her, then he looked down and saw that she still wore *Emonmistess*, he slowly reached for it.

"It still glows," he said as he rubbed his thumb on the silver surrounding the faintly glowing ember. He looked at her again, his hand moved to her cheek and he held it there for a while. Then he moved it back to the bed.

Kadreya wasn't sure what to think of all this and felt that she must say something, "What is your name?" she asked after deciding that he could be *Lacksteeg* and longer as it meant 'Black Stag' in Ahbrenian.

"Jairen," he answered.

Then the door opened and Lady Atalina walked in.

"Have you told her?" She asked Jairen.

He shook his head no.

"Now is the time." She walked back out.

The young people watched as she left, and then Jairen looked at Kadreya again.

"Kadreya."

She looked at him.

"The story of how I became the Black Stag is a long one, it seems so long ago." He took a deep breath then began, "I used to be King Jairen of Ahbren, but I was young and quickly became bored with being just King and began pirating, I became captain of the ship *Moonlight Shadow*."

Here he paused to see her reaction; she tried unsuccessfully to stifle a gasp. She may have grown up in a small village in the middle of nowhere but everyone had heard of the *Moonlight Shadow*.

He continued with more regret and sadness in his voice than before, "Lady Atalina threatened to make me stop pirating if I didn't stop on my own. I didn't listen and continued killing, stealing and kidnapping. Then one day she came back and turned me into a deer. She said that if I was meant to get a second chance then I would be killed and my heart would continue beating. Then Atalina would put the thought of burning my heart in the head of either my killer or someone close to him and I would be reborn from the ashes as the Black Stag. That was one of the reasons why I continued to ruin your fields, because I knew that eventually your family would get angry and wish me dead."

He stopped for breath before continuing; Kadreya was beginning to understand everything now.

"I was to give *Emonmistess* to the person of my choosing; I gave it to you because you did not fear me as a demon-like being. Even before you saw me you seemed so much stronger than everyone else. *Emonmistess* would glow when you were ready to find me and only the true mistress would be able to accomplish this. I was told that to turn back into a human the wearer of *Emonmistess* would have to care for me as I would them. Then I would be killed as the Black Stag and would turn back into a human."

He was silent, allowing time for her to let the story sink in.

"But you're not a king anymore," Kadreya said, then thought that maybe she shouldn't have.

70

"I am again. Here in Ahbren, when I became a deer time had stopped and now that I'm back it's like we're all picking up where we had left off."

"What about the people who came for me?"

"They were the people chosen to get the one I gave *Emonmistess* to."

She nodded understanding, "What happens now?"

He shrugged, "I don't know, you go home I guess," he said this last part rather regretfully. "I stay and continue to live a secret."

Kadreya stood and went back to her room. Leila was waiting for her there and the two women had a happy reunion. After the hugging and crying had stopped they sat down to talk.

"What will you do now?" Leila asked.

Kadreya took a deep breath before answering; "I'm leaving."

"Where will you go?"

"I don't know," Kadreya stood, remembering that in all the excitement she had never changed her nightgown, and quickly put on a simple gown that she found in her dressing room.

"Why don't you stay?"

Kadreya's back was facing her, but now she turned and answered in a quiet voice, "He didn't ask me."

"That doesn't mean he doesn't want you to."

Kadreya stood there silently, not knowing how to answer. Then finally said, "I'm leaving in a week."

Kadreya ended up lengthening her stay to two weeks, Leila convinced her to stay until Jairen's wound healed. So during that time, Kadreya reintroduced herself to all of the comforts of the place where she lived one year ago, when she looked back it seemed so far away.

Everyday she went to visit Jairen, after the constant persuading of Leila and because of the small hope that he might ask her to stay after all.

"How are you?" she asked one day, it was a week and a half since he had changed back into a human and his wound was not quite healed.

"Not bad after being killed twice," he grinned at the joke that he had made.

She smiled and went to sit down, he seemed so much happier now that everything was over.

He turned serious suddenly, "Have you decided what you're going to do yet?"

She shook her head, "No."

Jairen looked at the necklace that she never took off, "You can keep that you know."

"*Emonmistess?*"

He smiled again, "Think of it as a souvenir."

"What are you going to do when you're healed?" Kadreya asked, unsure of what else to say.

"Do things right, plan a future," he shrugged, "Not much else I can do. I learned my lesson."

The same look that he wore when he was the Black Stag covered his face now as he thought of the past.

Kadreya thought of something to say to turn his thoughts, "What exactly are your plans for the future?"

He shrugged, "I think I would like to go on a fox hunt, something like that. Like other kings do. Maybe give a few orders," he laughed, "No, I would actually like to take a trip through the country and see what needs to be done."

"It sounds like a good start."

"Yes," he said thoughtfully; "it does."

So that was the end of their conversation that day. Kadreya only felt more saddened by it because he did not mention her in his plans for the future. She was so downhearted that it did not occur to her that maybe he was feeling shy as she was, and unsure of her feelings for him.

It was the end of the week, the sun was just rising above the fog and shining on the dew covered grass. It would seem like a happy day, but it was not so for Kadreya. That day was the day she said her good-byes to Leila and all of the people whom she had spent those five memorable years with. She was just going to say an awkward good-by to Jairen when they met in the corridor.

"I heard you were leaving," he said.

"Yes."

He held his hand out to her, "Good luck."

She briefly shook his hand, then left; he watched her walk out the castle doors and didn't turn until they closed behind her.

Kadreya walked across the drawbridge, trying to hold back the tears. She walked through the field of bluets, remembering the day *Emonmistess* began to glow; she still wore the necklace. She looked at it now; it glowed brightly; though she didn't understand why. She had done her job in releasing him from the spell but now it was as if it was telling her once again to go find him. She was lost in her thoughts and did not hear the distant sound of horse hooves, then they became louder and she turned around. Jairen rode up to her and leaped from the horse.

"Stay with me," he said in a rush. He took a step towards her, she didn't know what to say, then suddenly everything that she had been holding in had burst out, she laughed and cried, then he began laughing and took her in his arms.

They stood out in the bluet field like that for a long time and lived in the castle for an even longer time.

Stories of the Black Stag and his Mistress will continue to be told, but now there is a new one, and that is this one, the true story of the Black Stag and his mistress.

# DOCUMENTATION OF A PHENOMENON

## Corey Melin

*Corey Melin. When he's not working, Corey spends his free time reading or writing. He just recently started writing what he's hoping will one day become his first published book.*

They all slowly walked up the hill toward the last standing building of the old world. They all wanted to see the phenomenon. They all wanted to see the days people once lived long ago.

The group consisted of photographers, artists, writers, and spectators. The photographers to take pictures as quick as they could, artists to draw as quick as they could, writers to document until their hands hurt, and spectators to stand in awe and to shed a few tears. All of them would shed some tears before the phenomenon ended.

The world had drastically changed since the days of old. Man in his ignorance had treated the land carelessly to the point that the land had decided to spew the man from it, almost wiping mankind from existence. Only a few survived to now live in a land that showed very little of what life for man once was like. Large tracts of land had heaved up and turned completely over, swallowing man and his makings. Mountains blew, covering the land with its innards. The oceans rose up and took chunks of land to lay hundreds of feet below the surface. Even the skies opened up, pouring acid rain, baseball size hail, and even fire onto the land. No one who still survived wanted to remember those days, but by just opening their eyes it would remind them. But then the phenomenon began and it brought hope to man.

They were nearly to the top, the younger helping the elder, and mothers carried their babies wanting to see the event that would give them a reason why they brought a child into this forsaken land.

A few glanced back at their homes down at the bottom of the hill. All they could see was the lights from inside their homes and a vague outline of their place. The time of day was continually stuck on darkness since the days of the wrath on man. Wrath on technology. Wrath on science.

They reached the top and started walking toward the building. It was quite bizarre that the land was wiped clean of man's doings in this area, but this building survived with little harm. They figured this building was once an apartment building and at one time thought of moving in, but when the phenomenon started they figured it would be a bad idea to move in. If they moved in the phenomenon could end and all lose hope. None wanted that to happen. In fact, all windows and doors were boarded up to keep out disobedient people, but those were few in number since they all knew it was that type of people, who brought the destruction.

They neared the building and came to the spot where it was best to see the phenomenon. Chairs were all ready set-up for the elderly to sit in and blankets lay out nailed to the ground in some spots. Most of the people brought their own stuff to sit or lie on. People started to do just that while photographers and artists with their assistants set-up quickly. Time of the phenomenon was near at hand.

Five minutes later they all stood, sat, or lay staring up at the top of the building. On top of the building was a billboard. The advertisement had blown away long ago leaving a white surface. It was this billboard that would display the phenomenon. They all waited in anticipation.

Suddenly the darkness in the sky split open and a beam of light struck the billboard, which started emitting bright colorful pictures to the watching crowd. Everyone saw a different picture of things each one of them would love to do just once in their life. To swim in the crystal clear water. To go hiking through the forest and smell the great outdoors. To take their child to a park on a bright sunny day. To just lie outdoors and look up at the stars or the shapes of white puffy clouds. To dance with joy. To see a happy face. They all watched, with the photographers taking pictures to later develop photographs of bright colors, artists drawing what they saw, writers documenting what they saw, and the others just watching.

For fifteen minutes they watched until the darkness of the sky closed back up. They all packed up and started the return trip to their homes. All had tears running down their cheeks. Oh, how they wished the days would come again like the ones they just witnessed. Maybe one day that day would come. Wished, they all did.

# FOREVER TWELVE

### Colleen Drippé

*Colleen Drippé has had many science fiction stories published, as well as a book. She also writes essays and articles and children's books. She is editor of "Hereditas," a Catholic literary magazine aimed at high school and older readers.*

*She has always been a fighter, Jamie thinks. She fights now.*
"-- a twilight existence at best," the doctor is saying. "But at least it is a life."
"She cannot mend?" Mack says. "There is no hope?"
"Life is hope," the doctor tells her. "Here they think; they make decisions. But not on the level they once knew."
*Jamie is twisting her hands together in her lap.* "They don't heal?"
"There isn't much to heal. We can't regrow a brain. Your mother is lucky to be alive at all. Surely you must know that. It was a terrible accident."
"But she will never be conscious again?" *Mack asks, trying to make it real.*
*The doctor gives them each a long look.* "I am trying to tell you. She is conscious. She experiences life in Sim. If she is a good subject, she will live many years. She may even link into the nerve nets, strengthen her grasp -- grow stronger. But she will never be able to reach outside. There is not enough left."
"Then she is dead to us," *Jamie says.* "Isn't that so?"
*The doctor nods.* "But she is happy. They all are. She isn't alone, you know."
"For how long?" *Mack demands in her incisive way.* "How long can she live in Sim?"
*A shrug.* "Who knows?"

*       *       *

"The things I like most is Xmas. And birthday cakes and rideing my bike. And playing Monapoly with my best frend --"

The pencil stopped moving. Slowly Laura closed the red leather diary. She clicked the latch where a tiny key was supposed to go, only she had left the key at home. She fiddled with the little metal pencil.

Christine was gone. She had moved away.

The spring sunshine made her mother's flowers glow, floating above tiers and shades of green where butterflies passed and bees hummed. April seemed to go on forever, though she knew it would yield to May and then June. School would be out and the summer would be, as all summers were, a ritual of joy.

Only it would be a summer without Christine.

She heard the back door slam and someone came running up the path. Laura rose, clutching her diary.

"Just got back from the store," Robby panted. "My dad was buying seeds and things." He came to a stop just short of the tulip bed. "Come and see what we got! Asparagus roots. They look like spiders." He glanced at the book she held. "That your diary?"

Laura nodded. "I was writing happy things," she said. "I wanted to think about things I like."

"I like Saturdays," Robby told her. "And ice cream." He looked up at her. "Why did you need to write happy things? I mean today?"

"You know. Christine."

"Oh, yeah. They moved."

"We've been friends since – well all our lives." Laura didn't know why she couldn't say since first grade. Maybe it was because she couldn't remember first grade. She had no memory of Christine small; Christine was always a freckled twelve-year-old, her hair as red as carrots, curled and stiff with a green hair band.

Laura followed Robby into the house and put her diary away. She could hear the whir of Mother's sewing machine in the library.

"I had a dream last night," Robby said as they skipped down the sidewalk, missing the cracks. "I dreamed about my grandfather."

"The one who lives in Philadelphia?"

"No, the other one. He's got a little office and – and some things in it."

"I didn't know about that one," Laura said. "I thought the other one lived on a farm."

"I know." Robby shook his head as though he needed to shake something loose. "But this was a *dream*. So he was in his office."

"What did he do there?"

"I think he was writing a book."

"That's funny," Laura said. "What was it about?"

"Oh, something boring. But it seemed interesting to me in the dream. I can't remember now except that I was typing. My fingers were moving and I could see words."

"You? I thought it was your grandfather."

"Well it was, sort of. But he was me." He gave a little laugh. "Maybe it is me when I grow up."

They turned in at Robby's gate. Laura felt a chill as she stepped up onto the porch.

"What are you going to be when you grow up?" Robby asked her suddenly. "Do you know?"

Laura didn't turn. "How could I know something like that?" she asked.

"Do you ever have dreams about it?"

And suddenly, for no reason at all, she burst into tears.

*  *  *

Their letters said 3:30 but of course they had to wait. Outside the day was darkening, the arctic cold closing in. Jamie fingered the heater control in the pocket of her opened parka. She would need it when they left the building. Beside her, Mack was staring straight ahead.

It was nearly five o'clock when they were called..

Doctor Bain rose as they came in, her eyes as intense as always, her cropped hair combed sleekly back. "Jamie," she said. "Mack." She always remembered their names. "Please sit down."

Jamie found she was crumpling her letter. In the oppressive silence, it was she who spoke first.

"What does this mean?"

The doctor looked up, her eyes warming as though someone had turned on a switch. "I'm sorry, Jamie," she said. "It means exactly what it says. Your mother is failing."

"How long does she have?" Jamie asked.

"Who can say? There was more damage than we thought and she is not going to be able to hold on at this level much longer. There is no use going on."

Beside Jamie, Mack sat forward. "She doesn't suffer. Not in Sim."

"She will."

"What," Jamie asked, swallowing, "will happen? I mean, from her point of view?"

"She'll stop. But things may deteriorate first and we want to prevent that."

"I've heard when they reach this point," Mack said slowly, "there are other levels. Infancy, early childhood. You can keep her going longer – use less energy."

The doctor looked down. "Those options are still in the early stages of development. Only one of the patients in your mother's group has been transferred so far -- at her family's request. Normally this alternative is offered to a different sort of subject."

"You mean guinea pigs," Mack said. "Social rejects. Retards."

This time the doctor winced and stopped smiling. "It wouldn't be in your mother's best interests."

"So what else can we do?" Jamie asked.

"The kindest thing."

"She would have put that in her will," Mack said flatly. "If she wanted us to kill her."

"I'm sure she never anticipated something like this."

"We don't know what she anticipated," Mack snapped. "That's the point. She lives. She makes choices. She reasons."

"Not to any purpose. She can't tell you what she wants."

"What," Jamie broke in hesitantly, "else can we do? If we don't sign for termination, I mean?"

"I told you." Bain stood up. "You *can* opt for experimental treatment. You are her guardians."

"But you don't think we should."

The doctor said nothing.

"How much time do we have?"

"I can't answer that," Bain said coldly. "But probably not long."

"Well?" Jamie asked her sister as they left the office. "Was she exaggerating?"

"About other levels in Sim? I don't think so. It's a risk."

Bracing themselves, they stepped out into the night where the cold wind met them and the frozen stars looked down.

*      *      *

It seemed as though school days flew by. One minute she was stepping out the door, bookbag in one hand and a bunch of tulips in the other -- and then the final bell had rung and Mother would be waiting with cookies and milk. Laura would tell her about the day, piling detail upon detail, laughing with her mother at the antics of the hamsters they kept in the classroom, eagerly reminding Mother about spring open house day and the field trip coming up.

But Christine's absence left a dark place in the story – a vacancy where shadows moved.

"Would you like to write to her?" Mother asked. "You could use the stationary you got for your birthday."

79

Laura thought of the lavender sheets, violets bunched at the top. There had been twelve candles on her cake and she had opened presents. Every birthday was the same.

"Would she write back?" Laura asked.

"Of course she would, dear." Her mother took the empty glass and plate from the table. "I will address the envelope for you."

Laura settled herself on the chair. Behind her, Mother was peeling potatoes and putting things in pots. A roast was already cooking.

*Dear Christine,*

Slowly Laura wrote the story of the days that had passed. She wrote things and she remembered them and they were so. She wondered what Christine would write back. Would there be a letter full of days? The days of Christine? Or would they only be days – days of no one?

"I will put in a flower," she said. She went out into the garden. The tulips were too fat for the envelope and so were the irises, so she took a few petals from an early peony. The afternoon sun gilded the leaves and the quickening earth gleamed like chocolate.

Later, she was soothed by the evening ritual – her father's return, his newspaper and his pipe, dinner and a quiet hour cutting paper dolls while her parents watched television. She was safe at the dining room table with the sounds of music and laughter coming from the set, a smell of popcorn, a rustle of paper. Outside the night was full of springtime – frogs croaked, an occasional car crept down the street, a dog barked. Her letter was finished and she would mail it tomorrow.

Her mother kissed her good night. "I think," she said, "you are a little warm. I hope you are not coming down with something."

Laura snuggled into the pillow. She was too old for a teddy bear but she always kissed her mother goodnight. She slept.

All night Laura wandered in springtime gardens, sailed story book seas, and played with Christine. "I know this is a dream," she kept repeating. "It must be a dream. You're gone – moved away."

"Yes," Christine agreed. "I have gone away."

In the moonlit garden she reached out one hand, groping for Laura's.

"It isn't real," Laura said, stepping back. "This is a dream."

Christine laughed softly. She was smaller than she had been.

"Stop it!" Laura cried. "Stop –" But she did not know what she meant. Stop shrinking? Is that what Christine had done? Had she *shrunk* away?

But Christine only smiled, her reaching hand unraveling in the moonlight, her hair moving slightly in the breeze.

"Stop," Laura said again, but this time in a whisper. She crouched down herself, hands on the earth as the stars wheeled above drawing her helplessly to a place where cookies were ashes, dolls bits of paper, mothers and fathers no more than the sound of the television playing in another room.

She woke, whimpering in the dark, and Mother was there, soothing her until she slept again.

*       *       *

"Social misfits, criminals," the doctor was saying. "But they are only children, of course. Some of them are even *real* children who can go no higher. They haven't the experience to create much of a world."

"Criminals!" Jamie whispered. "But –"

"At that level there is very little interaction," the doctor said. "But everything will be – it is a collective reality."

"Is that why we have to sign a release?" Mack asked her.

The doctor glanced at a holo on the wall. It was a jungle scene, counterbalancing the ice age in which they lived. "Yes. This is a very complicated technology," she said. "The brain itself is built into the interface, though the body lives on as well as it can with the help of machinery. But – but there has to be something to build with. I mean, the brain has to function at some level. We can't just have a flat line, you know."

"So the line," Mack said thoughtfully, "is flatter than it was?"

"You could say that," Bain agreed.

"In laywoman's terms," Jamie murmured and Bain looked at her sharply.

"And you reduce criminals to this level?" Mack said.

"Only if that has been ordered by the court. It is an alternative to the death penalty."

"So the world they build might not be very pleasant?" Mack asked.

"It depends on the early memories of those involved. Someone like your mother could have more influence than, for example, a child who had never lived a full life, or someone whose mental growth had been stunted. But how she would interact with criminals, I don't know."

"Children," Jamie murmured. "Only children."

"She could still have a fairly decent existence," Mack said, but she looked doubtful.

"She *could* – for the time she has left." Bain looked up at them once more. "Or," she added bluntly, "it might be a living hell. We just don't know."

Jamie felt a shrinking within herself. "Then maybe –"

But Mack's face went all hard and stony. "She taught us courage."

"But this –"

Mack turned on her sister. "We can't let her down."

*     *     *

Laura gazed in wonder at the ripening apples. Standing on her tiptoes, she set her teddy bear in the cleft where two big branches grew out. Birds sang and she could smell roses -- and garbage. To the right a high hedge grew, deep and mysterious.

"Come in now," Mother called. "Grandma and Grandpa are here and we are going to have your cake."

Forgetting her bear, Laura turned and ran back to the house. It was her birthday. Daddy was home and everyone sang.

Laura was four.

They gave her presents. But later, she could not remember unwrapping them or eating the cake. She could not remember saying thank you and goodbye to Grandma and Grandpa.

The days jumped ahead and she was playing once more by the apple tree when a little girl looked in from the alley. She had red hair and freckles and her mother was holding her hand. "Hi, Laura," she said.

"Christine!" Laura ran to the little fence. "Can you play?"

Christine looked up at her mother who said, "Christine can stay until lunchtime." It seemed a victory to Laura, something monumental. A piece of the world fell back into place.

They played house beneath the hedge and a stick scratched Laura. She licked off the blood.

Later it was autumn and the girls played in the leaves and Thanksgiving came. There were children in the alley and not all of them were nice. Once a little boy threw rocks. Some little girls fought together and said bad words. Laura watched and listened, her eyes narrowed, wondering.

Christmas came and the strange children threw snowballs. Daddy helped Laura and Christine make a snowman. Laura's face was thoughtful as she fingered the snow and watched a few flakes falling from the leaden sky. Her coat was not warm enough.

"But when I'm bigger," she said, "It will be different. I will make it different."

Daddy laughed a not very nice laugh.

Christine's birthday came and she was four. Laura and her mother bought her a coloring book and wrapped it up with white paper and a pink ribbon. They took it to her house.

Now there were even more children in the alley, staring over the fence. No one seemed to be minding them, though sometimes a mother would come and snatch a child away. Those mothers were not like Laura's mother.

In April there was a storm. Rain and hail dashed the flowers to the ground. After that it was chilly outside. Mother was busy more often these days and Daddy did not always smile when he came home from work. The little boy who threw rocks sometimes came into the yard -- and once a strange girl hit Laura with a stick.

"I wish Robby was here," Laura said. But then she forgot who Robby was.

Summer came. There were still flowers and butterflies but the bees stung and Laura no longer played under the hedge.

"Soon it will be my birthday," she told Christine.

"Will you be four?"

Laura thought about this, feeling the power grow in her, and shook her head. "No," she said after a moment. "I will not be four."

Christine gaped at her.

"I will be five," Laura said. Her eyes flashed a sudden challenge to the garden and the hedge, to the alley and to the child beside her. "I think," she said, reaching out into the roots of the world, "I will keep getting bigger until I am twelve." She did not say "again". But it was a number she knew. It *meant* something.

Slowly she turned, challenging the flowers and the apple tree, the fence and the house. "When I am twelve, I will teach the children in the alley not to throw rocks. I will take care of them because no one loves them."

The sun shone. The birds sang. And the world quivered with change.

*       *       *

"It isn't," the doctor said, "regrowth. But she is using the interface much more efficiently."

"Then there is hope?" Jamie tore at a loose fingernail, realized what she was doing, and stopped.

Bain shook her head. "Hope for what? It is a last expenditure of energy – a flare up before the end."

Mack raised one eyebrow. "You really don't know what is going on, do you?" she said. "You have no idea how things will turn out."

Jamie leaned forward. "She is using the interface. Making it part of herself. Isn't that it?"

"That's it. But what she is experiencing –"

"As I said," Mack repeated. "You have no idea how things will turn out."

At this the doctor smiled. "No," she agreed, "we don't."

# PICTURES ON THE WALL

## Danielle Weiss

*Danielle Weiss is eleven years old. She loves to write and says she doesn't know how she got the idea for her story, it just popped into her head. It is an amazing piece of work for such a young writer.*

"Beep, beep, beep, beep," the unsteady flow of the heart monitor kept blurting out. Josh's mother, Patricia, stared with a blank face at him as he lay on the hospital bed helpless, in a coma. A stream of tears fell from her eyes and she began whimpering loudly. All the nurses and doctors standing in the bland room turned around to see why she was crying yet again. They'd told her numerous times that Josh would be okay and he would wake up sooner than she thought possible. But Patricia knew they'd said that one too many times and couldn't grasp that the concept might in fact be true. So the tears kept coming faster and faster, the whimpering grew louder and louder, and her heart started to tighten in to one huge knot that seemed like it wouldn't ever come undone.

The frightening image of Josh on his bike kept replaying over and over in her head. No matter how hard she tried it wouldn't vanish from within her. Shrills began to fill her ears, she tried to block that out too. But it was no use, she knew the scene wouldn't go away until her beloved son Josh was awake and well again.

Patricia was so lonely without Josh. She was not married and he was her only child. She longed for the day when she would hear, "I love you, Mom," escape again from her twelve-year-old's lips. She wondered what Josh would be doing if he wasn't chained to an air mask and all of the machines that were keeping him alive. But what she was most curious about was what her son was thinking or dreaming. Was he just lying there with an empty head, she wondered, or was it filled with silly and impossible thoughts?

. . .

Josh began to hear faint music in his head. It began to grow closer and closer to him. It was as if someone kept turning up the

85

volume on a radio and putting it near his ear. Then he began to feel dizzy and as time passed he felt as if he was spinning faster and faster.

Wham! Josh landed smack dab on the cold tile in his mother's art museum. He looked around, assuming he would catch sight of his mom and some strangers who stopped by to see the famous paintings that were hung on the walls. But to his surprise no one was there. No fly flew around. No whispers were heard. He was all alone. All alone.

After sitting on the ground for quite some time thinking how it was possible that he was in the museum all alone, he began to get up from the floor. But a sharp pain shot through his whole body and he was thrown back down. He checked his body to see where the pain had come from and he was surprised to see he was wearing a nightgown. The kind that hospitals give out when you are about to go into a life-changing surgery. Nothing was covering his feet and he felt a fearful shiver race around his body.

Josh loved art and had always been thrilled that his mom owned an art museum. Knowing he could come and admire paintings all day long gave him a sweet feeling inside. Looking into a frame filled with color and objects always made him feel better no matter what kind of jam he was in. Josh knew that if he could gather up enough strength he would be able to reach the nearest painting. And maybe, just maybe, he would feel a bit better.

Josh moved towards the closest painting. He recognized it. It was one of his least favorites, *Sunday Afternoon on the Island of La Grande Jatte* by Georges Seurat. He could never figure out what was so special about this painting. To him it was just ordinary. Looking more closely he realized that he did, in fact, admire that up close the painting was made up of thousands of dots and then when you stepped back from the picture the dots formed people and landscapes.

With all the strength he had, he stood up and stretched his hand out towards the painting to get a closer look at the dots that amazed him. Then in one swift movement he was sucked head first, body following right into the picture.

Josh came off as a strong boy who wasn't scared of anything. But as he stood in Georges Seurat's painting he couldn't help but be more than a little frightened. He turned his head around and around, examining his brand-new surroundings. He couldn't believe it. He could have sworn his eyes were playing tricks on him. But they weren't. He really was in the painting, plain and simple. And if that wasn't enough Josh saw that he too was made up of millions of brightly colored dots.

Cruising through the priceless painting stunned Josh because he had never, in a million years, thought that he would ever be in a painting, let alone a world famous one. Josh found hidden details that he hadn't noticed before. For instance, he never knew the painting stretched back so far. He found other people holding umbrellas in one hand and swinging the other even though they weren't moving. As time ticked by Josh disliked the picture even more. He felt it was out-dated. He thought the clothes were too proper and looked very uncomfortable. Why couldn't Georges Seurat just put them in blue jeans and a colorful t-shirt? And what was the point of women holding umbrellas in the middle of July?

As Josh sat on the green, thick grass he wished to himself that all the people who were enjoying their bright Sunday afternoon were dressed in today's hottest and latest fashions and that rain would pour loudly and intensely down on everyone so the umbrellas would be useful. In the blink of an eye Josh's wishes came true, rain fell from the sky's lightless clouds and the guests on the island were suddenly wearing clothes he could recognize. Josh was utterly shocked and confused. How did these wishes come true, he wondered.

Just as fast as all these wishes came true Josh was whisked away, far away to a different painting. He fell from the gloomy and disrupted sky. It was filled with one monumental hurricane that was revolving around a few houses. He knew this painting really well. It was the first one you saw when you entered the museum. It was titled *Tornado Over Kansas* by John Steuart Curry. He could see the terrified look that was placed upon the face of each and every person scattered around the open and dull land. He could tell they were trying to reach someplace, anyplace where they would be safe. The dogs and the chickens were also running from the hurricane, searching for someplace where they could stay and survive to see what the next day would bring. It was quite visible to Josh that the animals were just as afraid as their owners.

As Josh watched the hurricane, his heart began to break, one tiny microscopic piece at a time. He just couldn't imagine being in the shoes of these innocent and loving people. Just standing there and thinking about his house being demolished brought tears to his eyes. He couldn't take it anymore...he just couldn't. So he began to wish again; this time he wished the houses wouldn't be destroyed by the weather. And with that, his wish came true again. The expressions of the humans' faces began to change. Their worried expressions became relieved and they were smiling. Josh felt like his work was done and he was very proud of himself for saving theses peoples' lives from tragedy.

Then Josh began to feel woozy, as if he had been running in circles. All of a sudden he fell and landed in thick plants that scratched his bare knees. He was very tired of falling from one place to another. He desperately wanted to stay in one place. He wanted to know, what, at that moment in time, was going on! Why was he falling and landing in various paintings? Why was it that when he wished for something it came true? But the question that he wanted an answer to most, was when was he going to see his mother again? It had troubled him all day and he couldn't take his mind off of it.

Josh felt something clench his finger and he looked down to see what it was. Sitting on his ring finger was a hairy spider. Even though Josh knew nobody would be able to hear him, he still screamed quietly to himself just in case someone happened to walk by. He then shook his hand until the spider was flying through the air. He was hoping it would land with so much power it would die of shock. That way the spider wouldn't come back and bite him again. After hearing a faint sound of the spider plopping to the floor Josh realized he needed to leave the bushes before he was really harmed by some other wild creature.

As he pulled back the leaves he found a man on his hands and knees. On his back was a woven basket, filled past the brim with pinkish, purplish flowers. Josh stared at the flowers, amazed that these things could bring such beauty to one's eye. But then he glanced back down at the man with the heavy load on his back and Josh felt sorrow for him. There was also a woman there. She was helping the poor man secure the basket so it wouldn't slip and fall to the dusty land.

To Josh this was just another painting that he was unhappy with and didn't like. But before Josh started to wish, the woman began walking away and soon she was out of sight. The young boy was startled, yet fascinated, by the action that just took place. He couldn't believe what happened. No character from any other painting just got up and left. He wanted to chase this woman down and get answers from her. So he ran closer and closer to where she used to be standing and was ready to run past the man on the ground when he abruptly heard someone yell, "Stop!" He looked around but no one was there except for the flower man. Then he heard the voice again, it was saying, "I'm down here, with the flowers placed on top of my back."

Josh slowly moved his eyes down to where the man was on the ground. "Who are you?" Josh was somehow able to spit out from his quivering lips.

"Me? Well my name is, is... well I'm not quite sure what my name is since the artist, Diego Rivera, never named me. All he named

88

was this painting, it's called, *The Flower Carrier*. So here I am, the flower carrier. But what about you? What's your name? Who are you?" asked the man.

"My name is Josh Staples. The last thing I can recall is riding my bike across the black, paved street and then I don't know what happened. Suddenly everything went dark and unclear, as if nothing was there. Nothing at all! It's as if my mind just turned off at that moment. I'm so lost and confused."

"So how did you wander into my home?" the curious man questioned.

"Well, I can't answer that question because I'm searching for that answer myself. All I know is that I keep jumping from one painting to another. The only thing they have in common is that they are hanging on the walls of my mother's art museum, Pictures on the Wall. I went to crawl over to the painting, *Sunday Afternoon on the Island of La Grande Jatte* and all of a sudden I was inside the painting. I made a simple wish to myself and then bam! it came true. Then as quickly as I came, I left the painting. Somehow I traveled into another painting called *Tornado Over Kansas*. That was a very sad painting but you don't need to worry, I made it so the citizens would all have a home to live in and each other to love. Then I ended up here, stuck and confused. The only thing I want to wish for now is to see my mother. But I've got no clue whatsoever on how to escape from here."

"Really?" the flower carrier asked Josh.

"Really!" Josh replied, a little irritated.

"There's no point in getting so riled up about it and besides I've got some good news," the man said cheerfully.

Josh couldn't help but smile after hearing this piece of information. "Go on sir, please, oh, please!"

"Okay, well I met another boy with the same issue as you. I was able to help him return back to his home and I think I just might be able to do the same for you. But the only way it's going to work is if you believe. Are you with me?" the man asked.

"Of course I am!" Josh said with as much conviction as he could summon up.

"Okay, first we have to figure out how you got here and make sure you're not... well, you know...dead!"

"I'm not dead. I'm sure I'm not dead," Josh spat out.

"Okay, let's see, you said the last thing you can recall is riding your bike. So you probably got hit by a car and you're in a coma," the man said as if it didn't mean a thing.

"What! That can't possibly be true! I don't feel like I'm in a coma. But what if I am? That could mean that I might die and then I wouldn't see my mom again. Oh, this is bad, but it can't be true, it just can't! I just need to forget about that for now because I still don't know how I got here or how I can leave," Josh blurted out to the man who now took the basket off his back and sat comfortably on the ground.

"It is possible you're dreaming but in a more realistic state." This made no sense to Josh. Noticing the look on Josh's face the old man continued. "I can see I puzzled you. Let me try to explain. I think you're in a coma and you're dreaming that you've jumped into various paintings. If this is true, to go back and wake up from this dream you have to really show you deserve to go back to your home, back to the ones you love and cherish," the wise man explained to the young boy.

"But I haven't done anything wrong! Why would I need to prove that I deserve to go back to home? I've done nothing wrong!" Josh protested repeatedly, although he was a little unsure if what he was telling the flower carrier was actually true because he didn't really give it much thought. He couldn't think off the top of his head of anything that might have caused him to be in this position.

"But a very reliable source told me you've been a very greedy and mean boy." the man told Josh

"Oh, and who is this 'reliable source'?" Josh demanded from the man.

"It's me, myself, who else?" the man said with a chuckle. "You see," the man went on, "The only way you would be here is if you had done something wrong. And you, my boy have been sent to me so I know you've done something wrong."

"Me, do something bad? I don't think so." the boy snapped back.

"Well you are sure wrong about that and until you're able to admit what you did wrong, you will live in this world by my rules. Oh, and one more thing. I am the one who changed the paintings to the way you wished. It's a little test to see if you are so arrogant that you change the work of others. Others who have worked on these paintings long and hard. Who spent their time and effort on them. And if a person is so arrogant that they decide to reconstruct a painting to better fit their needs, then I grant the wish so they can see what it would be like if it was their way. Of course the second you leave the painting it's changed back to its original form. But it really helps me to determine if you truly need to come to me so I can teach you right from wrong," the wise man was quick to point out. He was expecting to hear the boy babbling about him not doing anything horrible. Or to hear how manipulative it was for someone to be granting his every wish. But to his surprise, the boy was silent. Nothing came out of his mouth, he just sat there with his face shoved into his knees.

Josh didn't want to admit to the flower carrier that he was sitting there thinking hard to himself about what he could have done that brought him to this place. He was really perplexed about what he had done. He dug deep into his memories but couldn't figure it out. He knew he couldn't give up because he wanted to see his mom, the one who loved him dearly, and if the man said he did something wrong then he must have, he figured. So he sat there rocking back and forth, back and forth. Thinking. Thinking. Thinking back to yesterday, the day before that, last week, last month, and on and on until he began realizing things he was already regretting. Just last Wednesday he yelled at his mom because she wouldn't buy him the new Tony Hawk game. As Josh looked back upon this he couldn't believe that he actually screamed at his mom and told her she was mean for not buying him a game. He began apologizing to his mom as if she was standing in front of him.

Then there was the time when Josh's Mother told him to go to bed because it was getting late. But he talked back to her saying, "I don't care, I don't feel like going to bed and I won't." His mother was stunned by his words and took away his television watching for a week. He remembered that this had made him even more furious and he slammed his door so hard it caused the painting that was hung in his hallway to fall from its nail. Again Josh regretted his actions. And then he remembered the worst thing he had ever done. It was just yesterday. Josh wanted to ride his bike around the neighborhood even though it was already dark outside. He told his mom he was going to be riding outside for a bit but she explained it was too dark and dangerous and it got pretty busy on the streets at night. But Josh didn't take no for an answer. He marched right into the garage, opened the door, and started out the gate, forgetting his helmet in his rush. He knew his mom was chasing after him but that only caused him to pedal faster so he could lose her. He turned his head around while he was crossing the street to see how far his mom was lagging and then a glare of light fell on his eyes. And then there was nothing. It was then that Josh realized the flower carrier was right, he had been hit by a car. He finally understood why he was here, in this surreal world. He got right up and marched over to the man and began telling him his mistakes and regrets.

"Disobeying, talking back, scaring her half to death; these are the reasons why I'm here. But now that I look back on what I've done I realize that I should never had done or said those things. I know

91

now that I can't act this way anymore because one day it might go as far as losing someone I love dearly. And I know I'm not going to die because I understand and admit to my wrong actions. I understand that this is a warning. It's my one chance to learn from my mistakes and never act that way again." Josh said with all his heart and soul.

"Wise words, wise words indeed. I'm quite surprised you were able to understand all of that. I thought I was going to have to explain everything to you and you still wouldn't have understood it. I can trust that you have learned from the past and will not make these mistakes in the future. I must say goodbye to you and hope not to see you in here but out there," the flower carrier said with a smile on his face and pointed far beyond where the eye could see, as if that was where the world was.

. . .

"Josh, honey, are you there? Honey, honey? Please wake up!" Patricia pleaded. She put her head down on the back of her hands and began crying. Tears fell from her chin.

"Ms. Staples, Ms. Staples!" the nurse shouted out.

"What?" she snapped back.

"Look," the nurse replied kindly.

Patricia lifted her head and wiped away her tears because what she saw before her eyes was unbelievable. There was Josh, eyes open and trying to breathe.

"Josh!" Patricia screamed with joy as she gave her son the biggest hug he had ever received from her.

"Mom!" Josh cried out, still stunned that he was back home with the person he loved.

"Oh, honey, you got hit by the car and, and, and then you ended up here in a coma and I didn't know if you were going to make it but the doctors told me to keep my spirits going and..." Patricia blurted out, but Josh cut her off before she went any farther.

"Mom, I'm sorry, I will never, ever, ever, ever do those mean things to you ever again. If I would have listened to you I wouldn't be here right now," Josh cried out, but his mom cut him off just like he did to her.

"It's okay, the important thing is you're alive and well."

"Mom, I love you," Josh exclaimed.

"I love you too, Josh," Patricia told her son for the first time in what seemed like forever.

# THE FEAST

## Corey Melin

*Corey Melin. has been married two years. His hobbies are writing short stories and reading. He likes hiking on the plentiful trails in the great Northwest and also enjoys travel, both in the US and abroad.*

I clocked in and started walking up the stairs to my office to start another week of work.

What I didn't know was that this was going to be much different from other days.

James is the name and it's going on ten years since I started this job at the charter bus company. I started the job as a bus cleaner working everyday of the week either first thing in the morning or late at night.

After three years of cleaning and celebrating my twenty-third birthday I realized I couldn't stay in this job forever. I had become so comfortable with this position that I didn't realize time was quickly going by and that this was not the type of work to retire at down the road.

I looked into community college figuring there was no way I could afford going to a university. Spend years getting a degree that doesn't even promise you that a job will come your way that you can end your working days at and go on vacation.

Then one day as I was doing my errands I saw a school that will teach you office skills in less than a year. It was quite costly, but after going in and being able to set up loans I went for it.

When I finished I figured I would look for another job, but the bus company offered me an office position in charter sales. At first, I wasn't sure how I would do, being the shy type and not a big talker to people I don't know. It turned out that I enjoyed the position and got along with everyone I talked too. Even the ones who called very upset I was able to calm them and reassure them everything is going to be okay.

This went on for four years when I was offered another position. Dispatch. The one who did it before became quite ill and after five months of being in and out of the office, he called it quits and I was offered the job. At first I was reluctant to start a position that was more stressful than my current one. I eventually caved in and have done the job since.

There are many days that I have to come in at the crack of dawn to make sure all the drivers get out on time. This particular week was one of those times I had to start quite early everyday due to a big convention in town. Thankfully, I lived nearby so I was able to sleep until four a.m. to be up there by five a.m.

When I drove into the parking lot there were two other vehicles already there. One was the bus cleaner's, who comes in at midnight to clean, and the other was a driver, who was on a ten day trip.

I didn't see the cleaner in sight and figured he was inside a bus or inside his little cleaning shed.

I got out of my car and walked up the steps to the office building and unlocked the door. Immediately, the alarm started beeping, which I quickly went over to the opposite wall to the keypad and put in the code before the alarm went off and alerted the people in charge of security. As I punched in the code I wondered when they would replace the outdated system. Many times the owner is awakened in the middle of the night by security saying the alarm was going off. Every time it ends up either an insect or rodent setting it off or someone hasn't closed the door.

I went over to my desk and immediately started on my workload. If I didn't, for one I would fall behind on my work and secondly, I would end up falling asleep.

As the next hour went by the drivers came in and headed out for their daily run. Today, all of the drivers should be gone by seven o'clock on their merry ways. By eight o'clock the rest of the office crew would be here, plus the phones would start ringing away.

When I saw that it was close to seven I got up and went over to the window, seeing that all the buses were gone except for the one that was broken down. I also saw that the bus cleaner's vehicle was still here. Once the buses are gone usually he is gone.

I went outside and went down the steps, seeing that the door to the shed was wide open.

"Bill!" I called out as I neared the shed.

No answer and when I entered the shed there was no one around.

"Maybe he's in the honey bucket," I thought.

At one time the wash crew was allowed to use the restroom in the office, but when items started disappearing they locked the doors and stuck a honey bucket by the mechanics garage.

When I got to the honey bucket I knocked and called out his name. No reply. I pulled the handle and the door opened but there was no occupant.

"Where did he go?" I muttered.

I looked around the lot, seeing if he was sweeping the paved section or cutting down weeds. He was nowhere in sight.

The lot was surrounded by woods. At one time it was completely surrounded, but a couple of businesses were put in on the south side.

"Bill!" I called out.

No reply, but I heard some rustling sounds to my right in the woods.

"Bill!" I called out, looking that direction I saw a bush shake.

I started walking over, grabbing a shovel just in case.

"This better not be a joke!" I called out. "You'll end up getting whacked by the shovel I'm holding."

I neared the bush that started rattling again, but no distinguished sound telling me if it was human or animal.

As I slowly circled the bush I raised the shovel ready to swing if it turned out to be a wild animal. Especially one that could have rabies.

When I came to the other side I saw a strange sight. Lying on the ground with his hands and legs tied up with what looked like a vine, with leaves stuffed in his mouth, was Bill.

"What the heck is going on?" I asked, bending down to loosen the holdings.

He started to make noises and move around with a frightened look on his face.

"I'll have you out in a moment," I said. "Just hold still."

Bill continued to move around and I noticed he wasn't looking at me, but at something over my shoulder.

I started turning my head and felt something hit me on the back of the head and darkness welcomed me into its embrace.

I opened my eyes and blinked numerous times until my vision cleared and I saw I was somewhere in the woods. I looked around, almost blacking out from the explosion of pain coming from the back of my head. I closed my eyes and waited for the pain to subside. When it did I opened my eyes and looked around to see that I was not familiar with my surroundings.

There were a few times in the past that I would walk through the woods a ways just to get away from the monotony of everyday work. It was nice to feel like I had entered another world.

Now I sat there propped up against a tree, not knowing where I was and feeling the fright creep up on me. I quickly realized my arms were tied behind me and my legs were also tied with the same vines I saw on Bill.

"I have been kidnapped and there is a good chance I am going to die," I thought, remembering the crime movies I have watched.

I figured I better make my peace with God and pray that my death would come quick.

"I see you have awakened," a deep voice spoke out in front of me.

I looked up and to the left and right, but didn't see anyone.

"Who's there?" I called out. "Show yourself."

"A bit feisty, he is," a high squeaky voice to my left spoke.

Great. There were two of them. My small chance of possibly escaping was shrinking.

"I think he is handsome for a human," a feminine voice spoke to my right. The sound of the voice amazingly brought some comfort to me.

"A human?" I thought. "What am I dealing with here?"

"Is this the one we are having at the feast?" another rough voice spoke to my left.

"Attending the feast," replied the deep voice in front of me. "Not to consume."

Everything started to spin on me. In listening to this conversation I wondered if I was still unconscious, dreaming away.

"Should we show ourselves?" the high voiced one asked.

"I'm not sure," the deep voice responded. "Don't want to scare the poor fellow."

"Please tell me who you are?" I called out.

"We will tell you and we will show you, but you will not be expecting what you see," the feminine voice said, soothing my rapidly beating heart. "I will show myself, knowing that you will be fine with my appearance. Will that please you?"

"It will," I responded. "I hope," I thought.

I heard some rustling to my right and upon turning my head I saw a beautiful woman with long blond hair going down to her hips and wearing a dress that sparkled everywhere, making me squint to look at her. I looked at her face with the bright blue eyes, small nose, pert lips, and dimpled cheeks and felt at peace.

"Are you an angel?" I asked.

She started to giggle, which brought a joy to my heart.

I just wanted to leap up and start dancing with this beautiful woman. I believe I was falling in love.

"What is your name?" I asked her.

"My name by your language is Lillolyn," she replied. Then she looked around the woods and called out. "Everything will be all right. You may all come out." Then she looked at me once again. "If you become afraid just look at me and it will all go away."

I nodded then started looking around when I heard rustling sounds. I wasn't sure if I wanted to see the others, but as Lillolyn said, I could look at her and be okay.

When I looked straight ahead the trunk of the tree in front of me now had two brown eyes looking at me and a long pointy nose. Then to my left I saw a black bear come tromping out and beside the bear what looked like a human figure made of tree limbs. The head and the body looked like one branch and it had two arms and legs of smaller branches with three little twigs for fingers.

I stared at them for a moment before I quickly turned my vision to focus on Lillolyn as the fright started to overtake me.

"Never see a bear before?" the black bear growled out.

"I have seen plenty," I responded looking at the bear as it came within five feet of me and stopping. "But not one that talked and didn't attack a human."

"The ones you are talking about are my dense cousins," the bear said. "Most of them forgot their speech, letting out grunts instead. Quite a shame."

"Please introduce yourselves," Lillolyn said in her sweet voice.

"I am Blaggert," the bear responded.

"I am Sten," the walking stick squeaked out.

"And I am Oaknott," the tree spoke out.

"Now that you have our names," said Lillolyn. "What is yours?"

"James," I replied, becoming a bit calmer looking at Blaggert, Sten, and Oaknott. "Are there many of you?"

"There are many more of our kind," said Lillolyn. "We don't show ourselves to many humans and when we do we wipe your memory."

"So after this feast you will take these memories away?" I asked.

"I am afraid so," replied Lillolyn. "There are many good humans out there, but many bad ones who would cause us harm. Some unintentionally."

"That is probably a good thing," I said knowing that I would unintentionally mention this episode. It would be good for them and good for me since people would think that I went insane.

"We will untie you and you must promise not to run away," said Lillolyn. "We would hate to have to tie you back up or take you to the feast unconscious."

"I promise I won't run," I said.

Sten walked over and quickly untied me and helped me stand up.

There was a little bit of tingling in my hands and feet, but it quickly went away.

"Follow me," said Lillolyn turning around and starting to walk.

I followed her with Sten beside me and Blaggert a few feet behind me.

We walked for I don't know how long for when I looked at my watch it had stopped. I'm sure my co-workers were in by now wondering where I was at this moment.

"I'm with a group of forest creatures," I could hear myself telling everyone. "All is okay. They won't hurt me."

But then I thought possibly I was dreaming. I pinched myself a couple of times and closed my eyes, but every time I opened them I was still in the forest.

"I must be in a deep sleep," I thought.

"You are wide awake," said Lillolyn continuing to walk. "I understand it's hard to believe, but you should know this land holds many wonders that man knows little or nothing about."

"Why did you pick me for the feast?" I asked.

"You have a good soul," replied Lillolyn. "You respect life and treat your fellow man with kindness."

"Thank you for the compliment," I said. Overall, I practiced what she just stated, but there were moments I would say that I failed miserably.

We continued to walk on in silence for awhile with me still wondering if I would wake up or a bunch of friends would pop out, telling me this was a practical joke.

"Why do you need a human for the feast?" I asked Lillolyn.

"We have had our annual feast for a very long time and have every living creature participate in the feast. When humankind came along we invited one and have invited one since then."

"So every year you pick a human?"

"Our time is different from your time. Compared to your year I would say one hundred years have passed in our land."

"Are there many of your kind at this feast?" I asked picturing a large feast with all kinds of creatures dancing around a fire.

"I believe there will be hundreds," she responded. "You will be fine for I will remain by your side. None of them would think to hurt you, but the human kind is frightened of what they can not explain. They tend to lash out instead of welcoming."

I listened to her words, painfully agreeing. There were many out there who would end up running away or attacking the unknown. At first I was frightened, but as I walked along I was becoming more comfortable being with a life form I have never seen before or if I did it was in a fictional book.

"Wouldn't my kind see this large feast from afar?" I asked, knowing there were houses and businesses scattered throughout the area.

"They will not see us for we will not be here to be seen."

"Are you going to transport to another land or planet?" I asked wondering what she meant.

"We will be here, but the human eye will not be able to see or touch us," she responded. "Please do not try to comprehend the matter. Just enjoy the feast."

We walked on for who knows how long when there was a flash and next I was surrounded by creatures of all types. I stopped, my first reaction complete fright, but I looked at Lillolyn and my heart slowed down. A minute or two later I had enough courage to look around, seeing that many of the creatures were in fact wild animals. Wild animals conversing with other animals. There were other beings like fauns, satyrs, centaurs, Cyclopes, and other mythological creatures walking about and ones I didn't have a clue what they were and what they were made of. Some looked similar to Jell-O you plopped on your plate, one looked like two eyeballs with one above the left eye and one below the right floating around, and one that looked like a bunch of multi-colored sticks massed together slowly moving with the use of a larger black stick. The strange part is that I could understand everything they were saying to each other.

"I can understand their language," I muttered.

"We have allowed you to understand every language spoken at this feast," said Lillolyn. "No one here actually speaks the human language."

"Does everyone live here on Earth?" I asked.

"Most," she said. "Many of us live among your kind, but you won't recognize us since you do not know what to look for."

"Time for the feast!" a voice called out.

Everyone went to an open field where in the middle was a canopy of trees. Beneath the trees I could see platforms covered with trays of food.

"Let's go over and enjoy the feast," said Lillolyn heading toward the food.

I followed her and was greeted by many different kind of species. It was quite strange to bend down and use my pinky finger to greet two squirrels. There were a few I wasn't able to shake hands with for they had no hands.

As I neared the food I realized I was getting used to seeing the different kind of beings conversing throughout the area. I wondered if there were ones just like me seeing all the different races for the first time.

When we approached the food I saw there were all kinds laid out for the taking. There were fruits and vegetables throughout the area. I also saw platters of meat, which I wondered if it was someone's cousin.

"Don't worry," said Lillolyn. "No one's cousin was killed. These are simple creatures that we serve for ones who are carnivores."

At first I wasn't hungry, but as I walked past the numerous dishes my stomach started to growl. I began grabbing up food, putting it on a platter until it was full, then taking a goblet of unknown liquid that was sweet and brought a warm feeling to my stomach.

I followed Lillolyn out onto the field and sat down and started eating, enjoying myself. Here I was having great food and seeing beings no one else would ever see in their lifetime.

There was little conversation between me and Lillolyn, which was fine since I was looking around at all the different creatures.

I finally finished my food and I lay on my back looking up at the sky.

"Soon the music will play," said Lillolyn. "Just relax and enjoy."

"I will," I muttered.

It wasn't long before I heard the sound of a flute then the sweet sound of other instruments. I closed my eyes, listening to the sounds of the music that brought positive thoughts to mind. Soon I drifted away into wonderland.

"James," a sweet sounding voice called out to me. "James."

I slowly opened my eyes and saw Lillolyn standing over me looking down, bringing calm to my soul.

"Had a nice nap," she said with a smile.

I slowly stood up, seeing that it was dark outside except for a large bonfire on the left side of the field. There were creatures of all types dancing around the fire.

"Would you like to dance around the fire?" asked Lillolyn.

"I'm not a good dancer," I replied. "I would like to watch for awhile."

We stood there watching the merry scene before Lillolyn touched my shoulder, bringing a tingling feeling throughout my body.

"It's time to go back," she said.

I looked at her for a moment then at the party around me. I really didn't want to leave; I was having a lot of fun and just relaxing. It was like going to a nice sunny beach and lying there listening to the ocean waves.

"I can see you don't want to go back," she said.

I looked at her, feeling emotions I rarely experienced in life. This was a day of unique happiness and now it was over.

"I wish I could stay," I told her.

"Unfortunately, it is not possible," she said.

I looked around at all of the beings having fun, wishing I could enjoy this life, but it was not to be.

"Just close your eyes and you will return to the time you entered the woods," she spoke.

"I won't remember any of today's events?" I asked.

"Only in your dreams."

"Thank you for the experience."

"May you have a blessed life."

I closed my eyes and seconds later I opened them. I stood in the outskirts of the woods near the lot.

"What are you doing?" a voice behind me asked.

I turned around, seeing Bill.

"I don't know," I responded, shrugging my shoulders.

I went back to work having a wonderful feeling for some reason throughout the day and that night had dreams of dancing with mythological creatures.

# MOVE

## Sherri Fulmer Moorer

*Sherri Fulmer Moorer is a freelance writer in Columbia, South Carolina, and is the author of* Battleground Earth - Living by Faith in a Pagan World. *For more on her writing, visit her website at:* http://hometown.aol.com/bgearth/index.html.

"I was quite clear on this from the start. I want to be a stay-at-home wife and mother. I can't believe you want me chained to a desk!"

"You were not! A year ago you wanted to be a career woman! Then we get engaged and all you want that degree for is a decoration on the wall!"

Kayla looked at the young couple across the desk, reminding herself they were worth dragging in to work for on a Saturday morning. "Christine, are you saying you don't want to work at all after the wedding?"

"No, if I do that I'll be trapped into working full time the rest of my life. I want my home and family to be my life, not my job."

The man snorted. "At least that's what her mother and sister told her."

Pastor Jennings poked his head in the door. "I don't mean to rush you, but will you be done soon?"

Kayla nodded. "Sure pastor, give us ten minutes and we'll be done." She turned to the seething couple as Pastor Jennings shut the door. "I'm sorry, but we have a funeral in a couple of hours, and they need to set up the church. Between now and our next session, I want you to write down how you'd like to see your life in one year, five years, and ten years. You need to think about planning for your future together. Don't talk about this to anybody but each other. Remember, getting married is about building a life together based on who you are, not on what other people expect of you."

They stood. "Thanks Kayla." Ed said. "We appreciate you coming in to see us on a Saturday morning."

Kayla stood and shook their hands. "I'm glad to do it. It's normal to have such disagreements during your engagement. The important thing is to establish ways to work them out."

"Well done," Pastor Jennings said as the door closed behind them.

She dropped their file back in her cabinet. "Now I know why you require premarital counseling for all couples getting married. I hope they can get things worked out in the next five months. Every week, they're fighting over some new issue."

"I have no doubt you'll have them seeing eye to eye before the trees start budding."

Kayla shook her head. "I just hope they don't end out here for marriage counseling in two years, or worse yet divorced."

"I know it seems bleak when you see things like that, but have faith. Marriage is a wonderful thing when two are meant to be together."

She laughed. "I don't know. Seeing couples like that makes me glad I'm not married."

"Who knows, you may be walking down the aisle yourself one day. What about that boyfriend who gave you those beautiful earrings for Christmas?"

She shrugged. "We've only been dating five months."

"Diamond earrings are hardly a gift given by a casual acquaintance. The young man must think a lot of you to give such an exquisite gift."

Kayla grunted.

Pastor Jennings patted her on the back. "You're a good counselor Kayla, but sometimes you could stand to take your own advice. Joshua's actions show great affection for you. Give him a chance."

She pulled on her coat. "I'd best be on my way. You have a funeral to prepare for."

"Thanks for coming in, and take care. Make some time for Josh tonight."

"Will do," she said, opening the door to a blast of cold air and disappearing in the grey morning.

*** 

"Hey, you're up early," Lori said, balancing a baby on her hip. "Sorry the house is a disaster. I wasn't expecting anybody to come over."

"I had to meet a couple at the church for premarital counseling," Kayla said, studying the baby to figure out which one it was.

"It's Cassie. We just got Caleb back to sleep."

"I thought I'd drop by, since I was out. How's it going?"

"I haven't slept through an entire night in three months," Kieran said, stepping in the kitchen. Kieran was Kayla's twin brother.

"I haven't either," Lori said, running her hands through her messy hair and forcing a smile. "Don't get me wrong. I wouldn't trade my kids for anything. But having newborn twins is a challenge."

"Yeah, don't let her bloodshot eyes fool you. She envies that you get a decent night's sleep every night, and so do I," Kieran mumbled, leaning against the cabinet and drinking orange juice directly from the container.

"Don't do that!"

Kayla laughed. "Give up. He's been doing it for thirty years and I doubt he stops now."

Lori narrowed her bloodshot eyes. "I don't want the kids picking up that nasty habit."

"Look, I've done all the counseling I'm due for the week. Do you guys need anything?" Kayla asked.

"Sleep," Kieran mumbled.

Lori laughed. "No, we're okay. My parents are coming by later so we can go out to dinner." She bounced Cassie on her hip. "Come on Kayla, don't you want one of these?"

Kieran laughed. "I believe she's smarter than that after what you just said." He reached over to pick up Cassie. "I'm putting her down for a nap," he said, as he left the room with the sputtering baby.

"What's with him?" Kayla asked.

Lori shook her head. "He's moody. I think the stress of a new family is getting to him."

"That makes sense. How are you holding up?"

"You mean am I still depressed? Don't worry. The medication is working fine."

"That's not what I meant."

"I'm sorry," Lori said, dropping in a kitchen chair. "I suppose my nerves are a bit worn too. By the way, you look exhausted. How many hours did you work this week?

Kayla rubbed her eyes. "I don't know. Fifty, maybe sixty. It's the beginning of the year. We have a lot going on. Premarital counseling for twenty summer weddings, grief counseling for three deaths in the congregation, and keeping up with my normal patients has me swamped. Plus the secretary needed help getting all of those Christmas offerings processed. Perhaps I am a little overworked."

"And when was the last time you and Josh went out?"

"Lori!"

"I'm concerned about you. Come on, he lives in the same condominium complex as you."

"We're going out tonight."

"The guy worships the ground you walk on, and he's second to your job. What gives?"

Kayla sighed. "Please don't start on the speech."

"What speech?"

Kayla rolled her eyes. "The 'you need to get your priorities in order' speech. The 'you need to get married and have babies like everybody else in Midway' speech. You know, everybody's life doesn't follow the perfect pattern of education-marriage-family. Time doesn't move in the same linear pattern for us all."

"Kayla, your parents, your brother and I are concerned about you. You've turned down two engagements, and now you're dating somebody with great promise. Josh adores you, and those earrings are a pretty obvious hint that he wants to get more serious. Why are you having a hard time accepting it?"

Kayla sighed. "A broken engagement would scare anybody."

"I thought it was two?"

Kayla shook her head. "No, when Harry proposed I turned him down. We had just graduated high school. Trying to work and go to college at the same time seemed too overwhelming."

"Okay, you were too young then. But what about Daniel? What happened there? One minute you were engaged and the next minute you broke up. Why?"

Kayla stared out the window. "I think I was too hasty accepting his proposal. It's something I can't explain. Like something was wrong with him that I couldn't see, but I could feel." She lowered her head. "Perhaps it's the way he put that ultimatum on me. I always told him I wanted to be a counselor. Then the ring's on my finger and he wants me to quit graduate school to work as a secretary for his father's architectural firm. I thought I was clear with him from the start, but in three years of dating he obviously didn't hear me."

Lori mimicked Kayla's sigh. "You haven't had a serious relationship since then, and that was eight years ago. You've dated here and there but face it; you channeled your energy toward establishing a career. Isn't it time to focus your energy on a new goal, like the wonderful young man in your life?"

"Why is everybody in such a hurry for us to settle down? We just met." She had met Josh at the mail station six months ago, just after he moved in. They kept bumping into one another over the next month until she got sick with bronchitis and stayed home for a week to recover. Much to her surprise, he showed up at her door with a bouquet of pink roses, a pot of chicken noodle soup, a book she had been talking about reading, and several DVD's, to 'help her recover.' They had been dating ever since.

"I think marriage may be on his mind. Perhaps that's why your relationship developed so quickly."

"That's what makes me nervous. It's built up so quickly. I hope there isn't a big fall at the end."

Lori laughed. "Please, give me a break. A man wouldn't go to the trouble he has with you unless he were serious." She leaned forward. "I'm not criticizing you Kayla, just pointing out the obvious. Please think about it."

"Will do," Kayla said, standing and putting on her coat. "Look, I better get home. Josh and I are going out tonight, and I want to take a nap. I was up way too early this morning."

Lori hugged Kayla. "Thanks for coming over. Tell Josh we said hi."

"I will, and you try to get some sleep," Kayla said, getting in her car and driving off. She shook her head at the irony of it all. She was just as successful as her brother, but because she was single she was still seen as a failure. She had met all of her goals and built a good life for herself. So what if a husband hadn't fit in so far?

Still, some of Lori's words stuck in her mind. As she walked in her condo and laid down on the bed, she couldn't help but wonder if she had sacrificed too much for the life she had.

\*\*\*

Kayla woke to the doorbell ringing. Sitting up, she realized she was in a pink recliner in a huge room.

*Where am I? This isn't my condo.*

She stood up, knocking the newspaper out of her lap, and made her way to what she thought was the door. Looking out the peephole, she saw a woman about her age with long hair.

Kayla opened the door. The woman rushed in and hugged her.

"Hey!" Kayla said, jumping slightly.

The woman stepped back. "Well, you look better today. Getting adjusted to being home alone just when the Daniel's fixing to come home?"

Kayla shook her head. "I'm sorry, you must have mistaken me for somebody else." She looked around. "I'm not even sure where I am."

The woman laughed and led her back in the room she had come out of. Looking around, it was opulent – the house was obviously huge. Two recliners sat across from an entertainment center that took up the entire wall, complete with a big screen television, stereo system, and other gadgets and gizmos she couldn't distinguish clearly from across the room. The woman plopped in one of the recliners.

"You're home Kayla. And I'm Natalie, your best friend. Remember, we work together at the architectural firm?"

Kayla looked around the room, still confused. A picture on the wall behind her caught her eye. It was a wedding picture of her – and Daniel. Kayla sank down in the recliner.

*This isn't right. I'm not married, I don't live here, and I'm not an office manager.*

"Kayla, are you alright?" Natalie asked. She looked at the newspaper on the floor. "You fell asleep reading the paper again, didn't you? Kayla, what are we going to do with you? Every time Daniel and his father have to go to a job site out of state, you fall into bad habits. How do you expect to start a family if you can't take care of yourself for a few days?" Natalie got up and went in the kitchen. "Come on, I'll get you back on track."

"Excuse me, but I'm capable of taking care of myself," Kayla said, following Natalie into a large kitchen with fancy, stainless steel appliances.

"Good," Natalie said, handing her a pill bottle. "Then take your medication like a big girl."

Kayla looked at the pill bottle with a start. The prescription was for an antidepressant.

*This can't be real. I must be dreaming.* She slammed the bottle on the cabinet.

"I don't need that."

Natalie stared at Kayla. "I know you don't like it but face it, you're depressed. And I can see why. You're the poor little rich girl, and it's getting to you." Natalie motioned around the room. "Look at all of this. You have it all, but your husband works all the time to keep up this extravagant lifestyle."

Kayla shook her head. "Where is Daniel?"

"He's in Salt Lake City with his father, inspecting a job site." Natalie shrugged. "You know, you should go on some of these trips with him. He begs you to go every time, but you always bow out because you hate to travel."

Kayla sat in a kitchen chair. "How did it come to this, Natalie? What happened? I was going to be a counselor and help other people build better lives. But here I am, needing help."

Natalie sat across the table from her. "It happens to all of us. Remember last year when I turned thirty and got so depressed about not being married? You encouraged me to finish my education, and thanks to your advice I'll have my associate's degree by the end of this year. I'm trying to return the favor." She patted Kayla on the hand. "I know you have regrets about dropping out of school to get married, but take a look around. You have a picture perfect life. Heck, you only work part-time! Most women would kill to have this life." She took the pill bottle and spun it in her hand. "But no life is perfect. Daniel loves you, but he shelters you. Perhaps too much."

Kayla looked at Natalie. Searching her heart, she finally sensed what the problem was. "The world is caving in on me."

Natalie nodded. "You're in a rut, Kayla. Daniel loves you, but he has you trapped in this world he created. It's *his* house, *his* work, *his* life, *his* world. And you are living in it as *his* wife."

"And what about me?"

"Exactly," Natalie said, slamming the pill bottle on the table and taking her hand. "Do you even know who you are anymore? Daniel's done everything for you. Now for some women, it would be fine to be led by the man in their life. But I thought you were stronger that that. At least you seemed it at the start. You talked about going back to graduate school, but instead you took the promotion your father-in-law offered you and let Daniel use the money to build this mansion." Natalie leaned forward. "Don't you see? They offered you that job as bait to keep you in this life, and you took it! Now he's pressuring you to have children because *he* wants to have a family. Is that what you want, Kayla?"

*I gave up my life to live Daniel's.*

She had gone through with the wedding, and this was her life. She was married and financially secure, but she gave up herself. She lived as an extension of Daniel and not as herself anymore.

That's what put her off about him – his insistence on having his way. He didn't respect her opinions and didn't allow her to make her own decisions.

"I don't know what I want anymore," she finally said, her eyes welling with tears. "I'm so browbeat that I don't even know how to think for myself anymore." She grabbed a napkin and swiped at her face, disgusted. She didn't cry, at least not in the life she thought she knew. She had been happy. Lonely, but overall happy. She cursed whatever twist of fate put her in this miserable situation.

Natalie got up and patted her on the back. "It's alright. Everything will be okay."

"This isn't my life," Kayla mumbled, squeezing her eyes shut and trying to shut out the world around her.

***

"Mom? Are you awake?" Kayla woke to somebody gently shaking her. Squinting her eyes open, she saw a girl who looked a lot like she had in middle school.

"Hmm? I guess so. What happened?" she asked, sitting up. She didn't recognize where she was. She had a headache and hurt terribly, as if she had been in an accident.

"Take it easy. He's gone." She noticed for the first time that the girl had a black eye and a red mark on her cheek.

"Who?"

The girl looked at her with concern. "Dad. He left after his fit."

Kayla put her hand to her head and sure enough, her eye was slightly swollen. "I don't understand."

"We never do when he goes on his tirades," The girl sat next to her and hugged her. "Come on Mom, he won't be back until late. Why don't we take off? I'd like to see my grandparents again – *your* parents. Maybe they can help us."

Kayla shook her head in confusion and got up slowly, looking for the bathroom. Walking through the doorway, her eye caught a picture hanging on the wall.

It was of her, Hank, and the girl.

*No, it's not possible! I turned down his proposal. And I don't have a child!*

The girl followed her. "I know you're afraid he'll follow us and hurt them, but come on! If we don't get out, he'll kill us"

"You're awfully wise for your age," Kayla said, shaking off her shock and continuing to the bathroom.

The girl put her hands on her hips. "I'm in the gifted program, remember? They say I might be the smartest girl in the sixth grade!" The girl was stopped by a knock at the door. "I'll get that," she said, running down the hall.

Kayla found the bathroom, switched on the light, and recoiled in horror when she saw her reflection in the mirror. It wasn't just a black eye; the left side of her face was swollen. There was a small cut on her right cheek below the eye. There were also bruises on both of her arms. She sat on the edge of the dirty tub as the facts set in.

*This isn't possible! I'm not a battered wife.* She put her head in her hands and wondered what was going on. Just then, the girl appeared in the door with a woman about her age.

"Thanks Rachel, let me talk to you mother. Why don't you go to the library? We'll pick you up in an hour." The girl nodded and disappeared up the hall. A minute later, they heard the door close. The woman sat beside her and put an arm around her.

"Kayla, are you alright?"

Kayla shook her head. "Where am I? What's going on?"

"You're at home." The woman rinsed a cloth in cool water and pressed it against the Kayla's face. "That ought to help the swelling. That girl is your daughter, Rachel. She just told me Hank got passed up for a promotion at the textile plant last night, and he came home drunk."

Kayla reached up and held the cloth to her face. "Pardon me for sounding rude, but who are you?"

The woman shook her head. "I'm Natalie, your neighbor. Don't you remember?"

Looking in the mirror, she realized Natalie cast no reflection in it – it showed her alone in the room. Kayla took the cloth off her face. "No I don't. In fact, I don't remember any of this because it isn't real." She pulled herself up straight and looked Natalie square in the eye. "I'm no more a battered wife or mother than I am the wife of a wealthy architect. I have no recollection of you because you don't exist." She threw the cloth in the sink. "What are you? And what have you done to me?"

***

They were sitting in Kayla's office. Natalie was behind Kayla's desk, hands folded and studying her intently. "Congratulations. I wondered how long it would take you to catch on."

"Catch on to what?" Kayla said, jumping off the couch across the desk, where her patients usually sat.

"Kayla, what's the last thing you remember? What's the last thing you did that feels 'real' to you today?"

Kayla sat back on the couch. "Okay, everybody wants to play therapist with me today, so I'll indulge you. I talked to my sister-in-law, went home, and laid down to take a nap." She shook her head. "So what is this? A bad dream?"

Natalie looked out the window at the empty parking lot. It occurred to Kayla that there was supposed to be a funeral going on, yet the church seemed abandoned.

"Kayla, Pastor Jennings and Lori are right about one thing. You're good at giving advice, but bad at taking it."

"Is this about the marriage thing again?"

Natalie stood up and walked around the desk. "Kayla, you've sacrificed a great deal to get here and I think you're starting to realize that. You got what you wanted out of life. Why do you keep putting Josh off?"

Kayla wandered toward the window and looked out at the cold, gray day. "It's not putting him off; it's about giving things time to develop."

"How much time do you think you have? None of us knows. We may feel like we have many good years ahead, but some freak accident can take them all away in an instant."

Kayla sighed. "I've had my heart broken twice before, and I don't want it to happen again." She turned toward Natalie. "Harry and I dated for a year, and I did think a lot of him. But he was in a hurry to get married and move out of an abusive home, and I wanted to go to college. As much as I wanted to help him build a better life, I couldn't sacrifice my own future to save him. Then I met Daniel my junior year in college, and we were happy together. But he was a few years older and ready to move on with his life, and I wasn't. I couldn't sacrifice my future to give him the life he wanted. I had my own dreams. Neither of them seemed to understand or respect that."

Natalie nodded. "They got in the way, so you let them go."

Kayla shook her head. "I wanted to compromise and try to work things out, but they didn't want to give me time or space to build my own life." She looked at her college ring. "Most men don't want to stay with you when you've turned down a marriage proposal. At that point it's all or nothing." She sighed. "I knew it would come to this. You're right; basically I was telling them to take me on my own terms or leave, and they left." Kayla shook her head. "Sometimes doing the right thing feels wrong. All you have is the feeling deep in your heart that it was right."

Natalie walked behind Kayla and put her hand on her shoulder. "Are you're afraid it will come to that with Josh?"

"I don't know what it will come to. I wonder if he will expect me to give up my career like Harry and Daniel. Then that makes me question whether I did the right thing pursuing my career with such single-minded determination." She walked across the room and sank back on the couch. "You're right, it's fear. I do love Josh. But I've had two relationships that ended for practical matters, and I'm scared of my feelings for him because I'm afraid I might have to let him go, too."

Natalie dropped on the couch beside Kayla. "Then you finally get it."

"Get what?"

"Kayla, every time you make a decision it closes old doors and opens new ones. There's no way of knowing what options you have unless you move in a new direction. Josh has opened a new door for you, yet you're dwelling on what's behind you. That's not uncommon, but if you aren't careful, dwelling on the past will cause you to stagnate in the present."

Kayla nodded. "Which means doors to the future close."

"I've given you a gift today that few people get. I've shown you what would have happened had you moved on different paths. You could have married Daniel and had a nice home, but you'd be depressed. That door opened financial stability, yet it also opened regret for what you gave up to build a life with him. Could you get over your depression and accept the life you chose?"

Natalie stood and paced in front of her. "Or you could have accepted Harry's proposal on your senior trip. You could have helped him escape an abusive home. But you got pregnant on that trip and had to give up college to raise a child. The burden of working low-level jobs with a new family brings out what you hoped would never happen: Harry inherited his father's temper. In giving up your future, you put yourself and your daughter in the very place you meant for him to escape. So it comes to the day you just saw – do you take your daughter and try to build a new life, despite the risk that Harry will hurt you and anybody who helps you? Or do you stay and continue to live in fear to protect everybody else you love?"

Kayla slumped in the couch. "So now what?"

Natalie shrugged. "Whatever you want. You lament the past. Now you have a chance to change it. Do you regret the decisions you made?"

Kayla shifted in her seat. "All this time I imagined I gave up Prince Charming for my career. But after seeing this, I know I made the right decisions. They were hard, but they were right."

Natalie stopped pacing. "The right decisions are rarely the quick and easy ones. Often, they are difficult and painful. And they require extreme patience to see them come to greater good."

Kayla laughed. "I think I've told a few of my patients that. Maybe it's time to take my own advice."

Natalie smiled. "Good, I'm glad. I would hate to send you to another reality."

"Another reality? What are you? An angel or some sort of a spirit guide?"

"Just think of me as someone sent to show you the way amidst all of your confusion."

"Well, I appreciate it. Now what do I need to do to get back to reality – *my* reality? I have a date with my boyfriend tonight and I'd like to see if I can bring this relationship to a happier ending than my past ones." She paused. "You've shown me what would have happened if I accepted the other marriage proposals. Can you show me what might happen with Josh?"

Natalie shook her head. "That story hasn't been written yet. I can only show you what might have been; no the future." She patted

Kayla on the back as they looked out the window at the sun breaking through the clouds. "Your decision to move through this door could lead to the happy ending you want. The only way to know is to move on it now."

"Thanks Natalie, I appreciate it ..." she said, trailing off as she turned around to discover that she was in the room alone.

***

Kayla bolted upright with a start, startled by the doorbell. Pausing a moment to stare at the setting sun slipping through her bedroom window, she stumbled to the door to see Joshua standing there. She threw open the door and kissed him.

"Wow, that's the warmest welcome I've got yet!"

She pulled back. "I'm just glad to see you. Am I late meeting you?"

"No," he said sheepishly. "Actually, it's 4:45. I know you said you'd be over at 6:00, but I saw your car and thought I'd surprise you by coming over early."

"I must have overslept. I laid down to take a nap when I got back from work and seeing my brother."

"I'm sorry, I didn't mean to wake you. Are you okay?"

She smiled and kissed him again. "I'm fine. Just a bad dream. Actually, I'm glad you're here."

"I'm not usually one to wish nightmares on anybody, but if they mean the welcome I just got, I wish you'd have them more often."

She laughed. "That won't be necessary. You do deserve more warm welcomes." She turned toward the bathroom. "Give me a minute and I'll get changed into something more appropriate."

"What's wrong with what you're wearing? It's just dinner, not the prom. You look great. Come on, let's go."

She studied him for a minute. She was fortunate to have met such a wonderful person. Perhaps Lori was right – it was time to move forward. "Alright, if it's good enough for you, let's go," she said, pulling on her coat and grabbing her purse as they headed out the door.

# ONE-EYED TEDDY BEAR

### Linda Hudson Hoagland

*Linda Hudson Hoagland is a wife and mother who lives in a small Virginia town where she works in the field of education. Her novel,* The Little Old Lady Next Door, *has been published and is available on the Internet.*

"Hey, look at me. I'm over here!" he shouted to the little girl as she stood in the center of the room and turned herself around and around while she tried to take in all the sights of a giant toy room.

"I don't know which one I want to play with. Let me look some more," she pleaded with joy shining from her eyes.

"Hey, Lovely Little Girl, I'm over here. Right here! See! I'm winking at you," he shouted loudly and hopefully with a persuasiveness that couldn't be refused.

The little girl gazed at all of the toys in front of her as she pondered the problem of choosing one, only one toy, that she could share her time with as she waited for her mother to return to her from her visit with the doctor.

"Come on, Dearie. I'm the best of the lot. Please pick me," he whispered as the little girl reached for a doll with long raven hair and fancy clothes.

I knew she wouldn't pick me. I don't know why I bothered to get my hopes up. It happens every day, several times every day.

If I only had two eyes. If my eye hadn't been lost in the wash. Maybe someone would love me and play with me.

I remember when the children would almost fight each other to be able to hold me, hug me to their hearts, and talk to me like I was one of them. Now, no one wants to look at me, touch me, and talk to me except maybe to say that I'm ugly.

The one-eyed teddy bear felt dejected and alone in a room full of toys. He closed his one eye and tried to make himself small so that no one would be able to see how sad he was and how easy it was to make him cry.

He wanted to go to sleep and dream about all of the wonderful times he had when he was loved by everyone. He wanted to go to sleep and dream forever about good things and good times.

"Hey, One-eye, wake up," shouted the giraffe from the shelf above the one-eyed teddy bear.

"What? Hunh? Did someone say something?" muttered the one-eyed teddy bear.

"Yeah, I did," said the giraffe whose name was Duncan.

"What do you want?" asked the one-eyed teddy bear sadly.

"How many times did you get picked today?"

"Why?"

"I just want to know, that's why," demanded Duncan.

"How many times did you get picked?" returned the one-eyed teddy bear rather than answering the questions.

"I asked you first," whined Duncan.

"I'll tell you if you tell me first," said the one-eyed teddy bear.

"I got picked five times. They all love me. They can't keep their hands off me. Now – how many times did you get picked," he asked in a sarcastic tone.

"None," answered the one-eyed teddy bear in a barely audible whisper.

"I knew it. I knew nobody picked you again. How many days has it been since you've been chosen?"

"I don't know. I can't remember."

"You won't be around here much longer. Some one will come in with the big brown box soon and put all of the toy rejects in it. You'll be one of them. I don't know what they do with the rejects. Maybe you all get burned in the incinerator. Maybe they haul you off to the dump. But, I know you won't like it. None of the rejects ever gets to come back," said Duncan as an ugly sounding laugh escaped his stuffed body.

"You shouldn't wish that on any body, you know that don't you, Duncan? It could happen to you someday."

"No, never. I'm never going to go away. The kids really, really love me."

"You are getting a little dirty, you know. Maybe they'll do to you what they did to me. Remember that loose thread? That's how I lost my eye."

"No, it's not going to happen to me. What did happen to you? You never did tell anyone. Why don't you tell me now so I'll know if it happens to me?"

"It's too scary. I don't want to talk about it."

"Aw come on, tell me," pleaded Duncan as he looked as his dingy used-to-be-white fur.

"Well, they didn't put me in a box. The lady that works out front, the nice one with the brown hair, you know who I mean."

"Yeah, go on," snarled Duncan.

"Well, she picked me up very gently and carried me to her car. She put me on the front seat right next to her and drove me to her house where she carried me inside the house and placed me on the kitchen table. I sat there and looked around just enjoying the change of scenery for a few hours until she picked me up again and carried me to the basement. I think that was what that room was called."

"Okay, okay, what happened next?"

"I sat on the dryer for a while until she sorted a big stack of clothes that was laying on the floor. Then, she grabbed me up and put me on top of the clothes she had shoved inside the washing machine. She added a sweet smelling soap of some kind and closed the lid. The last thing I remember was the water. I could hear water running."

"What happened next?"

"I don't know. I can't remember."

"Were you scared?"

"I think I was, but I can't remember. I guess it is better that I don't remember because after I went to sleep in the washer, I woke up as she was taking me out of the dryer. I remember feeling clean and pretty except for one thing. I could only see out of one eye."

"What happened to your other eye?"

"It disappeared between the time I fell asleep in the washer and waking up in the dryer. I must have lost it along the way."

"You don't remember any of it?"

"No, Duncan, I don't."

"You don't think that will happen to me, do you?"

"Your fur is getting awfully dirty. That's what the lady said to me when she took me to her house."

"Teddy, can I call you Teddy? I didn't mean to tease you."

"Yes, you did."

"I'm sorry."

Suddenly the door to the darkened room opened wide and a woman entered carrying a large brown paper box.

The one-eyed teddy bear watched the woman with his one eye.

"This thing has got to go. Some of its parts are missing," she said as she shook the robot, forcing it to rattle loudly.

The lady grabbed a doll that had lost its arm and a truck that had only three of its four wheels. She roughly shoved the broken toys into the box and continued to search through the remaining toys for rejects to be disposed of.

The one-eyed teddy bear realized that the blank spot on his face where his missing eye should have been was plainly visible, at first glance, from the woman.

Oh, no, what can I do? She'll see me and throw me in that big brown box.

The one-eyed teddy bear was too frightened to move. He was afraid any movement would draw her attention even faster.

"That's definitely got to go. Nobody ever plays with it. It only has one eye," said the woman as she threw the one-eyed teddy bear into the big brown box.

More broken and mutilated toys were thrown in on top of the one-eyed teddy bear until the box was so full it would hardly close.

The lady pulled and tugged at the big brown box until she reached the lobby where she let the box sit, directly in the way, until she could get a note written to the janitor and taped to the top of it.

> *Harry,*
> *See that this box of toys gets taken to the dump.*
> *Thanks,*
> *Mary Turner*

"That ought to take care of it," she whispered as she left the office and then the building for the night.

"Help, help me," cried the one-eyed teddy bear from beneath the pile of broken bodies of toys.

No one answered. No one moved. They remained piled up on top of the one-eyed teddy bear. There seemed to be no life in any of his fellow toys. They were all dead, lifeless, except him.

"Help me, I'm not dead," he whimpered as a tear rolled down his cheek.

He dozed off to sleep and dreamed of being loved and being happy until his threads were worn bare and he no longer was able to hold himself together. He longed to die happy, smiling, and being loved. He wanted to be a favorite toy that was carried along everywhere and cried after when he was misplaced for whatever reason.

"Lou, I'm going to take this box downstairs. It looks like it's full of old toys. The note says to take it to the dump, but I think the City Mission could make use of these things. Maybe they could repair them and get them useable again. What do you think?"

"That's fine with me, Marty. We won't mention that it didn't go to the dump."

The one-eyed teddy bear felt himself gliding along, being moved. Suddenly he was jolted a bit as if the box was bumped against something.

Where are we going? What's going to happen to me? Am I going to be tossed in the dump?

The box stopped moving and it was placed gently onto the floor. The sound of keys rattling in a door, the pulling forward of the box over the threshold, and the motion of being carried again kept the mind of the one-eyed teddy bear busy. Finally the box was lifted and placed into a small area with the slamming of the SUV door, the noise of the outside world assaulted the one-eyed teddy bear's ears.

He was not able to move. He couldn't see that world around him. He didn't know where he was except that he wasn't in the toy room any longer.

"What's going to happen to me?" he moaned as he closed his one eye to shut out the scary world that was descending upon him.

The outside world seemed to settle down and go to sleep so that is what the one-eyed teddy bear decided he should do.

Moving? Am I moving again?

He felt the motion of the SUV as it traveled along a road. The sensation was calming but the idea that he didn't know where he was headed and what would happen to him after he arrived at his unknown destination had the one-eyed teddy bear worried.

Suddenly the big brown box was being moved, carried to another place to be left for whatever reason.

"I brought these toys to you to see if you could use them. I know some of them are broken beyond repair. There are a few in that box that someone's little kid would love to have to play with. I just couldn't see taking these to the dump without you guys getting a chance to take out what you can use."

"Thanks, Mr.?"

"Adams, Marty Adams. Don't thank me. They aren't my toys. I was told to take them to the dump. That would have been such a waste, as I see it."

"Yes, Mr. Adams, it would have been a waste," said the elderly lady who was tearing open the top of the box.

"Just leave them all here. We will dispose of the items that are beyond repair."

"Great. I'm glad you can use them."

The one-eyed teddy bear opened his eye to see what was happening.

The old lady was pulling one toy after another out of the box, separating them into trash and repair piles.

She peered into the box with her wrinkled face hanging over the edge of it like some grotesque shrunken head.

"A teddy bear. It's only got one eye. I've got just the thing to fix that," she said as she hugged the one-eyed teddy bear to her breast.

Thank you, thank you, for saving me, said the one-eyed teddy bear.

"What? Did somebody say something?" asked the old lady as she looked around the room.

"I did, Lady. I said thank you."

"You're welcome to whoever said that."

"Hey, Lady, you heard me, didn't you?"

"Heard who? Who said that?" asked the old lady with a look of consternation etched into her brow.

"Look down, Lady, I'm Teddy."

The old lady looked at the one-eyed teddy bear and shrugged.

"I'm going to call you Teddy. You will be my Christmas present. You're going home with me where you will be taken care of for the rest of your life and my life."

"I guess I didn't need that lovely little girl to give me a home. A little old lady named Ellen will do just fine," Teddy said as he smiled contentedly.

# FOR MY YOUNGEST GRANDDAUGHTER

## Yvonne Eve Walus

*Yvonne Eve Walus is a novelist, poet, freelance writer, mathematician, wife, and mother – not necessarily in that order. Published in the United States and England, her work is available worldwide. Her latest romance,* Small Price to Pay, *was published by Echelon Press in 2007. http://yewalus.kiwiwebhost.net.nz/index.html*

Should she open it, she asked herself. The door to the attic looked smaller than Amy had remembered. Smaller and less foreboding. Still, she hesitated. The fear with which she had learnt to live in the last few years, weighed heavy in her stomach. Escape, she needed to escape from it all.

As a child, she had climbed up here every day, longing for the moment when she would be allowed to enter the mysterious room beyond. But as the years went by, she discovered it was not that simple. Nothing was ever that simple. Marriage was not the magic adventure advertised on the Internet. People were not fair or prejudice-free. As for the attic door…Amy sighed.

Grandmama's instructions, attached to the key ring, had been vague yet firm. *For my youngest granddaughter, to be used only when a genuine need arises.*

Amy swivelled the hologram around her index finger. A genuine need, she pondered. Grandmama must have written those words in the late two-oh-sixties, decades before organic computers replaced the old-fashioned electronic ones. It was a time of great distress, when information hijacks and Internet monopoly threatened the fate of billions. That must have been the context of Grandmama's message. Not a failing marriage or two daughters who were social outcasts because of who they were by birth.

"For crying out loud, what's taking so long?" Ralph's voice was muffled by the narrow staircase, but the tone of irritation was not. "Did you find anything useful up there?"

Her husband was right. Envied and hated by their neighbours, laughed at and misunderstood, and lately persecuted, they were slowly sliding towards the abyss. The family heirloom, this birthright of hers, was their only hope. She should have realised it long ago. But she was like a frog in water that became imperceptibly yet relentlessly warmer. Degree by degree. Until it's too late.

Sometimes she wondered what her life would have been like if she had married somebody else. Somebody with less knowledge of course - but somebody who was liked in social spheres. Somebody whose children wouldn't be scorned on the playground, called names like Nanotechs and Learned and Infojunkies, and worse.     "Amy? Are you listening? Just open the damned door. Get it over and done with."

Amy moved forward. Now was not the time to dissect her emotions. It's not the real Ralph, she told herself. The circumstances are making him grumpy, is all. It must have been a blow to his ego to be sacked from the work he loved. Not because of negligence, but because of who he was.

It would be selfish to hesitate any longer. Presently, she would open the door and find - what? A shortcut to another universe? A Sesame full of Arabian treasure? That's what she had imagined as a child during all those afternoons up here, her eye to the black keyhole, her heart pounding with anticipation.

"Amy!"

The voice blared right behind her. Her heart raced in her chest. Her fingers clutched the key. She wanted to speak, and couldn't. Ralph was a stranger, a foreigner in her world of dreams. They had no words in common.

"Look," he said. "I know you said you wanted to do this alone. It's what you said the time you fell pregnant. And on ten other occasions. Only you never did do it, did you? Face it, you're never going to through with this."

Be it now or later, she would have to do it. But... but suppose this was a once-off chance, something to be saved for an emergency? The thought came unsought and unchecked, and Amy felt her cheeks burn. Because this was an emergency, at least from Ralph's point of view. And from hers, of course. This was her husband and she loved him. She did. Didn't she?

"The way you always carry on about this door," he said as he dug the key out of her resisting fist, "one would swear it opens straight into your soul." He chuckled, then chortled, then doubled over. A large stone tumbled to the floor, among the shards of broken window glass. The letters blasted on its inert surface screamed,

"Alien". Amy felt bile rise to her throat. The key protruded from the keyhole. She aligned it with the hologram inside the lock. The door shuddered with a gritty squeak, then slid into the wall.

She expected a musty, dark smell of abandon. But the hot afternoon sun laid its dusty blots on the old linoleum floor and unplastered brick, both of almost museum quality. Amy sighed. One couldn't very well sell an attic - not for money even, and certainly not in exchange for safety. Especially an attic that's the size of a walk-in closet. And no wonder - from the outside, the top floor of the house resembled a turret rather than a tower.

For a nanosecond, she thought the room empty and waited for a wave of disappointment to hit home. She felt nothing. Subconsciously, she must have expected it all along. Pirate maps of treasure islands usually lead to nowhere.

Then, in the shadow cast by the window's broad sill, she noticed a box. An ordinary plastic box, with a see-through lid and one of those old-fashioned airtight seals. On it lay a letter, a printout of Grandmama's electronic stationery on an ancient black-and-white reusable sheet. Amy tasted a rush of nostalgia. She remembered those sheets, made of minuscule particles that rotated to form the printed word. They were Grandmama's generation's answer to nature conservation.

*My youngest granddaughter,* flickered the pixels. *I'm sorry you're reading this letter, for it implies you're in need. Try as hard as I may, I cannot imagine the disaster you're facing. The world is a dynamic place, and what troubled our family in the past will probably never affect you.*

*Concentration camps and gas chambers were what awaited my grandmother, for example, once - long long ago. She was on a wrong continent and of a wrong race. She escaped her persecutors, but her escape channel was paved with her jewellery, and behind she left those less fortunate than herself.*

*My mother feared mushrooms. She thought doom would come dressed up in a nuclear mist and radioactive ashes. In the midst of the cold war, she hid all her valuables in a steel container and buried them in the garden. Some of them, you will find in this box.*

A soft pouch the size of her finger rested on the bottom. Amy untied the cord. Solid tears of diamonds glided into her palm. She dropped them impatiently. Every child knew how to grow diamonds.

*I myself thought I would see the Armageddon. On the last day of 1999, I gathered my tins of food, candles, canisters of petrol and hid in this attic. I know it sounds silly, but people got that way since the beginning of time whenever a series of man-made figures moved into a pattern. I was a software engineer and I feared the repercussions. Anyway, that was when I opened my grandmother's parcel addressed to me. I used her treasures years later, to bribe my way through the channels to get a license for a baby: your mother. As I write this, she is a beautiful young lady and I hope that by the time she starts a family, all the silly laws will be abolished and she will have many, many daughters. Children should not be punished for the sins of their parents.*

Amy's eyes stung. All the silly laws had indeed been abolished. But nothing had changed. Although she had been allowed to procreate, her offspring was considered second class. For every century must have its scapegoat. In the previous millennium, it had been the Jews with all their money and their unique way of celebrating life. Today, it was the Information Specialists with their computers. The way of the world since time immemorial.

*This box holds a collection of items from the past. Call it a time capsule if you like. My grandmother's diamonds and her passport are here as the twentieth century symbols of wealth and freedom. The passport in particular was what she held precious throughout her life, a tool that enabled her to move freely from what was then one country to another, in search of people who would accept her birth burden.*

Amy thought of Ralph, of the birth burden he had given their children. Knowledge, learning, information. And - for the first time ever - she felt proud of him.

*The sign of my own time is money. Not the money you have and hoard, but the money you spend. It's so easy with electronic shopping - one click of the mouse and you are a thousand credits poorer. So I add to this box my money card. I thought of preserving some of the latest technology wonders, but your generation will either have surpassed us in this respect, or receded so far back that you won't be able to appreciate it.*

*I also include some of my favourite items, objects of beauty or sentiment. Decorations, photographs, and the diaries of six generations. I hope something from this random collection will help you in your quest today.*

It was hours later that Amy walked onto the landing. Ralph still sat there. He extended his hand and she took it in silence. She felt the strength flow from her fingers, the strength of six generations of women who never gave up.

The key to the attic she left in the door. For her youngest granddaughter - to use whenever she liked.

# FOREIGN LAND

## Corey Melin

*When Corey Melin is not working, he spends his free time reading or writing. He just recently started writing what he's hoping will one day become his first published book.*

I crossed the great Negotto River to enter into the foreign lands of Agron.

"You come from afar?" the boatman asked with a questioning look at my attire.

"I was born way to the south in the lands of Merith," I replied, getting off my strong and trusted friend, Allanorn.

Allanorn is a pure white stallion that was given to me as a gift for helping a widow survive a harsh winter. One of the worst winters that has ever occurred in my life. At first, it was quite difficult to handle Allanorn, but after a few days he grew accustomed to me and all became well. Of course, this pleased me for I was able to continue my exploration of the lands around me.

"Traveled quite far," the boatman said as I looked down the river, seeing it stretch beyond what the eye could see. "Any particular reason?"

"I like to see the land," I replied. "See the different sites God has created."

"You picked a good time to explore the wonders for the entire land is experiencing peace. No need to worry about evildoers for the most part."

"For the most part," I repeated, thinking of the one encounter with a robber, who had to be over six feet tall, but was a walking scarecrow.

"All your coins now!" the robber, with a high pitched voice, had called out pointing a crossbow at me.

I wasn't good with the bow and only sufficient with the sword, but when it came to daggers I was an expert. By looking at the robber, who stood there with a slight tremble, which told me he was new at this, I knew it wouldn't take much to disable him.

"You sure you want to do this?" I asked him.

"Do it now!" he screeched out.

"Fine."

A second later the crossbow lay on the ground and the robber held his hand, which now had a cut across the top of it.

The robber cried out, turning around and running off into the woods.

The only encounter, so far, I had of anyone with evil intent. A poor soul trying to make it through life the easy way.

"May I ask your name fine sire?" the boatman asked.

"James Curstron," I replied. "James the explorer," I added with a chuckle.

"Sounds like the exploring is going well."

"Yes. Yes indeed."

It is hard to believe that fifteen years have gone by since I started traveling across the land. The decision was made a week after the woman I was to marry suddenly became ill and died. I was crushed, staying in my quarters for a couple of days with nothing to eat and very little to drink. I wanted to die myself and join my love in paradise. I wasn't sure what I wanted to do at first, having been a carpenter. I figured once I married we would move on to a more populated area. We would talk about our ambitions late at night as we sat together by the lake.

"You will expand on carpentry and I will be expanding physically," she would tell me with a smile, rubbing her stomach area.

"How many kids are we planning on having?" I asked, giving her a squeeze.

"Enough to take care of us when we become too old to support ourselves," she replied with a laugh.

Unfortunately, those days would never happen. My decision on what to do was made suddenly when my good friend, Santrix, paid me a visit.

"How are you doing?" he asked when I let him in.

"Trying to get myself back together," I replied.

"You probably should try to do that somewhere else."

"What do you mean?" I asked.

"Unfortunately, the troublemakers in this town have been spreading the rumor that you murdered Abrilla."

"What?!" I cried out. "Who is spreading the rumors?" I asked him, grabbing the dagger off the table.

"Hold up," my friend said. "It's too late to stop them. The word is out and people are wondering now."

"By leaving it would make the townsfolk more suspicious."

"The family knows you haven't done anything, but the people are a superstitious lot so you will always be looked at with suspicion."

I put the dagger on the table and sat down in despair.

"You always wanted to leave this town."

"Not so soon," I said but it turned out to be that way.

I wanted to leave the town on a horse, but that was not to be as I went through town getting many glares from people full of hate. Even the ones I considered good friends treated me harshly, telling me to leave at once.

"I know you had nothing to do with our daughter's death," Abrilla's mother told me when I went to see them before I left. "The townspeople around here are very simple and easily swayed."

"I must move on," I told them. "But I feel much better that the both of you do not believe in the lies."

"Where will you go?" asked Abrilla's father.

"I'm not sure. I believe I will travel around for a few years and eventually settle down."

"May God be with you at all times."

"Thank you."

I left on foot, stopping at different towns and cities as the years ticked by.

Now here I was going to one of the last lands that were known and considered safe for the most part.

"Almost there," the boatman said when we were three-fourths of the way across the river.

I looked over at the land of Agron and could see what looked like a gray tower off in the distance on top of a hill.

"Someone live in that tower?" I asked, pointing.

The boatman looked toward the tower then turned to me and I saw a moment of fright displayed on his face.

"No one, I believe," he replied. "At one time it was the ruler of the land residing in that tower. The last person to live in the tower was an evil man out to destroy everyone's lives. He was able to employ a band of orcs and create havoc in the land. Many say he was a powerful magician."

"How was he defeated?"

"A mighty army from the land east of here came and took care of him. The fool easily took over the land of Agron since it is scarcely populated, but then he became greedy and invaded the east lands.

They came and wiped out his forces and went home with his head on a pike."

"I'm sure you know much about this land," I said as we neared the shore.

"I have heard many tales of this land, but I have a feeling I know very little of it. There is a lot that is mysterious. You will either be on this land for a very long time or a very short time."

We reached the shore and I stepped off the raft with Allanorn.

"Some people call Agron the 'land of faeries'," the boatman called out.

"What do you think?" I asked tossing him a few extra coins.

"I don't know, to be honest," he replied with a grin. "I have never stepped foot onto this land and never saw anything from the raft. Only heard from people who have stepped onto the raft. Some of them are believable while others are quite mad. I'm sure you will find out quick enough what this land holds."

"Should be quite the adventure," I said, wondering if this might be the land of my new home.

"I hope so and good luck," the boatman said, starting to move back across the river.

I turned to the land, seeing the rocky terrain that went about a hundred feet before it turned into a grassy plain with trees sprouting here and there throughout the land. Off in the distance the trees grew closer, cutting off the sun from touching the ground.

"Let's go a little ways before we call it a day," I said to Allanorn.

I rode through the rocky terrain onto the grassy plain, heading toward the trees. As I galloped closer to the forest I saw that I wouldn't be able to ride through due to low hanging branches and the trees being quite close.

"I'm not sure you can get through this dense forest," I said to Allanorn, who shook his head up and down in agreement.

"You can travel west a little ways to enter the forest." A voice, sounding like a child's, spoke from the forest.

I looked around, but didn't see anyone.

"Who said that?" I called out. "Are you behind a tree?"

"Up in the tree," the voice spoke.

I looked up and saw on one of the branches a calico cat. I looked to see if there was a child to the left or to the right, but saw no one.

"I don't see anyone, but this cat."

"It is I who speak to you," the cat said.

I saw the mouth of the cat move, but could it be? The boatman said this land was mysterious. Was I seeing one of the wonders or was I losing my mind?

"Am I already losing my sanity?" I asked Allanorn.

"Possibly, since you are talking to a horse who cannot reply to you."

I looked up at the cat that started to lick his paw.

"Have you always spoken?" I asked.

"I believe so," the cat replied. "As far as I know since birth."

"This is remarkable," I said with excitement. "Many would give a lot to have you in their possession."

"They would if they knew I spoke, but only two know that I do. You are one and a young girl is the other. She is probably looking for me as I speak."

"Is there a village nearby?"

"Not far from here. A few people live there."

"I hope someone is with this girl if she is out in these woods," I told the cat, concerned. "If not, I should go and try to find her."

"I wouldn't worry for this area is quite safe. Nothing bad will cross her path."

"Do you plan on going back to her? I'm sure she is quite worried about you."

"I leave her all of the time. She has a free spirit so she likes to go out and explore, telling her folks she is looking for me."

"Do the parents worry about her going out alone?"

"You will find out this land is quite safe. There is nothing to worry about."

There was no land that was ever completely safe, but according to this talking cat all was good. Part of me still wondered if I was losing it.

"I believe I will move on," I told the cat. "One more question before I leave. Why did you decide to talk to me?"

"You have a good soul," the cat replied. "There are many with good souls, but you are one I don't need to worry about trying to catch me due to my gift."

"Thank you. I won't be bringing trouble your way. I also thank you for showing me where to go."

"You are welcome," the cat said and went back to licking himself.

I moved on, thinking that I had just experienced one of the strangest conversations ever. By tomorrow I would be wondering if I was dreaming it all up.

I rode west for a little ways before I saw that the trees started to grow further apart. I rode a little further to see if the forest opened up to the point where I wouldn't have to bend over or get my horse stuck. It wasn't far before I saw a path that led into the woods.

"Here you go," I said to Allanorn.

I looked up at the sky, seeing small white clouds here and there, seeing the sun was behind one large dark cloud. There wasn't much more time left in this day before darkness settled over the land.

"Go a little ways and hopefully find an open spot to light a fire and call it a night," I thought.

I started down the path, looking to my left and right into the woods to see if there might be any kind of wildlife out there, but there was no movement. I heard the sounds of birds ever so often, but otherwise it was very quiet. Maybe they were all checking out the newcomer to the land.

"Maybe they are all together having a feast," I muttered with a chuckle.

The path went straight as far as the eye could see, which worried me, as I was hoping to stop soon to call it a night. The path was only about seven feet wide so there wasn't much room to rest, especially if someone else came through. The woods were heavy with brush so it would be difficult to get off the path.

"Let's pick up the pace, my friend," I said to Allanorn, urging him on.

Allanorn started to gallop and eventually I saw the path curve to the right, hopefully to open ground. When I rounded the corner I saw off in the distance the path widening. I also heard voices. Very small voices.

I brought Allanorn to a stop and listened. At first it was like a buzzing sound, but little by little I could make out a word. The voices didn't sound like children, but were little squeaky voices.

"Who is out there?" I called out.

The voices quieted for a few moments, but started speaking again.

"Hello!? I called out.

The voices continued to talk this time.

I thought about getting off the horse and rushing through the bushes, but doing that would probably be a bad idea. If they were faeries, I heard they had magical powers and could very well turn me into a pig or worse.

"Best to move on," I muttered and urged Allanorn forward.

The voices continued to talk as I neared the widening of the path. Soon I saw there was an opening on the left, which turned out to be a small section surrounded by very large trees. The tree in the back was enormous, with a hole big enough for me to crawl in about six feet up. In the middle of the clearing was a ring of rocks where others had started fires.

"Looks like the perfect place to stay for the night," I said, getting off the horse.

As soon as I dismounted, the voices stopped speaking. I looked around, but saw no movement.

"Must have left," I thought. "Or they are watching to see what I will do next."

I started to go around and pick up small branches around the edges of the clearing. Soon my arms were full so I went over to the circle of rocks and dumped the branches next to them. A few moments later I had a stack within the circle of rocks and soon had myself a fire going.

I went over to Allanorn and started to take out everything I needed to rest plus some food to appease my grumbling stomach. I put everything by the fire then went over and fed Allanorn. As I did I heard a voice coming from the enormous tree with the large hole in it. I lay Allanorn's food onto the ground for him to eat and took a couple of steps toward the tree. The voice was coming from inside the tree.

"Hello!" I called out.

The voice stopped speaking for a few moments then a hoarse-sounding voice called out, "Who is there?"

"My name is James," I replied. "A traveler passing through the land."

There was silence then a white hairy head popped out of the hole. I had to keep myself from chuckling as the old man squinted at me, trying to make me out. His entire head was covered with hair except for his beady eyes, bulbous nose, and small lips.

"A traveler you say," the old man said, clearing his voice many times.

"Yes," I replied. "Traveling the lands to see the wonders."

The old man started to cackle with laughter.

"What is so funny?" I asked.

"You have come to the right land for wonders," he replied, once he stopped laughing. "Did you hear the voices as you traveled the path?"

"Yes. I thought they might be faeries."

"Little people they are," he said with a chuckle. "Never seen them myself, but I have searched for them numerous times. Never can find the noisy critters. Even when I'm in this tree sneaking a look out."

"Maybe they are invisible," I told him.

"Maybe so," he said with a laugh. "Or they are too small for the human eye to see."

I had to chuckle as the old man scrunched up his face.

"Why are you in the tree?" I asked.

"A nice place to live," he replied. "Would you like to come in? Quite cozy. Better than sleeping out there."

"I will be all right," I said picturing myself crammed in the tree with the old man.

"Suit yourself. I need to get back to my duties. Have a good night and keep the fire within the rocks. I don't want to have to go and find another tree."

"Will do," I said, as the old man disappeared into the tree. "Strange little man."

I went over by the fire and sat down and ate my meal then lay down and went to sleep.

I woke-up as daylight came back to the land. I slowly stood up, feeling a bit stiff from sleeping on the ground.

"I need to get myself a nice comfortable bed," I muttered, stretching out. "And probably a good bath."

I started up the fire and had a little to eat and fed Allanorn before packing up. I couldn't hear the old man speaking so I figured he might be still sleeping.

"Goodbye," I muttered, leaving the clearing after putting out the fire to continue my travels.

The path went on a ways before opening up to rolling hills. Off in the distance I could see a mountain, which meant there should be a river nearby.

I urged Allanorn on, already feeling the cool water washing over my body. Hopefully, I would find a small river or a lake to be able to jump into and clean up.

I went up and down the hills until the land flattened out and I saw more trees in the distance, but they were spaced further apart. Should be no problem riding through the forest.

To my left, I saw smoke slowly rise up into the sky. I saw a couple of more streams of smoke rise nearby, telling me it was a village. Possibly, the village the cat told me about.

"I'll check it out later," I thought.

I continued toward the forest, soon entering it. Now, far into the woods I saw a river about ten feet wide with a small wooden house on the other side in front of me. As I rode closer, I could hear what sounded like a woman screaming. I urged Allanorn to a gallop and when I got to the river, I saw a middle-aged man running out of the home, followed by a middle-aged woman with a broom that she was swinging at the man.

"You selfish fool!" she cried out, taking a swing at his head.

Luckily, the man ducked in time and ran off into the woods. The lady stopped, being a little on the heavy side, and threw the broom, hitting the man across the back. He yelped and picked up his pace.

"What seems to be the problem?" I called out to the woman.

With her hands on her hips she looked at me a moment with a frown, then at the man who kept on running, then back to me.

"What do you want?" she called out to me.

"It seems you are distressed," I said, looking down at the river to see if it was too deep to cross, but it looked like it was only a couple of feet deep. I was about to look back up at the woman, but I thought I caught a glimpse of a face in the water. I looked around, but nothing.

"I am quite distressed because I have a fool for a husband," she said.

"I'm sorry to hear that," I said. "I should probably leave."

"Wait!" she called out as I was about to turn the horse around. "You don't look familiar."

"I just entered this land yesterday."

"Did you enter by the boatman?" she asked, walking over to the river.

"Yes."

"Oh good," she said with glee, clapping her hands. "I was hoping he was still around."

"Why is that?"

"Because I'm going to leave and head back south to the lands I love."

"What about your home here?"

"You need a place? If you do, here you go. It's all yours."

"What about your husband?" I asked, as she turned around and went toward the house.

"Unfortunately, the fool will follow me," she replied, going inside the house.

I crossed the river and went up to the house and got off the horse.

"May I enter?" I asked, standing by the doorway and seeing her grab certain items and put them on the bed.

"Sure," she said, continuing to grab things. "It's your home now."

I wasn't sure what to say. When I first entered this land I didn't know if this is where I wanted to settle down, but as I traveled deeper into the land I had a feeling this would be my new home. I was a bit surprised that I was being given a home my second day here, but it looked quite cozy.

"What did your husband do to upset you?" I asked.

"You see that cage," she asked, pointing to her right to an empty cage. "Do you see the beautiful blue bird?"

"No," I replied, seeing the cage door was open.

"The fool let the bird go because he was jealous of it," she said, wrapping up all the items.

"He was jealous of a bird?" I asked, thinking that was quite strange.

"This was no ordinary bird," she said, walking up to me. "This bird would make the most beautiful sounds. The sounds would brighten your day. The only thing I had to do to keep the bird satisfied is to feed it sweetened bread once a day. The same kind of bread that my husband loved to eat."

"I'm sure the bird didn't eat much," I said.

"It didn't, but enough to make my husband upset."

"I'm sorry to hear about this unfortunate event," I told her, thinking this was quite bizarre, but maybe it was meant to be.

She took a deep breath and slowly let it out.

"It's probably a good thing," she said, going over and picking up her bundle of items. "I really didn't like this place. The bird was the only thing that kept me here and eventually the bird would have died. Let it enjoy its freedom."

"A positive way to look at the situation."

"Well, I am off," she said, walking over to the door. She went out and started walking away, but she suddenly stopped and turned to me. "Do you have loved ones?"

"Yes," I replied.

"If you think about them, look into the river and you will see them," she said with a grin. "I wouldn't look too much. You will want to go back home to see them. Maybe that will be a good thing."

"Thank you and good luck on your travels," I told her.

She turned around and continued on her way.

I turned around and checked out the place. I was still in disbelief that I now had a home. I wondered if this would truly be my new home and now I know this must be it.

"I must check this river out," I thought.

I walked to the river and looked into it. I started thinking about all of my family members and the one I messed the most, Abrilla. It wasn't long before her face appeared in the water.

"Abrilla," I said, tears appearing in my eyes.

I looked at her beautiful face for who knows how long before I turned away.

For the next few days I stayed around the home, moving stuff around. I saw they had a little garden so I attended to it. I sat down one night and looked around the place and realized I was very content with my life.

As time went by I decided to check out the village nearby. At first the villagers were a bit cautious, but eventually they welcomed me in. The best part of all and what erased any little doubt of living here was when I met Michelle in the village. My life was now complete.

# NEON

## Rebecca Cuthbert

*Rebecca Cuthbert lives in the Arizona desert, where she drinks a lot of coffee, refuses to grow up, and insists on remaining a mystery.*

I remember those nights we use to spend sitting on the bench out in front of the old theater, just watching the traffic go by. The neon-lit office building in the background, electrifying our existence. During the summer we felt like static from the humidity. During the winter we clutched close to each other, stealing each other's heat as we watched the busy world go by in the electric light. Electric like the stars above our heads. We hardly ever said a word. We just sat there and existed.

It's nothing like that now. There is no existence, and I wonder if there ever was to begin with. I use to be able to go outside and see beauty in everything. The trees, the grass, the sky, the buildings. Colors so real, they looked *un*real. Maybe it all was.

At this moment, it is only raining. There is no feeling as the rain beats down on my skin. No salty taste as I lean my head back with my mouth open to greet the falling droplets. Nothing. I don't even feel wet. I don't feel anything. No. I am longing for something. I am infatuated with the thought of being able to throw out my arms to each side and let the wind blow past me and take everything with it. To be free, invincible. Of this. Of you.

I sit down, looking at my life—if you'd call it that. My mother's sitting on the couch watching television. My father's in his room, sleeping. I'm not with them, but I know that is what they are doing. I'm trying to think of what you would be doing right now, but it's too hard to think about you. Every time I try, I think about that night, and I'm not ready to understand why I am here, alone.

I remember the funeral. I couldn't cry. God had taken the ability away from me after the accident. Maybe I don't need it. Everyone else was crying while your mother spoke. My mother sat silently, in a daze. I wanted to look at you, but I couldn't. I didn't want you to be there. *I* didn't want to be there. But I couldn't leave. I still can't leave.

The rain stops. For a moment quiet noise is all there is. A quiet so loud, it's all I can hear. A car drives past me and destroys the quiet. I smile, because I'm relieved. Someone yells from across the street. I turn, for some reason thinking it could be you. Of course it isn't. Why would you be here? I watch a man call over to someone sitting at a bus stop. They're too far away for me to hear what they are saying, not that it has anything to do with me. Nothing does.

I look up at the street sign that marked death, wondering why I always had to be here. Everyday I stand here and watch the people. The sad people, who walk depressingly and drive lethargically. People who dream of nostalgia like I dream for life. I stare down at the little white cross that was surrounded by candles that had long ago melted down to nothing. We all dream of nostalgia.

The clouds part from the night sky and I can see the stars barely shining through, competing with the street lights and their ever-changing glow. The asphalt reflects the city with the freshly poured rain. It is definitely the city that has dominance over the night. Who pays attention to the heavens anymore? I try not to. Then I would be admitting something that I am not ready for.

Two women walk by, one holding a little girl's hand. The little girl runs, trying to keep up with the giant steps her mother takes, avoiding small puddles. The woman with the child looks down at the little cross.

"Oh, how sad," she mutters to herself. This sparks up a conversation with her friend about drunk drivers and adolescents not being able to drive until they are twenty-one. The little girl looks at me. I smile. She smiles back, and says, "Hi". Her mother looks in my direction and tells the little girl to be quiet while she's talking. They all cross the street and disappear behind the traffic.

I pace down the street, in the opposite direction, trying to remember my innocence. Innocence. Like summer, and catching frogs, and having water balloon fights, and pointlessly running down hills. Like bliss, naïveté, simplicity. The world is so easy when you don't know any better. I hope that little girl never grows up.

A few steps later, I find myself back where I had started. I let out a sigh. I cannot escape this, but I know why I'm still here. I can't let go of you. Not yet. I don't want the last time I saw you to be a fading memory. A horrible memory of your body falling limp and I can't tell if you're okay, because my vision fades and I can't see you anymore. I'll never see you again, because I refused to say good-bye when I had the chance. I wish that you'd come back here, just once, to say good-bye to me. To save me from being numb all of the time.

I sit down on the pavement and stare down the street, towards home. I know you'll never come, but what else do I have? I close my eyes and remember feeling like neon. Neon, like our town's only tall building. I miss sweaty palms and shivering cold. I miss feeling alive, happy. It all leads back to you. The touch of your hand, the feel of your hair through my fingers, the smell of your skin, the feel of your skin, the feel of you. All like neon.

I open my eyes and the sun is peeking through blinding white clouds. I hug my legs to my chest, my back facing the parking lot of the convenience store behind me. What was this for? To have a cup of coffee that I'd give my life for—the best coffee in town? Untouchable liquid that I never even got to taste? I smile at the irony of it all.

The green waves of the palm trees overhead sway back and forth from the wind like a tide. Wind that refuses to wash over me; cleanse me. Maybe I'm not worthy. Or, maybe it's just too late.

I look up at the blinking red light of a radio tower, far off in the distance. Blinking like the ticking of a clock. Life buzzes by wearily, like a movie on fast-forward, and the sun is weakening, like everything else. Everything but the blinking red light, which only grows brighter. Brighter than a star. Another day gone by, and I didn't even notice.

I welcomed the night with a strange thought. I wondered if God had sympathy for me, or if He was smiling down on me. Why is he allowing me to still be here? Is it out of punishment or love? I looked up at the brightest star I could see and screamed at the top of my lungs. Lungs that had no air. I was drowning in nothing, and no one could hear my cry for help. I rest my head on my knees, still hugging my legs tightly to my chest. I hear more footsteps, but I refuse to look up. It's not you; it's never going to be you. The footsteps stop. Another spectator looking to see a life in shambles. A life that's gone. There's a long silence, and then the footsteps keep walking. I don't look up until I hear the same rhythm walking back. I watch you pace back and forth on the sidewalk, hands shoved into the pockets of your coat, head tilted up towards the stars, breathing in the cold memory of the rain.

All I can do is stare at you. I can't cry, I know that, but I want to. I want to pull your arms around me, to kiss you, breathe you in. But I can't touch you. I look up at the sky, as if I'll find an answer to anything. I never do.

You stop, and I can feel how much it took you to look, not at the memorial, but at the street of where it all had happened. I know, because that's how much it took me. To see the skid marks, and the broken pieces of glass that still glittered the asphalt. You take in a sharp breath, and I can see the tears in your eyes. Tears that I envy. I stand up and come near you. I reach for you, but it's as if you're just out of reach, no matter how close I am to you.

You stand there for a long time, just staring at the street. Then you lean against the wall and stare at the melted wax and white cross. You slide down onto the ground, a hand unconsciously grabbing at your hair. I sit beside you, wondering if you even know that I'm still here. If you know how long I have been waiting for you.

You rest your elbows on your knees and keep staring at the street. I'm staring at you, trying to memorize the outline of your face, every freckle, every hair on your head. You start crying, but you wipe the tears away quickly, and stand up.

"Good-bye," you choke out.

Your voice is crackled and distorted. You dig into your pocket and pull out a lighter and a small candle. You set the glowing candle off to the side so it won't be disturbed, and look down at it for a while.

"Good-bye," you say again, more clearly; as if you were worried that I hadn't heard you the first time.

"Good-bye," I tell your deaf ears. You shiver, and shove your hands back into your pockets.

Something clicked in the wind.

Your image starts to fade, and I know that, somehow, you had heard me. I look around and everything is deadening. I watch the traffic slowly go by, and all I can hear is the flame of the candle crackling. I look back at you and I see you closing your eyes. The numbness fades and I feel like air as the world turns to gray. Black dots clutter my vision, and I can remember what you feel like. I pull the memory around me for warmth as I drift, hearing the promises we had made each other throughout our lifetime echoing in the background of my mind. Cities we'll live in, things we'll see, things we'll do. How we'll always be here forever. How we'll always just be forever.

I look back at you, taking you in as I fade from non-existence. You start to walk away, and I can feel myself fading even more. I blink my eyes for a moment and you are gone. I look at the candle and feel myself fade. Fade completely. Erased from the world I loved. All I can see is blinding light, like the morning sun reflecting off of the clouds.

And electric blue static is all there is. Fake, familiar reality. Summer rain. Cleansing wind. Falling leaves. Velvet green grass. Sweaty palms. Warm skin. Brown eyes. Innocent bliss.

All that's left is neon.

# CIRCLES GO ROUND

## Darrin Cates

*Darrin Cates has an extensive background in writing. His recent short story, "A Lesson Learned," was published in* The Paper Journey's Anthology Blink Flash Fiction: Before You Can Bat an Eye.

I didn't like what I saw. The reflection wasn't being kind. It wasn't the wrinkles in my forehead, the lines stretching out from the corners of my eyes, or the skin that was starting to sag, showing symptoms of too much sun in my youth. Those were all evidentiary signs of my true age. Results of time that I couldn't escape. Results that wealthy people can wipe away with a few trips to the right doctor.

The aging reflection of a thirty-five-year-old, former corporate drone wasn't what bothered me. What bothered me was revealed somewhere in the midst of the dark circles surrounding my eyes.

I had spent the last two years consumed with a mission. A mission that had little chance for success. I pursued this mission with a fervor that left me little time to give much thought to my appearance. Or what I had become.

My brief moment of introspection was loudly interrupted, "Whachu lookin' at?" The voice came from the seat directly across from me and exuded plenty of attitude.

"Excuse me?" I came back with force.

"You heard me. Keep your eyes to yourself, if you know what's good for ya."

He was from Brooklyn. His navy blue suit said he worked in middle-management, probably somewhere downtown, but his attitude and accent revealed his roots. He was probably from a tough neighborhood. I'd seen a million people like him in the last six months traveling the trains in New York. Normally, I'm not staring at my reflection in the windows as I travel. I'm not that vain. And, I'm usually too busy looking for a sign – any sign – of her. But I had plenty of these types of confrontations on the trains and I had learned how to handle them. "What? I can't look out the window? You the window police or something? Or are you just that homophobic? Better not let your boss know. He may think you're trying to hide something," I replied with plenty of intensity, despite a real lack of passion for the cause.

"Yeah. Yeah. Whatever. Just keep your eyes to yourself." He immediately buried his head back in "The Times." I'm sure he was cursing me under his breath. But the bottom line was he was back to his business, having decided to leave me alone. He                wasn't intimidated by my appearance. I am physically fit and about six foot one. But I am getting older in years. Visually, I am not a threat. I'm more nondescript than anything. But the overly verbose traveler respected how I responded. I hadn't backed down. I knew how to communicate on his level. It was kind of a gift of mine. A gift I had since my formative years in college but its development had been enhanced in the last six months. If nothing else, the New York transit system can teach you about people. If you only listen.

Listening is an important part of being able to communicate with people of differing backgrounds, lifestyles and financial status. And what I heard from the pseudo bully sitting across from me was that he had issues. Issues with his boss. Issues with his job. Issues with his life and where it was going. But then again, don't we all?

Communicating with – and listening to – different types of people was a trait that proved to be of limited value to me as I slowly climbed the corporate ladder back in Fresno. Yes, I had achieved the esteemed title of Vice President of Human Resources for an overly bureaucratic medical supply company. There may not be a more boring title in the universe. But I was going no higher. Maybe that's why she left. Maybe being Vice President of a bank is more impressive.

* * * * * * *

"Oh, I'm sorry." The soft voice was smooth and seemed sincere. I smiled pleasantly. "It's okay. Really."

"I'm so sorry. It's this big bag," her tone was still apologetic as she settled into the seat next to me. "I don't know where it's at half

141

the time." She chuckled under her breath. "I guess the same could be said for me."

"I'm fine. Really. It actually probably helped my face." I said with a smile, trying to put her at ease. Self-deprecation helps soften the barriers surrounding most social circles.

"I promise I won't hit you when I get up. Unless, of course, you try and get handsy." She raised her eyebrows playfully. Even this couldn't hide her beauty. She was tall, thin, and had stunningly dark eyes. I couldn't quite place her origin. I wasn't sure where she was raised. But my guess was that the beguiling African-American may not have originally been from New York.

"It's no problem." I tried to evoke a demeanor that would give her a reprieve. I just wanted to get back to scanning the rest of the car. And I assumed she wanted some peace, while traveling. Of course, I was never very good at recognizing the motives of females. I could listen to them. I could empathize. But guessing their next move was like picking the next candidate the democrats would nominate for President. Lots of options, but no clear choices.

"I guess it's only polite of me to introduce myself. I'm Natalia." She smiled and her beauty multiplied.

"I'm Jesse." I tried hard not to reveal too much about myself in my occasional meetings on the trains. I justified this by deeming it a distraction from my mission. In truth, it may have been more about not knowing what – if anything – there was to reveal.

"So Jesse, what do you do?" A great question. Usually an easy answer for anyone but me. What I did and how I earned a living were two different things. "Currently, I'm a bartender. What about you?" Turning the topic of conversation back to her was again part of my gift – part of my ability to ease into a circle of which I really don't belong.

It wasn't that difficult. You ask people about themselves. Unlike me, most people love to tell others about who they are and what they do. Even if you only listen to part of what they say, you can quickly learn what really makes them tick, what drives them to be who they are. Or at least who they want you to believe they are.

"I'm a singer," she quickly replied.

"Well, that makes sense," I said as I looked past her to see if I recognized the female sitting at the end of our row. "You seem to have a great voice." I couldn't have spoken truer words.

"Thank you. That's very nice of you to say."

"What kind of singer?" I continued the conversation, along with my covert visual scan.

"Opera."

Before I responded, I suffered a slight jolt. I thought my search had come to an end. I thought I found what I had been looking for. But within a second I recognized my lack of recognition. I tried to recover quickly. "Really?"

"You seemed surprised," she said, almost amused. I was actually startled. Not because I had never met a real opera singer before. But mostly because of what I thought I had seen at the end of the train. An apparition. One I had seen too many times.

"Is that because I'm black?" She queried with some intensity.

"No." My eyes widened. "It's just that I've never met an opera singer of any color before."

"And you didn't picture them looking like me?"

"I don't know what I pictured." That was not entirely true. But I should have known that in the real world opera singers don't go around on the subway with braided long blonde hair flowing out from under a Viking helmet. That type of stylistic décor was usually reserved for other, more eccentric riders of public transportation.

She then went on to tell me about how she was a part of the cast of La Forza Del Destino. That she enjoyed it but really thought it was time she got a leading role. And how it was difficult for a woman of color to land such roles.

She was well-traveled. Spent some time in Paris as a backup singer for a French rap group. She was full of other great surprises. A wonderful, beautiful, unique person. Who didn't know it. She was insecure and was looking for validation. Unfortunately, she wasn't going to get it from me. I couldn't keep my mind from drifting to how I was going to find *her*.

"Look, I don't normally do this but I really feel like I can talk to you," she said as she started rummaging through her purse. She took out a pen and a legal pad, which probably shouldn't have surprised me since the bag did have room for that and one of those foldout tents that could sleep six. She started writing. "Here's my number. Maybe you can come to a show one night and we can go out for some drinks afterward. But I must warn you, music is my passion until…until I get a few drinks in me. Then, I display my passion in other ways." I don't know if I've ever heard a more sultry, seductive voice in my life. The offer was truly enticing.

Obviously, I never called. Obviously, I too have issues.

* * * * * * *

"Well, it's over now. Rivera's coming in." I recognized it as a response to the Yankee game that the elderly gentleman was listening to on his portable radio. An ancient piece of technology in today's world of iPods and satellite radio. But a piece of technology I'm sure as a kid he never dreamt he would own.

I nodded my response, showing agreement. Although I really didn't care for the Yankees and their game against a Pittsburgh Pirate team that was 14 games under .500. It was the last thing on my mind.

"You know, I never used to miss a game when they were in town. But this gaddamn inter-league play is a joke. Can't stand it. Won't spend a dime to watch a game between teams that shouldn't be playing until the World Series."

An elderly gentleman, clinging to memories of what he believed to be better days, didn't surprise me. After looking at the oxygen tank he carted around, I could easily see where – in his mind – everything about the days gone by was better.

"What about you?" His question did surprise me.

"Me?"

"Yeah. Are you one of those people who like this new baseball? Designated hitters. Free agency. All that hogwash."

I smirked. "The game doesn't interest me anymore." It was true. But I'm sure he thought it was due to a similar ideological stance about the great American pastime. In truth, it was simply because I had become consumed with my mission.

Feeling like he had a newly acquired kindred spirit, he went on to tell me about baseball's glory days. His glory days. Somehow, before his stop at 86th Street he managed to tell me about his family, his health problems and his routine of spending some time each week in Central Park – weather permitting.

When the train finally stopped, he asked me for help getting his cart off the car. I couldn't say no. And I felt obliged to help him make his way to the park. Maybe he did this on all his trips to the park, but I felt like he spent most of his time alone.

I can't say that my actions that day were completely altruistic. Maybe our trip to the park that afternoon was based on the fact that I was tired of my self-imposed sentence of seclusion. That, and there was always a chance I might see her there.

Once in the park, we walked awhile and then sat for awhile. But whether we were sitting or walking he kept talking. He filled the afternoon with stories from his life. He had done so much he was quite interesting.

For a moment, I thought about my own life and how little I had done and accomplished. I thought about stories I would be able to tell when I was his age. I wondered if I would have any to share. For the first time in the last two years, I was saddened by the thought of what

I had missed, rather than what she had done to me. Yet, I blamed her for that, too. I realized I had been robbed. And despite the saddening revelation, I realized my time in the park that day was the best time I had experienced in the last two years.

\* \* \* \* \* \* \* \* \* \*

"Hey barkeep. You gonna keep admiring your face in that mirror or are you going to serve me a drink?"

I turned slowly to get a visual confirmation of the familiar voice. "Mr. Tripp. I wish I could say it was good to see you, but I'm not really that good a liar."

"Yeah. Yeah. Yeah. You don't lie," said the tall, athletic man in the black suit. His short dark hair and a thin black tie gave him a look straight out of the movie "Men in Black." In fact, the only difference between him and one of the movie's main characters was the signature pair of Rayban sunglasses. Well, that and anything else remotely resembling the coolness of Tommy Lee Jones or Will Smith.

Not that Ray Tripp was a complete geek. He was what I would consider a typical FBI agent in his mid forties. Jaded by an up close and personal interaction with humanity's bottom-dwellers, as well as being overworked and underpaid, Tripp was a person who had a hard time believing in the goodness of people. In fact, he had a hard time believing promises from devout clergymen, Buddhist monks and Eagle Scouts. Let alone an enigma like myself. But from what I knew of him, he had me convinced that he did believe in justice. And the pursuit of it. Whatever that means.

"How could I forget that you never lie?" he asked skeptically as he leaned against the bar. "Yet, you have an uncanny ability to tell people what they want to hear." He folded his arms down on the well-worn bar and his demeanor turned a little more direct. "Or at least what you think they want to hear. A real skill for someone like you."

The words "someone like me" gave me pause. I wasn't sure what to make of that – or me – anymore.

"I guess. I'm not really sure what skills I have. I haven't found her, yet." I said as I leaned forward on the edge of the bar. I looked toward Tripp's glass and nodded. "Can I get you a drink? What is it? Crown and Coke?"

Tripp took a look around the nearly empty bar – not an uncommon sight for a Tuesday evening in the small, dimly-lit establishment on the upper west side. The sparse crowd was composed mostly of working people trying to do whatever they could

145

to avoid heading to wherever it is they call home. Tripp then checked his watch. "Ah, why not? I'm scheduled to be off the clock in about forty-five minutes anyway. Besides, maybe it will make you listen to me."

I shook my head and smiled. "I'm failing to see how you drinking while on duty is going to help me listen to you. It's the code of the bartender."

"Well, if I keep ordering drinks, you have to spend more time listening to me and my logic."

"Having problems with your wife again or are you getting ready to lecture me?"

"Lecture you?" He said, like he couldn't believe I would accuse him of such a dastardly crime. He loosened up his tie to help validate how offended he was by my accusation.

I turned to pick up a half empty bottle of Crown Royal and poured some of it into a glass half full of ice. "Don't act like you're not going to give me the 'you're wasting your time. If we haven't caught them by now, the chances are we're not going to. And we're not even sure they're in NYC,' lecture. I've heard that speech." I mixed in a splash of Coke – the way he liked it – and placed it in front of him before leaning back against the mirror behind the bar.

"Look, Jesse." He tried to use his most persuasive tone. "I know you've heard it before. But this really isn't your burden to bear. We have it covered. Yes, we have appreciated your help. And I'm sure that somewhere in the annals of the FBI there will be a mention of Jesse Blunt and his loyal dedication to this case. Without you, we probably would not have been able to trace them to here. But the lead is cold. Really cold. I mean, it was over a year ago when two of the twenty dollar bills stolen from that Fresno bank turned up. And what?" His eyes widened, to let me know that the following words were questioning my sanity, judgment or eyesight. "You think you saw her on a subway about six months ago? No verification, mind you. Just something you thought you saw in passing."

I straightened up and cleaned a spot on the bar with a wet rag. I didn't say a word. I knew nothing I could say would sound rational.

Tripp broke the silence. "Even you have to admit, that's not much to go on." He looked down at his glass, ready to take a drink, but paused as if the cubed ice spelled out a descriptive message. "You need to go back home and get your life back. Or just get a life. Whatever. But what you're doing now isn't healthy. And it's not helping us find them. The bottom line is we're probably not going to find them. Not until one of them gets seriously hurt or they make a big mistake. Something they haven't done in the last two years."

He looked a little concerned. A look I hadn't often witnessed. At first I thought my perception of his demeanor was influenced by the ambiance of the dimly lit bar. But a closer look revealed real concern.

He went on solemnly, "I'm sorry. But it's true. And I think you know it." He took a long drink, consuming about three quarters of the entire glass. He was probably trying to avoid any type of uncomfortable look or response from me. Fearing that I would voice my belief through words or glares that he had overstepped his bounds.

That wasn't the case. I didn't think he was out of line. It was something I had thought about. If not often, at least recently. When I started my journey, I didn't think much about the "why." Probably because the reason why I felt the need to chase my felonious ex-wife and her lover across the country was not clear to me. I don't know if I was seeking a vengeful joy knowing I had a part in seeing her and the Vice President of the Gold Bank of Fresno heading to jail for the $250,000 they embezzled. Or if I just wanted to see her again. Something that I'm sure some analyst somewhere would define as closure. Even as an educated, open-minded and sensitive male, I'm not sure I fully understood the "closure" concept. Is confronting someone who has wronged you closure? Is helping put them behind bars closure? And how in the world would that help me get over the hurt of having the person whom I trusted and loved blindside me by running off with a co-worker. A co-worker so lame that he often would tell me how beautiful my ex-wife Nicole was, reinforcing it by poorly singing Rick Springfield's "I Wish that I had Jesse's Girl." A classic now ruined for eternity.

"Can I get a Captain Morgan and Diet, tall?" A man had moved up next to Tripp at the bar, obviously trying to get my attention.

"Sure," I replied, trying to put a smile on my face. As I reached for a glass, I caught a glimpse of a female sitting down at the opposite end of the bar. I didn't think much of it until I started filling the glass with ice. That's when I looked up almost in shock. After a closer look, I was sure: It was her. Her hair was short and dark, different than the last time I had seen her over two years prior. But it was definitely her.

I had spent countless hours thinking about that exact moment in the previous two years. I thought about what I would say. What I would do. If I would run off a litany of pre-planned insults detailing each and every issue she had. Maybe doing it in a quiet, subtle tone or possibly screaming at her at the top of my lungs. Or maybe I would simply follow her and try to sabotage her life at every possible turn, repaying her for what she had put me through. Or maybe I would calmly ask her the simple question that haunted me – why?

While all of this was running through my mind, I continued to stare at her. She never looked up. She never recognized that my eyes were upon her. She was talking on a cell phone and checking out her nails. She was totally oblivious to anything other than herself. It was definitely her.

"Jesse," Tripp interrupted my gaze. "You okay?"

The lag between my answer and his question was miniscule in real time but seemed to drag on forever in my mind. Not only was I unsure about how to respond to her presence, to the culmination of the mission that had consumed the last two years of my life, but I was also uncertain how to answer his query.

Finally, I spoke quietly. "Yeah. I'm fine."

"You sure?"

I folded up the towel I used to clean things on the bar. I placed it neatly on the bar in front of him, completely abandoning the customer's request for his Captain and Diet. As I slid under the opening at the end of the bar near where we were standing, I calmly verbalized my realization. "It's her."

"What?" Tripp heard me but he couldn't believe it. After emerging on the other side of the bar I looked him square in the eye and without saying a word, I gave him confirmation.

"You're fucking kidding me," was his response.

I shook my head negatively, as I made my way past him. I walked directly toward her. My mind raced with what I would do and what I would say. Two years. Two years of buildup, hatred, passion and determination. My pace quickened as I got near her.

When I was but two steps away from her, I looked closely at her face. She never looked up, still talking on the phone. Rage filled me. My issues all ready to be solved with this confrontation. My life recovered in a single moment. One round would redeem everything.

I was ready. I had so much venom that I wanted to let out on her at that moment. Instead, I walked. I walked out the door. I walked down the block. I walked and walked and walked. And I never looked back.

# FORGOTTEN TREASURES

## Daniel E. Donley

*Daniel E. Donley was raised in a suburb outside of Pittsburgh, Pennsylvania. He graduated with a Bachelors of Science in Justice Studies from Arizona State University. He lives in Las Vegas, Nevada and is currently working on a 30,000 word novella called* Chloe's Secret.

It was a pleasant 75 degrees as a slight breeze from the south passed by the suburbs of a large east coast city. Two men sat on the bumper of a truck eating lunch.

The sun rested on Alex's shoulder. Mickey turned to look at him and squinted with one eye as he asked, "Is it the television sets?"

Alex replied in a non-committal mumble, "No."

Mickey unwrapped the cellophane from the chipped ham sandwich he bought from the corner deli. He was starved as he took a big bite out of his sandwich. The flavor exploded on his taste buds. Chewing on his sandwich and gazing into the sky, Mickey said, "Is it the couches, 'specially the ones with daybeds? Huh? They can be tough. They're heavy and tough to get a grip on."

Alex had no reply.

Mickey asked, "Is it the refrigerators? I know how you hate them."

With a bothered look Alex said, "No. It's not the refrigerators."

With one eyebrow raised and a disgusted look on his face, Alex said, "Just figure out the details for the job. Okay?"

A dejected expression took over Mickey's face as he replied, "Okay. You don't have to get all bent out shape about it."

Alex stared at Mickey with his right hand clenched in a fist, "Don't you want something more than thirty years of a nine to five job? Don't you want to do something more than putting shit into the back of this truck every day?"

A befuddled Mickey replied, "I guess I'm happy with the way things are. What you want to do is risky, takes a lot of time, energy,

149

and has to be done right or we'll both get screwed. Why don't you forget about any other work? Eat your corned beef sandwich and enjoy the day. There is so much good stuff here if you just sit back, relax, and enjoy the pleasure of breathing."

Alex looked over at Mickey and said, "When I had my head in a rut, you were the one that told me to set my sails for tomorrow because the sun had set on yesterday." Alex stood up and poked himself in the chest stating, "It's just not enough. I feel like I've been living in a haze the last three years. I need something more. I don't know how to explain it. This job is like being in prison. This job is killing me. It's like driving a stake through my heart. I just can't do this for thirty years. If we can get the jobs to work out, I feel there might be some hope for something better. I mean how hard can it be? I'm just like everyone else. I have two arms, two legs, and a brain. Why can't I have a better life? Why can't it be me that lives a better life?"

Calmly chewing on a pickle Mickey turned his head toward Alex. Squinting with one eye closed, Mickey said, "It looks pretty good to me. It's a beautiful day. I get to work with my best friend. We get a lot of exercise that keeps us healthy. This is a great place. The air is fresh. In the fall the trees will change and no matter where we go there will be a beautiful fall landscape. In the winter everything will have a blanket of white over it. This place will look beautiful."

Alex said sarcastically, "Everything is wonderful to you. You never think anything is wrong."

Mickey smiled knowingly and said, "It's the ice. I know, the big heavy truck and all. You're worried the truck is going to slide and fall off one of these hills. I can drive in the winter if you want."

Mickey got up from the bumper and they threw their trash in the back of the truck.

Alex said, "It's the stink, Mickey. I can't stand the stink. I do not care if they're rich or poor, Asian, Black, White, or Mexican, their garbage stinks." With a befuddled expression Alex asked, "Don't you smell it?"

An apologetic gaze came from Mickey as he said, "I probably should have told you this a long time ago, but my sinuses were screwed up when I was a kid. So I really don't smell anything. Sorry."

Alex sighed, rolled his eyes and shook his head. He opened the door to the truck and said, "Just do the work-up and meet me at the gym tomorrow. "

Early the next morning Mickey headed off to the gym for his workout. Alex was already in the locker room when Mickey arrived.

Alex asked, "Are you going to run by and check up on the warehouse this morning?"

Mickey answered with an inquisitive look, "Yes."

Alex slowly mentioned, "I wasn't sure you would show up today."

Mickey stopped stuffing his socks into his shoes and looked Alex in the eye saying, "I know this is important to you."

Alex explained, "I got your work-up last night. We'll have to make a withdrawal, so meet me at the bank around nine."

Mickey took off on his run through the streets that lined the industrial areas of the city. Thirty minutes later he stopped at a rundown warehouse bordering the docks. Pulling a key from his shoe, he slid it into the padlock, opening the rollup door. The car Alex was concerned about was in the middle of the floor. It was a 1979 280Z, a classic to some and to Alex. Mickey thought it was just another car. He turned over the engine and headed off.

Mickey snapped his wrist to check the time. A quarter to nine, he was late. Mickey knew that Alex would be getting impatient if he didn't show up soon. The bank was owned by a corporation out of France and was the most respected institution for international business in town.

Mickey thought Alex was far too stressed-out when he spotted the "Out of Order" canvas bag over the parking meter that Alex used in order to save the parking spot. But, this was a big deal for Alex. Mickey walked into the bank.

The bank had an open layout. To Mickey's left were six desks without partitions, enabling him to see the last desk without obstruction. The room was forty feet deep and eighty feet wide. The vault was to the right of the entrance. There were only two bankers at the desks and one of them was the branch manager. Two tellers stood behind the counter with their supervisor at a desk behind them. Several customers were lined up in front of the counter. Mickey asked to see the banker in charge of opening business loans. The teller told Mickey to sit down in the row of chairs that lined the wall to the left of the entrance.

Finally, Alex walked in with big grin on his face. He walked over to the desk in the middle of the room and started writing out a withdrawal slip. Mickey was called up to the manager at the second desk and sat with his back to the banker in the first desk. Mickey saw Alex make his way through the line to stand in front of a teller.

Alex pulled a hood over his head and drew a gun. He then instructed the tellers to put their hands over their heads. Mickey grabbed the back of the chair of the banker at the first desk and pulled her away from the desk so she couldn't trip a silent alarm. Pulling a hood over his head and drawing a gun, Mickey told the manager in front of him not to move.

At this time the supervisor came out of the vault from helping a customer put back a safety deposit box, when she saw two hooded men with guns drawn.

Alex yelled, "This is a hold-up. No one move. No one do anything stupid and no one will die." Mickey moved to the center of the lobby and yelled for every one to lie down on the floor, face first.

Alex got behind the teller's counter just in time, as the supervisor was about to push a button, triggering a silent alarm. Alex raised his magnum gun against her temple and said, "Lady, I know what you're thinking. If you press this button the cops will be here in seconds. But look, do you want to die for a paycheck?" At that moment the lady could not take the stress of the situation and fainted, falling on the button as she hit the floor.

Mickey had planned for such a contingency. At nine o'clock the police were making their shift change and they would all be at the police station. Mickey yelled, "We're on the clock: five minutes now."

Alex grabbed the hair of one of the tellers and instructed her to empty out all the drawers and put the money into a backpack. Both Mickey and Alex left through the front door as a teller in a separate room for the drive-up customers came out into the lobby and found her coworkers lying on the floor. Alex was carrying the money as they hopped into the brown 280Z.

He threw the backpack in the back seat and picked up a laptop. He looked around anxiously and said, "Okay let's go."

With one hand resting calmly on the steering wheel Mickey said, "Wait."

A startled Alex replied, "Wait? We're golden, let's go."

Mickey flicked his hand up, wiggling his fingers and said, "Patience, Alex, we got to get it right."

Alex replied in confusion, "Are you nuts? What are you thinking?"

Mickey wore a puzzled frown. "I'm wondering: should I load my gun now?"

A paralyzed Alex responded, "You robbed a bank without any bullets in your gun?"

With an inquisitive look, Mickey replied, "Is that a big deal? I didn't plan on shooting anyone."

Alex exclaimed, "I don't know who is more insane, the guy that robs a bank with an unloaded gun or the guy that follows him."

Mickey grinned. "See, now that you released all that tension, you're more relaxed. Now you can think clearly. What do you think? One or two bullets?"

Alex snorted, "Why don't we go nuts and put all the bullets in the gun?"

"Now you're being overly dramatic. Get a grip. Two should be plenty."

Alex shook his head and started typing on the laptop. The same laptop he used to break into the bank's wireless signal and re-position the bank's security cameras to point up at the ceiling.

Out of the rear view mirror Mickey spotted the flashing red lights of a patrol car behind him. Smashing the gas pedal to the floor, the tires spun with a screech as blue smoke came from under the wheel wells. The 280Z hatchback was easy to spot, darting out of the parking space.

Shifting through the gears, Mickey's feet danced on the pedals. The hatchback darted its way back and forth through the congested streets like a running back dodging defensive backs on his way to the goal line. Mickey was close to the docks where he knew the back streets and hiding places. He made a right at the red light and spotted the cop in a patrol car behind them. Two other patrol cars were now on parallel side streets and Mickey could tell they were going to try to box him in.

Mickey did what he does so well and exploited their weakness. He pulled hard on the emergency brake lever in the middle console, holding in the lever release button. The right rear wheel stopped turning sooner than the left. Mickey turned the steering wheel to the right. The car spun on a dime 180 degrees to face the oncoming police car. He dropped the emergency brake lever back into position as he accelerated toward the patrol car. Alex looked over to see a sinister smile hijack Mickey's face. Alex panicked and he grabbed the suicide handle attached to the dash.

Mickey knew the cops in this precinct. John McGuire happened to be the officer barreling down the street at him. John was a son of an alcoholic father that in tough times was nowhere to be found. John promised himself this would never be the case with his two sons and only daughter. Mickey knew John was a bully but would never jeopardize his family's future with a head-on collision.

Mickey closed the gap, causing John to make a snap decision. John slammed on the brakes and swerved, diving through an open parking space onto the sidewalk to avoid the oncoming car.

Mickey decided to make a break for the parking garage, one of his favorite places to shake the police. The garage had a pedestrian walkway that bridged two stand-alone garages, one on each side of the river. One floor below the roof, Mickey had stashed the getaway car. He pulled into the parking garage, tires screeching with each turn. Turning a corner Mickey looked in the rearview mirror to check on his pursuers.

An excited Alex yelled, "Look out."

Mickey returned his gaze to a pair of headlights on a collision course with the 280Z. Mickey slammed on the brakes with both feet and turned the wheel to the right as the back end swung around, coming perpendicular with the on coming car. Alex was braced for the impact when Mickey saw an empty parking space in front of him. Mickey eased off the brakes and the 280Z slipped into the space as the car passed within an inch of his rear bumper. Mickey threw the backpack over his shoulder and he and Alex made a break for the stairs. The bridge was at the top of the stairs, connecting the two roofs.

A police car skidded to a stop on the top deck as Mickey and Alex were crossing the bridge. The cop opened his door and yelled for Mickey to drop the backpack and freeze. Mickey, already halfway across the bridge, turned and popped off two rounds into the cop's radiator, forcing the cop to take cover. Mickey, standing in the middle of the bridge, was an easy target for the cop, who popped off two rounds, hitting Mickey squarely in the chest. The impact of the shots carried Mickey over the rail. Alex tripped and fell as he watched his friend fall from sight.

As the cop passed over the bridge, he could see Mickey's body float down the river. The cop came off the stairs as Alex got into the stashed getaway car. The cop drew down on the Nova, shooting twice. One round caught the bumper and the other rested in the concrete pillar.

Mickey floated up under the piers, his ribs sore from the impact of the bullets. He then pulled himself up onto a cross beam and started to rip off the bulletproof vest. He jammed the vest in the waterproof backpack where the money was kept.

The warehouse was not far, but it was upstream in a different precinct. It had to be the warehouse because dead bodies don't float upstream. As he started to swim, he could hear two cops talking above. One said Mickey was a goner and must have gotten snagged on something holding him under. The other said the current carried him away.

Mickey pulled himself out of the water and slid into the warehouse. Conveniently tucked away in a corner was his jogging outfit. Before he started his jog back to the gym, he concealed the backpack and all evidence within a hollow steel post used to support the warehouse. The gym was upstream so the cops wouldn't be looking for him in that direction.

As he entered the doors to the gym, Albert, a surfer "wannabe" and a trainer for the gym, stopped him. "Yo, dude, did you hear another bank was robbed down by the piers?"

Mickey hoped he looked shocked as he replied, "That's terrible."

A concerned Albert warned him. "Dude, you got to watch it when you're out there. Those kinds of people will rip your head off!"

Mickey smiled and said, "Well, we don't want that!"

With a wrinkled up face and cringed nose Albert said, "Dude, that must be some workout, you stink!"

Mickey thought, "Nuts. I'll have to come up with something to explain the smell. I don't want trainer/surfer dude to tell the cops I been swimming in the river." And without raising an eyebrow Mickey explained, "I slipped on some lard by the fish fry and fell into their garbage."

With raised eyebrows Albert said, "Yo, that's why you should use the indoor track."

Mickey, thinking of the money from the job, said, "I can't get the same benefits I do from running outdoors."

Albert remembered when he was a promising high school baseball player and trained outdoors when he said, "Fresh air, high and low ground, dogging stuff."

Mickey, desperate to get rid of the river stench, said with a smile and two thumbs sticking into the air, "Yo, yo!"

Albert, satisfied, simply said, "Later."

Mickey walked into the locker room and headed for the showers. After a long, relaxing shower, he toweled off and dressed.

Two hours later he pulled up to the front of the warehouse. Waiting until there wasn't a soul in sight, Mickey opened the front door and walked along the wall of the empty warehouse to find a large aluminum briefcase sitting in the corner. He pulled the backpack from the steel post. A small table and chair were in the corner where he sat to count the take. He packed all of the money into the briefcase and walked out of the warehouse. He opened the trunk and placed the case inside. Slamming the trunk closed, he found a policeman standing beside his car. The badge read Timpson.

A little startled and trying to calculate the odds of this cop being a part of the investigation Mickey said, "Hello."

With a noncommittal look Officer Timpson said, "You look a bit out of place."

Mickey replied worriedly, "I heard there was a robbery and wanted to check the place out. We're starting a new business and rent this place as a holding area."

The officer asked, "And that is?"

Mickey replied, "My friend and I go around picking up stuff people no longer need or find out of fashion. You would be amazed at the kind of stuff we get. Good stuff, too. With a little hard work it's as good as new." He paused for a moment and said, "We think of ourselves like fishermen, and the city is like a big ocean of oysters just for the taking. My friend and I pick up the oysters. Then we crack them open and extract the pearl, and polish it up."

Mickey watched closely as Officer Timpson asked, "So you pick-up other people's junk?"

An honest Mickey stated, "Well, we like to call ourselves Sanitation Engineers."

He looked in the officer's eyes and saw he had lost interest in pursuing Mickey as a suspect. Officer Timpson broke his gaze with Mickey and looked at Mickey's car.

Mickey thought he'd better change the subject and asked, "So the robbery happened at the other end?"

Officer Timpson said, "Yes, but we got one of them. The body is in the river. We are searching for it now. I think they are more worried about recovering the money than the body."

Laughingly, Mickey said, "It's probably worth more."

With a smirk Officer Timpson said, "There is my watch commander, I have to go." As he started to walk away, he said, "Take care."

Mickey thought to himself, "I do," as he said, "Have a good evening."

The watch commander asked, "What's up with that guy?"

Officer Timpson replied, "Nothing. He's a junk dealer."

Mickey drove to Jonathan Beckmore's offices on the corner of Too Rich and Not Rich Enough. Alex soon caught up with him and they entered the office together.

Mickey and Alex sat in front of Beckmore's desk. A perplexed Beckmore said, "Now, let me get this straight. I was to pay you $5,000 if you could get away with robbing my bank and not get caught by my high tech security cameras. Is that right?"

Alex said, "Yep."

Mickey acknowledged Jonathan by saying, "That is what we agreed on."

Receptive Banking President Jonathan Beckmore asked, "So, how did you beat the encrypted code of my forty-million-dollar wireless security cameras?"

Mickey simply stated, "I found out the name of one of your new bank managers. I then called a secretary at your I.T. department and convinced her that you would fire me if you found out I had lost the encryption code for the cameras. She being relatively new herself and not wanting anyone to lose his job, agreed to look up the code. I gave her a number and she called be back with the code."

An amazed Beckmore asked, "You mean my forty-million-dollar system was cracked with a couple of phone calls?"

Alex replied, "Yep. It's amazing what people will say to be accepted."

Beckmore was very sober as he asked, "What is your recommendation to prevent this from happening again?"

Mickey explained, "It's not hard. When someone calls for that kind of information, instruct your staff to tell them they will call them back with the information. Do not call them back with the number they gave your staff. Find out from the department directory the internal office number and call them using the directory's number.

A secretary walked in and handed an envelope to Jonathan Beckmore. He handed the envelope to Mickey, saying, "Thank you for your services and I believe this will be payment in full."

Mickey and Alex walked out of the building to their cars.

With a feeling of gratitude Alex said, "The money doesn't mean anything to you does it?"

A satisfied Mickey replied, "No, I have everything I need out of life. I have a family, nice friends and a good place to live."

An appreciative but confused Alex said, "Everyone thinks I'm still an alcoholic."

A somber grin fell on Mickey's face as he said, "I know more than anyone what you were. Remember, I was the guy that picked you up and got you to work. I poured you into the truck every morning for three years and did the job of two. You're not that person anymore. You kicked that habit." Mickey paused and said, "Do me this favor; believe in yourself and not what others think of you."

With much hesitation Alex said, "You're insane. You should have given up on me a long time ago."

With a pleasant, half-laughing grin, Mickey said, "You didn't think I was going to throw away a good friendship just because of a little distress and abuse."

Alex raised his fist as if he had a mug of beer in his hand and Mickey gently tapped it with his own.

Mickey asked, "See you at work tomorrow, five o'clock? Alex walked off, replying, "Five o'clock."

# GHOSTS OF CIENFUEGOS

## Susan Coppola

*Susan Coppola has been writing since early 2005 and has already been a finalist in five writing contests. She is working on a creative nonfiction book based on the life of Hall of Fame Jockey Joe Notter. You may view her work at www.susancoppola.squarespace.com*

The ambulance flew up Twelfth Avenue. Its siren scream hung in the humid night air like a wet towel on a shower rod. With lights flashing, the fluorescent yellow Miami Dade Fire Rescue truck pulled up to the entrance of the Ryder Trauma Center. Outside, taking a breather from a hectic night shift, I looked up at the moon rising on the eastern horizon. Thoughts of my father and Cuba filled my mind like a mushroom after the rain. I pictured people strolling along the Malecon in Havana making secret wishes to the glowing golden orb, only ninety miles, but worlds away. Watching as the EMTs unloaded the gurney and pushed it through the automatic doors, I followed them inside.

"Thanks. I'll take him." I grabbed the clipboard, looked for the patient's name.

"Mr. Sanchez, I'm Dr. Maria Benitez. I'll be taking care of you. Where do you hurt?" The man's face, ruddy brown like fine tobacco, looked pinched with pain. His body swathed in white sheeting, an IV line trailed from his hand to a clear bag at his side.

"Oh . . .All over. Please help me. I'm in a lot of pain." He said in Spanish.

"Si, mi amor, un momentico mas." I turned to an intern.

"Carlos, take him up now, give him two cc's of morphine after his CAT scan."

I was turning away when something caught my eye; on his upper arm was a tattoo of the Cuban flag, the words "Brigada 2506 Nunca Olvidese" underneath. I scanned the pre-admission record and found his date of birth: 4/12/35, Place of birth Cienfuegos, Cuba. Making a mental note to visit Mr. Sanchez after he was admitted upstairs, I finished my shift a few hours later, headed home and called my mother.

"Hi, Mami. Just got home, I'm so tired, going straight to bed but I have a quick question." Setting my keys on the counter, I rubbed my neck, kicked off my shoes where I stood. I'd lived alone since med school. One failed engagement was enough for my already wounded heart. It was my mother's one unspoken disappointment in me, no husband, more important, no family.

"Si, mi cielo. What is it?" Her voice as sweet and warm as cafe con leche.

"Did Papi know a man named Raul Sanchez?"

My mother paused. "Raul Sanchez, such a common name, I don't know. I might know him, where's he from?" Her tone was evasive.

"His pre-admit said he was born in Cienfuegos like Papi, about the same age, too. He was brought in tonight. Hit by a car on Eighth Street. Had a tattoo with *Brigade 2506 Never Forget* on his arm." Portable phone in hand, I stood at my sliding glass door scanning the electric skyline view from my newly purchased condo.

"Yeah, maybe I have heard of him. Perhaps, he was with your father at the Bay of Pigs." Her voice trailed off like a hiker unsure of the right path.

Just the mention of the name made me wince, the saddest moment in our bittersweet legacy as exiles. I remember the sepia toned photos of my father and his comrades looking Elvis Presley handsome in their silver frames atop our television. Lost count of how many times I heard him say, we came so close, if only we'd had a little help – we would have made it, a free Cuba.

"God, it never goes away, does it?" I said.

"What do you mean? Why do you say that?" I heard the anger rising in my mother's voice.

"Because it was always the same sad song. I loved Papi very much, but sometimes it just seemed like loving Cuba was more important than loving us."

My mother snapped, "You know that's not true. He loved us very much."

"I know, you're right, I know, I'm sorry. Por favor, let's change the subject." My mother wavered, let it pass.

"So, how is this, Mr. Sanchez? Was he badly hurt?" she asked.

"Yeah, very bad, broke his leg and some back injuries. I'm going up to visit him tomorrow. Talk with him about Papi." My mother's response surprised me.

"Why do you want to talk to him?" Her voice was agitated, had been since I mentioned Raul Sanchez's name.

"I'm not sure. Just curious, see what he remembers." I sat back at the counter, thumbing through forgotten mail.

"Why stir up bad memories? Remember, hija, be careful what you wish for." She was starting to annoy me. I cut her off.

"Mami, por favor, I'm tired. I don't want to fight with you. I'll talk to you tomorrow. Hasta luego. Te quiero."

"Si, si, hasta luego. Good night, te quiero."

I hung up the phone feeling drained and empty like a soup bowl in a homeless shelter. My mother and I always disagreed when it came to my father's death. She accepted the story Metro Dade Police told her. He was killed, execution style, by Castro's terrorists. Case closed. Not for me. I wanted more. I wanted a name and a face to go with the hand shooting a gun out a car window. I wanted justice.

After my father's release from Castro's prison in '62 and joyous return to Miami, he and my mother worked and saved, eventually bought a small house in Little Havana. They dreamed of the day they would return to a free homeland. That day was not to be.

Coming home from the bakery early one January morning in '78, he was gunned down in front of our house. The white bakery box filled with guava pastries landing in the roadway like a misplaced gift. I was seventeen and just getting up for school when I heard the shots, ran outside and saw him. I remember screaming over his prone body, being led away. Within minutes, cops, paramedics and nosey bystanders filled the street. Shot four times in the back, my father died instantly. The police suspected his killing was linked to anti-Castro activities, but no one was ever arrested. In my grief and shock, I retreated from the world. There was no sense to be made of an unsolved murder, but school made sense. There were always answers at school. I studied hard, became a doctor. If I couldn't save my father or his beloved Cuba, I would save someone else.

The next morning I pulled into the parking garage, unanswered questions circling in my mind like planes in crowded airspace. I didn't get to visit Mr. Sanchez until late in the afternoon when the emergency room finally quieted down.

"Francisco, I'll be up on six west. Page me, if you need me." I said to the head nurse on duty. I took the elevator up, found him alone when I entered his room.

"Senor Sanchez. How are you feeling? A little better?" I asked in Spanish.

"Yes, a little. Thank you." The man's eyes looked tired and sleepy, his pain relieved.

"Mr. Sanchez, I told you my name was Maria Benitez, but I didn't tell you my father was Osvaldo Leon Benitez."

At the mention of my father's name, Raul Sanchez lowered his head.

"Ay, lo siento. Your father was a brave man. He loved Cuba very much . . ." His words trailed off.

"I know he did and I loved him very much. Mr. Sanchez, is there anything you can tell me about my father's death? Anything at all?" I asked.

"What has your mother told you?" His leathery tan face wrinkled into a frown, his gray, bushy eyebrows creased in a furrow.

"Only what the police told her. That he was killed by terrorists for Castro." I said.

"And your mother knows you were coming to speak with me?"

"Yes, but she wasn't happy about it. Do you know why?"

"La puerta, por favor." He motioned for me to close the door. I sat back beside his bed, pulling my chair up close to the edge to better hear his frail voice.

"Please try to understand. Your father was a good man with a confused heart. His love for Cuba blinded him to the truth." His eyes, sleepy and sad stared down at the nubby fabric of the blanket, his right index finger tapping the surface.

"I don't understand. What did he do?" The air in the room felt stagnant. I was gulping to catch my breath.

"Got involved with some bad people, Colombians dealing cocaine. He was introducing them to people who would buy their drugs and they were paying him off in guns that were smuggled into Cuba. We tried to tell him he was crazy, but he wouldn't listen. The Colombians got greedy, thought they didn't need your father anymore and killed him." The words hit me with the impact of a bullet.

"If you knew all this why didn't you tell my mother? Why didn't you tell the police?" My anxiety was now replaced with anger.

"I did tell your mother." My heart jumped at his words.

"You told my mother? When?"

"We talked right after your father's funeral. She already knew most of it. Figured it out on her own. She begged me to keep quiet for your sake and for your father's memory. What difference would it have made? The Colombians were long gone back to Medellin. So we buried the truth with your father." The room grew quiet, the only sound the beeping of medical machinery. I struggled to compose myself, but failed.

"Oh! Papi, always for Cuba." Speaking to an unseen presence, I put my head down and cried. Raul Sanchez reached out and gently touched my shoulder.

"Ah, lo siento. For some men, Cuba is like a beautiful ghost that haunts their lives. It was your father's curse, but also his greatest gift. Please find it in your heart to forgive him." His fingers picked at the tape holding the IV line on top of his hand, not knowing what to say next in the stilted silence.

"Thank you Mr. Sanchez. I'm sure I will. It's just so much to take in. I'll need a little time." Wiping tears with the back of my hand, I got up to leave.

"Of course, of course, I just hope the truth will bring you some peace at last . . ." He squeezed my hand, surprised me with the strength of his grip.

"I hope so, too." I leaned over, kissed him on the cheek and left the room. My mother's words, be careful what you wish for, haunting me.

Finishing a long shift, I headed to the parking garage, got on the Dolphin Expressway, reaching my mother's house as the sun rose on the downtown Miami skyline. She was making coffee as I came in the kitchen. The smell of freshly brewed Pilon scented the air. I felt a wave of sadness as I looked around the tiny room. Porcelain roosters, Cuban good luck charms, stood in a row on a shelf above the table. My parents' lost dreams of a free Cuba echoing in every corner. I kissed her hello.

"Good morning, mi cielo. This is a nice surprise. Quieres cafecito?" Her smile lighted her face.

Good Morning, Mami. Yes, por favor." She poured the strong dark liquid into small white espresso cups, set them on the table and sat down. I looked at her face, so beautiful as a young woman, now careworn, but with a kindness still in her amber colored eyes.

"I talked to Mr. Sanchez. He told me everything, about Papi and the Columbians? All these years and you knew. Why didn't you tell me?" My voice tinged with the hurt and betrayal I felt.

"You don't know how many times I wanted to, but I thought it'd make you feel worse, not better. I'm so sorry. I was hoping you'd never have to know." Her eyes looked down as if weighted by her shame.

"Well, anyway, you were right. You know, be careful what you wish for? I didn't get justice, but I got the truth." My mother looked at me with a sad smile.

"I know, hija, and what you said about Papi loving Cuba more than us? Hurt me to hear you say it. Sometimes I felt that way too, but I forgave him years ago. I hope you can too."

"Si, Mami, I already have." We sipped our coffee in silence. I touched her hand and made a wish for the day when Cuba would be more than just a ghost.

# HAPPILY EVER AFTER

Lily Foster

*Lily Foster neé Gillman grew up in Seattle, Washington, where she co-published three books of poetry written for and by children. Lily now resides with her husband, Keith, in England.*

Once upon a time I was falling in love...

I've heard it said that you don't choose love, it chooses you. I believe this with all my heart.

The first time love chose me – I mean really, totally got under my skin so that the man I loved was not everything in the world; he *was* my world – I was only nineteen years old. It was a beautiful thing. We did everything together. We traveled, we went to movies, we played cards, we talked, we laughed, we made love. He was my best friend.

There were, of course, problems in our relationship. There are always problems in any relationship, even the very best. But to me, it was simply a matter of learning to compromise. As far as I was concerned, I loved him and he loved me, and as they say, love will find a way.

So I was as patient as I am able to be. I was not one of those women who got angry and then told my spouse, "you *know* what the problem is." I knew he couldn't read my mind and I didn't expect him to try. So if he upset me in some way I told him exactly why I was upset and asked him to please try to avoid the problem in the future.

Unfortunately, for all the things in which we were of like mind, this was not one of them. For one thing, if I was upset about something that he wouldn't be upset about himself, I was being "stupid." If, on the other hand, he was upset with me over something, he would keep it to himself, let it fester for a few years, and then dump it on me so long after the fact that there was nothing I could do to rectify the situation.

This was further exacerbated by the fact that, in my deluded belief that his love for me had remained as strong as my love for him as time passed, I went to extreme measures to try to get him to understand that this was upsetting to me. Had I opened my eyes and realized that his love had diminished over time, I would have known that extreme measures meant nothing. It only made him love me less. Adding to this the fact that my extreme measures really *were* stupid did nothing to help repair the rips and tears appearing in the fabric of our formerly nearly ideal relationship. Over time I developed nerve problems that seemed to get worse and worse as our relationship deteriorated.

And so it came to pass that, after nearly a quarter of a century together, he was through with me. I was summarily dismissed from his life. I was cast out. I was a divorced middle-aged woman, still deeply in love with her ex-husband. I spent over a year of truly bad luck trying to find a new home so that I could "give him back his life." In essence, I was waiting to be exiled.

During my year of the worst luck of my life, my nerve problems increased and, as a result, my health diminished. I lost my ability to concentrate on work, in fact as time went on I found it harder and harder to work at all, eventually losing my income. It seemed that everything I tried to do to get out of the situation fell through. Whether I was trying to buy a cheap (not inexpensive – *cheap*) home or just trying to rent an apartment, something always happened to keep the deal from going through.

Sometimes it was my own fault. My nerves were so bad and my concentration level so low that keeping focused on all the various procedures for relocating was a nearly impossible feat. Sometimes it was definitely *not* my fault – luck of the draw, the alignment of the planets, Mother Nature, or the very gods themselves laughingly flaunted even my best efforts. I told friends and family, "I won't believe I've really got someplace until the key is in my hand." This is when the gods truly laughed.

When I finally was able to sign a lease, pay first and last (and damage deposit, of course), and had a key firmly placed into my palm, that's when lightning struck. Key in hand, boxes nearly packed, I received the call from the property manager, telling me that the apartment had been struck by lightning; all the appliances were blown, the brand-new carpet was severely burned, and the door was demolished. The door to which I held the key which allowed me to believe that the move was finally going to happen.

In the meantime, still staying in the house that used to be my home, the house I had cleaned and painted and in which I had lovingly cooked meals for my beloved, the house in which we had made love in each and every room, while still surrounded by the ghost of my life, I became officially divorced.

The property manager offered to rent me a unit in a different complex. I told her (and everyone else) that I would wait for the repairs to be done because I had had so much bad luck with getting a place I would rather keep the one that I had gotten so close to moving into. The truth of the matter was, my nerves were much too shattered to go back to square one, or even backward at all. Simply waiting was all I could cope with.

Three weeks later, on my birthday, I woke up for the first time in my new surroundings. Although on the first day I managed to somewhat make the place livable, I found that my ability to go through boxes filled with memories and place what meager remains there were into a new environment became harder and harder. As the months passed I began to doubt that I would ever really make my little apartment into a home.

My ability to work and make money also deteriorated. I would sit in front of the computer with every good intention present. I *will* work today. I *will* get through the most time-sensitive jobs. I *will* make money. But ultimately, day in and day out, I would sit at the computer playing games and crying. It was not that I wanted to play games, and certainly not that I was enjoying myself. It was more like I was paralyzed. It was the thought that the person who completes me was thirty-five miles away, probably not even thinking about me, that kept me from completing even the simplest tasks.

My memory has always been very vivid. Throughout our entire relationship I would suddenly find myself in the middle of a memory, reliving the moment as if it was currently happening. There has never been any particular trigger or reason for a memory to come to the surface – it just does. When we were together, this was wonderful. I never tired of remembering days at the beach or discussions of movies we had just seen, or that really beautiful five minutes we spent standing under a tree while a pouring rain came down all around us, and we just wrapped our arms around each other and laughed and kissed and waited.

But sitting alone in strange surroundings, hearing neighbors walking or running past my door, talking to each other in English or Spanish or hip-hop slang, vivid memory truly became a curse.

My shattered nerves got worse as financial issues started to catch up to me. There is only so long you can live on credit and then they actually expect you to be able to pay them. I may have been "stupid" to have had feelings that my ex-husband would not have had, but I was not so stupid as to believe that I could explain to creditors, "You have to stop calling me. You see, I'm having nerve problems and I need to calm down in order to work to make money so that I can pay you. So you see, you're only making it worse by calling me." So I stopped answering the phone. When it would ring I would cringe and think, "go away – go away – go away."

Sometimes I might have been lucky enough to have been actually getting something done prior to the phone ringing. This would end *that* lucky streak. I would then wander through the kitchen, looking for something that I felt I might be able to eat. If I found something (or even if I didn't) I would then turn on the TV (just for *one* show) and sit down on the couch to eat, or not eat, as the case may be. But work was done for the day.

They say that time heals all wounds. They say that it is better to have loved and lost than never to have loved at all. They also say that absence makes the heart grow fonder. And of course, John Greenleaf Whittier said, "of all sad words of tongue or pen, the saddest are these, it might have been." I guess it depends on who you are and who you love as to which statements are true and which are bullshit.

I found that I was jealous of widows and widowers. How wonderful to spend your entire life, until the day you die, always believing that the person you loved also loved you. Always being able to hear the words "until death you do part," without bursting into tears. Never having to know that you love someone who used to love you – but no more – and never again. Never having to be just someone that your love used to know, long ago, somewhere in the distant past; just someone of no consequence now. Never having to look back upon happy memories and wish that you could rip them forever from your brain, just so that you can sleep through the night.

I promised myself one thing – an actual sacred vow to whatever remained in me of myself – that if I lived through this, that if I ever repaired the damage to my nerves and my health and my mind, I would *never* allow anyone to hurt me again.

So I truly believe that you don't choose love, it chooses you.

You, my love, were a surprise.

Do you remember how hesitant I was to even speak to you in the beginning? Do you remember how, after I finally consented to that one – *one* – date, you had to literally beg me for a second? I remember. I have a very vivid memory.

Do you remember what I said the first time you told me that you love me? I told you that that could change, and that I wasn't willing to take the gamble. I told you that I could never stand to lose love again and that, if you really did love me, you would go away before I loved you back. And do you remember what you answered me, my darling, my love, my life?

"Love, I could never stop loving you. You are the part that was missing from my soul. You are the one thing that I have always lacked but was never able to name until I found you. If I had to believe that I would never hear you tell me that you love me, there would be no purpose to my life. You are the entire universe to me and without you, I could never be really myself again. Because 'myself' is nothing more than one-half of us."

This is what finally began the process of my falling in love with you. These words, these feelings, were exactly what I had felt (and unfortunately never stopped feeling) for my ex-husband. Although my love for him had never dimmed, and my life was miserable and incomplete without his arms around me, I found that I had room in my heart to include you. The very fact that you were able to articulate the feelings that had racked my nerves and nearly killed me, made you special to me.

And the years since that day have been filled with so many beautiful, warm and wonderful memories that they could fill volumes in my mind. Volumes that, without warning, without a trigger, without a reason, fill my head throughout the day and night into my dreams. I remember each happy moment that we have shared and I want to live each of these moments again.

But apparently that is not an option. I do understand, my love, what you are feeling now. Or rather, what you are not feeling. I've heard it before. I know that what you want to tell me is not something that I am capable of hearing again.

I understand that you wanted to have this "serious, heart-to-heart" talk to tell me something that will make my life unlivable. And as I told you, I promised myself that I would never let anyone hurt me again.

So I thank you for allowing me to tell you all of this first. It gave me time. I thank you for giving me the time to let the wine go through your system, along with the little something extra that I added. I think that maybe, by now, you are probably much too tired to tell me what you wanted to tell me.

And I want to tell you just a little more.

I love you.

I will always love you.

And I know, now, that you will never tell me that you no longer love me.

Darling, until death us do part.

# THE HOUSE OF MY DREAMS

## Yvonne Eve Walus

*Yvonne Eve Walus is a novelist, poet, freelance writer, mathematician, wife, and mother – not necessarily in that order. Published in the United States and England, her work is available worldwide. Her latest romance,* Small Price to Pay, *was published by Echelon Press in 2007.* http://yewalus.kiwiwebhost.net.nz/index.html

The house seemed familiar. I tried to listen to the agent's sales pitch, but I knew that I'd seen this carved door before, the bay windows, the cliff. Which was strange, because as a newcomer to New Zealand I have never been in this area before.

If only I could stop thinking about it, the memory would come back.

The property was magnificent. Two and a half stories, terraces running halfway around on the first floor, just high enough for a view of the Pacific Ocean and the isolated beach at the end of the garden. Truly, a house of one's dreams....

I flinched. How did I know that the terraces were high enough? How did I know that the ocean was just over that rise beyond the garden?

I wanted this house. For some strange reason though, I didn't want to buy it from this particular agent. She seemed as friendly as all New Zealanders, yet there was something about her...

It couldn't have had to do with the nagging suspicion I'd had on first seeing the house, could it?

The house agent and I went up the outside stairs, and she quietly pushed the front door open. I felt a twinge of surprise that she hadn't rung the doorbell and that the door was unlocked. The house was completely empty. The door opened onto a large hallway, and I admired the healthy light colour of the wooden interior. We crossed to a splendid lounge with a genuine stone fireplace. Instantly, I knew that the solid chimney reached all the way down to the workroom adjacent to the garage.

By now I was sure that my Christine would fall in love with this house. But I didn't want to show too much interest. The agent hadn't uttered a word since we'd entered. Nothing of the usual enthusiastic sales-pitch. Instead, she was studying me with what I considered to be undue interest.

"Why is the house on the market?" My words echoed in the silence of the empty walls.

"I -" hesitated the agent. "I'll have to check in the file. If you're interested in the property, that is."

I thought it safer to change the tack.

"Can I see the workroom downstairs?"

I got an uncanny idea that she had anticipated my question. As though it were the most natural thing in the world to view the basement rather than the ocean.

The chimney did indeed start in the basement. What's more, there was a furnace in the large base of the conical stone structure.

"How is it possible that smoke from down here doesn't fill up the living room through the fireplace?" I enquired.

The agent shrugged. "I'm not too sure. But if you recall, there are absolutely no signs of blackening on the ceilings up there."

Finally she began to sound more like an estate agent. Her voice was bright and encouraging when she opened her eyes very wide and asked, "So, are you considering making an offer?"

And it was right then, in the semi-darkness of the workroom, when suddenly I recalled where I'd seen this house before. You see, I have an almost photographic visual memory. If you need a reliable witness, say for one of those ridiculous line-ups in the movies, I'm your man.

I felt a chill in my spine as I recalled the details. The house had been the scene of a series of cruel murders that had shocked the peaceful New Zealand, a country in which the word "car-theft" doesn't exist and the most serious criminal offence on a Saturday night is a ten-year old driving his passed-out father home. The picture of the house had appeared in the papers just after we'd arrived in our new country and Christine had suffered her back injury. I suddenly remembered what this furnace had been used for, not to mention all the equipment that had once stood in this very room. The news flash had so disturbed me at the time, that I even had recurring nightmares about this house. The same dream over and over again, night after night. I couldn't quite remember the dream, except that it had an unpleasant ending.

I realised three things with a shock.

One, the murderer had never been apprehended. In fact, nobody knew who he - or she - was. Two, the house had been uninhabited and on the market even when they had found... those remains. Three, I didn't know where that atypical agent had suddenly disappeared to, but the furnace was fully stocked with coal.

Overcome with an irrational bout of fear, a more primitive part of me decided to bolt. The sense of relief at making it all the way to the garage without an injury made me reel. The pressure inside my twenty-nine year old chest was unbearable. I frantically struggled to open the garage door with both hands, scrambling to release the latch. The heavy door budged. I squeezed under it and ran over the driveway pebbles, then threw myself into the long grass. My heart was pounding. The agent could be hiding here, too, and I wouldn't see her until too late. I looked over my shoulder, half-expecting something sharp and looming. Get away! Get as far away from this place as possible, preferably to an open area, where I'd stand a chance even if she had a long knife.

Carefully I made my way uphill. I hoped she wouldn't be able to follow my progress from the terrace. But what if she had a gun? Cresting the hill, I would be completely vulnerable to a shot from the house. I froze. I should have remembered this cliff overlooking the sea from my nightmares. Yet here I was again, pinned between a fatal drop and a homicidal estate agent.

There was no other option. I ran down the hill. My back felt like a target on a shooting range. Fortunately, I had the beginnings of a plan.

If I had only an ounce of luck today, the agent would have left her keys in the ignition, the way most New Zealanders do. Especially out here, where there were no other people.

Make that - where there were no witnesses.

I reached her car just in time to see the agent walk down the driveway. She wore a grim, determined expression. Something glinted in her hand. I jerked open the driver's door and fell in, bumping my head on the frame. Good, the keys were in. As I frantically tried to start the unfamiliar car, the agent broke into a run. She was shouting something. She raised her hand....

The engine roared. I ground the stick into first gear. The car lurched forward, wheels screeching. It hit the approaching woman head on. She flew into the air and over the bonnet, crashing heavily into the windscreen before passing overhead.

I braked to avoid the half-lifted garage door. In the rear view mirror, I saw the agent struggle onto her knees.

Adrenaline surging, I put the car into reverse. Aiming straight at the limping figure, I accelerated the car into a high-pitched whine. The body passed sickeningly under the car, lifting it twice, the way a speed hump might have. I took my feet off both pedals, and the car stalled with a shudder.

Oscillating between relief and panic, I got out of the car. Very cautiously, I approached my victim and looked at the crumpled body. Yes, she was clearly dead. And all she'd had in her hand was her gold-rimmed diary. No glinting pistol or even a bread knife.

My mind reeled. How would I explain this to the authorities? I had no idea what the penal codes were in my new country. And I couldn't put Christine through any more upheavals.

Then I remembered where I was. As though I had done all of this before, in a nightmare or in a previous life, I went into automatic.

It was surprisingly easy to drag the body back to the furnace room, stoke up a big fire, and get rid of most of the evidence, including the diary. The driveway had come off relatively unscathed, but I hosed it down nonetheless.

Now all I needed to do was get rid of the agent's car. There were lots of isolated cliffs nearby, overlooking the sea. I drove as far as I could, then got out and shoved.

I stumbled back to the house on foot. My body was aching, my head spinning. I tried to keep my mind on concocting a feasible story. Now I remembered the news bulletin in full. Estate agents. All the victims were estate agents. And the murderer - or were they multiple murderers? - had never been discovered.

Concentrate, I told myself. The agent, my agent, was working on her own, a one-woman business. She would have written my name in her diary, and the diary was no more.

Would she have mentioned me to her family by name? Unlikely.

Of course, she would have told someone - even the police - that she was going to the notorious house and with whom. Except that the viewing had been a spur-of-the moment thing, on our way back from looking at other properties, when I had spotted an overgrown driveway with a "For Sale" sign.

I decided to take my chances. And I decided to buy that house. The house of my dreams.

I turned around for one last glance before the long walk to the nearest town.

It was odd, though. I couldn't shake the impression that my new home seemed extraordinarily pleased with me.

# MAN OR MOUSE

## Chris Blizzard

*Chris Blizzard was born in Michigan but currently resides in Arizona. He is a single father with two teenage boys. He has just finished his first novel. "Man or Mouse" is his second short story and his second published story.*

Sherman and Dan were brothers and my best friends. We did everything together. Sherman was the younger brother and was thin and mouthy. He was good at starting fights and not so good at backing up his mouth. Dan was older, bigger, and tougher. He didn't take lip from anyone.

On one particular day, we just finished smoking a joint next to the river on our way home from school and were headed back to their house for cereal and cartoons. When we got to the top of the railroad bridge that divided Island and Nelson Park, we saw Gimbo. I don't remember his real name. I'm sure he had one, but that was not our concern. What was our concern was that he was walking along and minding his own business. The nerve! Here we are doing our best to catch a buzz, and here he is giving us a casual nod and continuing on his way. It was as if The Rules of Picking on Gimbo didn't apply to him! Our seventh and sixth grade pride and our buzz demanded we fix his casual attitude and remind him that he sucks.

"What's up, Fatboy?" asked Sherman.

"Just walking home," answered Gimbo.

"Why don't you swim home?" asked Dan.

I knew what he was thinking. We all did. Twenty feet below the train bridge we were on ran the Chippewa River. The three of us looked at each other and shared the same thought: *Gimbo plunging into the river from the bridge.*

This was a favorite summer diving platform for us. It was early spring now, and way too cold for swimming, but since it was Gimbo that would be doing the swimming, it seemed like a good idea. Sherman walked towards Gimbo with his fist cocked.

174

"You ARE going in that river!" he bellowed.

"No way, man," came Gimbo's response. Then he stood and froze. Apparently he was not born with a fight or flee gene. He simply stood there and did neither. He really could have used the flight gene. As it turns out, I wish he had it, too.

Dan got in his face and stood there with fists clenched. He pointed at the river and told Gimbo to get out on the ledge. There were two steel cables that separated the walkway from the ledge. Instead of doing anything logical, like running or fighting, Gimbo set down his book filled backpack and climbed through the dangling cables. I really wish he hadn't done that.

"Now jump, motherfucker!" yelled Dan. All three of us stood there with fists clenched and death looks in our eyes.

"No way!" Gimbo shot back. "I could be killed!"

"You're going to be killed if you don't jump!" Sherman responded.

This went back and forth for the next few minutes. Gimbo didn't seem to grasp his inevitable decision. Sherman, growing weary of the senseless banter, proposed a question to Gimbo designed to show him how limited his choices really were.

"Are you a man or a mouse?" asked Sherman. It really was a basic question. There were only two possible answers. It came back to his flight or flee gene. His response was a thing of comedic legend.

"I'm a mouse! I'm a chicken shit! I'm a freak!"

That one sticks with me. He was given two choices. He picked one and added two electives. When he added the *chicken shit* and *freak* options, we lost it. I'll give him this much, he was funny. But funny is funny and joking time ended with that remark.

"Time to get wet, Freak!" I yelled as I went to kick him in. I took a three step approach and telegraphed my kick. He saw my foot coming and made the only decision he could. Either he was going in with a few cracked ribs, or he was going in with some air still in his lungs. But he WAS going in.

He jumped off the bridge backwards. In mid-dive/jump/plunge, he turned to face death. He straightened out his legs and I thought he looked pretty good. Then he bent at the waist. Not just a little either. His body was bent in a ninety-degree angle as his arms pin wheeled. His legs went in the water straight and with his body he did an enormous belly smack. We could hear it from the bridge. It was loud. We all looked at each other and cringed.

"Man, that had to hurt," Sherman said. We all let out a laugh. For Gimbo to jump into that cold water was funny enough, but for him to do a loud belly smack made it hilarious!

175

Then it turned bad. All of our fun ended. The water was flowing strong and clear that day. We could see Gimbo a few feet under the surface doing his best to swim up stream and towards the opposite shore. All he needed to do was swim ten feet to his right and he would be back on land. We would walk down there; call him, a *mouse/chicken shit/freak* and walk away laughing. It was a very simple plan. But Gimbo was trying to swim up stream and towards the other side. Not only that, he was trying to do it under water!

All three of us looked at each other in horror. "He can't even fuckin' swim!" exclaimed Sherman.

"Why didn't he tell us that?" I asked the group. "He would have had a better chance of getting out of this shit with that then he would have with the whole *freak* thing."

"If that fucker drowns," said Dan, "You know we are all going to get blamed, don't you?"

At that, we looked at each other with knowing faces. He was right, of course. Now it was up to us to save Gimbo. The only way to do that would be to jump in.

"No way, man," Sherman, answered the unasked question. "I'm not going in to save his dumb ass."

"What choice do we have?" asked Dan. "If he dies someone might have seen us push him in." That spoke volumes about our character. We could really care less if Gimbo dies, but if we were going to get grounded over this we had to act.

"Who's going in?" Sherman asked. It was a question we all shared. It was obvious that one of us had to jump in the freezing water and drag Dumbass to shore.

"We all go in," I said. "It's the only right way to do this." We exchanged looks that were pleads for someone to speak up and volunteer to do it alone. No one did. "Let's just do it," I finally said.

This got us moving. We climbed between the cable ropes and stood on the ledge. We looked at each other while still hoping that one of us would volunteer to do it alone. Being that we were the same group that had just kicked a fat kid off the bridge for minding his own business, this group didn't have anyone that selfless.

"No one stays!" Dan warned. It was a thought we had all considered. *Hey, why not stay back and let the other two jump?* I had decided to hold back from the jump until I knew they were both going in. On the count of three Dan and Sherman jumped. I was surprised they both did. They turned to me on their way down with hate in their eyes. They were already ten feet under me, so I jumped out far enough to clear them on impact.

I nearly hit Fatboy when I landed. The water felt like ice! It was cold to the point that it pulled the air out of my lungs. My feet touched the bottom of the riverbed and I sprang towards the surface. When I finally reached air, I gasped. I couldn't breath! I had a moment to wonder how Fatboy must feel. The water must have pulled the air out of his lungs as well.

Then he grabbed me by the legs and started to pull me under. I let out a yell and tried to kick him off. It was no use. He was holding on as if his life depended on it! I let out a scream and Dan and Sherman came to my rescue. They both went under and helped Gimbo to the surface. When his head reached air, he coughed out a lung full of water and gasped. He was in a total panic and tried to latch on to all of us. Sherman slapped him hard to bring him under control. It didn't work. Gimbo yelled at us and struggled harder. While the current was pulling us down stream, we worked the victim to the shore. He kept struggling, but that didn't deter our valor. Once we got to where our feet could touch bottom, we let go of Fatass. All four of us walked on to shore.

Gimbo yelled at us, "I could have died you fuckers!"

"Why didn't you tell us you couldn't swim?" asked Sherman. It was a reasonable question. We might have let him go if he would have said that. *I'm a mouse! I'm a chicken shit! I'm a freak!* That was not going to save him. *I can't swim.* That would have at least made us pause.

"I can swim!" Fatass yelled back at him.

We stood there looking at each other with blank expressions. Gimbo looked back at us with what appeared to be genuine anger. Apparently, shoving him off a railroad bridge wasn't enough to upset him, but insulting his backstroke was.

"You call that swimming?" Dan asked in bewilderment.

"I swim under water!" Gimbo retorted.

Despite how cold, pissed, and confused we were, we had to laugh. It was the perfect comeback. Thinking back, that was exactly what he was doing. He was trying to make the opposite shore against the current, under water. The dumb bastard picked an odd topic to get proud on. He was a mouse, a chicken shit, and a freak. But he could swim under water!

"The next time we see you," Dan said, "We are going to kick your ass. And if you are on this bridge, you are going back in, Dickface!"

On that, Gimbo scurried up the hill and back to the top of the bridge. I figured he needed his backpack and then was going home alive and cold.

"This is bullshit!" exclaimed Sherman. Dan and I exchanged quizzical looks.

"What's bullshit?" I asked.

"We just jumped off a bridge into icy cold water to save that fuck. He is alive because of us! Did any of you hear a *thank you*?"

"We'll settle that score the next time we see his dumb ass," I said. "Let's get out of here. I'm freezing!"

"You know what's worse than being wet and cold?" asked Dan.

"What?" Sherman and I asked in unison.

"I lost my fucking buzz!" Dan scowled.

On that we all laughed and headed back to the brothers' house. Their mom was at work so we didn't need to invent a story about all three of us falling in the river. We dried off, smoked some weed, and watched cartoons.

I wish I could say that this was a life-altering event. It may have been for Gimbo; heck, he might have gone on to learn to swim above water, but my life went unchanged. We never pushed anyone else off a bridge, but we never really had the opportunity either. We agreed that if we ever did, we would make sure he could swim first. To this day, when I think about the story, my mind still hears Gimbo pleading: *I'm a mouse! I'm a chicken shit! I'm a freak!*

That memory alone is almost worth the jump. Almost.

# A PIRATE'S CHRISTMAS

## Susan Coppola

*Susan Coppola has been writing since early 2005 and has already been a finalist in five writing contests. She is working on a creative nonfiction book based on the life of Hall of Fame Jockey Joe Notter. You may view her work at www.susancoppola.squarespace.com*

I surfaced from a stormy sleep and stared at the alarm clock. It glowed a turquoise digital message; four-thirty. The air in the room was heavy and stale, smelled of too many spilled beers in too old carpet. Same nightmare, same time, been this way for two weeks now. Every night, a long dark wall looks shiny like it's wet; lots of fog and then she's there, a woman in a trench coat walking along the wall and rubbing it as if she's looking for a secret passage. I walk up behind her, touch her on the shoulder. She turns and it's him, the poor SOB in Danang, the pilot, and I always wake up sucking for breath. I could tell this was gonna be one hellava week in group down at the VA.

Served me right for what I did, but shit everybody did it; scavenge, pirate stuff off of bodies after recovery. My first recovery, I was new in country, new to warfare; didn't know the way things worked, but I found out quick enough. As a Navy SEAL, part of UDT -14 we were sent in to relieve UDT-12, operating out of Danang team headquarters. It was a screaming hot afternoon with streams of heat shimmering off the tarmac like spirits released from purgatory. I was unloading my dive locker.

Our platoon leader, CPO John MacAfee, yelled, "Hey Tank... gotta a dead pilot... overshot the North Island runway, plane's about twenty feet down. Grab someone and go retrieve the body."

Tank McNamara, a veteran frogman, got up and motioned to me with his hairy arm.

"Come on kid, your first search and recovery."

We headed down to the pier, put on our fins, tanks and masks and slipped under the water. I could see the jet sitting on the bottom tangled in reeds. We paddled our way down and found the pilot still strapped in. His head was bent like a lollipop on a soggy stick, his neck probably broken on impact. . The guy's skin was wrinkled and white from being under. His eyes were milky blue. I acted like this was no big deal, but inside I was screaming. I watched McNamara pull out his dive knife, thought he was going to cut the straps and free the body. Instead he started sawing on the guy's finger that was clenched in a fist. In a few clean strokes the finger came free from the hand, McNamara took the man's ring, pocketed it in his wet suit. I was too stunned to do anything but finish the job. I cut the straps and we pulled the body to the surface and then onto the pier. I threw my dive mask off and glared at McNamara

"What the hell did you do down there?" I wanted to deck him, but knew better. He gave me a cold stare and a sly smile.

"Hell, I left his watch." He deadpanned. "Lighten up kid, Welcome to Terry and the Pirates." He threw me the ring. I stashed it in my pocket, and then buried it later in my gear.

I kept my mouth shut for the next six months and learned. Survival was job one. Hell, I joined onto the SEALS as a sort of insurance policy, figured my odds were better in a tight group of elite warriors. I was right. I did two tours, but it wasn't just the training that got me through. Conventional training could only carry you so far in an unconventional war. BUDS and Hell week gave you the endurance and will to survive physically. How to survive mentally? You were on your own with that one. Thank God for Johnny Walker and reds; they kept you from thinking too much. Thinking let fear in. If you thought too much, you'd stop doing it; just quit and join the fleet.

McNamara was one of the hardened SEAL lifers. All heavy drinkers, in Nam they found themselves infiltrated with ex-college jocks that'd been around performance enhancing drugs from their playing days and hippie stuff like acid and pot. We were an odd mix. The drinkers didn't understand the jocks and the jocks didn't trust the drinkers. Hangovers made them slower out of the box. There were no hangovers with pot. I did psychedelics three times in country, bad choice; hell, the place was naturally hallucinogenic. Tripping was just redundant. We struck a happy medium between us when we all settled on Johnny and speed.

We'd get our briefing the night before, share a bottle while we cleaned our weapons, then crash. We'd wake up to another shot, two dexies; then suit up and go. No thinking at all and speed kills a memory as well as booze. After six months of that every night you didn't fit in well anywhere. No where to go but here type of deal.

That's the way they wanted it and the brass looked the other way. Long as you were doing the job nobody cared. Hell, what were they going to do, send us to Viet Nam?

After my discharge in 1970 with a few stops along the way I put my life back together. I kept the ring in my drawer alongside my medals. I'd take it out every Memorial Day and think of the guy who wore it. It was his Naval Academy ring, black Onyx with a trident insignia on either side. His initials M.P.M. were etched inside the band. His name was Michael Patrick Murphy. I'd never forgotten it from his transport papers. He was from Boston. After I got back I tried to find his family, but had no luck. Instead I just stashed the loot in my drawer like the pirate I had been.

And then a few weeks ago, after thirty-five years, the dreams started. There had been others before this, other spectral nightmares, but none as real and compelling. The timing was right, too. I was involved in a talk group at the VA. They'd asked some of us Vietnam era vets to come speak to the guys returning from Iraq and Afghanistan, share what we experienced. It was supposed to help them and wound up helping us all in the end.

"Hey, Charlie, How are you?" I walked in the office of Charlie Turk. He was our liaison counselor, worked with all branches of the military, could say he was an equal opportunity nutcracker.

"Fine, Andy. How you doing? Need something?" I liked the man's style, smart and direct. He had helped me dance through a few tangos with terror over the years. I wouldn't trust my brain to anyone else. I got up and closed his door, drowning out the PA system with its garbled announcements and syrupy Christmas music.

"Yeah, got a new screenplay running in my head the past few weeks. I don't care much for this movie. Got something to show you." I reached in the front pocket of my jeans and laid the ring on his desk.

"What's this?" Charlie picked it up, started examining it.

"Something that needs to be laid to rest." I told him everything, the recovery, McNamara, the dream. When I finished he got up and went over to his window like he needed to move away from me.

"And you tried everything to find his family?" He looked stunned, like he'd been blindsided.

"Hell yeah…been to all kinds of military sites on the web, but no luck. You know how many Michael Murphy's there are in Boston? A lot." I answered my own question.

"Give me all the specifics you have. I'll hunt around, see what I can find." I jotted down Michael Patrick Murphy, March 1968;

Danang. I pocketed the ring, then got up to leave. Charlie called to me as I reached the door.

"Hey, Andy, you did good here. Hellava thing to carry around. I'll call you if I find something."

"Thanks Charlie. I appreciate it." I walked down the hall and out the door before the last chorus of "I'll be Home for Christmas" came warbling through the air.

The drive home through late afternoon traffic left me testy and tense. I was happy to get in the door and pop a cold beer. The phone rang as I finished my third one.

"Hello?"

"Hey, Andy, its Charlie. I got some news about your flyboy." It sounded funny Charlie referring to Michael Murphy as "my" anything.

"Yeah shoot. I'm all ears" I smiled to myself. We put a nasty spin to that phrase in the teams, used to take ears and teeth, even scalps after kills as souvenirs. A guy said he was all ears meant that was his preferred part. Like I said nasty, real nasty.

"I located his widow." He paused.

"Shit that was fast; how you do it?" I was surprised.

"Being a bureaucrat has its perks sometimes. I made a few calls and pulled a few strings. I got his social and I tracked her through her widow's benefits. She wants to meet you. Are you okay with that?" Now there was a loaded question.

"Yeah, after all these years how can I not be? What did you tell her?"

"Well I didn't tell her the whole truth. No need to at this point. Just said I had a vet who has her husband's Naval Academy ring."

"What did she say? What she sound like?" I reached in the fridge and popped the tab on another cold one.

"She sounded relieved, like she knew this was coming. She said. 'Oh good, when can I meet him?' Actually kind of weird now that I say it."

"Yeah it is kind of weird. This whole thing is kind of weird, though. So how did you leave it with her? Where we gonna do this hookup?"

"She gave me her number, wants you to call her. She wants to meet you at The Wall in D.C." His last words hit my like a mortar round to the chest.

"Ah fuck… The wall? The memorial? This isn't the Paris Peace Accords. Why can't I just mail it to her?" Charlie's answer nailed me where I stood.

"Because you're her hero, she wants to talk to the soldier who brought her man back home for her. Remember she doesn't have the whole story; thinks you snatched the ring from another guy's gear to protect Michael's honor."

"Thanks Charlie, for giving me respect I didn't earn, but I will now, at least I'm going to try. Give me the number." I jotted it down and hung up. I didn't feel much like drinking anymore. I didn't feel like much of a hero either, but for the sake of Mrs. Michael Murphy I was going to act like one. I picked up the phone and punched her number.

She answered after two rings.

"Hello." Her voice sounded stronger than I'd imagined. I guess the widow thing had my mind going in a wrong direction.

"Hello, Mrs. Murphy. This is Andy McCaren. Charlie Turk told you about me?"

"Yes, sure, and you can call me Karen... Hey, I'm real glad you called. I can't believe you had Mikey's ring after all these years. Can't wait to see it again. I was there the day he got it..." Her voice faded, her mind probably somewhere else, long time gone. Sounded strange to hear her call the guy Mikey, made him more real for me.

"I'm glad, too. Charlie said you wanted to meet at The Wall in D.C.; any special reason?"

I was picturing a person to go with the voice, tall, dark haired, and pale skinned.

"I know this is gonna sound crazy but I've been having this strange dream over and over for the past few weeks and I'm always standing at The Wall where Mikey's name is and this man walks up to me and hands me something. I always wake up before I get to see what it is, but it feels so real. The other day I woke up with my fist clenched like I was trying to hold on to it, bring it back into my waking world or something. See I told you it was crazy. Now tell me Andy... Are you tall and thin with a gray beard and long shaggy hair, kind of like an old timber wolf?"

I pulled the phone away from my ear, like it had stung me and stared at it in disbelief. It took a lot to rattle me, but this stranger, the wife of a dead pilot from over thirty-five years ago had been seeing me in her dreams.

"Oh God... I think we got to go there, to The Wall I mean. When you want to meet? I live outside Baltimore. I can drive up in an hour." I walked over to the freezer and pulled out a bottle of Absolut. I needed a drink, not a beer.

We made plans to meet the following Monday. I'd never been, never wanted to. I'd battled my demons and moved on, or so I thought until this latest dream. And then it hit me, my dream, and the image of a woman at a long wall. I'd dreamed it all, now I was going to live it.

I got into D.C early Monday morning, checked in and took a cab over to the memorial. She was waiting for me at the East Wall. She had on a long tan trench coat as I knew she would. She was smaller than I'd imagined, but walked with a quiet strength about her like she had answers to questions that nobody asked. Her hair, pulled back in a pony tail, was a rich brown streaked with gray. The weather was bitter cold and felt like snow with dark heavy clouds hanging low in the slate colored sky.

She walked right up to me. "Mr. McCaren?"

"Mrs. Murphy?" I put out my hand. She reached up and hugged me tight.

"Thank you for coming. Wow, you look just like I dreamt you." She let go and started smoothing down the front of my jacket with trembling hands. I let my head drop, weighted down by shame then we turned, facing The Wall. It was all decked out for the holidays with wreaths, ribbons and flags. A flow of people, some hushed, some talking quietly, and some crying, walked trancelike in front of us; their images reflecting back off the sleek black granite surface. I reached in my jacket pocket, pulled out a ball of tissue paper and handed it to her. She opened it and began to cry.

"I told myself I wouldn't do this. After all these years you'd think it'd get easier." She fumbled in her coat pocket, came out with a tissue and wiped her eyes.

"I guess some things aren't meant to be easy." I took her hand. "Come on, will you go up with me? I've never been."

"Of course." We walked up. I looked at my reflection in the polished black stone. I touched the name of Michael Patrick Murphy and rested my head against the cold tomblike surface. The tears started to flow along with the memories and like a kayaker shooting the rapids I was just along for the ride now, trying to hang on. Karen rubbed my back. When I turned away from the etched testimony to so many lost lives and dreams I saw it had started snowing and I knew this pirate had finally made it all the way home.

# SHORT TIMER

## Warren Jamison

**Second Prize – contest of December 2006**

*Warren Jamison has written, coauthored or ghosted more than three million words in forty-five nonfiction books, one-third of them issued by major publishers. "Short Timer" is his first success in fiction.*

It's really unfair, the fix I'm in. The only murder I ever did happened when I was only nine years old. Knife stab below the belt. Not a planned thing—it just happened. I'll bet a smart lawyer could squeeze it into self defense or find some other BS way to get me off. Never came to that. If it had, there wouldn't have been money for a smart lawyer.

Now I'm a short-timer, real short—tomorrow's the day. I've been a short-timer before, in 'Nam. Only way I can handle what went on over there is to pretend like it happened to another person. Sometimes that even works.

Funny thing about time. When you want it to go fast, it drags; when you want it to go slow, it races. That's what it's doing now, racing.

The thing I hate most about this whole business is that I've never had what I've always wanted most—to be part of a family with mother, kids and a father who would take care of us because he loved us. I could be one of his kids—but that card wasn't in the deck when I was little. Later I could have created the family—settled down with a good woman and raised some kids right—but I thought I had plenty of time.

So I'm going to spend the night writing my story. I finished my dinner—a really good one—exactly what I wanted. So I have all night to get my story down on paper—what I'll be doing tomorrow doesn't call for alertness. But it's important to me to tell you exactly why that fatal stab below the belt happened because I don't want

185

people to think I'm a bad person, even though they call me Blake the Snake. That tag got hung on me for no reason except it rhymes.

I was always hungry as a kid, not ambitious hungry—I had the worst kind of hunger, for food. In those days I mostly thought about food, and how to get enough of it.

You grew up on three squares a day, didn't you? Probably only got hunger-cranky when your parents took you on a long drive to Disneyland and the peanuts ran out. So maybe you don't understand the real hunger I grew up with. It's not something you learn from a book. Sure a TV flash of bony faces and bloated bellies on kids in Africa will show how starvation looks, but not how it feels. The only way you can get to know the gut-wrenching agony of real hunger is to go to the near edge of it yourself. That's a lesson you don't need, and I hope you never learn it.

I know that welfare is a dirty word to some well-fed folks, but not to me. Say welfare and I see skinny little kids eating. Mom's scant earnings mostly went to pay the rent because you can't steal rent. But you can steal food, and we all did. It was steal or starve, not a hard choice to make is it?

Get a job? Oh yeah. Where we lived most of the men had no jobs and would jump at any chance to make a few bucks working. Hey, I was hungry as far back as I can remember.

We used to go to this little deli a few blocks from where me and my three half-sisters lived with Mom. My Dad? Mom was always vague about him so I guess he was like the other guys who were my mother's downfall. Mom is a wonderful person but she always hooks up with boozer-losers. She would put up with a lot from the men who floated in and out of our lives but she wouldn't stand for them messing with us kids.

We had a cold-water flat in Chicago's worst neighborhood—in a grimy brick building on a grimy brick-paved street. Back then I thought the whole world was grimy brick.

Hugo, the guy who owned the deli gave us food for doing little jobs around his store. I was in there a lot with my friend, Mike. We'd carry out trash and wash windows while Hugo handed us things to eat. But I was leery of Hugo; there was something wrong about him. Already I knew there are a lot of bad creeps in the world. One day Hugo comes into the restroom where I'm cleaning the toilet and tries to molest me.

Hugo was drunker than usual so he was slow. I managed to kick him where it really hurts and broke away. Mike and I ran out of the deli. Kids in my neighborhood never thought of going to the cops with anything. And I was too ashamed to tell Mom. Dumb, huh? It's not like I had done wrong.

A few months later me, Mike, and a couple other kids were across the street from Hugo's Deli. It was hot; we were thirsty. We wanted to buy some cold drinks, and we had a dollar. We stood there looking at Hugo's for a long time. Nobody wanted to go in and get some Cokes because we all knew how Hugo was around boys.

Somehow I got volunteered. I remember walking across the brick street. It was dusty because it hadn't rained for a long time. You've heard of the asphalt jungle; back then ours was a brick jungle. Dreary brick-paved streets between drab brick buildings where nobody except strangers to hope lived.

The sun's brightness had no sparkle; just made it hotter, drier, and dustier. Along with my fear of going into Hugo's, I remember the sour dry smell of the dust.

The door was open but it was dark inside, black actually, because I came out of the glaring sun and the lights were off. For several seconds I couldn't see anything. Talk about scared! I was all alone in the dark den of the molester. But when you're nine, your eyes adjust fast.

I call out, "Hello, anybody here?"

Dead silence.

I walk around the store, stuffing candy bars in my pockets. Yeah I was stealing food because I was hungry and my friends were too. I keep walking around the store, moving slowly so I won't trip over something and make a racket. Now I'm really scared because not only am I deep in Hugo's lair, I've been stealing from him, and the proof is in my pockets. I keep looking at the light coming from the doorway, making sure I got a clear path to run the hell out of there.

I walk around behind the counter where he kept a tray used as cash register. I feel for money and jam some bills in my pocket. Of course I know it's wrong to steal, but what's the worst crime, letting kids go hungry, or stealing food? Thing is, I knew I'd be hungry tomorrow and so would my sisters.

Behind the counter I'm close to the butcher's block where Hugo chopped meat. His big knife gives off a faint gleam in the dimness. It's a wicked thing, sharp edged and pointed. I pick the knife up, intending to drop it by the door when I run out, but I'm still a scared little kid, standing there in the dark, all my senses boosted to fear-driven sharpness. My nose picks up a variety of odors, some of candy's sweetness, more of sour sweat. Even tonight I can almost taste the funky sweet-sweaty stench of that place.

187

I hear a sound behind me like someone moving and whirl around as a shape comes at me. I opened my mouth to scream but nothing came out. I know it's Hugo. The thought of what he would do impaled me like a gigantic icicle slammed into my gut. Without thought—I stab hard at the shape and jump back. If there was a sound from the shape I don't remember it. Dimly I saw the shape fall back across the chopping block.

Now I'm so scared I can't move. Just stand there, not a cell in my brain working. Seems like a long time passed but it probably wasn't more than a few seconds. I hear a gushing sound. I don't think I saw it but somehow I knew human blood was flowing off the butcher's block and spilling on the floor. Terror keeps me rooted to the spot.

I hear ghostly breathing from the butcher's block. He's alive!

No, the breathing sound comes from further away. With the leopard's vision of terror I make out Hugo slumped on a couch about ten feet from me. His mouth is open in the stupor of drunkenness I've often seen on men in the neighborhood. Guys that far gone don't know where they are, don't know whether they're alive or dead. Most importantly, Hugo doesn't know I'm there.

Blood keeps dripping off the butcher's block. A sudden urge to run hits me and I'm out of there like a rifle shot. My friends waiting across the street race away with me, all of us going like cats with dogs snapping at their tails.

A block or two away from Hugo's Deli we stop running because our throats are unbearably dry. We buy soda pop from another store. When we go outside to drink it, I tell my friends how dark and scary Hugo's Deli was. Nothing more. Even then I knew the best way to keep a secret is to tell nobody.

After a while we heard sirens go by toward Hugo's. We walked back to see what the commotion was. Nobody paid any attention to us.

Something was carried out on a stretcher; covered from head to foot by a blanket. Right behind came Hugo, handcuffed and too blind drunk to know or care what was happening. The cops shoved Hugo in the back of a squad car and roared off.

Open and shut case, right? Drunk found passed out a few feet from his stabbed-to-death wife. An officer had picked up the bloody knife on the floor near the body. Fingerprints? The cops rarely bothered, certainly not in obvious cases in that neighborhood where stabbings and shootings went down almost every day.

Hugo and his wife had been drinking vodka and chocolate milk all night and into the morning, I learned later. Much later I heard that

Hugo was convicted of second-degree murder and got a long sentence. The low-life deserved what he got even though he wasn't sent up for his real crimes against kids. My part in what had happened wasn't the kind of thing I wanted to tell my mother; she already had enough worries. In fact, I've never told anyone before now.

Far as I know, Hugo's wife was just a harmless drunk, so I've carried the burden of her death all my life. She was dead for no reason but nobody cared; people in our part of town had energy for very little beyond their daily fight to survive. If someone didn't— tough.

Before I was old enough to steal food on my own, we lived on what Mom could get hold of one way or another. Our landlords lived above us; they always had eggs. Mom would go in their flat when they weren't home and take a couple three eggs. She'd mix them with a potato and make a pretty good meal for us kids.

One time I was out in the hall when Mom came down from the landlord's flat with some eggs in her apron. Just then the woman who lived in the other flat above us started up the stairs. Mom let go of the apron and raised her hand in greeting. I saw the eggs fall. "There goes my dinner," I thought. I can still see those eggs falling.

Lots of times we didn't lose dinner because we didn't have any to lose. I got real sick about this time, and somehow Mom got hold of enough money to take me to a doctor. He examined me and told Mom, "There's nothing wrong with this kid except he's starving. Feed him or he'll die." That doc was a good man; he wouldn't take any money; said Mom should use it to buy food.

People throw a lot of good food away in this country. For anybody except a little kid, it's not hard to keep from starving if you're willing to work at it a little. Go to the back of restaurants until you find somebody willing to give you food if you'll help do his greasy job. So I'd beg some here, work for food there, and if all else failed, steal.

When I turned eleven, I started earning money and from then on I not bought my own food, and I saw to it that my sisters ate regular too. This wonderful change came about because I started hanging around a used car lot run by the Mafia. I did little things for them like washing cars. They'd give me a few bucks, send me out for cheeseburgers, and let me get one for myself.

Before long, I had a steady job as a lookout. They ran a poker game in the upstairs office. When someone showed up to look at cars, I'd press a buzzer and one of the wise guys would come down to handle the customer.

At about this time I saw another opportunity. A different gang had vending machines all over. They were legit if you don't count the way they got rid of competition and skimmed the profits. Every week a fat, tough-looking little guy called Wingy would go around and collect the money from the vending machines.

Wingy always got to each machine at the same time every week. Afterwards, he'd park his car in the same spot while he had his mid-afternoon coffee and pie. He always went to the same little diner where he could see who came and went in the alley leading to the parking lot behind the diner.

He always parked beside a storm drain—one of the concrete-lined channels that cut through town. Across the channel, one big old tree still stood. Some kids tied a rope to one of the tree's branches, and if you climbed to the right place, you could swing almost across the channel.

I practiced early in the morning when Wingy was never there and I could be sure nobody would see me. Over time I worked up to where I could sail over the channel and land near Wingy's parking spot. A stub of rebar sticking up from the channel's concrete wall allowed me to tie the rope so it would be there when I needed it.

One day Wingy parked as usual and hurried into the diner, his mind on the pie he was there for. Soon as he was inside, I swung over the channel, reached into his car, grabbed the leather satchel he kept his collections in, and sailed back across the channel. Before Wingy discovered the impossible had happened, I was giving the money to Mom. It was a bit over two hundred dollars, a fabulous sum to us at the time. In today's money it would be more like two thousand.

Mom said, "Where'd you get all this money?"

"Better you don't know. Hide it."

She did, and spent it wisely—slowly and carefully, buying food in different markets.

Wingy's boss blamed him. After Wingy got out of the hospital a few months later he walked with a bad limp. The Mafia guys also had people on the street watching for anybody who was suddenly rich.

I did crap like that until I was eighteen. Then I got a job as a driver/bodyguard for a beefy old guy who had a piece of the action in a Las Vegas casino. Every midnight—on the dot—he and a bunch of other guys showed up in a back room at the casino to get their slice of the skim. It was done very fast; anybody who wasn't there had his share split among the others.

After a year on that boring job, I got interested in going to college. The army would pay for it if I enlisted. which is how I got to

Vietnam. When I came home I gave college a year and then sort of lost interest. Dumb choice.

Then I fell in with three guys who knocked over banks in California. After I got the picture of how vicious those guys were, I pulled back.

Me and my girlfriend were lying beside the pool at a Lake Tahoe motel one summer day when all of a sudden we're surrounded by a dozen cops pointing guns at us. Turns out the bank robbers I knew had messed up a job in Los Angeles real bad. Cop got shot dead. They all said I had been the shooter. I'd been in Lake Tahoe, hundreds of miles from the bank when it happened. Didn't matter. My girlfriend's testimony might have saved me, but she took off like she'd been fired out of a cannon.

She also took off with all my money, so the only lawyer I could get was a public defender. He advised me to plead guilty and throw myself on the mercy of the court. I'm not that dumb. But I got convicted of first degree murder anyway. That's my story, and now I'm so sleepy, I can hardly keep my head up.

*We found these pages when we came for Mr. Blake. We had to wake him up for his short walk to the long sleep.*

*—James Henry Hardin, Correction Officer, San Quentin Prison, California*

# AN UNCONDITIONAL LOVE

## Dawn Wilson

*Dawn Wilson is from Connecticut and now lives in Milan, Italy, where she teaches and tutors English as a second language. She thanks her five children – Courtney, Alex, Collin, Emily and Molly – for being her "biggest fans," along with Del for his constant encouragement.*

"Bev! Oh my God, Bev!" He ran down the stairs as quickly as he possibly could to where her body lay lifelessly on the entryway floor. As he reached her, he carefully turned her over, and noticed that her neck appeared to be broken. There was also a large gash on her forehead from where she had hit it on the entryway table when she had fallen. "Oh Bev," he sobbed as he cradled her in his arms. He gently laid her back onto the floor, and after taking his jacket from the coat rack, he rolled it into a ball and placed it under her head. As much as he hated to leave her lying there by herself, he knew that he had to call an ambulance. "I'll be right back, sweetheart," he said softly, even though he was fairly certain she was unable to hear him.

He went into the kitchen, reached for the phone and quickly called 911. "This is Henry Fallon. I live on 246 Peach Tree Lane," he stammered into the phone.

"I'm sorry sir, but if you can, please try to compose yourself. I'm having difficulty trying to understand you," replied the police officer on the other end of the phone.

Henry took a deep breath before continuing. "I'm sorry, officer...but it's my wife. She fell down the stairs ...and now she's just lying there..." his voice broke off as he began to sob.

"It's okay, sir. Try to remain calm. We'll have someone there as quickly as possible, but just be careful not to move her."

"You don't understand. I can't feel a pulse and she has a large cut on her forehead. I think she might be..." and he stopped. He was unable to bring himself to say the words.

"Okay, sir. I understand. We'll be there as soon as we possibly can." Henry stood there motionless for a few seconds before hanging up the phone.

As he walked back to the entryway, he stood over his wife, looking for some sign of life. If it weren't for the gash on her forehead, she almost looked as though she was sleeping. He slowly lowered himself to the ground and placed a thumb on each of her eyelids, gently prying them open. "Bev?" He whispered, but as he looked at her eyes, he was certain she was dead. "Don't worry, Bev. I'll stay here with you until the ambulance comes," and he watched as her face became wet with his tears.

They had known one another since they were just kids and had attended school together. He had loved her even then. He was two years older than she was and he had waited until her sixteenth birthday to ask her out on a date. One date had turned into several, and before they knew it, they were an item. While she had been in her last year of high school, he had enlisted in the service, and before leaving for Korea, he had asked her to marry him when he returned. She had said yes and promised to wait for him, but six months before he returned home, she had sent him a letter, telling him she was marrying somebody else. It had nearly killed him at first, but in time, he adjusted, and he returned home a town hero, having been decorated with a Purple Heart.

He had never married, although he came close a few times, and ten years after he returned from Korea, he had learned from his sister that Bev had been divorced for well over a year. He took it as a sign and called her, asking her out to dinner. When he saw her after all the years that had gone by, he thought she was even more beautiful than he had remembered, and in a short time, they had become very close. She had two little girls that he simply adored, and it was obvious how they felt about him. Less than a year later, he had asked her to marry him, and she had said yes. Although he had been head over heels in love with her, he had known clearly the reason for her acceptance, and it had had nothing to do with love. She had liked what he had been able to offer her and her girls. Henry had always been level headed, a hard worker and a good provider. But he was crazy about her, had lost her once and wasn't about to let it happen again.

Life with Bev had been extremely difficult almost right from the very beginning. She had controlled every instance of their life together and was always the final decision maker. Henry had worked hard six days a week before semi retiring and sometimes twelve-hour days. Sunday had customarily been his day off, but Bev had always made certain Henry kept himself busy. Henry had been a carpenter and a good one, too. When he wasn't at work, or fixing their own house, Bev had him doing side jobs for other people. It had saddened him to never be at home in the beginning, especially when the girls were growing. He had wanted to be real father to them, but he was grateful because he knew that they loved him and treated him as though he was their real father, so he rarely complained.

There were many things about Henry's life that upset him. He had been a man with many interests. He had skied, fished, hunted and enjoyed boating and scuba diving, but Bev had made sure that there was no time for hobbies or leisure activities. They had never taken a vacation together, unless it was over a Labor Day weekend, and it had always been some place that Bev had chosen.

And then there had been the other men in Bev's life. At one point, she was even seeing her ex-husband. It had hurt him to know that people were laughing at him behind his back. He had left her a few times, but had always come back because of his love for her, and eventually had decided to look the other way. They had argued a great deal of the time, and once he had had more than he could take and had given her a beating, which had landed her in the emergency room for a few hours. After that, he had vowed to never touch her again, no matter how angry she made him.

As far as their intimate life, there was none. They had now been married for over forty years, and he couldn't remember the last time they had made love or even held one another, but he knew that it had been more than fifteen years. Fifteen years ago, they had retired to South Carolina and not once since they had been living there had they even so much as slept in the same bed. They had separate bedrooms right from the very beginning.

After moving to South Carolina, Bev had mellowed somewhat, and Henry had assumed it was because of the milder weather. Although they fought less, there was still no real closeness between them. Bev had her own life and her own friends, most of whom were widowed. They would often go shopping together and stop for lunch, and every few months or so, she would go away for a few days on some trip they had planned, which was usually a gambling excursion. It had upset Henry at first, as Bev never wanted to spend her free time with him, but as the years passed, he adjusted, just as he had adjusted to everything else Bev tossed his way.

Although he was seventy-two years old, he had worked until a little over a month ago, doing maintenance at an animal theme park, but it had been something he had enjoyed, and it had seemed like a vacation compared to the work he had done when they had lived in Pennsylvania. Up until four weeks ago, he had worked from eight o'clock until four, Monday thru Friday, and had punched out everyday at noon for an hour to have lunch. He enjoyed the work, he liked the people and although the pay wasn't much, they offered a health insurance plan, which had become extremely important, especially in recent months. Reporting to work everyday had given him a sense of purpose and made him feel needed. And for once, he was able to enjoy himself again, even if it had been without Bev. He had bought a small boat and fished on the lake, and had been on a bowling team with some of his friends from work. He had a dog, and although Sam didn't make up for what Bev didn't give him, when Henry returned home from work each afternoon, Sam would run to the gate, wagging his tail to greet him. Henry would go into the house and say hello to Bev, grab a cold beer and a few dog biscuits for Sam, and he and his dog would sit outside together in the backyard, where Henry would listen to the radio.

Dinner was always at six o'clock, and twenty minutes before dinner, Henry would go in to the house to shower. Once dinner was finished, he'd go back outside with another cold beer and sit with Sam, or do some work in the backyard until it got dark. At about nine o'clock, he would retire to his room and sit in a chair to watch some TV, and when he began to nod off, he'd climb into bed, but not before saying goodnight to Bev, who sat in the den watching television. Every evening was the same, except for Wednesdays, as that had been Henry's regular bowling night. The following morning, he'd be up early and pretty much do the same thing all over again, although he never complained. But the weekends were sometimes a bit different, as that was when Henry would go to the lake and think while he spent his mornings fishing. Although he had asked Bev several times in the past to come with him, she always refused, so he eventually stopped asking. In recent months, the lake had become even more important to Henry, as it gave him the time he needed to be alone to think and make plans for the future.

You see, in recent months, Henry had been diagnosed with cancer. Although initially the doctors had been optimistic, they had never given him any guarantees, and now, eight months later, the cancer had spread. He had done everything the doctors had suggested, including chemotherapy, but to no avail …he was dying. But the amazing thing was he continued to work because he knew how important the insurance was, and when he was gone, he didn't want to leave Bev with a pile of bills. He tried to carry on as though everything in his life was normal, but he silently watched himself waste away, as did those around him.

Although Henry was seventy-two years old, prior to the cancer no one would have guessed it. He was in excellent shape, and was a handsome man, but in recent months, the cancer had eaten away at him, and he had become extremely thin. When he looked at himself in the mirror, what he saw were two huge brown eyes staring back that seemed too large for his face, and the once muscular body was far too thin. His clothes now seemed several sizes too large, and it reminded Henry of a boy trying on an older brother's hand me downs that he hadn't quite yet grown into. Bev had told him on several occasions to go out and buy new clothes, but Henry had never bothered, because he quite simply saw no point to it. Finally, one day Bev had taken matters into her own hands. She had returned home from a shopping trip with her friends, and had thrust a bag at him. When Henry had looked inside, he had been surprised to find four pairs of new pants along with several t-shirts. He had smiled and thanked Bev, but it hadn't taken him long to understand why she had bought them. It had been to save her from embarrassment on the rare occasion that they should happen to be seen together. Even now, Henry tried to be upbeat, but inside he knew that he couldn't run from the truth. He was declining rapidly and there wasn't much he could do about it.

Although Bev had always been cold toward Henry, she had now become even worse. She snapped at him constantly, and when he was unable to do things that he had previously done, he often saw a look of disgust on her face. One day after lunch, Henry had caught her adding bleach to the water in the sink before washing his dishes. Another time he had watched as Bev wiped off the telephone after he had finished talking on it. Henry had laughed, and asked if she thought what he had was contagious, but Bev hadn't bothered to answer. She just continued with what she had been doing, as though Henry hadn't spoken a word.

In recent months, work had been kind to Henry. He was well liked, and it had hurt his co-workers to see him deteriorate before their eyes, so they had made sure that they had given him less strenuous things to do, but they had continued to treat him in the same way. They had known that Henry had a lot of pride, and they hadn't wanted to do anything to injure it. Last month, Henry had had an accident. He had been leaving work and had driven his car into a tree on company property. Henry had said he didn't know what had happened, but the truth was he had blacked out for a few seconds. His supervisor had called Bev and had asked her to come and pick Henry up. It was just a short drive and months back Henry could have easily walked home…but not on that day. He had hated that Bev had to come drive him home, but he had had no other choice. She had come into the office and had talked politely to Henry's boss, but once in the car she had treated Henry scornfully, belittling him and had demanded that he give her his keys. He had started to offer an excuse, but had quickly backed down, as he hadn't the strength to fight back...especially with Bev.

A few days later, he had returned to work, but Henry's doctor had advised him to stop working altogether after he had become dizzy and fallen. Although Bev hadn't said much, Henry knew she was angry, and she now treated him as though he was a stranger in his own home, so he spent most of his days outside, with Sam tagging along for company. He couldn't stand to listen to Bev as she talked on the phone, complaining to friends about this bill and that, and wondering what they were going to do with no insurance, now that Henry was no longer working. He especially hated it when the mail was delivered, as he would have to listen to Bev as she ripped open the bills and wondered aloud, how she was going to pay what Medicare wouldn't cover. It made Henry angry to hear Bev talk like that. They had a beautiful home, and several insurance policies, and money in the bank. He had made sure years ago that she would be well taken care of in the event of his death, but it never seemed enough for Bev.

Last weekend, he knew it would be his last time at the lake. He had become too weak in recent days to continue to go alone, and he knew asking Bev to take him was out of the question. He had thought about killing himself that day...but he knew if they discovered he had taken his own life, Bev wouldn't be able to collect the money from the policies they had. So, he came up with another plan.

As he bent down to hold Bev for one last time, he heard the ambulance off in the distance. "They're almost here now, sweetheart. You don't have to worry anymore. I've taken care of everything." Gently, he touched the cut on her forehead. "I hope that you didn't have too much pain from your fall, and I'm sorry if I pushed you too hard. I just had to be sure that everything went as I planned." Henry turned at the sound of the doorbell, and looking back at Bev, lowered his head and softly kissed her cheek. "They're here now. I love you Bev and you'll see. It won't be long before we're together again. I think the police officers will understand when I tell them why I had to do what I did. Surely they'll be able to see how much I love you. I just couldn't let you live worrying the way that you have."

Henry slowly got up from the floor, and before opening the door, he looked back at Bev, and smiled a sad yet grateful smile.

Finally, he had been able to show Bev how much he loved her. Yes…
surely the police officers would understand…he was certain.

# YOU'RE DEAD, MR. COLLINS

## Linda Hudson Hoagland

*Linda Hudson Hoagland is a wife and mother who lives in a small Virginia town where she works in the field of education. Her novel,* The Little Old Lady Next Door, *has been published and is available on the Internet.*

Arnold was astonished when he saw Mr. Collins lumbering up the sidewalk towards him, mainly because he had forced himself to sit through the man's dull funeral just the week before.

"Mr. Collins, is that you?" he asked, forcing the words from his mouth while he squinted from the glare of the setting sun. Arnold held his hand above his eyes to shade them so he could get a better look at what he thought was an apparition.

"What did you say, boy?"

"You're dead, Mr. Collins."

"What's that?"

"Dead."

"Who's dead? What's dead? What are you talking about, boy? You're not making any sense."

"I went to your funeral. Your body was in the casket."

"What funeral are you talking about?"

"Yours."

Mr. Collins reached across the small space between him and Arnold, looking as if he were going to grab Arnold by the shoulders and give him a good shake.

Arnold stepped back quickly. He didn't want a dead body to reach out and touch him. Maybe he wasn't talking to a dead body but a ghost. That's it, the ghost of Mr. Collins walking the streets to find the person who torched his house.

"I'm not dead. You can see that I'm not dead."

"Yes, sir."

"If I'm not dead, how could there have been a funeral?"

"I don't know, but there was one. There weren't very many people there. I didn't see a single person shed a single tear in the whole place. The only family in attendance was a nephew from out of town."

"What nephew? I don't have a nephew."

"Mr. Collins? Is that you, really you?"

"Don't be stupid, boy."

"But, I went to your funeral?"

Mr. Collins looked at Arnold and saw the sincere confusion and fear etched onto his round, sheet-white face.

"Arnold, let's go to my house and you can tell me all about this funeral and how I died."

"Your house has been burned down. They found your body inside. That's why I went to your funeral. You are dead."

"Well, let's go look at where my house used to be standing, Arnold. I haven't seen it yet. I just got back into town."

"I don't know, Mr. Collins. What if somebody sees us?"

"Okay, what if somebody sees us? I didn't die. They are going to have to know sometime or another," he said, as Arnold started to back away from him again. "Arnold, it's really me. I'm not dead and I'm not a ghost."

Arnold was a scared, so scared that his fight or flight mode had kicked in and he was getting his nervous feet ready to run.

"Here, touch me. See for yourself," said Mr. Collins as he reached for Arnold.

That was all it took. The outstretched arm with the hand dangling on the end of it. Arnold was running and not looking back.

Arnold was a fifty-year-old man who always found it very difficult to keep a steady job because he was a little slow. Mr. Collins knew that Arnold had problems with thinking things out all the way to the point where he could understand them. Mr. Collins paid Arnold to do little odd jobs for him around his house to keep the poor man in spending money. Most of Arnold's income came from the government in the form of social security disability. That kept him fed and put a roof over his head, but that was about all. There was no extra money from the government whatsoever.

Mr. Collins, his first name was Delbert but not many people knew that bit of information, continued to walk up the main street of town toward his burned out house. At least, Arnold said it was burned out. He had returned from a bus trip that had taken him to the Veterans Administration Hospital about a hundred and fifty miles away for a check up. He had fought in the Vietnam War and was being bothered with some problems that could have been caused by

Agent Orange, a defoliant that had plagued many of his fellow soldiers.

The hour was getting late and he wanted to see his house, or what was left of it, before it was too dark to get a good look.

The street was quiet, not a soul moving around anywhere. They seemed to have rolled up the sidewalks in this little town to discourage trouble as soon as the nine to five working hours were done. It wasn't like the big city he had just come from where there was always noise and people to be seen.

He continued to walk and look, hoping to see someone, anyone, he could talk to and find out what had happened in the few days he had been out of town.

When he reached the end of the business section, consisting of several store fronts, he made a left turn onto a side street and continued walking down the quiet lane. He passed houses where he saw interior lights shining against the shades and window blinds. The front doors of the houses were closed and the inhabitants were sitting down to dinner or helping the kids do homework or talking on telephones or just plain living the lives of families.

A frown appeared on his face when he thought of family. He had none. He was the last limb on his family tree and it appeared that someone had already eliminated him, if he could believe Arnold.

Another half mile of walking would get him home and into his own comfortable bed.

He smelled something odd. Something had burned. Plastic, wood, paper, he couldn't put his finger on the particular odor.

He continued to walk and worry. Maybe Arnold was right. Maybe his house had burned. But why would they think he was dead, he mused as his steps seemed to become heavier and harder to do.

The closer he got to his destination, the stronger the burnt smell of old fire that wasn't quite finished.

He stared at the large black area that was still smoldering.

His house was gone.

There was yellow police tape across the front of the lot telling him not to enter. He pushed the tape down far enough to climb over it and walked up his sidewalk to what used to be his front door.

He walked around carefully, kicking aside pieces of charred wood, overturning what looked to be slabs of drywall that hadn't crumbled until he touched them, moving God knows what as he looked for something that hadn't burned.

He arrived at another cordoned area that was outlined with yellow police tape. He guessed that was where his body was found.

He didn't disturb anything within that small area. He didn't want to mess up any clues that might have been left that would explain why he died such a horrible death.

He took a step towards where his bedroom had been and felt his foot slip out from under him causing him to fall onto his backside where he landed on what looked like a fallen burned wall that tilted with him throwing him face first into the black, sooty muck and mire. He pulled himself up and wiped at the wet black water running down his face with an equally black and sooty hand.

"Goddam…" he said as he flung his hands to his side waving them in the air to remove any dripping liquid if that was possible.

Suddenly a scream pierced his aggravation with and concentration on his nasty appearance.

"Mrs. Fields, it's me Mrs. Fields – Del Collins. Don't be afraid. It's me Del Collins."

Mrs. Fields ran inside her house and slammed the door, making sure to lock it so no one or no thing could enter her domain.

She ran to her telephone and dialed 911 asking to speak to the sheriff.

"This is the 911 dispatcher. What is your emergency?"

"There is a ghost roaming around the burned out Collins house. Send somebody over here now."

"There is no such thing as a ghost, Ma'am."

"I'm telling you the ghost of Delbert Collins is poking around in the remains of his burned out house. Get somebody over here right now."

"All right, all right, I'll dispatch a deputy right away. What is your name?"

"Betty Fields, I live next door to the burned out mess of a house where Mr. Collins died. I saw his ghost over there. I swear to God I saw his ghost."

"What's the address?"

"1218 Cypress Lane. That's my address. The burned out house is next door to me. Please hurry. I'm afraid to go outside."

"Yes, Ma'am. I've already dispatched the call to a deputy. He should be there any moment. Stay on the telephone with me until you hear him knock at your door."

"Okay, but what can they do about a ghost?"

"I don't know, Ma'am. That is a decision the deputy has to make."

"I see the flashing lights. The deputy is right out front."

"Okay, Ma'am. You can hang up the phone now."

"Thank you," said Mrs. Fields absently as she placed the receiver on its cradle to disconnect her line from the 911 dispatcher.

The deputy did not knock at the door of the Fields house.

"Hey, you!" he shouted at the soot blackened figure poking at the burned site.

"Yes, Deputy."

"Who are you?"

"Delbert Collins."

"Delbert Collins is dead. What's your real name?"

"Delbert Collins."

"What are you doing poking around in this crime scene?"

"This is my house, or this was my house, Deputy."

"Let me see some identification."

Del Collins reached into his back trouser pocket and withdrew an old well worn black wallet.

"Here, see! I'm Delbert Collins."

"Then who did we bury?"

"I don't have any idea."

"You need to go with me to the sheriff's office, Mr. Collins."

"That's fine with me. I need to have some questions answered myself. Before we go, could you go over next door and tell Mrs. Fields that I'm no ghost."

"In due time, Mr. Collins. Right now we need to take a drive," said the deputy as he started walking to his patrol car.

"I'm a mess, if I get into you car I'm going to get it all black and sooty from poking around in the ashes trying to see if I had anything left."

"No problem, Sir. Just get in the car. You can wash up at the sheriff's office."

The deputy kept looking in his rearview mirror as he drove back to headquarters. He doubted what he was seeing. He wanted to make sure the man he put in the back seat was still there when he arrived.

When the patrol car pulled into the parking lot at the sheriff's office, a crowd had formed awaiting the arrival of the dead Delbert Collins.

"Deputy, why are all of these people here?"

"News travels fast in this little town. They are here to see if you are Delbert Collins and they want to see it for themselves. They don't want to take anyone else's word for it."

"Like you, Deputy? You still don't believe I'm the real Delbert Collins and not an imposter or ghost."

"You're dead, Mr. Collins. At least, that's what is written on the death certificate."

"Let's go get this over with. I need some questions answered by the sheriff."

One by one the crowd was gathering size and people were staring with their mouths open in astonishment.

"Del? Is that you?" came a shout from the onlookers.

Delbert Collins turned his head towards the direction of the question.

"Yeah, it's me," he answered not pinpointing the questioner.

"If you don't have business in here, go away," shouted the deputy above of crowd noise.

Most of the onlookers stepped back but no one left the area.

"Deputy, you need to show me where I can wash my hands," said Del as soon as they entered the building.

"Over there, second door on your right," he said as he pointed down the hallway.

Del walked in the pointed direction while the deputy waited for him, standing near the front door to keep out the crowd.

"Let's go see the sheriff, now," said the deputy when Del reappeared with a clean face and hands.

Sheriff Thompson was waiting for them in his office.

"Hi, Tommy," said Del as he entered the office.

"Del, nice to see you're alive and kicking. Have a seat and we'll have a talk," said the smiling sheriff.

"Who did you bury with my name?"

"Who do you think it was?"

"I wouldn't have any idea. Is anybody missing around here?"

"No one has been reported as missing."

"What made you think for sure that it was me?"

"Well, number one was that it was your house. Next, when the body was discovered it was in such bad shape that the coroner wasn't able to confirm the identity. There wasn't even any dental work to compare it to. Sort of left us with nothing else but the idea that it was you."

"I was at the VA Hospital for a check up. I'll give you the doctor's name and the phone number if you need to check it out."

"That would be a good idea, just to cover all the bases," said the sheriff.

"Now that I'm dead, how are you going to make me undead?"

"I'll straighten that out except that you'll need to contact your insurance company so they won't pay your nephew the hundred thousand dollars."

"What hundred thousand dollars? What insurance company? For that matter, what nephew?" snapped Delbert Collins.

"You don't have a nephew?"

"Nope, none that I know of. What's the name of the insurance company?"

"Some place out of New York. I don't remember right off," answered the sheriff. "I guess I'll need to check that out in the file."

"My insurance is for burying only and it's local. Was that used to bury the stranger?"

"No, money was used from your checking and savings for that."

"You're kidding me?"

"No, your nephew showed us the power of attorney and he wrote the checks."

"Do I have any money left?"

"I don't know. You'll probably have to check with the bank."

"My house has burned down and I probably don't have any money. What am I supposed to do now?"

"Is there anyone, family member or friend that you can stay with until this is cleared up?"

"No, not unless you want to put me up, Tommy?"

"Sure, we have an extra room. You can stay with us until we get some answers. I'm sure my wife won't mind."

"Maybe you had better ask her first."

"I will. But she'll say it's okay. But you don't have any clothes or anything?"

"Just what I had with me at the VA Hospital. That's all."

"What are you going to do now?"

"Just walk around and look some more at the black hole where my house used to be."

"If you come back here at five o'clock I'll drive you to the house."

"Okay, can your deputy take me back to the ashes?"

"Sure, no problem. Be back here at five, okay?"

Delbert Collins was driven back to the ashes where he continued sifting through the sooty material remains of his life.

Del searched and sifted but found nothing that could tell him who died in his place or why. He wasn't a wealthy man. Most of the time he just barely got by. He did have a little money in his checking account but he knew that was gone to the nephew he didn't have.

He left the burned out home site and walked to the sheriff's office so he could get a place to sleep for the night. He was too tired to puzzle out the problem of who died and why. He would get some sleep and start over tomorrow, was the last thing he thought before he crumpled to the ground in a big, black, sooty heap.

Usually his short cuts through back yards and alleys got him to where he was going much faster than taking the sidewalk route. That day the shortcut very nearly got him dead - again.

"Mr. Collins? Mr. Collins? Are you all right?" asked a worried Arnold who was hovering over Del, looking directly into his face and pretty near taking all of his breath away.

"Hunh? What? Owww!" said Delbert Collins as he reached for his head.

"Are you okay, Mr. Collins?"

"Arnold, what are you doing standing over me like that? What happened?"

"The sheriff sent me out looking for you. You didn't show up at the jail. He was really worried," said Arnold as he nervously danced around Del.

"How long have I been here?" said Del as he glanced at his watch. "It's after six o'clock. I was supposed to be at the sheriff's office at five."

Del struggled to get himself up off of the ground.

"Let me go get help, Mr. Collins. Your head is bloody. Did you fall or what?" Arnold asked excitedly and every part of his body seemed to twitch and shake at the sight of the blood.

"No, no, Arnold. I didn't fall. Someone knocked me down by hitting me on the head. I don't need a doctor. I just need to get to the sheriff's office. Why don't you walk back there with me, okay?"

"Sure, Mr. Collins. I'll walk with you and – Mr. Collins - uhhh, uhh – Mr. Collins..."

"What is it, Arnold?" Del said as he took a deep breath to bite back the irritation that was trying to surface in his voice.

"About running away earlier, I'm sorry about that, Mr. Collins. But, I went to your funeral and I just knew you were a ghost. Mr. Collins, I'm afraid of ghosts."

"Forget about it, Arnold."

"Who hit you, Mr. Collins?"

"I don't know."

"We're almost there."

"Yeah, I know. I see the sheriff is still waiting for me."

"He said he wasn't going to leave until you were found."

"That's awful nice of him."

Arnold held the door for Del and they both presented themselves to the sheriff.

"Del, what happened? Sit down here. Nancy, get a wet towel," shouted the sheriff to his secretary in the next office.

"Someone hit me over the head. I was walking back here somewhere between four and four-thirty. I took a shortcut through the back yards and alleys. Near the Smith back yard, that's where it happened. I don't have any idea who did it. I didn't see a soul."

"What about you, Arnold? Did you see anybody?"

"No, I didn't see no one, sheriff," answered a concerned Arnold as he emphasized his negative answer with the shaking of his head.

"Del, do you know of a reason someone might want to hurt you?"

"No, I don't bother anybody. I keep to myself and mind my own business."

"Do you think you need to go to the emergency room to have you head checked out? It looks like you've wiped away most of the blood with that wet towel."

"No, I don't want to see no doctor. I just want to take a hot shower and lay down for a while."

"Let's get in the car and I'll drive you to my house where you can do that except that you will eat dinner first."

"That's fine, Tommy. I am a little hungry after I think about it."

The sheriff pulled his wallet from his back pocket and extracted a ten dollar bill.

"Here, Arnold. Thanks for finding my friend for me."

Arnold's eyes brightened as he reached for the money.

"You take this money and go on home. It's too late for you to be running around. Go home and watch TV, okay?"

"Sure, Sheriff, and thanks," said Arnold as he walked with the sheriff and Del out the front door of the office.

Very few words were exchanged between Tommy and Del as Tommy drove them both to his home. Upon arrival at the house, Del was welcomed warmly by Adele Thompson, the sheriff's lovely wife.

"Let me show you where you can clean up, Del. I'll get some of Tommy's clothes for you to wear. You and he are about the same size. Close enough anyway. When you're ready, we'll sit down to a warm, belly filling meal."

Del stood under the warm fingers of water spraying from the shower head and tried to think about what had happened to his life within the last twelve hours. The actual time span for the events might have been longer, probably more like a week, because that was how long he had been away from home. The twelve hour span covered the time period he had lived through, and almost died, since he had come home to the black, burned out house where he had spent many years of his life.

"The nephew, it's got to be the nephew. I've got to find out who that is."

He finished his shower, dressed, and raced downstairs to tell Tommy.

"Does anybody know anything about my so-called nephew?"

"No, not really. I guess we could check with the insurance company. I have the name of the New York company in my file at the office."

"I need to find him. He's got to be the reason all of this is happening to me."

"You're probably right, Del."

"Was there anything in the paper about me dying?"

"Sure, an obituary, I have a copy of it over here. I also have the little printed card they handed out at the funeral. You could have that, too," said Adele as she handed the items to Del.

"It says his name is Jerry Collins. That would mean he would have to be the son of my nonexistent brother, wouldn't it?"

"Sure does," answered the sheriff.

"I'll do some checking with some family members from another branch of the family tree since my branch dies with me. Maybe there was another Delbert Collins, which I sincerely doubt, that really does have a nephew named Jerry Collins."

"You can do that tomorrow. Right now it's getting late and I'm sure you would like to go to bed," said Adele was she stood to leave the room.

"That's a great idea. Good night and thank you to both of you for lending me a helping hand."

Del tossed and turned through the night. His mind was exploring possibilities and his overactive imagination wouldn't let him rest.

The morning finally arrived after he had worn himself out again with his attempt at sleeping.

"Ezra Collins, please?" Del said into the telephone loudly.

"Who are you?"

"Delbert Collins. Ezra is my cousin on my daddy's side."

"You're dead, Mr. Collins," said a sarcastic voice on the other end of the telephone conversation. "Who is this really?"

"I'm Delbert Collins and I ain't dead. Now, let me speak to Ezra," demanded Del, as he was losing his battle to remain calm, cool, and collected.

"I don't think I should. Who is this?" whined the unknown person.

"If you don't let me talk to Ezra, I'm coming there and wrapping the phone cord around your neck. I'm going to pull the cord so tight that you're going to fall over dead while you're clutching that phone. Now put him on the phone!"

"All right, all right, but don't get him upset. You hear me. Don't upset him."

There was a pause as the female, whoever she was took the necessary steps to place the telephone receiver in Ezra's hand. Ezra was about eighty years old give or take a year or two. He was hard of hearing and you really had to yell at him to get him to understand you at all. It was best the talk to him face to face but Del didn't want to take the time to do that.

"Hello?"

"Ezra, this is Delbert. I need to ask you some questions."

"Who'd you say?" asked a weak, old voice.

"Delbert, you know, Martha and Clay's boy."

"Somebody told me you were dead. Millie told me you were dead and you were buried a few days ago. Millie, didn't you tell me Delbert Collins was dead?" he asked his care giver.

Del could hear a barely audible affirmative reply.

"Yeah, yeah, she said he died. Now, who is this?"

"It was a mistake, Ezra. Somebody else died in that house fire. It wasn't me. Honest Ezra, I'm still alive and kicking and I want to know what the hell is going on. Can you help me?"

"I don't see how?"

"Is there anyone else in our family anywhere that has the name Delbert Collins or Jerry Collins?"

"You're the only Delbert I know of. You say you didn't die in the fire?"

"Of course not. You wouldn't be talking to me if I was dead."

"Yeah, that's right, isn't it?"

"What about Jerry Collins? Do you know Jerry Collins?"

"Let me think about that for a minute."

"It's real important, Ezra. Somebody told the sheriff here that he was my nephew, Jerry Collins. I don't have a nephew."

"I believe there is a Jerry Collins somewhere in the family. I don't know where but I'll have Millie look at the family Bible. We've tried to keep that up over the years, you know. I can't see too good anymore so she'll have to do it for me."

"Do you trust her, Ezra?"

"Sure. Why shouldn't I?"

"No reason except that somehow, somewhere, and for some reason someone wanted me dead. I need to know who that someone is and I don't know who I can trust."

"Millie can be trusted. She doesn't lie about anything. She's a fine Christian lady. Millie, get the Bible and see if you can find the name Jerry Collins written in it anywhere. Del's going to hold onto the phone and wait for an answer. So get a move on."

Del held the telephone to his ear for at least ten minutes as he waited for Millie to get the Bible and read through the many handwritten names to find the answer.

"Mr. Collins, Delbert, there is a Jerry Collins who appears to be a very distant cousin of yours. He lives in the next county over, I think. His mommy and daddy were Thelma and David Collins. Do you know them?"

"No, I guess I should have been going to the family reunions. Then maybe I would know something, don't you think?"

"Is that all you need?"

"Have you ever met Jerry Collins, Millie?"

"No, I don't believe I have. We don't get many visitors, you know. Seems the family don't want to be bothered with the old folks. Too busy. Got too many things to do. You know what I mean."

"Yes, I do. Millie, are you a relative somewhere along the line?"

"No, sir. I was homeless, looking for a place to stay, and a job when Ezra asked me to stay with him. I don't know what I would have done without his help. I really don't know."

"How come you were homeless?"

"My husband died of cancer and the bank took my house because I wasn't able to keep up the payments. The medical bills just about ate me alive. I met Ezra at church. I went there looking for help, any kind of help I could get. He helped me then and I've been helping him ever since."

"I'm glad you found Ezra."

"Thank you, Del. That's what Ezra calls you. Is that all right?"

"Sure. You don't have an address for Jerry Collins do you?"

"No, I'm sorry."

"Thanks for your help, Millie. Thank Ezra for me."

Del immediately dialed the phone number for the sheriff's office.

"Tommy, can you get an address for Jerry Collins in Russell County?"

"Is that the same Jerry Collins who said he was your nephew?"

"I don't know. That's what I'm trying to find out."

"I'll contact the Department of Motor Vehicles and have them send me a photo if he has a driver license. Then I can have a look at that Jerry Collins to see if he is the one."

"How long do you think that will take?"

"Couple of hours probably."

"I'm going to go up by my burned out house and do some more checking."

"Okay, but be careful Del. Ask Adele to let you use her cell phone so you can call for help if you need it."

"That's not necessary, Tommy."

"Maybe, maybe not. Don't take any chances, Del."

"See you later, Tommy."

Delbert didn't ask Adele for the cell phone. He didn't want to bother her. She was upstairs straightening up the bedrooms so he scrawled a note and left it on the kitchen table next to her coffee cup.

He slipped out the back door quietly and started walking along the narrow country road that would take him to the main road that led into the heart of town. It wouldn't take more than a half hour to walk to his house if he wasn't sidetracked along the way. He would be on foot a few more days because when he left to go out of town he placed his car in the worthy hands of the local car repair shop for some work. He didn't have any money to get his car back, not yet anyway.

The morning was just cool enough to make walking such a long distance a real pleasure. The steady rhythm of his footfalls lulled Del into a comfort zone that allowed him to think.

Jerry Collins? Did he know Jerry Collins? He really needed to look at a picture of him so he could see if he knew Jerry Collins.

How did Jerry Collins know that he was going to be gone for a few days? How did he know it was going to be long enough for him to collect on an insurance policy?

"Hey, Mrs. Collins!" shouted a familiar voice.

Delbert turned to look behind him and spotted Arnold running wildly behind him trying to catch up.

"Hey, Arnold. What do you want?"

"I saw that Jerry Collins fella a few minutes ago."

"You did? Where?"

"His picture came in on that machine at the sheriff's office. It was the same man who said he was your nephew."

"Did the sheriff send you after me?"

"No, he didn't know I saw the picture. It was still laying right beside the machine when I left."

"How did you know to find me here? Did the sheriff tell you?"

"No, I just figured I was going to walk to the sheriff's house since you stayed with him last night and try to find you so I could tell that I saw the fella."

211

"Thanks, Arnold. Now, you go on home. I don't want you getting hurt hanging around with me."

"No, Mr. Collins. No one can hurt you. You're dead, Mr. Collins."

Del shook his head and walked on with Arnold at his side.

"Arnold, have you see Jerry Collins in town since you saw him at my funeral?"

"Yes, sir."

"When?"

"Just before I saw the picture at the sheriff's office. I think it was him. He had the same kind of car."

"Did he see you?"

"Sure, I was walking along the sidewalk and I waved at him."

"Did he wave back?"

"No, he didn't. He must not have seen me."

"Did you see him after you left the sheriff's office?"

"No."

"What kind of car does he drive?"

"A blue one. Sort of new looking."

"Is it like the one behind us?"

"Yes, that's it. That's your nephew."

"Run, Arnold, run as fast as you can," shouted Del as he raced from the road to an empty field.

"Why?"

"Just run. He's not my nephew. He might want to hurt you. I know he wants to kill me."

Running off the road was what they needed to do. The car couldn't follow them and they could keep walking or preferably running until they could get some help from somewhere.

A pop and something zinging past Del's ear caused him to crouch down as low as he could go and still be on his feet running.

"Get down, Arnold. Someone's shooting at us," Del shouted at the frightened Arnold.

"Why, Mr. Collins? Why is he trying to kill us?"

"I don't know. But, get down lower. No wait a minute. Get behind this tree and just stand there until I tell you to move."

Arnold tried to stand still but he was too scared. His body parts seemed to want to jerk about like he was a puppet and someone was indiscriminately jerking on the strings.

Del stepped into plain sight and stood there not moving a muscle.

"Shoot at me, you idiot, so I can tell where the shots are coming from," he mumbled under his breath.

A pop and a zing and the crackle of glass as the bullet went past Del and into the window of the house he was standing in front of. The house was empty so he wasn't worried about the bullet hitting anybody. As a matter of fact, it was surprising to see that there was still a window that hadn't been broken out by vandals.

"Over there towards the pond, Mr. Collins. That's where the shooter is," shouted Arnold excitedly.

"Yeah, I saw that, Arnold. That guy pretty well has us pinned down I think."

"Looks that way."

"Arnold, did you get a look at him?"

"No, sir. I didn't."

"Keep your eyes open. He might try to get around behind us. We'll just have to try and wait him out."

"I see a car coming up the road there, Mr. Collins."

"Can you see who it is?"

"It's not the blue car."

"Let's go wave the car down and see if we can get a ride to the sheriff's office."

Arnold and Del started running toward the road waving their arms at the car. The driver slowed to see what was wrong.

"Bob, we need to get to the sheriff's office right away," said Del as he ran to the passenger side of the car with Arnold trailing close behind him.

"What's wrong?" asked Bob Martin, the owner of the hardware store.

"Someone's trying to kill us," shouted Arnold as he scrambled into the back seat.

"Is that right?" he asked with a smile.

"Yes, Bob, someone is trying to kill us. Please drive us to the sheriff's office," Del said sternly.

Bob screeched his tires as he accelerated rapidly with the encouragement of Del.

"I see it. The blue car is behind us!" shouted Arnold.

"We're almost there, Arnold. Get down so he can't see you."

Bob Martin drove right up to the front door of the sheriff's office. He slammed the gear into park and climbed out of the car with Arnold and Del.

"Sheriff, sheriff, he's trying to kill us!" shouted Arnold as he ran through the front door.

"Slow down, Arnold. Mr. Collins, Mr. Martin, what's going on?" asked a surprised deputy when he saw the three men running into the office.

"He's trying to kill us! The man in the blue car is trying to kill us!" shouted Arnold as he looked for a place to hide.

"No one is going to kill you. Not in here, Arnold. Take a deep breath and tell me what's going on."

"Deputy, Arnold is telling you the truth. Someone is trying to kill us and he is driving a blue car," said Del as he tried to confirm Arnold's excited utterings.

"Who is trying to kill you?"

"Jerry Collins. He supposed to be my nephew except that I don't have a nephew. Is Tommy here?"

"You mean the sheriff?"

"Yes, I mean the sheriff who is also my friend Tommy."

"No, he went home for lunch. I'll give him a call if you want me to."

"I want you to. We've been shot at, Deputy. We need all the help we can get. The three of us are not going to leave here without some kind of answer."

Bob Martin had no idea what was going on so Del tried to fill him in with the little bit of information that he had.

In a matter of minutes, the sheriff returned to the office after receiving the telephone call from the deputy.

"Del, I need to talk to your alone," he said as he nodded at Delbert Collins. "You others wait outside on those benches. Won't take but a minute or two."

He motioned towards the door in an effort to get Bob Martin and Arnold out of the room.

"I received this photo from the DMV, Del. Take a look at it and see if you recognize this guy," said the sheriff as he handed the photograph to Del.

"Yeah, I've seen him but I didn't know he was a Collins. I thought his last name was Walter."

"He appears to have been using his mother's maiden name of Walter. He was born with the name of Collins."

"Is he the one who is trying to kill me?"

"I've done some checking with the insurance company. It seems he took out a policy on you since you have no other close relatives. Then he found a body and planted it in your house while you were gone to the VA Hospital."

"He had to know I was coming back, didn't he?"

"Well, I'm guessing that he was going to stop you before you left the hospital but you left earlier than he expected."

"Yes, they told me I could leave the next morning but I went ahead and left the same day. I guess I messed up his plans."

"You were gone long enough for him to kill you, get you buried, and collect the money in your checking account."

"What about the one hundred thousand dollars insurance?"

"He hasn't got that yet. That's why it's so important for you to die."

"How are you going to stop him?"

"I guess we're going to have to let him kill you."

"What?"

"Let him think he's going to get his chance. That's what I mean."

"How?"

"He seems to be getting information from someone. I'm guessing it's Arnold. I don't think it is intentional. That is, I don't think Arnold means you any harm. But, you know Arnold, if someone asks him a question, he will answer it."

"Yeah, he is honest and truthful to a fault."

"Arnold seems to always pop up whenever there is trouble. Seems a little strange, don't you think?"

"Come to think of it, the first person I always see is Arnold. But he does odd jobs for me and helps me a lot. In return I help him. That's how he makes his spending money."

"I know, but I think Arnold is innocently telling this Walter or Collins guy everything he has needed to know to get this far in trying to kill you. Why don't you go outside to the bench and keep Bob Martin company? I'll have a friendly little talk with Arnold."

"Arnold wouldn't do anything to harm me, Tommy."

"Just go on now, Del. So I can talk with Arnold."

Delbert Collins left the room with a scowl on his face. A few moments later, Sheriff Thompson appeared in the doorway and beckoned Arnold to enter the room.

"Sit down, Arnold. I need to ask you a question or two."

"Sure, Sheriff, sure."

The sheriff held the picture up before Arnold.

"Have you seen this man before, Arnold?"

"Sure, he said he is Del's nephew. He was at the funeral."

"Have you seen him anywhere else?"

"Yeah, I saw his blue car driving through town the other day."

"Have you ever talked to him?"

Arnold looked down at his feet and paused.

"Arnold, when did you talk to him?"

"I talked to him a long time ago and again after the funeral."

"How long ago was the first time?"

"I can't remember, been a while, maybe a couple or three months."

"What did he say to you?"

"He wanted me to tell him all about his Uncle Delbert."

"Did you tell him about Del?"

"Yes, I got into his blue car and he took me to get a hamburger, fries and a cold drink both times. I told him everything I knew about Delbert Collins."

"What did you tell him?"

Arnold looked directly at Sheriff Thompson and asked, "Did I do something wrong?"

"No, Arnold, you didn't do anything wrong. I just want to know what you told the man."

"Everything I know like Mr. Del lives all alone. Where he does his shopping. Where is does his banking. That he goes to the VA Hospital every so often for a check up. Stuff like that. None of it's really important, is it?"

"No problem, Arnold. You didn't tell any secrets. Have you talked to that man in the blue car since Del came back to town?"

Once again Arnold looked down at his feet.

"Yes, sir, I sure did."

"When, Arnold?"

"A little while before I found Del after he was hit on the head."

"Did you tell him where Del was?"

"Yes, sir. Was that wrong?"

"No, Arnold. But if that man finds you again and he asks you another question this is what I want you to tell him."

Arnold's eyes glistened with excitement. The sheriff wanted him to do something. He would do whatever the sheriff told him to the best of his ability.

"You go on now, Arnold. You go see if you can find Del's nephew," said the sheriff as he slightly pushed Arnold to the door.

"Bob, I'll have one of my deputies take you where you need to go. You leave your car here for a day or two. I think that would be the safest bet for right now. I wouldn't want anyone taking pot shots at you, would you?"

"If the deputy would take me home, I'll get the pickup truck so I can go about my business, if you think it's safe, Sheriff."

"Should be safe, Bob. The shooter wasn't after you."

"Del, come back in here. We need to talk some more."

"What now, Tommy?"

"I sent Arnold on an errand. I don't think the guy will hurt him because he needs to talk to Arnold to get all the information he can get about your whereabouts. Arnold is the one who has been telling your so-called nephew about where you are and what you're doing. He didn't know he was doing anything wrong. He really wasn't doing anything wrong. You know Arnold. He wouldn't hurt you, Del, for anything."

"What has he been asking Arnold?"

"He's been bribing Arnold with hamburgers and fries to tell him where you are when the killer can't find you."

"Doesn't take much, does it, Tommy?"

"Like I said, Arnold wouldn't hurt you, Del."

"I know. He is such a simple soul. People shouldn't take advantage of him like that."

"No, but not all human beings are like you and me."

"I guess not. What is Arnold supposed to tell this guy?"

"Where he can find you."

"And that is?"

"My house. I told my wife to go visit her sister for a couple of days."

"Are you sure you want to do that? He's already set one house on fire. What if he does that to you?"

"Del, you and I will be waiting for him. Arnold will tell me as soon as he talks to Mr. Walter or Collins. We'll be waiting."

"This guy won't hurt Arnold?"

"No, he needs Arnold to keep track of you."

"Arnold won't spill the beans, will he? You know how he is."

"No, I told Arnold what he is to say. He isn't allowed to say anything else. He could only tell the killer where you are and then he had to leave and come to tell me."

"You want me to hang around here until you hear something from Arnold or whoever?"

"Yes, I think that would be best. I don't want anyone taking aim at you until or unless I'm there with my gun to shoot back. I want this guy. I don't like anyone shooting at my friends."

The remainder of the day passed quickly. Del occupied himself with watching the comings and goings of the deputies and people who had business with the sheriff's office.

"I wonder what's keeping Arnold?" asked Del as he and the sheriff were getting ready to leave the office.

"I told him not to come back until he talked to the man. Maybe he hasn't found him yet. Or, the man hasn't found Arnold."

"I hope the guy didn't harm Arnold."

"He will be one sorry piece of humanity of he did," growled the sheriff.

The ride to the sheriff's house was a short one but it was nerve wracking because they had to be constantly vigilant trying to make sure they didn't get shot by a killer hiding behind some bushes or a building.

"My wife picked up some fresh lunch meat before she left for her sister's. We can eat good even if I can't cook very well."

The lunch meat was spread out on the table along with the condiments and fresh bread when there was a loud knocking at the front door.

"Who's there?" shouted Sheriff Thompson as he held his service revolver in his hand ready to fire.

"Arnold, Sheriff Thompson, it's Arnold," came an excited shout from the other side of the closed door.

"Are you alone, Arnold?"

"Yes, sir."

The sheriff opened the door slowly to admit Arnold into the darkened living room.

"Come on in, Arnold. Del and I are just sitting down to eat. You want a sandwich?"

"Sure, thanks, Sheriff," said a smiling Arnold.

The sheriff led Arnold to the kitchen and set a cold soda pop in front of him,

"Help yourself, Arnold. Get what you want to eat on your sandwich."

Del wanted to know why Arnold was there. Had he spoken with the killer? Should they be guarding the doors and windows with gun in hand?

After Arnold had prepared himself a hefty sandwich Sheriff Thompson started asking him questions.

"Did you see Mr. Collins or Walter or whatever he's calling himself?"

"Yes," answered Arnold between chews.

"What did you say to him?"

"Just what you told me to say. I told him Del was staying with you until he could find another place to live."

"Did he want to know anything else?"

"Yes, he wanted to know where I was going after I left him? So I told him I had to go find you, Sheriff. That was all right, wasn't it?"

Del looked down in disbelief.

The sheriff noticeably bit his tongue to keep himself from reprimanding Arnold.

"That's fine, Arnold," the sheriff responded with a sigh.

"I did something wrong, didn't I?"

"No, no, Arnold. Don't worry about it. Did you see anybody follow you out here?"

"You mean did I see the blue car?"

"Yes, that's what I mean?"

"No, I didn't look behind me. I was in a hurry to get here. Should I have looked behind me?"

"No, no, that's okay. We better finish eating, don't you think, Del?"

"Yes, we might have some company some time soon."

They were clearing off the table when a gun shot broke the window and embedded itself in the wall directly opposite the opening.

"Everybody get down," shouted the sheriff. "Del, did you see where that came from?"

"No, I didn't."

"How about you, Arnold? Did you see?"

"No," Arnold answered in a shaky voice.

"Just stay down, Arnold. Del and I won't let him hurt you. I guess we'll have to wait until he gets another shot off. I have my cell phone. I'll call and get us some help."

The next sounds they heard were sirens. The deputies were showing up all at one time.

No more shots, no more killer. He was gone and they had no idea where he was standing when he fired the shot.

"If he used a rifle with a scope, it's hard telling where he was," mumbled the sheriff to Del.

The deputies looked around the area but found nothing. After a couple of hours of kicking at the grass and looking at the ground, they left with no evidence.

"Arnold, you need to stay here for the night. I don't want you running around out there where he could take a shot at you."

"Yes, sir."

"Del, why don't you try to get some sleep. I'll wake you up in a couple of hours and then you can take over watching and listening."

During Sheriff Thompson's watch all was quiet. At two in the morning he woke Del and asked Del to take over the watch. The sheriff had barely fallen asleep when all the commotion started.

"Tommy, Tommy," said Del as he was trying to waken his friend, "the barn is on fire."

The sheriff jumped up and blinked himself awake. Arnold awakened and, without any thought about what he was doing, he raced to a window so he could see what was burning.

A shot rang out and Arnold slumped to the floor.

"Del, check on Arnold. Keep low."

Del scrambled to Arnold's side. He pressed his fingers against Arnold's carotid artery.

"He's still breathing. I can't see where he was shot. Give me a flashlight."

The sheriff tossed the light he found in the cabinet drawer to Del.

"It's on the side. Hopefully he didn't hit anything important."

"Here are some towels. See if you can stop the bleeding."

'What about your barn?" asked Del.

"Just got junk stored out there. Nothing too important. He set that fire so he could pick us off one at a time. I hope he thinks murdering us and the unknown man in the fire at your house is worth only a hundred thousand dollars. If it were me, a hundred thousand wouldn't be enough."

The sheriff poked his head up over the window sill.

"I see him. He's standing off to the right by the tree over there. Maybe I can get off a shot at him."

The sheriff popped his head up again and was grazed by a bullet at his temple.

"Tommy, are you all right?"

The sheriff reached to where the pain was centered.

"Just a scratch, a little blood, that's all. Stay down or he will try to part your hair."

"Where's your cell phone? Maybe we should call for help."

"It's not in my pocket. I must have dropped it."

Del started searching for the cell phone. He snapped the flashlight to life and heard the whistle of a bullet as it passed his head and struck a wall. Del extinguished the light. "I'll feel around and see if I can find that phone," he whispered to Tommy.

"Don't turn that light back on."

"Don't worry, I won't."

"Del, do you smell smoke?"

"Of course, the barn is burning."

"No, I mean in here," whispered Sheriff Thompson as he tried to pinpoint the location of the stronger whiff of smoke.

"Yeah, yeah, I do. Did that nut set the house on fire to get us out of here?"

"I bet he did. Can you see out a window?"

"I'll crawl to the window in the kitchen. Maybe I can see something out there," said Del as he started moving as rapidly as he could on all fours.

"I'll check the bedroom in the back," said the sheriff.

"The fire is under the kitchen window, Tommy. Do you have a broomstick? I'll need a clothes hanger and something round to look like a head."

"What are you planning to do?" asked the sheriff.

"I was thinking that if I held up a figure that looked like you or me, he would step out far enough to get a clear shot, and then you could get him with your revolver."

"It might work."

"The fire is starting to burn pretty good under the kitchen window. We had better pray that this idea does work."

Gathering the necessary items together took a few minutes. During those few minutes the fire under the kitchen window was getting brighter and brighter.

"I hope he can't tell this is a decoy when I hold it up to the window," said Del as he whispered a silent prayer.

"Try to make it look like you just found that fire."

"Okay, here goes," said Del as he made the decoy suddenly pop up from below the window sill to get a good look at the flames outside the window.

"Pull it back down fast so he thinks it truly is me," said the sheriff. "I wouldn't be holding myself in plain view for any length of time. It would be too dangerous."

Del pulled the decoy down and waited a few moments while Sheriff Thompson got himself into position where he could cover as much of the territory as possible outside the kitchen window with his eyes.

"Now, Del, put it up now."

The decoy popped up into view and Sheriff Thompson spotted movement to left where he aimed his revolver and fired. A bullet broke through the double panes of glass of the window and tore through the decoy, as the sheriff's bullet penetrated the body of a man who crumpled to the ground.

"Del, I'm going to check on who I hit. You get the bucket from under the sink and start throwing water on that fire."

"Be careful, Tommy. He might not be alone."

"Oh, I don't think he has any help. He wouldn't want to share the hundred thousand."

Del ran to the sink to get the bucket. He filled it with water that he threw on the fire through the broken window.

He saw the sheriff standing over the crumpled body of his distant cousin checking for movement after he removed the rifle from within reach.

A few moments later, Sheriff Tommy Thompson entered the kitchen and reached for the wall phone where he heard no dial tone after pressing the receiver to his ear. He then walked to the next room where he found his cell phone and dialed 911.

"This is Sheriff Thompson," he told the dispatcher.

"Send the body wagon to my house along with an investigating team. Also send the fire department because my barn is burning and do it now."

"He's dead?" asked Del somewhat relieved but also disappointed.

"Yeah, I hit him close to the heart."

"Did he say anything about why he did this?"

"No, all he said was he had some bills to pay."

"Nothing else?"

"He said, 'I'm sorry.'"

## EVERY MAN WANTS A
## YELLOW DUMP TRUCK

### Big Jim Williams

*Jim Williams, author of* THE OLD WEST *and* TALL TALES OF THE OLD WEST *audio books, has written for Western Horseman, Shoot!, Texas Livestock Weekly, American West, Orchard Press Mysteries, Radio World, and other magazines. He announces at KZSB, Santa Barbara, California. E-mail:* bigjimwilliams2@cox.net.

Henry J Taggert bought a ten-wheel, double-axle, long-bed dump truck, the kind used for hauling earth, asphalt and boulders. He saw the beat up yellow behemoth parked on a vacant lot next to a service station.

'74 Mac Dump Truck
Ten-Ton Capacity
Double Axles
$4,000

He bought it on an impulse; full price in cash. Impulses were Henry J's downfall.

"Why?" asked Rollo, his bowling buddy. His name was Francis, but a permanent baby-fat body in kindergarten forever branded him "Rollo" in small-town Clarkston.

"It looked lonely," explained Henry J. "I couldn't leave it there."

Henry J was short. Rollo was shorter and with bulging love handles.

"I've always wanted a big dump truck," continued Henry J. His blue eyes studied his pin-split at the end of his pockmarked bowling lane.

"You going into the dump-truck business?" Rollo swallowed the last of his jelly donut and Lone Star beer.

"Nope."

"You've had too many beers."

"Rollo, ain't never had too many beers." Henry J studied the 7-10 split and bounced his green bowling ball down lane five of the Kwik-Lunch and Hip-Hop Bowling Emporium. "Be twenty-eight next birthday. Who knows how long I'm gonna live?"

"My uncle made it to 92."

"Had a cousin who died at 22."

"Being hit by a train don't count."

"Train or old age, they ain't coming back."

"So you bought a dump truck."

"Yep."

The ball wobbled between the two pins.

"Damn!" sputtered Henry J.

"An eight." Rollo smiled and did inaccurate pencil-stub totals. "Beat you by forty. You owe me a burger and beer." He burped and scratched his overhanging stomach. "Buying a dump truck when you ain't going into business is kinda--"

"Wanna go for another ride?"

"Sure." Rollo grabbed a fresh Lone Star.

"I wanted a red one." Henry J's small frame slouched behind the steering wheel in the high cab. "But yellow's okay."

He ground the truck into first-, second-, third-, fourth-, fifth-, and sixth-gear, but not in that order. He grunted the manhole-size steering wheel into a turn, vacated his three parking spaces, and cut across the parking lot. His right rear wheels climbed a curb, smashed a planter, and snapped off two sprinkler heads.

Rollo's curly head poked out the window and surveyed the damage. "I think you left your transmission and two geysers back there!"

Both laughed as the rig gained speed, turned onto the two-lane highway, and left the Kwik-Lunch and Hip-Hop Bowling Emporium and Clarkston behind.

"How ya gonna afford gas--"

"Diesel," interrupted Henry J.

"—to run this thing," continued Rollo, "if you ain't going into the hauling business?" He gulped his beer.

"Using divorce money. My half from the house we sold outside of Fort Worth. Living with my folks now, so don't need much."

"They got a paper box factory in Fort Worth?" Rollo worked in an auto parts store. He added his empty beer bottle to the roadside clutter.

"Yeah, but I ran an all night gas station mini-mart. Hated it. Ever try sleepin' days with two twin babies squalling in the next room?"

Henry J's only claim to fame was he'd once sat in a car Elvis had thought of buying, or so the salesman said. He couldn't remember the color or make, but he did remember being drunk at the time.

Rollo's claim to fame was his rock collection, an odd assortment gathered along the railroad tracks that divided Clarkston. It filled two cigar boxes under his bed next to his comic books.

Henry J enjoyed driving the behemoth around Clarkston since buying it two weeks earlier. He'd go to the grocery store, put a six-pack of beer in the cab, a bag of potato chips in the huge lift bed, drive home, and dump the chips on his folks' driveway.

The neighbors shook their heads. They'd frown and ask: "What do you need a big dump truck for?"

Henry J smiled and waved. "Why not? Life's short. Ask the people in the cemetery. If you want somethin' and can afford it...buy it."

Then the neighbors really complained when...

"Rollo and me," said Henry J, "been putting six-packs of warm beer in the truck bed--"

"Cheap beer," interrupted Rollo.

"--and dumpin' 'em. Man, that beer's so shook up after it hits the ground. Open a can—-"

"It'll shoot a hundred feet."

"We've had some great beer fights." Henry J popped an imaginary can and sprayed Rollo.

"Great times!" agreed Rollo.

"Mom didn't like us having beer fights on the front lawn."

Rollo laughed. "Neighbors complained."

"Mom said we looked like a bunch of spoiled kids. 'So?' I said.

They both laughed.

"The first time it happened," added Henry J, "I'd forgotten we'd put a six pack in the truck bed with our tortilla chips."

Rollo elbowed his buddy. "Nothin' like a cold-beer shootout on a hot day."

"Yeah, but if you leave it in the sun and shake it up good, it'll maybe go half the length of a football field."

"Love a good beer brawl."

The truck came with broad waist-high steel bumpers, a grunt-climb cab, dented metal dump bed, squeaky tailgate, chipped windshield, expanding rust, and dual rear axles with double-mounted wheels. It clanged and rattled, and spewed black smoke from two cab-mounted vertical exhausts like Vesuvius signaling Venus. Its giant diesel engine rumbled like an angry Tyrannosaurus rex, action Henry J's right foot controlled with the grace of a prima ballerina.

He named the truck "Belcher," because of its bowel sounds and black smoke. Others called it "Big Yeller."

"What kind of mileage do you get?" asked Rollo.

"No problem. Use my credit card."

Henry J's logic defied Rollo. But he was his old school buddy who liked bowling, beer, wrestling on television, eating burgers and fries, and talking about Rollo's rock collection. He was glad Henry J was back in Clarkston after nine years. In high school they had cruised for cats in Rollo's old pickup. Belcher would get more cats.

Decaying "Save the Whales" and "Dukakis for President" bumper stickers flapped from the truck's tailgate like loose skin. Henry J added "Go Clarkston High Badgers" blue-and-gold stickers, but replaced the word *Badgers* with *Boogers*.

He planned to enter Belcher in Clarkston's annual July 4th, Veteran's Day, Founders' Day, and the high school's homecoming parades...if they'd let him.

At stop signs he shifted to neutral and rocked the accelerator. His big ears welcomed the roar.

Mac Truck's chromed bulldog trademark posed like a stud atop the radiator, a system big enough to cool half of Clarkston's water needs in August.

When Henry J showed his family what he'd bought, his older brother, Myron, said Henry J's grin reminded him more than ever of "Alfred E. Neuman on the cover of Mad Magazine."

Most everyone thought Henry J resembled Alfred E. Neuman with his round face, freckles, red hair, large ears and wide gap between his front teeth.

"Henry J's always been strange," said Mrs. Taggert. Her frown created enough dark lines to trigger a barcode reader. She watered her artificial flowers and began washing imaginary dishes in a waterless sink.

"Your side of the family's stranger," declared Mr. Taggert. He nodded toward 40-year-old Myron, who, jobless, still lived under their roof, watched reruns of "Gilligan's Island," read comic books, and left the toilet seat up.

"Stranger?" questioned Mrs. Taggert. "How about you? You named our other son after a 1951 model car!"

"The Henry J," acknowledged Mr. Taggert, "was ahead of its time. Small, compact, excellent gas mileage. Wish I still had mine." Then he added: "You're damn lucky I didn't name that boy Ford Fairlane!"

Then Mr. Taggert quoted, by memory, from the encyclopedia: "The Henry J was produced from 1950 through 1953 by Henry J. Kaiser, who, after World War II, switched from producing U.S. warships to making the Henry J, a stubby car with fishtail taillights."

Mrs. Taggert rolled her eyes, and added more water to her artificial flowers.

Henry J drove his truck to his forklift job at Clarkston's paper-box factory, to his ex-wife's home to see their five-year-old twin sons, and to church Wednesdays for what he called a night with "Saint Bingo." When he went to the drive-in movie theater, the last one in the county, the manager made him park in the back, to avoid blocking anyone's view.

"My twins," said Henry J, "love riding in the dump truck and blowing the horn. Even Betsy likes it."

Betsy Plummer was Henry J's new girlfriend. She didn't say much about anything. She came with long blonde hair and black roots, a shy smile, a supervisory job at the paper-box factory, and an apartment with HBO. She believed in UFOs, Ouija boards, Saint Bingo, and that Elvis was alive. So did Henry J. They got along fine.

"Why a dump truck?" asked Betsy, when first seeing the big yellow machine.

"I've wanted one since I was a kid watching big trucks and earth movers on the Learning Channel."

Red lettering on the door proclaimed: CLAPPER & SONS TRUCKING. "Dirt & Rocks are are business."

"Shouldn't that be our business?" asked Betsy.

"Guess so. But who cares."

Henry J's frequently uttered 'who cares' words helped destroy his marriage.

Betsy was pushing twenty-five and Clarkston offered little in potential husbands. Henry J was considered a good catch, though a daydreamer, divorced and without much of a future. She'd left a short marriage, something she refused to talk about, except to say it was "physically abusive."

"You just never know when you may need a dump truck," continued Henry J. "If you need one and don't have one you're in trouble. But if you need one and have one...you're not in trouble!"

Henry J's illogic logic puzzled Betsy. But no one else had asked her out since her divorce a year ago. She sighed, shook her head, and enjoyed her burger, fries and strawberry shake at the Dairy Queen.

Lust and two missed periods had sent Henry J and Gracie Pirouette to the altar nine years earlier. But that pregnancy ended in a miscarriage.

Now his divorce was final and he was seeing Betsy, who had been five years behind him at J.B. Clarkston High. They met at the box factory.

Betsy tried climbing onto the high running board. Her tight skirt revealed white thighs.

Henry J leered.

"You just wanna see up my dress!" she huffed.

He lowered his eyes and attempted a Humphrey Bogart imitation. "Ain't nothin' there, babe, I ain't seen before."

She blushed, scowled, and fought back a smile.

He grinned and helped her into the cab.

Betsy hated to admit it, but loved riding in the truck, looking down on all the cars.

"The radio plays cassettes, too," said Henry J.

"Everybody's got CDs now."

He ignored her and shoved a Frank Sinatra tape into the deck. "Strangers in The Night" blared from big speakers in the dash and doors.

"Love ol' blue eyes." Henry J's high-pitched, off-key, nasal voice clashed with the Chairman of the Board's mellow sound. He laughed and pressed a button on the dashboard. A big chromed horn on the hood blasted out the first few notes of "Strangers in The Night."

"That's what really sold me," he said.

He played the horn again, attempting to match it with the Sinatra recording.

"Listen to this." He pressed the center of the steering wheel. Twin air horns from the cab's roof broke the sound barrier.

Henry J stuck his head out the window and yelled: "Move over world! Here comes Henry J Taggert...and Betsy Plummer!"

He gave the horns another blast.

Three cars pulled over and let him pass.

Two miles out of Clarkston he floored the accelerator. The truck raced down the two-lane highway. The warm wind of summer churned through open windows, scattering Betsy's hair like golden straw.

Flashing red lights appeared from a side road, followed with the piercing sound of a siren. A motorcycle swung behind the truck.

"Damn!" Henry J slowly eased the big yellow machine onto the shoulder of the road and stopped.

A uniformed officer climbed off his motorcycle. His polished boots crunched the roadside gravel. He tried, but couldn't put his right foot on the truck's high running board.

"Where you think you're goin', sir? Is there a fire someplace I don't know about?" He snorted at the dented truck. "Or are you in a hurry to dump something...or this truck?"

Betsy curled out of view and remained silent.

The officer slowly pulled off his gloves and helmet, revealing a hairless pointed head.

Henry J wondered how the pointed head fit into the round helmet. Then he stared at the pudgy officer.

"That you, Ponch?"

"Ponch?" The officer removed his dark glasses and squinted up at the boyish face in the cab. "Nobody's called me Ponch since high school." He shielded his eyes against the sun. "That...That you Henry J?"

"Mighty snappy uniform you got there, Ponch." Henry J's extended hand was ignored. "You always wanted to be a cop."

"Highway Patrol Officer!" corrected the lawman.

"You loved that old 'ChiPs' TV show with Ponch and what's his name?"

"Sir, you were five miles over the--"

"How ya like my dump truck, Ponch? Ain't she a beaut?"

"The name is Highway Patrol Officer Raymond P. Gossper, and you should well know it, Henry J Taggert."

"Ah, come off it, Ponch. We went through school together—-almost. If I hadn't put that stink bomb in—"

"You were speeding, sir." He flipped open a pad of traffic tickets.

"Only doin' sixty."

"Fifty-five's tops for dump trucks." He began scribbling.

"Ponch, you're taking this 'ChiPs' stuff too seriously."

"Registration and drivers license, please."

Henry J produced both, including his commercial driver's license. "Just got that," he said with pride.

Ponch took his time studying the pictures on the licenses, and then chuckled.

"What's funny?" asked Henry J.

"You still look like Alfred E. Neuman."

Henry J snatched the papers back from Ponch's offered hand. "No, I don't!"

Ponch returned to writing. "Last I heard about you Henry J you were in Fort Worth."

"Got back a couple of months ago."

"Heard you were working in a paper-box factory."

"Mini Mart. Ponch, you still gonna give me a ticket?" Henry J's voice climbed toward soprano.

"The law's the law--"

"Damn!" Henry J pointed an index finger in Ponch's face. "You've never forgotten I whipped your ass in tetherball in the seventh grade...and in the twelfth grade took Gracie Pirouette to the senior prom."

Several cars slowed down. There wasn't much else to see or do in Clarkston on a July afternoon.

Henry J smiled and waved. Some waved back and honked.

Ponch motioned the cars away. "Nothing to see here, folks," he yelled. Then turned back to his speeder. "Whatever happened to her?"

"Who?"

"Gracie Pirouette."

"You still got a thing for her, don't ya?"

Ponch blushed. "She...She was kinda cute."

"Damn! Well, Romeo, she's back--"

"In Clarkston?"

"--and available. Came back months ago, old tetherball loser."

"Yeah, I...I liked her," admitted Ponch. "Wish I'd married her instead of that lemon I got...or had."

"Well, you ain't hobbled now, I see." Henry J gestured toward Ponch's left hand. "No ring. Hell, you had a crush on her like a steamroller on ice. This is your lucky day, Ponch, because, like I said, she's 'back and available.'"

"How do you know?"

"She signed divorce papers six months ago. She's still 5-1. Yours if you want her, all 215 pounds now. But she cries, nags and bitches a lot. She comes with two great kids, though. Twins. But you haven't lived until you've met her mother, Godzilla."

"How do you know so much about Gracie Pirouette?"

"She's my ex-wife."

Ponch muttered an expletive, ripped off a ticket and handed it up to Henry J.

"You're still gonna give your old classmate a ticket after I've told you all about Gracie?" Henry J pounded the outside door of the truck.

"With pleasure."

"Come off it, Ponch. Just bought this rig. I'm tapped out."

"That ticket's only the beginning."

"What?"

"Every time you drive this yellow elephant I'll be shadowing your ass!"

"Why you——"

"That tetherball game was mine! I should of won that blue ribbon. And I should have taken Gracie to the senior prom...not you!" He strapped on his helmet, and slipped on his gloves and sunglasses. "Welcome back to Clarkston, Henry J!"

Ponch lifted his booted leg over the motorcycle seat. The Harley-Davidson roared and kicked gravel as it fishtailed onto asphalt and headed back toward town.

Henry J thought he heard Ponch laughing.

"I know elephants with shorter memories than yours," he shouted. He turned to Betsy. She shivered in the corner. "What's wrong?"

"I can't stand that SOB."

"You know Ray Gossper?"

"Since I moved back here three years ago."

"I don't understand." Henry J was concerned.

She rubbed her eyes with a white lace handkerchief. "He's...He's my ex-husband."

# ANAMIKA

## Shivaji K. Moitra

*Shivaji K. Moitra is a young government servant from India with a passion for sharing the beautiful moments of life with people across the world who have a little time to stand and stare.*

When you are young and alone and you come to an unfamiliar corner of the country to earn your living and face the queer world all by yourself, you're frightened of loneliness which creeps into your heart as soon as you have finished your work for the day. The dusk and the leisure that comes with it are a perennial source of concern when you are new to a place where you do not know even a handful of people of your taste and predilections and where the avenues of entertainment are rare and rudimentary. So you have but one thing to do between dusk and dinner--maunder along the river or just hang around some public place such as the marketplace, the jetty or perhaps the temple to look at the people go about their business, talking and laughing and may be the pretty girls in colourful dresses, giggling and discussing animatedly their latest affairs with some spectacular flourish of their mehendi-decorated palms while their beautiful faces lightened up with bizarre expressions of mock anger, joy or embarrassment. It certainly lifted your spirits and kept the suffocating grip of loneliness at bay for the time being.

There was a fairly wide river flowing by the eastern margin of the town where I had been sent to work. I had been a poor young man not presently in the best of spirits and alone. I was disappointed at my failure to find a decent job which besides coming up to my expectations would allow me to take care of my aging parents. So each evening I emerged from my office after work gingerly as a rat that was still afraid of the last rays of the setting sun and trudged up to my one room apartment to wash up and change into my evening dress. Then I often headed straight for the quaint Radha-Govinda temple standing on a knoll at the bend of the river. It was a picturesque location from where you could get a beautiful view of the town below and its jetty a little down the river where boats of different colours jostled for space and passengers from dawn to dusk.

The temple was always crowded with devotees who either sat in rows on the long portico facing the alter, meditating quietly or listening passionately to the devotional songs being sung from time to time or just milling around the veranda to relax in the heavenly peace and tranquility that surrounded the place. Mostly I sat facing the river on one of the long marble stairs leading to the temple to spend the evening perfunctorily watching the devotees rather than the deities while listening to the canorous chimes of the temple-bells and kirtans (choir in accompaniment of cymbals). The fragrance of flowers and the perfume of incense sticks offered to the Gods mixed to produce that uniquely mystic aroma which wafts around any place of worship and it rendered me philosophical for the rest of the day. So at times I sat brooding over my future, my chin resting on my palms turned skywards and my elbows supported on my knees.

It was on such a time and place that I made the acquaintance of Dasanan Pal. Rather it was he who made the acquaintance of me when he said, "Young man, that's what I call an ugly posture! In the prime of youth do not sit thus like an old man who has difficulty in carrying his head over his feeble neck." I was ashamed and I turned towards him shyly. Sitting two stairs below me was an elderly man perhaps in his late fifties, tall and erect and wearing a disarming smile above his white trimmed beard. He had small round eyes set on a big, plump face and his large forehead receded to blend smoothly with his bald head. His fair pate glistened from the reflection of the temple-lights and produced the impression of a kind, wise man. The vestiges of his once robust body were discernable. I returned his smile sheepishly. "I have been watching you for some time, my son," he continued lightly, "and I hope you didn't take umbrage at the piece of unsolicited advice from this stranger."

"Oh no, never," I stammered, running my gaze swiftly over him.

"My name is Dasanan Pal and I have been at this place for a considerably long time. I am an ex-serviceman and I am a bachelor," he went on, "and I come here to watch the Arti (paying homage to the Gods with burning lamps and frankincense) twice a week. Without having the least inclination to snoop into your personal troubles I just want to say that I hate to see morose looking young men and women who appear to have lost all zest for life even before they have reached their thirtieth birthday. They stoop as if with the burden of all the worries of this world. Do not let the small adversities of life snatch the smile out of your lips." He paused ostensibly to make out if I was squirming to escape his speech. But when he guessed I wasn't an unwilling listener, he asked with a twinkle in his eyes, "Shall I tell you a real-life story to drive home my point?"

I nodded to convey that I wasn't averse to hearing one. "Well then, my young friend," he continued, "let me tell you that in this world full of surprises and contradictions there are people, a good many of them, whose cheerful faces and ungrudging attitude would confound you the moment you happen to get a ring-side view of their immensely tragic and aimless lives. All your pains and troubles then suddenly pale into insignificance before their sufferings and sorrows and you realise how lucky you are.

Thirty years ago I chanced to meet such a person precisely here. Her name was Anamika. She used to stand here under this old Banyan tree which has been standing since time immemorial with all its myriad arms flung around. Everyday she arrived with her two young sons at around nine in the morning when the fierce Indian sun was still hours away from attaining its threatening posture and the air was cool and the temple had been brimming with activity. Then emptying her baskets of clay idols of Hindu Gods and Goddesses, dolls and the figures of various animals she laid them on a patch of cleared ground beneath the Banyan tree on display before her customers---the devotees and their children. Those days I was a young man and I used to work here in the Postal Department.

Since the day I first saw her, two curious things about her struck me. The first shocking thing was the very incongruity of her presence here in such a fashion and the other surprising thing was her ability to keep a smile alive on her lips in spite of her many cares and needs. She was too fair and pretty to escape your eyes and I guessed she hadn't yet crossed her thirties.

It had become a pastime for me to observe her twice a week seated on one of these stairs and every time I couldn't help appreciating her beauty and surmising what great misfortune had befallen her which had brought her to such a state. I pondered how charming she was under the veil of her poverty, her faded raiment and of the dust that collected on her at the end of the day.

She never seemed to grudge her destiny which she dismissed with a sweet yet restrained smile which always clung to her lips. No wonder, the young and old both liked her and most of them bought an idol or two or a clay animal after a visit to the temple. She earned enough everyday to keep her body and soul together, I presumed. Being a young man those days and moody, perhaps like you, I used to be very much moved and amazed by the kaleidoscopic nature of life, its ups and downs and the unpredictable course life takes when you least expect it to do. I used to read a lot of Somerset Maugham and

Maupassant and the lives of people, their aspirations and frustrations, their pains and sufferings, their cowardice and fortitude in the face of tragedy and their love and despair, everything greatly interested me.

So one evening while somewhat pensively looking at the colourful reflections of the setting sun in the river I decided to take a peek into Anamika's past which I strongly believed could be replete with queer twists of fate and many a surprising event. So in the course of my weekly sojourns to the temple when I had made quite a good acquaintance with her I allowed myself to indulge in short conversations with her, to which she never seemed to object or mind. However, I never pressed her to reveal more than she wished to about her life, her present and her past.

The fact that I seemed to care about her worries and her past gradually made her believe I was a sort of kind, eccentric person. Flocks of wild birds regularly descended upon the Banyan tree to eat the juicy figs and they made a mess of the ground below by dropping a rain of ripe and decaying fruits. Then it was the job of Anamika's two little sons to hold the broom and clean the spot at regular intervals where she displayed her clay items for sale. But it had been a gang of black-faced Indian langurs that really bothered her from time to time. They stormed the temple premises for tasty handouts from the devotees and scampered across the small garden on the frontage and over Anamika's fragile wares to finally raid the Banyan tree. Sometimes I happened to be there at the right moment and I scared away the animals to save her wares from being trampled and destroyed. No doubt, she thanked me for the endeavour each time.

She used to live at the edge of the town in one of the shanties cluttering the river bank which was called Mechopara, 'The Village of Fishermen' which has long been devoured by the expanding town. It was a couple of miles from the temple and could be reached only by a narrow dirt-track which during the long rainy season simply vanished under slush and wild grass and weeds. Those days a mile of bush-land separated the temple from the borders of the town.

Of her two sons the younger one was only three and the older was a boy of nine. The younger had light skin and was a handsome kid while his brother was dark with tribal features. The marked contrast among her children was hard to overlook and one day when she no more felt shy of exchanging a few words with me I casually observed, "Your big one is damn smart and healthy but so much darker than his brother." Anamika smiled. Then she said almost in a whisper, "Yes, I adopted him. He is an orphan and he used to live by polishing shoes at the station and sleep on the platform of Bilaspur Rail Station."

"Bilaspur?" I exclaimed, "You mean in Madhya Pradesh, 750 kilometers. away?"

"Yes, he's a very good boy. I took pity on him when I chanced to see him one night while waiting for the train as he prayed to the Gods before eating his dinner of just bread with a piece of cucumber. Then he shared his morsel with two mongrels with whom he slept during the winter. I asked him to come and live with me and ever since he calls me mother."

It's only the poor perhaps who have the courage to help others of their tribe and who in spite of their meagre resources never seem to be short of kindness and generosity, I mused.

Dasanan fell silent for a few seconds, looking vaguely at a group of strangely-clad ascetics who were smoking ganja sitting a few steps down before us and shuffling the pipe among themselves. Then, having collected the pieces from his rusty memory and sewing them up in order, he began from where he had left.

"On some Sunday afternoons in the winter months of November, December and January, when basking in the warm sun is a luxury you can enjoy for free, I took Anamika's seat in jest and hawked her wares before the devotees and visitors who reacted with jokes and laughter but ended up buying something each. One day in course of such light-hearted activity I asked Anamika when and from whom had she learnt the art of clay modelling. I knew it was certainly not her husband, who I had come to know was a habitual drunkard and a vagrant sort of person of questionable reputation.

"I learnt to run my fingers on clay from my former husband; he's a very good sculptor and a famous artist," she said without hesitating. Then looking askance at the furrows of surprise on my brow as if secretly relishing my suspense she embraced silence. But she had already left the door of her past ajar and the smell of some sad event, some nasty betrayal came to my nose.

It was not my habit to embarrass a hapless woman by making an unwanted intrusion into her personal life and I knew it ill behooved me to be overtly curious. So I dropped the subject that day.

The call of duty took me to another town more than a hundred miles away and I had almost begun to forget Anamika when the event of a promotion brought me back unexpectedly after a gap of three years. The monsoon rains arrived along with me and it was not possible to visit the temple for a few days. But upon my first visit to the temple since returning, to seek the blessing of the Gods, the giant Banyan tree quite naturally drew my attention. Immediately I saw Anamika at the same spot where I had been used to seeing her. She had not changed at all in the years of my absence, neither did her warm, interminable smile. But her children had grown bigger and healthier. She greeted me with a 'namaste' and a lot of smiles and pleasantries and told me that nothing worth mentioning had occurred in the last three years.

Then a month later it happened. It had been raining cats and dogs for the last two days, the type of vicious monsoon rain that has scant respect for time, that disdainfully ignores umbrellas and man-made barriers, that envelops the sky, the earth and the mind in a suffocating haze and hides the sun for days, reducing your visibility to within a metre or two. Then after pouring what seemed to be an inexhaustible supply of water for nearly sixty hours at a stretch the clouds cleared at last around noon on Sunday and the sun shone again. The people, exasperated by long hours of confinement within the four walls of their homes and maddened by the continuous ruffle of the downpour, immediately emerged to breathe the fresh air and take benefit of the few remaining hours of daylight to complete their daily chores. I had slept late into the morning like all lazy people do when the rains come as a Godsend excuse for doing nothing and I did not wish to get groggy in the evening by spending the afternoon in slumber as well.

So after lunch I clutched a book of Tolstoy's short stories and set out for the temple, intending to read it sitting in a serene corner of the temple-lobby.

As soon as I entered the arched gateway of the temple I found a small crowd under the Banyan tree, a quiet crowd of locals and keepers of the place, that apparently was concentrating on something. Casting an indifferent glance at it, I was approaching the marble-paved lobby when Anamika's elder son stopped me. "Uncle, uncle," he cried, "my mother has been bitten by a cobra; what shall I do now?" His voice trembled in fear.

I saw her sitting calmly on the grass with her left leg folded up and blood was oozing from a spot just above her ankle. Somebody had rightly and wisely tied up her leg at two places above the wound with a piece of cloth and a string but I understood that the first right step was being diluted when someone told me that they had sent for the Ojha---a person belonging usually to the tribe of snake-charmers who is believed by the villagers to wield supernatural powers capable of rendering the venom ineffective and thus saving the victims of snake-bite.

Without wasting time I took her to the hospital. It eventually saved her life. After Anamika returned home her husband appeared one morning at my door. With trepidation he asked me if I could accept his invitation for a cup of tea at his hut. It was against my nature to disappoint anybody and I assured him that I would come some day. It was the first time I looked closely at his face.

He was a short, stout and swarthy man in his mid forties. His large rosy eyes were set upon a muscular face with high cheeks and a high nose and his hair was black, long and wavy, which he combed backwards. A brief lull in the spate of rains offered a few days of dry weather and sunshine and the soggy grounds and streets became dry and walkable again. On such a nice day Anamika's man arrived to escort me to his humble house. He and Anamika expressed their deep gratitude to me for the little duty I had done to save her life and then we talked of all those things that concern only the poorest of the poor and which rarely merit more than a moment of thought from people like us. Thereafter, I thanked them for the cup of tea and emerged from their quaint hut whereupon the melodious slosh of the surf came to my ears.

Dusk was closing in and Anamika's husband wanted to escort me back home. On the way I asked him, "Look, you're lucky to get such a good wife; why don't you work hard and become a worthy husband?"

"Yes sir," he replied, "she is a virtuous woman and she comes from the family of a rich Sarpanch (village headman). But while in her teens she did the mistake of eloping with a farmhand of his father. The youth was good-looking and was reportedly a good sculptor and painter and somehow she fell in love with him. Then after two or three years of hopping around miserably he went to Bombay, leaving her behind. There, Anamika had come to understand through his letters that lady luck had smiled on him and miraculously he grew famous and rich by displaying his talent. But quickly she lost track of him and he never returned to his wife again. Now, you know sir, what happens to a little-educated, forsaken woman, beautiful and alone. I bought her back and rescued her from a brothel I used to frequent when I came to know her plight. I set her free but she said she had nowhere to go. Her parents and her village had disowned her and she thus agreed to be my wife for an honourable life. Ever since, she has stubbornly refused to live upon my earnings until I revealed the source of my income. And I have not done that yet." He spoke not a word more and asked my leave at the gate of my house.

"A strange family indeed!" I mused. Later however, in the course of my journey through life, I realized to my amazement that among the most disadvantaged and ignored peoples of our society such makeshift families of convenience, held together not by the force of money but by the glue of real benevolence and magnanimity are by no means a rare phenomenon.

Next weekend when I met Anamika again I gazed at her smiling face with awe and disbelief as never before. There was on her mien not even a hint of the storm that ravaged her youth, not even a furrow of disgust or discontent on her brow for the travails of her present. She appeared perfectly in harmony and peace with her destiny. In my eyes she was still pure and innocent as a bud and her life was sublime.

Life continued without much of an ado for me and for Anamika. But I was getting restless and disillusioned with my uninspiring sedentary job. Then six months later the prospect of an exciting career in the Indian Navy made me resign from the P&T job.

About a fortnight before I was to embark on a different voyage of my life, startling news hit the townsfolk in the morning. I heard that a special team of CID officers had arrived from the district at night and had taken away Anamika's husband in a prison van just after dawn. Some of those policemen had told Anamika's neighbours that he was a gaolbird who had escaped from prison and was a notorious highway robber. It seemed so incredible, impossible. I was the last man to believe such crap until the next morning's newspapers unfortunately proved me wrong. A drunkard and a habitual gambler was the worst I could think of him. But it took quite a while for me to imagine the apparently peace-loving man in the garb of a dangerous criminal, a fugitive from law.

Naturally, you know, from shame Anamika stopped coming to the temple. So on the last day of my stay I went to meet her in her house for one last time.

Looking at her face now stripped of that inseparable and familiar smile was very very painful. Discreetly, I asked her about her future plans.

"You know sir," she said gravely, "after all this shameful incident I cannot think of staying in this town any longer; everybody knows me. Moreover, for a young woman living alone without her man is disgraceful and such women are considered immoral in this society and are often looked down upon with suspicion." She looked thoughtful.

"So where do you intend to go?" I enquired.

"I have an old uncle of my father who used to live at Kharagpur. I will try to find him out," she replied sombrely.

There wasn't much I could do. I gave her five hundred rupees to facilitate her journey which she accepted reluctantly.

I landed on the deck to begin a new life that took me across three oceans and many seas, I visited many a distant shore, ran into many queer people and caught wonderful glimpses of their strange lives, I fought a war, fell in love and emerged out of it a couple of times, disoriented and puzzled like a man who has just regained his memory after a bout of amnesia and all along newer reminiscences kept accumulating on the older ones, pushing those wilting memories towards oblivion.

It was only at times when a similar sounding name came to my ears did Anamika and the temple rise from the floor of my remembrance to float before my eyes. Occasionally, standing on the bridge of my ship INS Vikrant and while looking at the limitless expanse of the blue waters before my eyes I wondered what had happened to Anamika. Was she still alive?

Nearly two decades later, by one of those unbelievable accidents that happen in life, I met Anamika again at the most unlikely of places on earth.

A comrade of mine had died of kidney ailments. Being his buddy I was chosen in keeping with the custom in the Forces to accompany his body to his home at a coastal town called Baleshwar. And in the evening along with his bereaved family members I went to the cremation-ground on the bank of a river.

A pyre was burning in the gathering darkness and the dom (people who help cremate bodies as a hereditary profession) attending to it came up to arrange another pile of wood in its trembling light for my dead friend. Half-an-hour later my friend was stripped naked (because Hindus believe that a human being comes into the world naked and therefore must leave it in the same form) and laid on the pyre and dedicated to the Fire-God. As the tongues of fire leapt to consume the mortal remains of my buddy, a woman emerged from the surrounding darkness and ambled up to the dom. Her back was towards me but I could clearly hear her speak.

"Go, your tea and tiffin is ready; I will look after the pyres," she said to the man, who I presumed to be her husband. The man went away and the woman took a long bamboo pole and poked the fire to make it burn properly. Then she turned and immediately we saw each other in the bright orange glow of the pyre. For a moment a thunderbolt of surprise left both of us paralysed as we recognised each other.

Then she said, "Sir, I never thought I will see you again. But when God wishes to play a sweet trick, such impossible things can happen and I am so happy."

The spontaneous disarming smile so familiar to my eyes still hung to her lips and even in the afternoon of her life the vestiges of a pretty face were clearly discernible. But by no length of imagination

240

could I understand what mysterious event had flung her to such a bleak corner of the world.

Sitting on a brick platform built under a large Neem tree for the waiting relatives of the dead, she told me that she had searched out her uncle who, being a man without a family, happily gave them shelter. But he retired from service soon and returned to his ancestral place at Baleshwar where they lived together on his pension until he died suddenly just five years later.

"God snatched away my shelter a third time," she perorated broodily, "and I had nowhere to go again. With the help of a neighbour and my young sons I somehow cremated his body. But struck by the speed of the misfortune I had perhaps lingered a little too long at the gate of the cremation-ground that rainy evening which prompted Vikram, the person who has been making the pyres here to ask me if I really had nowhere to go. He had heard my sobs and wails and when he knew the truth he sent his old mother to persuade me to share his modest hut along with his mother and a deaf-and-dumb sister for as long as I wished. The rest is history and the story of his kindness. He was a very young man then, perhaps younger to me by several years but since then I have found peace and happiness here."

In the prevailing darkness which was thrust back only by the glow of the pyres I could see the reflection of the leaping tongues of fire in her moist eyes.

"Your sons?" I whispered.

"Yes, they are big now and happy. I had a son with Vikram and the three brothers run a kiosk and a shop on the highway," she replied in a happy note.

What a place to find happiness! I mused with a shudder.

The clang of the closing temple-doors made Dasanan spring to his feet.

He looked at his watch and exclaimed, "My God! It's dinner-time. Forgive me brother, for holding you back till this unearthly hour."

And he rushed down the flight of stairs dragging me along.

# THE BLAZER WITH TWO RIGHT SLEEVES

## Dan Sullivan

*Dan Sullivan teaches English at St. Mary's Ryken High School in Leonardtown, Maryland. He has published three short stories so far. Dan is proud that Supawadee is his wife, Laura and Mark his children, Kyleigh and Erica his granddaughters, and Ploy his stepdaughter.*

The Lynch twins were late for everything—weddings, job interviews, family picnics. On each occasion, they would arrive rumpled and out of humor to make their separate but identical apologies. "I'm really sorry we're late, but you know how my brother is."

Procrastination was a life-long character defect of the middle-aged bachelors. Their dear, departed mother, in tears, had often tossed up her hands and guessed that it probably started even before they were born with the two of them rough-housing inside her, losing track of time and finally arriving three weeks after their due date. She had always been at a loss on how to correct it. Prayer, fasting, novenas, threats, icy silence, sweet talk—nothing worked, and to her dying day, she considered herself a bit of a failure that her dear, sweet boys could be so inconsiderate to let her leg of lamb get cold each and every Sunday.

Nor did Catholic grammar school do anything to correct the problem. Sister Arcangela, Principal of Nativity Grade School, was fond of announcing after the first bell, "Ah, here they are!" And with that, the stately Franciscan—also now long departed—would use the twins' arrival, as if on serendipitous cue, to illustrate the downside of "tardiness"—a lesson which always ended with the admonition, "Ron and Walter Lynch, you two will be late for your own funerals."

Actually, she wasn't off by much.

Ron wasn't late for his own funeral that day, but he *was* about a half an hour late—give or take a few minutes—to welcome the mourners at his twin brother Walter's wake.

Ron had promised himself the night before that he *would* be on time, that he *would* go to an early morning AA meeting, that he *would* get his jacket pressed early enough so he could get there and have a word or two with Walter before the mourners arrived.

But he broke every one of the promises he made to himself and went instead to an AA meeting at noon, which left him with only about twenty minutes to spare. Then there was the traffic in Georgetown. And when he finally got to McCawley's Funeral Home, the tiny parking lot was jammed. Only a prayer to his sainted mother helped him find a spot three blocks west on 37th Street.

Then it came out of nowhere—the urge to have a cold one. Not just any beer, but that lovely Foster's, the one he had had a lifetime before. It was July 1960, a year before they buried their father. The three of them—Walter, their father, and Ron—had been laying sod at a country club. Ron was working his way up what must have been a thirty degree incline with a loose-handled spade, thrusting into the yellow lawn under the roots, jacking up the sod, pitching slabs into the barrow, staying ahead of the muffled thumping and tamping that grew louder behind him.

When the job was done, they sat in the cab of their truck and shared beers so cold that their throats burned. That was the one he wanted, the one he was craving now, but Ron knew that he had dallied far too long so he said the Serenity Prayer…again and again and again.

The craving began to dull as he had reached the front porch of McCawley's, rumpled, out of breath, and angry.

His program of recovery had taught him that it wasn't the thirst at all that drove him to drink. Beneath the urge for drinking and carousing was procrastination, and beneath the foot-dragging was more than a little vanity and a lot of anger. And Ron's anger and irritation had found, by high school at least—probably earlier—an available target in Walter, his twin, and a workable medium: disputes over verifiable facts all clouded by obstinacy and aging memories.

*Ron, for your information, Don Larsen pitched his perfect game in the 1956 World Series.*

*Wrong again, Walter. It was the **1955** series because Dad was still in the hospital and we were only freshmen at John Carroll High School that year.*

Cherished nieces and nephews had tried to intervene. At Christmas and on birthdays, they would bear neatly wrapped peace offerings in the form of books—more recently software—crammed with facts and dates and other trivia. Encyclopedias, almanacs, sports history books, trivia, dictionaries of sports, *The History of Golf,*

*Saints of the Roman Faith--Before Vatican II*, Mel Kiper Jr.'s *2007 NFL Draft Guide* were all presented in the vain attempt to keep pace with the disagreement *du jour.* They never did. Over the course of years the neglected presents began to overrun the bachelors' apartment.

*I can't believe you said that, Walter. It was* **Laura** *who gave us "The Complete Encyclopedia of Sports."*

*Wrong again, Ron. It was* **Eileen.** *Laura gave us the...*

Ron took a deep breath and then removed his glasses before going inside McCawley's. You just never knew when Janet or Susan Whelan from the old neighborhood just might show up even though he hadn't seen them in forty years.

The black and pink shapes of the mourners against the side walls of the parlor where Walter lay floated past Ron as if he were walking on the floor of the sea. At the casket, he felt as if he had stepped into a cave of flowers, and the place where he stood was oddly lambent—vague and out of focus yet somehow far too bright. It was like the time that Sister Archangela had summoned Walter and him on stage to sing "Wild Colonial Boy" at Nativity's St. Patrick's Day assembly. He was aware of the parlor full of mourners and that he and Walter were now center stage with him playing the mourner and Walter acting dead.

Ron made the Sign of the Cross and kissed his thumb before he knelt at the casket. *Our Father...*

It took a little time, but finally Ron looked at Walter. As best he could, without his glasses, Ron saw his own face, still and powdery, his own head resting on a white satin pillow in the casket. He kept waiting to see if Walter would flinch or tighten an eyelid or move a finger, signaling that it had all been a mistake, that it was time to call the whole thing off, that they hadn't properly rehearsed this. But there was no sign, just Walter asleep in the casket, his waxy hands folded just above his waist and fingering a rosary—still and waxy forever.

*Walter, you're an idiot! It was 1956 when Carl Perkins released "Blue Suede Shoes" on the Sun label. Presley was the one who covered it in 1957. If you had half a brain, Walter, you'd be dangerous.*

*"...forgive us our trespasses as we forgive those...."*

*And by the way, genius, it was Laura who gave us the...*

*It was no use continuing. Even in death, Walter aggravated Ron so much and then made him feel so guilty about it to boot that he couldn't even say a prayer for his own departed, aggravating brother. But the failed prayer did give Ron a chance to slip his glasses back on and inspect the corpse. After all, he was paying handsomely for the arrangements.*

Ye gods!

Danny McCawley, owner and mortician, must have been deep in his cups when he did Walter. There was no other explanation. It was either that or Danny had turned one of his interns loose on Walter: he looked horrible!

Just an hour into the wake, give or take a few minutes, and already the powder had begun to cake at the corners of Walter's mouth. Then there was Walter's expression—the one they would remember him by, the one Walter would carry to the seat of judgment.

Ron had told them he wanted his twin brother to look "noble"— in fact "noble" and "calm" were his instructions. But McCawley's Funeral Home had rendered Walter neither *calm* nor *noble*: somebody had fiddled with Walter's mouth—setting it in a kind of devilish grin for all eternity. Then the *piece d' resistance*—the presentation of Walter.

In the "Coronado" casket—a mid-point in quality, size, and price between the "El Camino Real" and the "Pobrecito"—Walter was laid out in his navy blue blazer—the one with two right sleeves, the one he had bought over the Internet for $24.99—plus shipping and handling. They laid Walter out—not in the clothes Ron had bundled up and given to Danny three days earlier, but in the clothes Walter was wearing the night he died of a heart attack at Arthur Murray's. Probably nobody but Ron would notice the stubborn eddies of fabric on what was supposed to be the left sleeve of Walter's jacket. Still…

*"Ron, come here. Look at this."* On the monitor in Walter's room was a cartoon figure with a magnifying glass examining a suit. A caption trumpeted, "Even the pickiest shoppers have a hard time finding anything wrong with our clothes. Clothes for a song. Men's Blazers starting at $24.99 plus shipping and handling! Clothes on line—www.sullyzclothesline.com."

*"Read between the lines, Walter—'have trouble finding fault with'—doesn't that tell you something? Doesn't that say to you that they're selling you a piece of…"*

*Within a week, Walter's navy blue blazer arrived by UPS, and, except for the sleeves, it was perfect.*

*"You've got to be kidding me. You're not really going to wear that thing out in public, are you, Walter?"*

*"Of course. Besides, I'll just be wearing it at night anyway."*

245

By the time Ron blessed himself and stood, his Aunt Annie Maguire, their eighty-year old godmother, who never could keep the two of them straight, was waiting to extend her hand and condolences to Ron. Ron kissed her forehead and squeezed her skinny hand. The skin felt loose and delicate like crepe.

"Walter, I know how much you loved your brother. But he's in a far better place. And I have to say that Ron looks just wonderful. Danny did such a wonderful job. So calm. So..."

"Noble?"

"Exactly!"

...Ron had come home early from Safeway that day. Their supervisor in the Meat Department had placed Ron and Walter on separate work schedules. Cleavers, cutting blades, and the Lynch twins on the same shift—it was a formula, their boss half-joked, for headline news. Ron and Walter returned from the Army in 1967, and Safeway Foods hired them as meat cutters as part of a program to give jobs to returning Vietnam veterans. When Ron entered the living room, he saw Maria from down the street, the Austrian nanny with platinum hair, her arms around Walter's neck, chiding him playfully in a deep, husky voice as they stopped dancing to the Five Satins' "In the Still of the Night."

"Vat's 'rong?"

"Nothing..."

"Vat's 'rong, baby?"

"Nothing..."

Ron's early arrival had had a chilling effect on Walter and his chance for romance. It seemed like minutes of silence, then Maria muttered and noisily collected herself before marching toward the front door. Walter followed, imploring. Maria over her shoulder called back, "Vogeddit, buddy." Walter at the front door, and Ron from a living room window, watched her as she clomped down the front walkway, out of their life, in a yellow sun dress and clogs.

"I guess you screwed up your chances with her, Walter," Ron said brightly with a can of beer in his hand.

"Not really, Ron, I told her I was you."

With one hand cupping her elbow and the other holding her upper arm Ron guided his aging aunt onto the kneeler and stood awkwardly behind her in the odd light near the casket. When Aunt Annie had finished mourning the wrong godson, Ron hoisted her up from the *priedieu*, and they turned away.

The parlor was now packed. And if Ron wasn't mistaken he thought he recognized Walter's cologne—the overpowering blend of sandalwood and witch hazel—asserting itself over the flowers and feuding scents of the mourners.

Besides the Lynches, almost every other family from Nativity Church—their old parish—was there. And after about an hour or so of mixing and reacquainting, Monsignor Tommy Wallace, who had gone to school with Walter and Ron, intoned the Sign of the Cross, and there was a grand, extended rush as the able-bodied mourners knelt.

"We are here this evening to offer the Sacred Mysteries of the Most Holy Rosary for the repose of the soul of Walter Lynch and for the needs of Walter's loved ones…"

Ron stole a look at Walter who still held his look of malevolent humor about the whole affair.

*…late summer just before the start of fourth grade. They had just turned nine. Ron was tired of always being with Walter, dressing like Walter, playing with Walter, eating with Walter, sharing birthdays with Walter. Ron wanted just to run away and stop being Walter's twin. After practicing the speech several times in his mind, he announced to Walter in the alley behind their house that they couldn't be friends any more, that they were getting too old to be playing together, that some of the guys said they were 'weird,' always with each other. Ron declared that they both had to be on their own and find girl friends, now that they were about to turn nine, and play sports. Ron remembered looking at his other self: Walter was lost and stunned at first. Then his own face—Walter's face— shattered. At the far end of the alley, a black man in a red flannel shirt swung an ax and buried it in a log. But the sound didn't reach them until he had raised the ax once more above his head. Walter's face was twisted in rage and pain. And he balled his fists and started to cry. "I hate you, Ron, you stupid moron." Walter ran away down the alley toward the man who again silently buried his ax in the log.*

It was the second Sorrowful Mystery. Ron knew that if you looked long enough and hard enough at something lifeless it would almost seem to move. That had been the case with his father when Ron could have sworn that their father moved two or three times during his wake. Ron had been looking at the corners of Walter's eyes since they started the prayers to see if there would be the slightest signal that it was all a mistake. But Walter lay motionless as if petitioning for his own cause with a rosary in his floury hands.

"Holy Mary, Mother of God…"

The rhythm of Monsignor Wallace's lead and the mourners' response made it sound, when Ron closed his eyes, like the rush and retreat of the sea.

247

"Holy Mary, Mother of God, pray for us sinners, now and at the hour of..."

*...Walter and Ron had taken their assigned places in the den for the family Rosary that night. Walter and Ron nudged each other all during the First Joyful Mystery, but it was Ron who finally got exiled to the hallway by the end of the Second Joyful Mystery, and after the Rosary, their father sentenced Ron to bed, even though it was only 7:30. But it was delicious being alone in their room under the cool sheets—away from Walter, alone with the light of early evening on the bedroom walls. He heard Walter and the D'Archangelo kids next door chasing each other across the yard, back and forth...back and forth...They had cornered Ron on a mesa in the blazing sunlight. It was either death by torture—and the Apaches had so many cunning ways to torture a man to death—or death by leaping to the boulders below. But that was suicide and a mortal sin. When Ron woke up, it was dark, and he was tangled in his sheets at the foot of the bed. Walter was asleep. Ron shook Walter awake and asked, "Walter, can I please sleep with you? I'm having a bad dream." Ron climbed into Walter's bed, and they held each other. Walter patted Ron's shoulder and muttered sleepily, "Don't worry, it's just a dream." The eight year-old twins and best friends huddled fast asleep. That was the year before Ron put an end to play in the alley.*

For the first time since Walter's heart attack, Ron cried. His grief sounded foolish and reluctant like a sneeze among strangers. He pictured the nine-year old Walter, his face twisted in pain and rage, balling his fists then running away down the alley. The sneeze came again and again, and then he couldn't hear any more the rush and retreat of Monsignor Wallace and the mourners in prayer.

He and Walter had been together since the first division of cells, side by side, taking careful note of the virtually identical genetic instructions from their parents. They had huddled and tumbled together as they grew inside their mother, kicking and touching and grappling. Ron was delivered first, then Walter—three weeks after their due date. Now...

*Walter, what am I supposed to do now, you idiot?*

Several elderly mourners were straggling through the concluding devotions after the fifth and final Mystery of the Holy Rosary. Monsignor Wallace blessed himself. Then there was an extended rush as the mourners stood and by degrees the parlor emptied and Ron thanked each one for coming. No sign of the Whelan sisters.

Finally, Ron was by himself with his back to the casket. He decided against going back again. It was slippery enough for him tonight, and he'd probably have to say the Serenity Prayer about a million times before he got to bed.

It was ten o'clock when he got home. He called his AA sponsor but got his answering machine. Still just making the call had steadied Ron enough to face the apartment alone. For the past week or so with making arrangements for Walter's funeral and notifying Walter's creditors and getting to meetings he hadn't had time to deal with the day-to-day of his own living. For one thing, he hadn't even checked his e-mail. He turned on his computer, and there were 15 unread messages waiting for him. There were messages offering season tickets to the Redskins at outrageous prices, which he deleted. There were daily GREETINGS! from his goddaughter Laura, which he saved. There were several UNDELIVERABLES FROM the SYSTEM ADMINISTRATOR, which he had no idea what to do with, and a promotion from the on-line clothes company sullyzclothes.com that had sold Walter the blazer with two right sleeves. And finally there was a message from *w.lynch.*

Ron said the Serenity Prayer and scrolled down and opened the message Walter had sent from his office the day before he died.

It was 1957, you moron!

*Easter Monday, the first day of their weeklong vacation from Nativity School. Everything was yellow and jungle green in the April sunlight. Sister Brendan, their third grade teacher, had assigned no homework, and they were free. Ron followed Walter as they hopped from one bunker to the next at Fort Stevens where Abraham Lincoln almost got shot by Confederate snipers. Back and forth across the bunkers, two gentle eight-year-olds hopping and yelling—whatever they felt like doing in the sweet April breeze. Before you knew it, it would be Daylight Savings Time, then the school picnic, then exams, and out at last for the whole summer. They hopped down from a bunker and lay in the grass that had become tall and thick while they were asleep the night before. Walter draped his arm around Ron; Ron did the same to Walter. They squinted at the crystal sky. They were copies of each other in every way—the same brown, wavy hair, the same slanted blue eyes, dressed the same: long sleeve polo shirts with red and blue stripes, blue corduroy pants, and black high-top sneakers.*

*"Do you think Esther Williams is pretty?"*

*"She's okay."*

*"How about Marilyn Monroe?"*

*"Oo la la..."*

*They laughed and punched each other, then jumped up and scaled a bunker. This time Walter followed Ron. Back and forth across the bunkers at Fort Stevens...*

Ron picked up a framed family photo from his desk. He touched the spot where Walter stood among the Lynches. Then Walter suddenly became small and began to float behind what seemed like smeared glass. Then he flamed out from the others and grew closer, and a feeling like whiskey bloomed inside Ron. But it wasn't whiskey: Walter was reaching out to his brother from an Easter Monday far away... *And beneath the anger was a feeling he had no name for, but it came on at times like twilight, in the alley behind their home, and it never failed to fill his eyes; it had something to do, he guessed, with the losses in his life and the time he put an end to play with Walter, fifty years before.*

Ron closed his eyes and whispered in his heart where he knew Walter could hear him.

*"Oh by the way, genius, I hate to disappoint you, but it was 1956."*

BRUISED APPLES

Debra Purdy Kong

*Debra Purdy Kong has published more than eighty short stories, essays, and articles. She has also published a mystery novel called "Taxed to Death." She lives in Canada's Pacific Northwest. See her website at www.debrapurdykong.com.*

"What's wrong with the women in this house?" Granddad yells from the living room. "Why can't you all get along?"

My footsteps falter on the thick, mint green, carpeted steps in my grandparents' home. His baritone shouts always startle me. Even Mom and my aunts stop arguing.

From his big chair, Granddad turns and spots me. "Come in, Marla. They've managed to shut up for now."

As I enter the room, I spot Mom gulping the last of her sherry. My Aunt Connie fiddles with one of the green rhinestones fastened all over her poofy red hair. My youngest aunt, Ann, strolls to the dining area at the far end of the room, looks at the remains of her twin's wedding cake, then drags her finger through the white frosting.

Granddad's question won't be answered. He's asked it so often during family gatherings, I doubt he expects a response anymore. Still, he always asks. It's a habit he can't break any more than he can quit smoking. Maybe he asks because he knows his daughters don't have an answer. This way, Granddad gains precious moments of silence.

"Marla, clear the plates, will ya?" Aunt Ann licks frosting off her finger. "Place is a mess."

I'm surprised she's waited this long to ask. As the eldest niece, I've been the family servant since I was seven. Cleaning up is better than sitting around listening to them bicker, though. I gather cake-stained plates from the mahogany coffee table.

"If Ann hadn't thrown herself at my husband, nothing would be wrong," Connie blurts, glowering at Ann. "Find your own man. Jane has one now. Surely you can land a husband, or are you plotting to steal hers?"

Swearing at Connie, Ann stomps out of the room on clumpy sandals.

Granddad mumbles, "Four daughters. Where did I go wrong?"

Another infamous question. Granddad's brothers had sons, and since he already had two daughters, Granddad desperately wanted a boy. He wound up with twin girls.

"Yes, Daddy, we're all a huge disappointment to you for not being born male, yada-yada-yada." Connie's face turns almost as red as her hair. "Like we had a choice."

Mom hiccups and raises her empty glass. "Marla, bring me the sherry, honey."

She points to a decanter containing amber liquid. Mom's not big on drinking until she's with her sisters. Thankfully, these visits don't happen often. I put down the plates at the bar, then lift the decanter with the delicate leafy pattern. Afraid of dropping it like I did two years ago, I use both hands. Sometimes, my aunts still call me the clumsy one.

"Thank you, honey." Mom takes the decanter from me.

This is my first wedding reception. It would have been nicer if Mom and my aunts left when the other guests did, but my mother and her siblings can't leave a gathering until one of them's in tears.

I should have gone downstairs to play ping-pong with my sisters and Aunt Connie's five kids, but their ongoing Supreme Player of the World tournaments bore me.

I walk around Granddad's outstretched legs to retrieve his plate. He props his elbows on the arms of his chair and entwines his gnarled fingers. To avoid his scrutiny, I focus on his empty coffee cup.

"Would you like more coffee, Granddad?"

He looks at the china cup and saucer rimmed with gold. "Thank you, dear." Tired blue eyes peer at me. "You aren't getting married any time soon, are you?"

"I'm only sixteen, Granddad." Seventeen next month.

"A young lady then." His smirk stretches below the bushy mustache. "You've always been mature for your age, you know that? Intelligent too. Smartest one of the bunch."

Judging from Mom's and Aunt Connie's laser stares at Granddad, another battle's brewing.

"You want to be some sort of scientist, as I recall," he adds.

"A marine biologist."

"Hmmmm." Granddad's brows scrunch into a long furry line, as if he isn't sure this is an appropriate choice for a young lady. "What are you studying in science these days?"

"Genetics."

"I've read about that." He nods. "At least one woman in this family will lead a useful life."

Why does he bait them?

"For crying out loud, Daddy." Mom plunks the stopper in the decanter. "I was doing laundry and grocery shopping at thirteen because Mother was busy with the twins. Now I'm raising three daughters on my own and working full time."

"When will you stop that pathetic self-pity act?" Aunt Connie removes a mirror from her purse, then checks for wayward strands and rhinestones.

A pointless gesture. Her hair hasn't moved all day. Must have used half a can of spray.

"It's not self-pity, it's fact!" Mom's voice rises. "No one's had it harder than I have."

Granddad snorts and turns to me. "Your mother's been singing that tune since she was your age, you know that?"

"I never was your favorite," Mom mutters.

"What are you talking about?" Connie shoves the mirror in her purse. "You've always been the favorite!"

"Here we go," Granddad grumbles.

Item number thirty-nine on the list of sibling feuds. Why can't everybody just play ping-pong? Have some laughs and forget old grudges.

"Marla." Aunt Connie holds out her dirty plate. As I stroll closer, her bloodshot eyes study my face. "You've lost all your homeliness."

"Thanks." This is the kindest thing she's ever said to me.

Plates and cup in hand, I push open the kitchen door with my shoulder, then freeze. My grandmother stands by the sink, trying to strike a match for the cigarette dangling from her lips. I had no idea Granny smoked. Her rigid stance and scowling face suggest she's had enough wedding celebration for one day.

"Don't tell Great Granddad I'm smoking," she says in a hushed tone.

"I won't."

Granny's seventy-four years old. Great Granddad's nearly a hundred, and he's asleep in the guestroom. Why does everyone here worry about what others think?

"Leave the dishes by the sink, honey. I'll do them."

"You want some help?"

"That's sweet of you, but I'll have them washed up in no time." As she exhales the smoke, relief dissolves some of the lines on her face.

I knew she'd insist on doing the dishes, but thought I should offer anyway. Granny's learned to stay in the kitchen when the family gathers. She's taken too much it's-all-your-fault-mother abuse over the years to risk more attacks.

After refilling Granddad's cup, I take a deep breath, then head back to the living room.

"You're a good girl." He watches me place the cup in the gold-rimmed saucer. "But if genetics is the big influence scientists think it is, you won't be for much longer, you know that? All those guys have proven is that the apple doesn't fall far from the tree."

"You're probably right, Granddad." He likes it when people agree with him.

While collecting plates from the dining table, a thought occurs to me. Maybe what's wrong with the women in this house is that the apples haven't fallen far enough from the tree.

I stare at the wedding cake. The once gorgeous three tiers with pink roses have been reduced to a mangled layer of chocolate cake surrounded by globs of frosting.

Aunt Connie's heavy footsteps come closer. I turn and watch her remove a cigarette from the pack next to Granddad's coffee. "You have more respect for your grandchildren than us. It's not fair!"

And whining about it's supposed to help? I drag my finger through the frosting. Aunt Connie's ample back blocks my view of Granddad and Mom. Before I know it, I'm flicking frosting at her poofy bullet hair. A tiny clump sticks a rhinestone. Two white dots land below it. Aunt Connie's so busy lighting her cigarette she doesn't seem to notice.

I lick my finger, gather more plates, then hurry to the kitchen before the adults discover that this little apple just hit the ground hard.

# FLOWERS for WALTER

## Dan Sullivan

*Dan Sullivan teaches English at St. Mary's Ryken High School in Leonardtown, Maryland. He has published three short stories so far. Dan is proud that Supawadee is his wife, Laura and Mark his children, Kyleigh and Erica his granddaughters, and Ploy his stepdaughter.*

To Myrtle's way of thinking, they did one sorry job of keeping up the gravesites at "Green Pastures of Southern Maryland." For the third year in a row, she had to get down on her hands and *knees* and clip last summer's grass away from Walter's headstone. The plastic trash bag she brought from home was about half filled, and she would make sure she plopped it in full view of the caretaker's office on her way out, and God help anybody who dared say a word to her. To tell the truth, though, Myrtle was just hoping someone *would* say something. She had been itching for a good fight for years over the care of Walter's gravesite. *Shovel-leaning idlers, that's all they were. Must be nice...*

Myrtle brushed off her knees, opened her Bible, and read from John, Chapter 20, a favorite of hers. She even had them put on Walter's stone, weathered after fifteen years, part of verse 29: *Blessed are they who have not seen and yet believed.* Next year, she would see what she could do about cleaning the headstone herself.

She put the Bible back in her straw carrying bag, said a prayer for Clint—Walter's boy now in his thirties who had drifted off years ago—and then spoke out loud to Walter.

"Blind your eyes, Walter McCarty. You stuck me with a mailbox full of bills, no *in*surance, and ..."

Myrtle could never bring herself to say out loud the last words she was thinking, but she remembered. And every time, it felt the same—like a slap across the face.

She remembered finding the magazines down in the cellar within three days after she had buried Walter. She wasn't one who could just sit around and mope. She would go crazy if she didn't stay busy.

On the day after his funeral, she washed every last window in the house and scrubbed the upstairs floors. On the second day, she washed, ironed, and folded every stitch of Walter's clothes, which she planned to give to the Salvation Army. On the third day, with a bandana across her mouth and nose, she started sweeping the cellar and clearing out his junk. After her eyes adjusted to the shadows, she found them—the magazines—stashed in three cardboard boxes in a closet next to Walter's workshop.

She pictured Walter just below her at that moment, a lump in the darkness, on his side, pulling a quilt of leaves over his left shoulder, burrowing to stay warm from October. Myrtle stamped her foot twice. She was not about to let Walter enjoy the luxury of eternal repose—not yet, not when he had left her alone with a closet full of those filthy magazines—just the filthiest things a person ever laid eyes on.

And even after six years of marriage, plus the fifteen years since his death, it was the pictures she remembered.

Without her reading glasses, in the cellar's darkness that day, the glossy photographs from Walter's "girlie" magazines at first had been a garish blur of curves and colors—pink and blonde, tan and chestnut. She had held the first magazine away from her and studied it with shock and fascination—the way she felt once seeing cars swerve around the body of a homeless man in the middle of a street in Washington, D.C. She turned the pages and glimpsed at Walter's fantasy world of perfect young women, a world that she had been shut out of for the years of their marriage. This is what he must have wanted all along, and she was what he had had to settle for—a bony spinster in her forties with a bad temper and flab around her middle. And all those nights, alone, and full of rage…

On Walter's workbench that day, numb and weak, for only God knows how long, with boxes of *dirty* magazines at her feet, Myrtle saw her six-year marriage to Walter narrow into focus. Every thought and memory of him became filtered through that moment in the cellar.

All the nights, she had gone to bed after the eleven o'clock news, to shower and put cream on her face and hands and feet and wait—wait for Walter. She finally gave up, but she always stirred when Walter, at about midnight, came padding softly into their bedroom. She remembered how careful he had always been to slip into bed and not touch her, turning on his left side away from her before going off to sleep. And the more time Walter spent in the cellar, the fussier Myrtle became, and the fussier she was, the more Walter stayed to himself.

So she talked it over with Ruthie, her sister. The verdict was that Myrtle needed to put more *spice* in her marriage, and Ruthie had "just the thing." The next day, Ruthie brought by a videotape of a TV talk show on sparking romance in middle-aged marriages. A skinny woman therapist with a New York accent said that women needed to be more assertive and put "the intrigue and the exotic" back into marriage. She recommended romantic nightgowns and perfume, makeup and jewelry, and above all torching those flannel pajamas. But when the therapist held up a can of whipped cream, right on television, and said, "Now, girls, if you or your fella has a sweet tooth…" Well, Myrtle had never heard of such a thing in all her life, and she stopped the tape right then and there. Still, the next week, she and Ruthie went shopping. And after Ruthie called Myrtle a "prude," Myrtle finally broke down and bought a black nightgown from Natasha's Sleepwear in Waldorf. Myrtle also got a permanent that day from Huong's Chopping Block, and, after supper and the dishes, with Clint at his cousins', she showered and sat on the bed waiting for Walter, waiting with fresh make-up, a new hair style, and sleepwear from Natasha's. When he finally scuffed in, she came over and put her arms around his neck. But he pulled away, gently, with a faint smile, kissed Myrtle on the forehead, then announced that he still had some work to do in the basement.

He closed the door after himself, and she crumpled on the bed and hid her face. After a time, she balled up the nightgown, threw it in the trash, and stood naked in front of the mirror, regarding her own body with shame and disapproval. She was flat where she should have had some meat, and she was flabby where she had no business carrying weight. She noticed the permanent she had gotten that day, especially the curls above her ears. At that very moment, she looked silly to herself because she had been so hopeful. She turned on the shower so Walter couldn't possibly hear and she stood in the tub, letting the water stream down her body, hearing her own sobbing that made her feel even weaker.

When she finally stepped from the shower, something burned white and cold inside of her. Later she even pictured her heart glazing over like ice then becoming as hard as enamel. She promised herself that she would never again give Walter or anyone else that much power over her. He had crushed her that night, and she promised herself she would never let that happen again. Then he went and did it to her all over again down in the cellar three days after she had buried him.

Well, that was a long time ago, and if you asked Myrtle, Walter had never been anything to write home about either—a big, heavy man, ten years her senior, with rumpled clothes and scuffed shoes—Mr. Pitiful—a man whose first wife ran off with a bass guitar player from Hagerstown. She could still picture Walter scuffing in and out of Glad Tidings Bible Church in La Plata each Sunday with his serious little boy in tow.

Pastor Armel Armbruster and all the ladies at Glad Tidings had felt that Myrtle was just what Walter needed—Walter and his sad little boy, Clint. Her friends all called her a "firecracker," with enough energy and spunk for any three couples, and of course, for a man and a little boy who both moved about half-dead, Myrtle was considered the perfect cure. She was organized, not afraid of a little hard work, had a good heart, and in her fussy, bustling way, she would, in the words of the pastor's wife, "bring Walter and his little boy back from the grave."

*Myrtle and Walter married in the middle of autumn. Myrtle wore a beige taffeta dress—a white bridal gown was simply out of the question at her age. Walter wore his navy blue suit, which she insisted he get dry-cleaned before the ceremony. She had bought Walter and Clint boutonnieres of white roses. They honeymooned alone—over Walter and Clint's objections—in Ocean City, Maryland. It was Myrtle's idea because she loved the sea. Her sister Ruthie said it would be romantic. Besides, it was off-season, and the price of rooms was less than half the summer rates, which made perfectly good sense to Myrtle. After the first night, Walter apologized, but she told him that it was alright. It was not that big a deal. It had been a busy day and a long ride. She had been tired too. They could wait. They had an entire lifetime together.*

Then once they got back home, they began to settle into a routine that was largely of Myrtle's design—breakfast at six-thirty sharp, home-cooked supper at seven on the dot, Clint's daily chores and homework done by eight, lights out after the eleven o'clock news. And all the while, Myrtle had held her temper in check. It was her bargain with the Lord to have Clint like her and Walter love her. She knew God was still working with her on that temper of hers, and she never wanted to cause Walter or his son any pain—they had already gone through enough. Still, Walter scuffed and puttered about, settling in, calling Myrtle "mother," until she felt like she was going crazy.

At first, she had felt that the bedroom business could wait. It was all the other little things. Walter would throw his socks and underwear on the floor *right in front of the clothes basket! Now how in God's name...He had to be blind not to know he had missed.* He would leave his dishes in the sink after lunch on weekends. At first, she tried to make a joke out of it, "Walter, the downstairs maid called in sick today so you're gonna have to take care of those dishes yourself, hon." And always Walter would scuff back to the kitchen sink with a weak smile on his face—Walter, the victim. And Clint of course was taking it all in.

Walter never helped when he should, and then when she needed a little peace and quiet and space—usually when she was on the phone with Ruthie—Walter would start his mindless and noisy puttering about the kitchen—looking inside the refrigerator, opening and closing drawers, rearranging items in the pantry. And just as soon as she got off the phone, derned if Walter, without a word, wouldn't scuff on downstairs to his workshop.

Myrtle stamped his grave again. She pictured Walter starting from sleep, throwing off his quilt of leaves and sitting up in the casket with a guilty look on his face, afraid to look at her, in his sorry boxer shorts and black socks.

"Walter McCarty, you left me with a mailbox full of bills, no *in*surance, and a closet full of dirty pictures." At that moment she pictured Walter looking down at his hands with that sad little smile on his face—Walter the martyr.

"Oh, no, you don't, Walter. Don't you *dare* pull that martyr bit on me!"

And then of course there was Clint who long ago had drifted away. Just when she thought that Clint was beginning to accept her, just when her prayers were beginning to be answered that the little boy—then eleven—would like her, just when Walter was at least beginning to act a little more like he had some life in him, she had to go and ruin it all.

Myrtle covered her face in her hands. *Oh Lord Jesus, forgive me for the dern potato chips!*

She had come home one Saturday afternoon, arms full of grocery bags, to find Walter and Clint watching *golf* on television and eating potato chips out of one of her good bowls. The *one* thing she had asked Walter to do—in fact the *only* thing she had ever asked Walter to do—was to clean out the cat box, which of course he never did. If Walter and Clint insisted on having cats, which Myrtle personally hated, since they were just about the sneakiest things that the good Lord ever let loose on the face of the earth, then Walter and

Clint needed to clean out the litter box *every single day*. So there she had stood with grocery bags in her arms, with no offer of help from a soul, with the smell of ammonia overpowering the basement, and the sound of the two of them crunching potato chips without even saying hello…She let them have it.

The blast from Myrtle—to this day she couldn't remember exactly what she had said—was so loud that both Walter and Clint started from the couch at the same time, her good bowl took flight, and potato chips scattered about the family room like a flurry of leaves. They cleaned up the potato chips and the cat box right away in silence, but Myrtle sensed she would never have another chance with Clint. After that Saturday, Clint spent more and more time in his room, never again said a voluntary word to Myrtle—only answered her questions. The softness she had been noticing in his eyes—before the potato chip business— turned back to that scared look—the same way he looked the day she moved in. And Walter of course plodded and puttered about the kitchen whenever she was on the phone, only to return to his workshop for longer and longer periods. In hindsight, maybe if she had been able to bridle her tongue, as Scripture warns, maybe…But lonely and hurt and stung beyond words after Walter had left her alone in the bedroom, like a fool in the forest, Myrtle fussed more and more—and louder. It got so that it was almost as if she were living in a rooming house with strangers keeping to themselves behind shut doors—driving her crazy. Then after six years of this, Walter had died in his sleep.

At the funeral, Ruthie and Mrs. Armbruster both told Myrtle how blessed she had been. Ruthie admitted that Walter was no ball of fire, but he was a decent man who seemed to treat her well. Mrs. Armbruster, the pastor's wife, went so far as to praise Walter, "Walter never ran around, Myrtle. He never had affairs with other women."

The consensus at the gravesite on the day of his funeral was that Myrtle had been fortunate to have such a God-fearing man as Walter. All the compliments and well wishes, though, seemed to crowd and bump against her, but she said nothing about how lonely she had been and how stung and angry she had come to feel living like a roommate with Walter who had vowed in the sight of God and man to be her husband.

Myrtle got the image of Walter sitting on the side of his casket, now in his pajamas and slippers, looking up at her, hoping that the memory of his advocates, his witnesses at the funeral six years before, might carry some weight with Myrtle now. She stamped her foot again. *Don't dare pretend that you're as pure as the driven snow, Walter, 'cause you're not.* The image of herself alone in their bedroom flashed in her mind, and she took a deep breath.

The wind scraped some rusty leaves up against Walter's headstone. Myrtle stooped to brush them away, leaned forward and, without really knowing what she was saying or why, blurted out, "You didn't have an affair with anybody else, Walter. You had an affair with yourself."

Myrtle kept brushing the leaves away from the headstone, but each time she did, the wind would rush more of them over the grave. It was no use; she wouldn't fight it any longer. She just stood there with the wind swirling leaves around her.

When she finally left Walter, she couldn't see his headstone. It was like looking through glass smeared with oil. She couldn't see the caretaker's office either as she placed the half-filled plastic bag gently on the walkway; still it felt as if she had stepped into a well-lighted room. For the first time since his death, Myrtle let herself remember a night when she and Walter had come back from Glad Tidings. Pastor Armbruster had been holding a revival, and that night Walter seemed softer and lighter. He had even hugged Myrtle and told her how sorry he was that he hadn't been a better husband. He promised to try harder. Myrtle allowed that memory to stay a moment, and then the image of Walter back on the side of his coffin returned. The quilt of leaves was now about his shoulders, and Walter sat there with that same soft look she had been refusing to recall for so long.

*Walter, it's o.k. And Walter...from the bottom of my heart, I want to apologize about those dern potato chips.*

On the bus back to LaPlata, she wiped her eyes and told herself that she would try to get in touch with Clint—just to say hello. And next year, for the first time since Walter had passed, she would bring flowers—probably a pot of yellow mums.

She would need a little more time to work her way back up to roses.

# THE GRAY GHOST

## Kelli A. Wilkins

*Kelli A. Wilkins is a multi-published author in a variety of genres. Her short stories and novels have won or placed in several contests. To learn more about Kelli, visit her website at: www.KelliWilkins.com.*

Dwight zipped up his thick winter coat and quietly pushed open the screen door. "Come on Shadow, let's go," he whispered.

He didn't want to wake Grandpa or Mom. His mother wouldn't want him leaving the house to explore, but he couldn't sleep. He'd slept most of the way here last night while Mom drove from their house in Cleveland to Grandpa's farm in Kentucky. Mom had said that she couldn't bear to stay home this weekend because the house held too many memories. Dwight frowned. If Dad were still alive, they'd be home now. Thinking about his father made him sad, and Mom wouldn't want to see him crying this weekend. After all, it was Thanksgiving.

Dwight broke from his thoughts as Shadow's warm wet tongue tickled his fingers. He rubbed the dog's head. No matter what, he still had Shadow. Since Dad's death two weeks ago, he had slept with the dog curled next to him at night. He cried into Shadow's short, gray coat when the sadness and sense of loss took over his heart.

He closed the screen door behind him and stood on the porch. The crisp early-morning air tickled his nose. He knew he shouldn't walk too far from the house. If he did, Mom would fret that he'd exerted himself and baby him, just because he had asthma. Shadow padded next to him, his pink nose sniffing the air.

Dad had surprised him with Shadow last month for his eleventh birthday. He had always wanted a dog, and Dad had come through for him. That Wednesday he'd gotten up for school and found the unusual-looking two-foot tall gray dog waiting for him at the bottom of the stairs.

"He's a Weimaraner," Dad said.

262

"A Weim-a-what?"

His father laughed. "A Weimaraner. They're called 'gray ghosts.' A friend of mine at work is moving and can't take the dog with him."

Dwight pushed the memory aside. Sometimes it hurt to remember. He picked up a wet stick and tossed it ahead of him. "Fetch, boy."

As Shadow vanished into the cold, misty morning, he understood how Weimaraners earned their name. Shadow seemed to disappear and reappear when he wanted.

He blinked back tears as he recalled the last few weeks he spent with his father. They had trained Shadow to follow simple commands. As a joke, they'd taught him how to fetch his asthma inhaler. Mom called it gross, but Dad thought that it was funny. It was during this time that Dad had explained that he was sick inside and the doctors couldn't help him.

He remembered his father's words. "I'm not going to be able to watch you grow up. But Shadow will be here for you, and he'll remind you of me. It'll be like a part of me is still here watching over you. Take good care of Shadow and he'll help you when you need him."

Shadow returned with the stick, and Dwight waved it over his head, making the dog jump. He threw the stick again and Shadow charged after it. Dwight crossed the yard and headed in the direction of the woods. Frost-covered oak and maple leaves crunched underfoot as he followed an overgrown path.

"Come on, boy." He tapped his leg and Shadow came to his side, carrying the stick in his pink mouth. Dwight patted Shadow's strong back and sighed. How could he celebrate Thanksgiving when he felt so miserable inside? He'd be a lot more thankful if Dad hadn't died and if Mom didn't cry every night when she thought he was asleep.

Shadow stopped walking and sniffed the ground in front of him. Suddenly, a brown rabbit dashed out of the bushes and darted across the trail. Shadow took off, chasing it into the underbrush.

He ran after Shadow, calling his name, but gave up as a familiar tightness in his chest forced him to stop. He reached into his coat pocket for his ever-present inhaler and relaxed. He hated not being able to go anywhere without his medicine. It made him feel weak and helpless. It was bad enough that he was short and thin, but he couldn't even breathe like other kids in school.

He glanced at the undergrowth and shrugged. His gray ghost would be back. He hiked through the woods and made his way across a field. An old, run-down house stood in the distance. He hurried toward it. A secret place! He'd always wanted a hideout of his own. Now he'd found one.

Tall weeds surrounded the three-story, weather-beaten house. Dwight hopped over the two missing front stairs and climbed onto the sloping porch. He cupped his hands around his eyes and tried to peek through a gap in the boarded up windows, but he couldn't see anything inside. Dwight jumped off the porch and walked to the side of the house. The bottom part of a small side door was broken in and he crawled inside. This would be fun. He could play and explore all he wanted.

He wiped off his grimy jeans as he stood and looked around the dim main room. The house smelled like mold, and his nose itched. Mom would have a fit if she knew that he'd come in here. She was always concerned about mildew and dust triggering his asthma.

He wandered into the rooms in the lower half of the house and examined three broken chairs, a half-chewed rug, and a few empty cardboard boxes. He wrote his initials in the thick dust on the kitchen counter and spotted a staircase leading to the second floor. Should he? He hesitated. Maybe he should leave now, find Shadow, and go back to Grandpa's house before Mom started looking for him. He could always come back after dinner.

He shook his head. It would be dark by then. If he explored now, he'd know all the good places to play this weekend. His body tingled with excitement. Who knew what treasures might be hidden upstairs?

The ancient wood creaked under his sneakers as he climbed the steps. The upstairs hallway was littered with bits of fallen plaster and rotten cardboard boxes. He tried to imagine the family that might have lived here. Why did they move? Did they have kids who played here?

Dwight entered one of the three bedrooms and ran his finger along the rusty iron bedframe. The stuffing had been pulled out of the mattress and lay scattered on the floor. An old trunk shoved into the corner captured his attention and he stepped toward it.

Suddenly, the floorboards cracked and collapsed beneath him. Dwight screamed and frantically grabbed the edge of the bedframe as his legs and torso dropped through the hole. His heart thundered as his chest tightened. No, not now! He couldn't have an attack now.

He clutched the bedframe and kicked his feet, hoping to find something to stand on. His sneakers swished through space. There was nothing beneath him. "Help!" he shouted. With a sinking feeling, he realized that there was nobody who could hear him. He was alone.

He swallowed hard. He'd have to pull himself up onto the floor, but how? He wasn't strong enough. His arms ached and felt like they would rip from his shoulders. His sweaty hands slipped on the cool metal, and he yelled again.

He took a breath and began to wheeze. The doctors had told him that stress and fear could trigger his asthma. How long could he hold on? What would happen if he fell? He might break his legs or his back. It could be hours before anyone thought to look for him. If only Dad was here, he'd know what to do.

"Shadow will help you when you need him," his father's voice echoed in his mind.

He closed his eyes and whimpered as his hands cramped. Shadow had to be close by. He licked his lips and whistled as loud as he could. Dogs had excellent hearing. Shadow would find him. "Shadow! Here boy!" he croaked. Dwight counted to fifty, then called out again. Where was Shadow when he needed him most?

What seemed like hours later, Shadow charged into the bedroom. His nails clicked on the hardwood floor as he approached Dwight's side. Dwight let go of the bed with one hand and wrapped his arm around Shadow's shoulders. Weimaraners were strong and solid. Once, Dad had told him that Shadow almost weighed as much as he did. "Pull, boy!"

Shadow walked backward and Dwight struggled from the jagged hole, inch by inch. He collapsed onto the dusty bedroom floor, wheezing and gasping for air. He fumbled in his coat pocket for the inhaler he so desperately needed, but felt nothing. His pocket was empty.

He clenched his fists as his chest burned. Now what should he do? Shadow's amber eyes searched his. "Fetch it, boy," he whispered. Maybe it was the smell of the medicine or Shadow's natural hunting instincts, but the dog knew how to find the inhaler. Shadow whined once and left the room with his nose to the floor.

Dwight tried to relax. If he didn't move, the attack might pass. Sometimes he got lucky and everything returned to normal in a few minutes. But sometimes things got worse, much worse. What if Shadow didn't find the inhaler? He coughed a few times as he lay on the floor, listening to his heart thundering in his ears.

A few minutes later, Shadow appeared with the familiar blue inhaler clenched in his mouth. He dropped it on the floor and wagged his tail. Dwight snatched up the inhaler and wiped it off before taking a deep breath. He felt his chest loosen, and air filled his lungs. He blinked back tears and stroked Shadow's head. "Good boy."

Shadow flopped next to him and licked his cheek. Dwight

draped his arm over Shadow's back and closed his eyes. He'd have to save his energy to make it back to Grandpa's house. Today he had something to be truly thankful for.

***

Dwight let the screen door slam behind him and entered the warm kitchen. Shadow's nose went up in the air as he sniffed out the delicious aromas of turkey and freshly baked pumpkin pie. Dwight's mother closed the refrigerator and rushed over to him.

"There you are! I was worried about you. Where have you been?"

He let her fuss over him. Right now, he wanted the attention. Dwight gazed into his mother's blue eyes. She didn't need any more worries. He shrugged. "Out playing, exploring."

"Oh, okay. Go wash your hands. You can help me peel potatoes." She smoothed his hair behind his ear and hugged him close. "I'm going to mash some turnips for dinner. They were your father's favorite. It just wouldn't seem like Thanksgiving if I didn't make them." She smiled. "I know it sounds strange, but I feel like he's here, watching over us."

He swallowed the lump in his throat and patted Shadow's head. "I think so too, Mom. I really do."

# THE LAST RAIN DANCE

## Big Jim Williams

*Jim Williams, author of* THE OLD WEST *and* TALL TALES OF
THE OLD WEST *audio books, has written for Western Horseman,
Shoot!, Texas Livestock Weekly, American West, Orchard Press
Mysteries, Radio World, and other magazines. He announces at
KZSB, Santa Barbara, California. E-mail: bigjimwilliams2@cox.net.*

Raindrops splattered Damien Steven's windshield like a
million angry bugs. Frayed wiper blades fought to keep the glass
free of the downpour.

Damien pressed the accelerator. His old sports car coughed
and bucked forward on the freeway. A wall of water engulfed the
small vehicle as he fishtailed around an eighteen-wheeler that
plowed through the storm like Moses parting the Red Sea.

Grace had sounded desperate with her sundown call. She
gasped out a sad, pathetic cry for help. Then abruptly hung up, a
manipulative skill she had honed to perfection.

He didn't know what she had done. It must be serious. It
always was. He prayed she'd still be alive.

There had been suicide attempts: pills and slashed wrists.
He'd rushed her to the hospital using driving skills that helped save
her life. Now racecar driving was a hobby he could no longer
afford, partly because of Grace, who, unfortunately, never
produced a dull moment.

Two miles later Damien exited the freeway of speeding cars
and shimmering lights. He swerved down a ramp and slid to a stop
at an intersection that was more river than road. The swaying
overhead traffic light remained forever red to Damien. He
nervously watched in his side- and rear-view mirrors as the same
big rig from the freeway squealed to a stop behind him. Its
searchlight eyes sent shafts of blinding light across its massive
bumper into Damien's small car. Wind rocked his vehicle as water
leaked through its top and windows. He'd wanted to replace the

canvas and window seals. But, being jobless, couldn't afford it. The college had claimed computer programmers were in demand, but had neglected mentioning the tight job market.

His fingers drummed the steering wheel. The low-slung car sputtered. "Don't die, baby." He revved the engine, and prayed it wouldn't die in the flooded intersection. A tune-up was something else he couldn't afford.

"Come on! Come on!" he shouted at the wind-tossed stoplight. Its red glow danced through his fogged windshield. He cleared a circle with his gloved hand.

Then red became green. Damien looked left and right, then carefully maneuvered his car through the swamped crossing onto a familiar country road that disappeared north beyond his high beams. The truck didn't follow. It lumbered left toward warehouses fronting the freeway. Damien could now make better time. He increased speed slightly, fighting the endless downpour blanketing his car and obscuring his vision.

Grace needed him. That was all that mattered; lovely Grace, so soft, warm, fragile, and--conniving.

"Could you help me with this month's rent, Damien?" She had cooed like a peace dove on Valium. Then it was a dental bill, the need for a thick winter coat, and a fashionable evening dress before that. It was something almost every month.

"I'll pay you back, honey," she smiled. Her soft voice came with a touch of slight southern accent but trowel-thick charm. Damien could still smell her jasmine perfume in his car.

He had loved her. Had said so. That ended with him broke, and Grace baiting her hook, trolling for a new lover with deeper pockets. Her latest, "Karl," came with looks, a Mayflower pedigree, money, and a new sports car.

Forgetting a beautiful young woman with a sultry voice wasn't easy. She always called Damien when she wanted something. He always answered because he needed something—-her. He still hoped they might get back together.

Another thirty minutes and he would reach Grace's remote lakeside home, a big lodge inherited from her father.

He could have shaved off minutes if the storm had lessened. It had been raining for days like a rehearsal for Noah's flood. Rivers had broken their banks, and several towns had been evacuated. The downpour now equaled fire hoses at a three-alarm fire.

Overflowing ditches on both sides of the narrow road lapped at the white line like high tide, and spread into adjacent farm fields.

"Dammit!" he yelled. A big green station wagon suddenly

darted from a side road, pulled in front of Damien, and slowed to a crawl in the middle of the road. The top of a bald head above the driver's seat glistened like a shiny melon under Damien's headlights.

"Stupid idiot!" cursed Damien, horn blaring. "Must be a midget driving that damned gas-guzzler!"

He had driven the two-lane twisting road countless times, but never during a thunderstorm, or behind a snail-paced driver.

He honked again and flashed his lights. The lone driver's speed remained unchanged. Damien lowered his window, stuck his head out, and yelled: "Move over you old son of bitch!" Water splashed into his face. He choked and coughed.

"Road Hog!" he screamed. The other driver didn't respond. Yelling lessened Damien's anger and frustration.

Again he beat his horn and flashed his high beams. The other driver stared straight ahead, seemingly unconcerned, the crown of bald head the only sign life behind the wheel.

"That driver must be a hundred years old!"

The front vehicle remained unhurried, despite Damien's incessant horn honking. Every time it came to a side road it stopped, and the driver leaned over and peered out the passenger window.

"Now, what's he doing?" Damien shook his head. "Why...why the old fool's lost. He's reading every road sign!"

The green car slowly advanced. Its driver ignored Damien's protestations.

Damien tried to go around the big car, but couldn't. "Dammit! Move over!" he shouted into his flip-flopping wiper blades. He cussed and slammed his steering wheel with both hands. "Should've brought my cell phone."

When Grace had called, he'd tried to call her back, but her line was busy, probably off the hook. She'd done it before when threatening suicide.

A stop sign loomed ahead. It marked a familiar crossroad within three miles of Grace's home. The station wagon stopped, still hogging the road.

"Now!" yelled Damien. He jammed his foot on the accelerator and splashed around the green behemoth. His left wheels slipped off the shoulder into a watery roadside ditch. His wheels spun, tossing mud and gravel. He gunned the engine, broke free, and flashed the driver the bird. "You old son of a bitch!" he yelled, his voice muffled behind his passenger window. As his mud-caked wheels left the flooded intersection, his rearview mirror caught the wide eyes and open mouth of a small, bald headed man in wire-rimmed glasses peering through a steering wheel.

Damien careened down the road, and slowly increased his speed. But within minutes the green car was behind him. Its lights knifed through *his* rear window.

"What the hell?"

The big car rode inches from Damien's rear bumper. It flashed *its* lights and blew *its* horn.

"What's he doing?"

Damien accelerated. So did the station wagon. "Get away old man!" he shouted. "Stay back!"

The second car's engine roared; its lights blinding as it dogged the smaller car.

"I'll fix you, you bastard!" A smile twisted across Damien's face. He stomped the accelerator. His sport car leaped forward. The gap between the cars widened.

A hundred yards later Damien yelled: "Watch this you crazy old fool!" His taillights flashed red as he slammed on his brakes and turned his steering wheel. His car spun around and stopped. Its glaring headlights faced the oncoming wagon. Unable to stop, the second driver braked and deliberately drove off the road. His car splashed into the roadside ditch, his right headlight beam dulled under water. The remaining headlight illuminated the ditch and rain-splattered road. The wagon's engine coughed and died.

Damien drove past the tilted wagon, spun his car again, and stopped alongside. He leaned over and rolled down his passenger-side window. Rain soaked his car seat. He didn't care.

A small, wide-eyed man in a thick overcoat stared from the tilted, partially submerged car. Shaking hands gripped his steering wheel. Twisted glasses dangled below his open mouth.

"How do you like them apples, old man?" shouted Damien. He laughed and drove away. The wagon's Cyclops' eye blinked, then died as water shorted the car's electrical system, and night engulfed the site.

Another few miles and Damien would reach Grace. He was worried, but smiled, thinking about the old geezer stranded in knee-high water. "Good riddance!" he muttered.

Minutes later he skidded to a stop at Grace's tree-shrouded home. All the lights were off. He grabbed his flashlight, splashed through the graveled driveway, and climbed the porch three steps at a time. He pounded on the thick door.

"Grace!" he yelled. "It's Damien. Open up!"

Stone silence came from inside.

He tried to shine his flashlight through a crack in the double wooden doors, but couldn't see a thing.

More pounding. Then the door slowly opened, revealing the large dark foyer. Grace looked pale under the beam of Damien's flashlight, but was still beautiful. Her long blond hair flowed to a flowery silk robe that covered her full breasts and perfectly proportioned body and hips, but ended above stiletto-heeled black pumps.

That's strange, thought Damien.

"Oh, Damien...thank God...you're here." She clutched her stomach, stumbled backward against an opposite door, and knocked it open.

Damien was suddenly blinded by bright lights, followed by shouts of...

"SURPRISE!" and a hundred people singing, "Happy birthday, Damien!"

After champagne, Grace stood with her arm around Karl, but kissed Damien on the cheek. "Damien," she said, "the surprise birthday party was the least I could do for all the wonderful things you've done for me over the years. The times you saved my life." She handed him an envelope. "Here's all the money I owe you."

"How did you get all my friends here?"

"Weeks of planning. Never expected a storm, though."

Lightning shook the sky as more rain pounded the lodge.

"I'm sorry," continued Grace, "you didn't get to see your special birthday cake. Our baker's made cakes for my family for years. Should have been here hours ago. A little old man, can barely see over his steering wheel. I'm surprised you didn't see him on the road. Drives a big green station wagon."

271

# LIFE'S CHANGES

Jeanette Hollman

*Jeanette Hollman is a wife of forty-one years, a mother, and a grandmother. She has been editor of a college newspaper and reporter for her local paper. She now writes short fiction.*

The area encompassing the fifty-year-old frame house first appeared unchanged as we pulled into the long gravel driveway. The oak post fence in front looked a little dog-eared--its bark no longer smooth, but splintered and festering, and the once pure white shingles on the house were gray and dotted with spots of mildew. But that was to be expected since Mother Nature's hand is never still. And just like the changing seasons, life's changes are also inevitable.

It was our daughter, Chris, who first noticed a difference. "That house on the left is new," she said. "That lot was still empty when Grandma died."

"That's right," I said. "That house was under construction the last time your dad and I were here, but you weren't with us then."

"This area sure has changed since Grandma and Grandpa first moved here. I remember when it was mostly woods and there were no other kids around to play with," Chris responded.

"I remember going hunting with Dad back in those woods," Joe sighed. "And now there's a shopping mall there. I guess that's progress for you. Nothing stays the same."

It was evident that the new neighbors had already moved in by the occasional puffs of smoke coming from the bar-b-q grill off the large wooden patio deck. The sprawling townhouse with its pristine, white, vinyl siding towered above my in-law's two bedroom ranch. The two-car garage housed a John Deere riding lawnmower and an assortment of tools and gardening supplies. A brand new SUV and a minivan were parked in the driveway. A large above ground pool took up most of the backyard which was surrounded by a six-foot tall cedar fence.

In the backyard of the lot on the other side, a young mother gently pushed a baby in a swing while older children played nearby on a jungle gym set. A child's red wagon sat idle on the grass. The lot was void of trees or shrubs, a direct contrast to the shadiness provided by my father-in-law's large cedar trees and bushes that surrounded his house. The attached two-car garage housed a mini-van and a brand new pickup. On the side, was a large camper—the kind you pull behind a pickup.

At the end of my in-law's driveway, Dad's small wooden unattached garage looked out of place sitting parallel to the neighbor's new camper. The once white paint was peeling and some of the wood slats in the double doors were splintered and cracked. A wasp nest dangled from the overhang. On the other side of the driveway, the giant maple tree stood with its bare branches outstretched next to the house. Layers of golden yellow and rust colored leaves covered the walkway to the basement door.

Dad's two American Eskimo dogs were tied up under the tall cedar trees in back of the house. Neither of them barked as we got out of the car--a sign that they had now become accustomed to humans within close proximity to their fenceless boundaries. Chris and I walked over to the runt, Sissy, who wagged her tail excitedly and rocked her pint-size body in anticipation.

"Hi there, girl. You look like you could use a bath and a good brushing," Chris said as she stroked the runt's matted and dirt laden fur. "Mom, remember when Grandma got in the bathtub with her to bathe her? Do you think she misses Grandma?"

"I'm sure she does," I answered as I bent over to pet Sissy. The runt licked my hand excitedly and a big gob of saliva drooled from her mouth. I could see the crusty tarter at the base of her gums. "It's been a long time since you've had one of Mom's big soup bones to gnaw on, huh girl?"

Snowball, the runt's mother, was tied up a few feet away. As Joe walked over to pet her, the old dog greeted him with a blank stare as if she did not recognize him. Her once husky physique showed how time and passivity had taken its toll. Her feeble legs wobbled as she stood while Joe brushed his hand over her matted and dirt-laden, once snow-white coat. Somewhere, from deep down inside her, you could sense the yearning to once more feel the rush of wind on her face as she raced though the countryside.

As we walked around toward the front, I was saddened to see how neglected Mom's flower garden had become since her death. She had always been so proud of her garden, but now it was overgrown with weeds. The tall zinnias no longer stood in even rows, but were slumped over like wearied soldiers at the end of a long battle. Their once brightly colored blooms were now a withered and crusted

273

brown. The chrysanthemums' once lavish blooms were now coarse and dry and the dying branches of the peony bushes drooped over, their heads buried in clumps of brown leaves. Much of the grass leading up to the porch had turned brown from lack of rain, and most of Mom's petunias in the large clay flowerpots were already dried and withered from the cool evenings.

As we mounted the rail-less concrete steps, the door swung open and an elderly figure emerged. Wearing his familiar gray sweater with its worn sleeves and torn pocket, Dad greeted us with a slight smile. He tried to hide the pain, but his slow gait, and tired swollen eyes, and furrowed brow gave him away, evidence that the last few months had taken its toll on his body as well as his mind. His frail frame shook as he leaned forward to give each of us a hug and kiss.

"Are you still okay with this, Dad? You know we're doing the right thing, don't you," Joe asked as he gently helped his dad down the steep concrete stairs and over to the spot where the dogs were tied.

Dad just nodded his head sadly and mumbled, "I know it has to be done, son. I just hope she understands."

Chris brought over a lawn chair for Dad while Joe picked up Snowball and gently placed her on his father's lap. Tears filled the old man's eyes as he gently patted the old dog's head and rubbed her matted coat. Whispering softly, he said, "Goodbye old girl. Someday soon we'll all be together again." He kissed the top of her head and she licked his hand. She seemed to understand and laid her head on his hand as if to let him know it was okay. She was ready. She would once again feel the wind as she raced though green fields. No more suffering, no more pain. Joe carried her to the car and gently placed her on the blanket we had spread out in the backseat. Chris climbed in next to her while Joe and I helped Dad back to the house. As we backed out of the driveway, we saw Dad sitting on the porch glider with his head down. We knew that this would be hard for him, almost as difficult as dealing with Mom's illness and funeral. And then, after we returned from our appointed duty, we knew Dad would be facing another difficulty—deciding what few mementos to take with him and grieving over what was to be left behind.

# THE LOVE POTION

## Sanjaya Mishra

*Sanjaya Mishra works as a geologist, engaged in exploration of ground water in remote parts of India. His works have been published online in desilit.org, dispatchlit.org, runesmag.com, and in print media, as well.*

As the sun descended from up above the sky, the activities at the weekly village market waned. The herds of gathered cattle disintegrated, each group escorted by its respective owner. The cheap clothes were again bundled together. The heaps of rice, dal and different seeds were meticulously transferred into the sacks and the vegetables, now losing their shine by the heat, were neatly gathered in the baskets.

Under the banyan tree, the nomadic salesman still displayed his wares – dry leaves, seeds, barks of different sizes and colours and even stones - all claimed to heal a variety of diverse ailments. Beads of light, created by thin pencils of sunrays streaming in through the dense tree, flickered over them like twinkling stars in a night sky.

Sitting in the jeep, I could see a girl of around thirteen, in a worn out dress, approaching the nomad salesman and I heard her ask, "Have you got Mohini?"

"What?" the salesman asked, amused.

"Mohini," the girl repeated.

"You know what it is? Why is it is used?"

The subtle movement of her head was the affirmative gesture - but to me it looked so out of place, so incongruent with the innocent stare of those two black eyes.

Two men, gingerly sucking at their biris looked in her direction, their faces displaying bafflement bordering on rage. One of them said harshly, "You devil of a girl...at this early age you already think of roping in a man...can't wait anymore..."

"Get lost you bitch...you are going to bring disgrace to your family and disrepute to our village," the other one joined in.

The salesman looked on amused, not minding his prospective customer getting shooed off by these villagers.

The commotion had started to attract the attention of others so the girl sheepishly turned to go and just then her eyes fell upon me and they looked as pure as the driven snow, betraying no signs of shame.

One of the villagers drew nearer me and explained as if to clear any confusion, "You know sir, Mohini is a potion that is used attract men by the women. A pinch of it sprinkled on the man unobtrusively or better still if administered through food by the girl, will do the trick."

The nomadic salesman waved his head proudly in agreement.

"And this young girl wants it…all the morality in our society has been thrown to the dogs," the villager went on sermonizing, his dark tobacco-stained teeth in perfect harmony with the torrent of expletives that were also let loose in between.

While on my way back from the village in the evening, I found the girl sitting on the edge of the pond; throwing small rocks to the water, with a forlorn look on her face. Still not able to conceive the fact that this girl could behave in such way, I approached her.

The downcast glance at seeing me coming bespoke of some trace of embarrassment on her part, but she remained where she was and kept on looking at the waves the rocks formed in the water.

I also took some rocks in hand and joined her in the act, hoping it would put her at ease.

"I didn't need it for me sir, it was for Pami," she said suddenly.

"A friend of yours?" I asked.

"Yes, our cow," she replied, laughing.

"For your cow!" I exclaimed, bewildered.

"Yes, ever since she hasn't delivered, we are in dire state, with no milk to sell…I thought maybe this thing would attract the village bull towards her and she will deliver."

I stood there dumfounded and it took some time for me to comprehend the whole thing.

She was still throwing away rocks aimlessly to the pond, as I drove on, ruminating about the fallacy of the adult mind.

# LOVE IS SUICIDE

## J. Matthew Nespoli

*J. Matthew Nespoli follows his passion at the UCLA Writer's Program. He aspires to publish a few novels that will affect the thought processes of his readers, and elicit some laughs along the way.*

Tonight was nothing more than the day after yesterday, another unavoidable obstacle on my road to the after-life. It was the thirtieth day since Melinda stomped on my heart, the thirtieth day in a row that I'd spend drinking myself sick...

There are various ways to kill oneself slowly.

I was out alone to see the band, Crooked Fingers. Music was the only true love in my life, and the only thing that wouldn't hurt me.

There were only about twenty other people there at the Viper Room, but the air was thick with greatness in the legendary venue. The walls were stained by the breath of icons like Johnny Cash, Iggy Pop and Springsteen, all of whom had performed there. Wrapping the bar in a chilly darkness was the lingering soul of River Phoenix, who'd died only meters from where I sat.

The emcee stepped on stage. "Please give a warm welcome to the night's first performer, Joanna Garucci!" he said.

The curtains parted and there stood Joanna, alone with her guitar.

And then the world stopped.

It was just her and me.

Vulnerable waves of want moved through me.

And I wasn't comfortable with how I felt...

When my father was alive he used to tell me, "A broken heart never heals. Falling in love is suicide."

He wasn't lying...

Allison was my first. I met her eight years ago in homeroom when she sat two seats away from me on the first day of high school.

I stared.

I forgot my name, forgot what I had for lunch, forgot what planet I was on. I couldn't avert my eyes; not because Allison was the most beautiful girl, but because she was the most interesting to look at. For the first time in a long time, I was sure about something; I wanted to be with her.

Our first year as a couple was amazing. The conversations were almost as good as the sex. Once, we snuck out of a class, taught by Allison's dad, and had sex in the back of his van. After, Allison fell asleep on my shoulder, and I watched her until my arm went numb. I carefully slid my arm out from beneath her and turned onto my other side. Without waking, Allison rolled toward me and slung her arm around me. That was my first experience with love...

A month later Allison came at me with, "I have to break up with you."

She'd found somebody else, somebody that, "understood her."

"It's not personal," she said.

Like hell.

There's scars where Allison once was.

I swore off love. I decided it was best to fall in lust over and over, and get out before things went bad. After Allison, came Theresa, Erika, Terry, Monica, Susan and Kim. They were all the same versions of each other in different packages. I kept a safe emotional distance and the relationships were purely physical.

Then Melinda came around. Melinda was a beautiful exotic orgy of ethnicities; her parents' DNA blended into something spectacular. I tried to avoid falling in love with Melinda, but she tried that much harder to make me fall in love. Melinda coddled my broken heart, nurtured it and kissed it's boo boos until it was healed... Then she reached down my throat, ripped my heart out and stomped on it until it was a worthless lump of flesh. She rammed the dead thing back into my chest cavity and disappeared, leaving me alone to stitch myself up.

That bitch Melinda ruined me in four weeks flat.

Last month, Melinda came to my work, uninvited and unannounced. I yelled at her, she disappeared, and then I caught her having sex with my co-worker in the bathroom. I kicked his ass, lost my girl and my job. A month later she told me that she was pregnant with my child and that she'd aborted it.

She did it to hurt me. It worked; that pain will stick with me forever.

Tonight, Joanna, by simply stepping onto stage, caused a whirlwind of inner conflict for me.

I don't believe in love at first sight; I don't believe in love at all. So what is feeling inside me?

With Joanna on stage, and my eyes on her, all my beliefs about love hung in the balance of the next few minutes. Joanna was sickly beautiful, like an injured fawn lying on the side of a freeway. Her face was poetic, wonderful and disturbing, like a terrifying movie that would mess with my dreams for weeks.

The way she strummed her guitar sounded soft yet obsessive. Joanna sang the first verse.

> "Pink pills in a purple bottle, can't stop lead foot on the throttle.
> You lied when you said you loved me, me believing you hopelessly.
> Life's not about easy escapes, like to think there is give and take.
> I felt emotionally raped, a victim floating in your wake.
> So don't fucking ask for charity. I hate you and I hate me."

Her voice was passionate and haunting; it made me think of cancerous tumors, spoiled food, and decapitated puppies, but even more powerful than all that. I wanted to pluck sound out of the air and keep it in my pocket for later when I needed to hear something moving.

Then, after her verse the tempo changed, and Joanna spit out the chorus like it was venom.

> "My empty dead body, I've forgotten how to long.
> Music is my weapon, I'll kill you with my song."

I felt that Joanna gave a true depiction of her world rather than prettying it up. The beauty of her song provided a counterbalance to her pain. Her suffering, I felt, was the inspiration behind the song, and this suffering begat beautiful art, giving a positive element to her pain...

She played only one song, and I felt like I knew her. Then, she sang a love song which completely threw me off. Her third number was pop-punk, and her fourth number couldn't be labeled; it was pure energy, hatred soaked in gasoline.

Joanna was an odd fusion of The Ramones, Blondie and Motorhead with a pinch of Alanis Morissette. She didn't fit a genre. The closest I can come is to say that she was the kind of punk rock that asks the question, deep inside us, that wonders why the fuck we're in this world, and when we've exhausted all possible answers, we give up and scream, "Fuck you," as loud as we can to the tune of three miserable chords...

After Joanna finished her only set, Crooked Fingers took the stage. I couldn't stop thinking about Joanna.

I rushed to the bar between sets. "Sorry," I said after accidentally plowing into someone. When I saw who it was I got a lump in my throat.

"Joanna?"

"That's me."

"You put on an amazing show," I said.

Joanna was as beautiful up close as she was on stage. I wanted her to like me; it was the first time I cared what someone thought of me in quite a while.

"Are you touring with Crooked?"

"No. Just opening for them tonight... I wish I was touring."

"You should be touring. You're really great."

"Thank you... What's your name?"

"It's Dylan... What are you drinking?"

"Beer."

"This round's on me," I said and signaled the bartender.

"Thanks. I've got to use the ladies' room. I'll be back," Joanna said.

Joanna walked away, her voice resonated in my head, and I tried my hardest not to fall in love again, because, as I learned before, love is suicide.

## MR. DEARBORN'S BIG VACATION

## Philip Loyd

*First Prize – contest of June 2007*

*Philip Loyd resides in Houston, Texas, and is the author of thirty-seven short stories. His work has appeared in eighty-three publications in seven countries, with one story even produced for radio in Australia. Included in his numerous awards is the Hemingway Center Short Story Prize.*

The ocean waves crested against the Caribbean sky, swirling and sudsy behind Anna as she came splashing to the shore. She smiled and waved to Richard, stretched out on the beach sipping his margarita. He waved back. She was a vision of loveliness, the image of simple virtue and supple charm altogether. She was everything he had ever dreamed of. Seeing her smile as she kicked up sand running towards him, he wished this moment would last forever. But just as all good things must come to an end, so too must all honeymoons.

This is what Mr. Richard J. Dearborn remembered as he sat daydreaming behind his busy desk. For the clutter of penholders, picture frames, and paperweights, there wasn't even room for his feet.

The door to his office opened abruptly and in the same motion a woman of great bearing came bursting through, the secretary saying "Good morning, Mrs. Dearborn," all the while Mrs. Dearborn yammering on and on, as was her way.

"Oh, the traffic--frightful. Why is there always such a crowd down below? Bums. Oh, they call themselves musicians, or artists, or some other clever names like bohemians, or avant-garde, but they're all bums, just the same."

"Now, dear," said Mr. Dearborn.

"Don't dear me," snapped Mrs. Dearborn. "This city has gone to hell in a handbasket, overrun by hoodlums and hooligans alike."

"But--"

"But never you mind," she said, changing moods at the drop of a hat, as was her way. "How has your day been, dear? Are you ready for the Gates merger? Everything in order?"

Mr. Dearborn walked over to the window.

"Why, look at your desk," said Mrs. Dearborn, "you've not even your papers together."

Mr. Dearborn looked out the window toward the park.

"How do you expect to..." Mrs. Dearborn began, and Mr. Dearborn tuned her out altogether.

Down in the park, a dog was barking, running, jumping, and catching a Frisbee. Richard had a dog when he was a boy, a bright-eyed beagle named Smokey; but Mrs. Dearborn would have no part of it, said she was allergic to the dander. A thirty-something couple strolled along hand in hand, pushing a baby carriage. Mr. and Mrs. Dearborn had tried to have a baby once, but after the miscarriage they never spoke of it again. Mrs. Dearborn had never been fond of children anyway, though she did often donate money to several orphanages and literacy programs. A college student lay beneath a sprawling oak, his head resting upon his backpack while he scribbled something in a notebook. Poetry, most likely, Richard thought. Richard used to write poetry. In fact, people used to tell him he was quite good. That was back in college though, when Anna and he first met. Mr. Dearborn saw a young couple playing footsie on a blanket below. It reminded him of Anna. For their ragged jeans and wrinkled T-shirts, they couldn't have had more than two dollars between them. Oh, how wonderful it must be to be penniless and in love. But Mr. Richard J. Dearborn didn't know about such things anymore.

"So how do you?" said Mrs. Dearborn. "How do you expect to be prepared for the Gates merger when you've not even your papers together?"

"Dear," he said, "we need a vacation."

"A vacation?" she said. "You've the Gates merger in less than an hour. Your papers are a mess. How do you expect to..." Mrs. Dearborn began, and Mr. Dearborn's eyes drifted to a picture on the wall. It was a photo of Anna and him, and her parents. It was taken on Thanksgiving Day at their estate in the country. Anna's father was a banker, her mother the head of the local garden club. Both played bridge religiously and never drank. Richard had dreaded the inevitable meeting, but Anna and he were going steady by then.

That time in the countryside was the first vacation Richard and Anna had ever taken together, and it wasn't until dinner Thursday that the conversation took an uncomfortable turn for him. The unavoidable questions had finally surfaced.

"So what are you studying, Richard?" asked her father.

"English," said Richard.

"English, why that's fine. Of course, you plan on attending graduate school, then attaining your Ph.D. There's no real money in teaching unless you obtain a professorship at a university. Then what, perhaps make dean, or chancellor maybe?"

"No sir," said Richard, "I want to write."

"Write?" said her father. "What, like for a newspaper or a magazine?"

"No sir, poetry, short stories perhaps."

"Poetry?" snapped her father.

"Richard's an excellent writer," interjected Anna, "everyone at school says so."

"But a man can't make a living writing poems. Why, you might as well be a juggler, or a mime on a street corner. I hear the new president of Czechoslovakia is a poet. Is that what you want to be, Richard, president of Czechoslovakia? Maybe you could learn to play the spoons, or get a monkey and…" and until they left her parents' house on Sunday it went on like that. He didn't mind, though, not really. He knew this was the girl he was going to marry.

"Well," said Mrs. Dearborn, "how you expect to be ready for the Gates merger when you've not even your papers together is going to be a fine feat indeed."

"Dear," said Mr. Dearborn, "we really do need a vacation."

"You're not going to start all that again, I pray."

"We could go to your folks place in the country. Remember the lake, the moonlight?"

"I don't understand you," said Mrs. Dearborn. "You know as well as I that the Gates merger is our biggest deal yet. How on earth could you be thinking of vacation at a time like this? They'll be here in less than half an hour. Honestly, Richard Jonathon Dearborn, I just don't understand you sometimes. How do you intend to…" she began, and as she did his eyes wandered toward a paperweight on his desk, a smooth, flat rock he had found while they were hiking out West one summer while on break from school.

He was completely out of breath when inspiration shot through him like the cold, thin air burning in his chest. "Wait," he told her, "don't move an inch."

He scurried about, looking for…she didn't know.

"What are you up to?" she said.

"Anna," began Richard, "I've loved you since the very first time I laid eyes on you."

"What are you doing?" she said.

"I'll never forget that day. You were wearing a white sundress that was hiked up just enough so I could see your legs. Your hair was resting on your shoulders and you turned and smiled at me." He knelt before her.

"Oh, my God," she said.

"Anna, I've known ever since that day, we were meant to be together, always."

She was about to cry.

"Will you please do me the honor?" he said, and she said YES.

Richard placed the rock in her hand.

"What's this?" she said.

"Well," he said, "I know it isn't the rock you were expecting; but right here, right now, it's all I have to give."

"It's perfect," she said.

Richard made her promise they'd come back every year. Anna thought it was a splendid idea. They never did come back.

"Well," said Mrs. Dearborn, "how do you intend to absorb all the merger information before the Gates brothers arrive?"

"Dear," said Mr. Dearborn, "we could go hiking."

"Hiking?" exclaimed Mrs. Dearborn. "Richard Jonathon Dearborn, have you lost your mind?"

"We could go out West, the mountains, remember?"

"This isn't the time to be playing Sir Edmund Hillary," said Mrs. Dearborn. "The Gates brothers will be here in fifteen minutes. How do you think you can possibly..." she began, and as she did he looked over her to the mounted sailfish on the wall. They'd caught it on their honeymoon.

Richard was talking to the boat's captain about something in Spanish, something he didn't fully understand, when suddenly Anna's line caught, nearly yanking the pole from her hands while she hooted and hollered, hopping all around. Richard came running to her side. "Give it some slack," he said. "Let it run with it."

Nearly two hours later, working in shifts and sometimes together, Anna and Richard reeled in the great fish. It had put up a valiant fight, and it was still fighting now; but its death was not so glorious, now flopping on the deck as the captain clubbed it repeatedly.

They danced all night.

"You know what?" asked Anna. "We should just stay here."

"What, for another night?" he said.

"No, forever."

"Forever?"

"We could open up a cafe, or a cantina. I have money. Then we could fish all day and dance all night. We could sip margaritas on the beach and make mad, passionate love until sunrise. What do you think?"

"I think you've been in the sun too long."

"You don't like my idea."

"Sure, I like it; but what would your father say?"

"Oh, phooey on him."

"Well, you're not the one who is going to have to see him every day. He expects me there bright and early Monday morning. It was your idea, remember?"

"Yes, I remember," she said. "It was a wonderful idea, though, wasn't it?"

"What, me taking a job with your father?"

"No, our staying here forever."

"Yes, it was divine."

"Well then, let's make tonight last. Let's watch the sunrise one more time."

They had spent their last night on the beach. There was a full moon.

"How do you think you can possibly be prepared for the merger?" demanded Mrs. Dearborn. They hardly ever made love anymore, only after hostile takeovers and auspicious mergers.

"Dear," said Mr. Dearborn, "we could go south of the border, to that ocean-side village where we honeymooned."

"Richard Jonathon Dearborn, now I know you've lost your mind," said Mrs. Dearborn. "The Gates brothers are surely on their way up as we speak. If daddy were only here, why he'd… Now straighten your tie; you look a mess."

Mr. Dearborn turned toward the window. "Dear," he said, "we must take a vacation."

"Lord have mercy," said Mrs. Dearborn, "we just went to London not even a month ago, the Bigsby merger, remember?"

"A real vacation, just the two of us."

"We're going to Japan next month," said Mrs. Dearborn, "you know, the Hioto deal."

Mr. Dearborn just stood there, staring out the window over the tall buildings across the park.

"You're just tired, dear," said Mrs. Dearborn. "Tomorrow is Saturday; you can sleep in.

"Now," she said, "get your papers ready. The Gates brothers are surely in the lobby by now."

"Yes, dear," Mr. Dearborn said, but he didn't need to go over any papers. What is that old cliché about a fool and his money? The Gates brothers had a lot of money, and they were quite the fools.

If you were to walk through the door of Mrs. Anna Dearborn's house on 1 Stanford Lane at or around four p.m. that Friday you'd swear there was a riot in progress. Imagine a hundred chickens in a room, beating their wings frantically and bouncing from wall to wall with their heads just having been hacked off, or the frenzied floor of the New York Stock Exchange as the numbers plunge amid widespread panic. Now imagine somebody moving slowly in the midst, someone who could not only make sense of it all but was in complete control. That someone was Mrs. Dearborn as she gave orders here and ordinance there: the flowers in the foyer, the settings on the tables, the food, the wine, the lighting, the music... She said something to the caterer, then like a shot from a cannon exploded through the kitchen door. Her caterer wondered why she hired her at all. She was the most expensive in the city, but had barely lifted so much as a finger. No matter. When Mrs. Dearborn was in the cast, she directed the show. You dare not get in her way.

After a short stint terrorizing the chef and his staff, Mrs. Dearborn came bursting back from the kitchen. She rearranged the flowers again, checked the lighting once more, and wondered if her new drapes really matched her carpet, or if the carpet went with the sofa, or if the sofa complemented the chairs. She lined up the waiters, busboys, bartenders, cocktail waitresses, and coat-check girls like a drill sergeant and inspected them one by one: comb your hair; trim your nails; brush your teeth; tie your shoe; change your panty hose; and to the last, trim the hairs in your nose, and your ears. Everything was ready. Everything was in place. Nothing could go wrong. Tonight would be perfect. What could possibly go wrong?

Tonight would be a disaster, she thought. She went over everything again. She would get her husband on the governor's committee and he would forget all that nonsense about a vacation. She was determined that this night be special. It would indeed be a night they would never forget.

The phone rang and a young, professional woman came shouting through the ranks, "Mrs. Dearborn, telephone.

"I'll take it in my study," said Mrs. Dearborn, staring all along at the foyer as if the Queen of England herself would soon be passing through. "And what have I told you about shouting?"

"That it's very unprofessional."

"And most unladylike."

"Yes, ma'am. Sorry, ma'am."

Mrs. Dearborn stood statuesque, arms akimbo, then removed one daisy from a vase while saying "there," to no one at all.

"Yes, this is Anna Dearborn," she said into the phone at her desk. "No," she said, "I ordered two, one for the pool and one for the gazebo. Lord in heaven, can't you people get anything right?"

She spun the daisy between her fingers as she listened, staring at Richard's portrait on the wall.

"I don't care what your invoice says;" she said, "I ordered two."

Richard's eyes stared right back.

"Just a moment; it's in my purse," she said.

She took a piece of paper from her purse. What's this, she thought? She then dropped it on the desk. "Here we are," she said, unfolding the invoice. "Two, it says right here, two."

She picked up the strange piece of paper from the desk.

"Well you had better, otherwise I'll see to it you never work in the free world again, or the whole world for that matter."

She unfolded the sheet of paper.

"Yes, that will do fine."

She read the title.

"Apology accepted," she said, hanging up the phone, hypnotized by the words on the paper. It was a poem Richard had given her long ago, and not just the same words, but the actual poem, the very same piece of paper, now wrinkled and yellowed. But how did it get into her purse? He must have slipped it in there. He must be suffering from fatigue, what with all this talk of a vacation and all. And now his slipping this poem into her purse? Maybe he did need more than just a good night's sleep. Maybe he did need some time off. Just get him through tonight, she thought; just get him on the governor's committee and then they would take some time off, perhaps even an entire week. Anything, just get him through tonight. She wondered how the Gates merger had gone.

She dialed her travel agent. There. Everything was set. They would spend a week in Hawaii before the Hioto meeting in Japan. There was a hotel in Waikiki she had been thinking of buying for some time now. She stormed from the office, almost knocking over the caterer.

"Mrs. Dearborn, we still have to finalize the--"

"You take care of it," Mrs. Dearborn said on her way out the door. "What am I paying you for anyway?"

The caterer did not know.

* * *

When Mrs. Anna Celese Dearborn came to the revolving door at 1136 4th Avenue--she felt like saying--no, she felt like screaming it. Bums! And the crowd had grown even larger, now stirring about as there seemed to be some commotion in the mix. She would have called the police, as was her way, but she just didn't have time.

287

Bolting out the elevator, she blew by the secretary--as was also her way--the secretary saying "Good evening, Mrs. Dearborn" as Mrs. Dearborn burst into the office.

"Marsha," shouted Mrs. Dearborn

"Yes, Mrs. Dearborn."

"Where is Mr. Dearborn?"

The secretary said something, but Mrs. Dearborn couldn't make it out for the noise below.

"Speak louder, dear."

"I said, he should be in his office. He hasn't passed this way since the Gates meeting."

"Well, he's not here."

"Maybe he's in the lavatory."

"No, dear. The door's wide-open. He's not in there."

"Then I don't know. I'm sorry, ma'am."

"All right, then," said Mrs. Dearborn.

"Is that all, ma'am?"

"No," said Mrs. Dearborn. "I want you to call the police. I've had it with all the commotion below."

But someone had beat her to it. The sound of police sirens now drowned her out.

"Never you mind," said Mrs. Dearborn. "Just put Mr. Dearborn through if he calls."

Mrs. Dearborn walked over to the window. The fumes from the cars below burned her eyes. She never did understand why Mr. Dearborn always kept the window open.

She looked to the street below. Bums! Now, they would get theirs. There were two police cars and an ambulance. Strange, she thought. She leaned forward and, with one hand on the rail, brushed against a piece of cloth. It was a torn piece of shirt. What? It was a blue pinstripe strip of starched cotton. It was just like the shirt Mr. Dearborn was wearing today. She knew; she had picked it out herself. Her heart began racing. Her face became flushed. She screamed in horror.

"Have a nice evening, Mrs. Dearborn," said the secretary as Mrs. Dearborn tore through the office toward the elevator, faster than was her usual way. Did Mrs. Dearborn still want her to call the police? She didn't know; she couldn't make out the last thing she said for all the noise below. She would close the windows on her way out the office, just like always. Those two really do need to take a vacation, she thought, as she went about her paperwork.

# RESCUED

Daisha Seyfer

*Daisha Seyfer is originally from Pierre, South Dakota. She is currently completing her pediatrics residency at the University of Iowa. She enjoys writing in her spare time.*

Missy ambled slowly along next to the busy highway. Cars and pickup trucks roared quickly past, but to anyone watching, Missy seemed oblivious.

"HONK!" squawked the horn of a semi-truck as Missy moved one step too close to the cacophony of traffic.

Missy jumped, seemed to recognize the danger speeding past two feet to her left, and quickly turned and began walking in the opposite direction.

Thunder rumbled overhead. It was April, and thus far, it had been a damp and chilly spring. Missy had been homeless for over a month now, sleeping under bridges and eating out of trash bins. She had lost weight, and her ribs were easily visible. Her hair, once thick and shiny, was now dull and falling out in spots. To make matters worse, she had been attacked by a gang of youth the previous night. Missy bore significant purple and crimson bruises across her chest and back, as well as a deep cut above her right eye that was now covered with dried blood.

In the past, Missy might have been seen by someone to have the cut stitched up. She also might have had a bath to be cleaned up. Those days seemed long ago; Missy had not had a bath in ages. It was apparent from people's reactions on the street that her odor left something to be desired.

The clouds opened up and it began to rain. Missy continued walking. It soon began raining harder and the air, which had felt cool prior to the rain, now felt positively freezing. Missy began to shiver. She spotted a bridge not far ahead and quickened her pace. She briskly reached it and crawled underneath. She was chilled to the core and continued to shake for several more minutes. She soon curled up

289

and fell asleep, the exhaustion from the morning's effort having overcome her.

She awoke with a start at the feel of a hand on her neck. It grabbed her roughly and dragged her out from under the bridge. A male voice boomed, "That the one?"

"Yep, that's the one," another male voice answered.

Missy, now fully awake, began to struggle, but a hard month on the streets had severely weakened her. A few feeble noises emanated from her throat. She was shoved roughly into the back of a truck, the door slammed, and Missy passed out.

When Missy awoke, she looked around to find a tiny but clean room. The door opened. In walked two women, one of whom bent down to where Missy lay. "She looks terrible. What happened to her?" the woman murmured.

"Don't know. Picked her up under a bridge last night. Looks like she's been abandoned."

The woman lifted the sorrowful-looking head and read the tag on the canine's collar. "Missy," she read aloud. She looked deeply into the heartbreaking brown eyes for one powerful lingering moment. The woman's eyes welled with tears. "I have a home for you," she whispered.

# A SADHU'S POLEMIC

## S.K. Moitra

*First Prize – contest of March 2007*

*Shivaji K. Moitra is a young man from India, working for the
government but with a passion for writing to share with people who
have a little time to stand and stare.*

The train had been running at a good speed that winter night.
Only the continuous rattle of its wheels on the rails pervaded the
peaceful silence within the dimly-lit coach. But to the ears of the
sleepy passengers the noise came as a lullaby rather than a nuisance
in the quiet of the night. They were all sleeping inside the crowded
coach in all possible ways and positions, some sitting and leaning
against the bodies of their fellow passengers who had been dozing off
in the same position, some stretched with their arms under their heads
and legs folded up and sleeping with their heads in opposite
directions so as to accommodate two on a single berth and still some
curled up on the floor of the passage and corridor with their knees
tucked up to their stomachs. Most of them were headed for Allahabad
where one of the biggest spiritual events on earth was to take place--
The Maha-Kumbh Mela. It takes place once every twelve years,
drawing some ten million pilgrims and holy men from all over the
country of India.

I yawned and closed the Bengali novel I had been reading in the
feeble light of the electric lamps to drive away sleep. But there was
no place to recline for a nap. So I looked at the only other person still
awake in the coach. He was a sadhu, sitting calmly on the corridor
just to my left. He was a middle-aged man with a lean body, a light
skin and a face older than his age. His beard was dark and long and so
was his hair that was neatly coiled like a serpent on top of his head
and tied with a string of beads. He wore a piece of saffron cloth
around his waist which crossed his knees like a frock and another
piece was thrown over his bare body in the fashion of a towel. A long

chain of rudraksha-beads hung from his neck that rested on a book of religious scriptures he had been stooping over to read.

It was only an hour after midnight and a long night still threatened to pull down my heavy eyelids. Yet there was only one thing I could do to stop myself from tumbling over the other passengers--draw the holy man into a tête-à-tête. But sadhus live a spiritual existence and share no common interest with worldly people like me whom they generally try to avoid. Most of them come to renounce this world after being stung by some painful tragedy in life or some unfortunate incident that has robbed them of the very aim and purpose of their lives. When a man has no one waiting for his love and compassion, no one to bestow on the sweet fruits of his labours and no promises to keep, the meaning of life changes irrevocably and he becomes a sadhu in pursuit of the ultimate truth--God.

"Babaji," I said after much hesitation, "I am going to Kumbh. But I am a lesser mortal trapped in the quagmire of ignorance, greed, lust and envy; can I hope to hear a few words of knowledge from your pious lips?" The sadhu raised his head slowly, looked at me with his piercing eyes and when he was sure I wasn't jesting, a stiff indecisive smile appeared between his drooping moustache and his copious beard. "My son," he commenced in a soft voice, "perhaps the two most precious gifts from God to Mankind are silence and loneliness. No wonder, it is only when a man is alone amidst the peace and serenity of nature that he is closest to the Almighty. And it is only then that his mind grasps the unique beauty and mind-boggling diversity of nature on our planet and endeavours to appreciate the power of God.

"Man being himself the most wonderful product of nature cannot live detached from it. However, it is only when one becomes sad and is all by himself that he can find time to stand and stare at the uniqueness of the earth, the moon and the sun and everything else which points towards the majestic hand of that Grand Creator called God.

"Aloofness and tranquility help your mind to get detached from the humdrum of your hectic life, your unending duties and desires and float freely into the domain of imagination. Then you get to ponder over yourself, your own very existence or may be your triviality against the backdrop of the huge earth, the solar system, the limitless universe and the endless space in which all float. It isn't surprising that all the great ideas of man emerged only in times of his aloofness and the concomitant placidity of mind, be it Newton's Laws of Gravity, the Principle of Archimedes or Darwin's Theory of the

Origin of Species. Moreover, when Man thus finally starts to think great, he grows wise and comes to understand the great truth that his self-esteem, his ego, his riches, his victories and failures have no place whatsoever in God's scheme of things. In His kingdom of eternal time and limitless space the existence and the pride of humanity are but dismissed with a whiff of indifference.

"However, Man is thoroughly indebted to the Almighty for the simple reason that he has been endowed with a mind sophisticated enough to comprehend it. And perhaps that is why he toils incessantly to unravel the mysteries of the origin of the Universe and his own self as well.

"Nevertheless, God speaks to you through the moaning of the wind blowing across the woods, the resonant murmur of brooks gliding down their pebbly course through the mountains and the humming of bees fleeting over the racemes of redolent wild flowers. He never fails to show you your place in the cradle of Nature.

"It isn't astonishing then that when you are confused and your mind is agitated or sulky, the mountains beckon you and the seas draw you towards their timeless shores. At every step He reminds you that you are inseparable from Mother Nature and warns you against riding on your misplaced pride and arrogance to establish a separate identity away from the vivid colours of flowers, the songs of birds, the swashing of the seas and the pristine silence of the woods. But unfortunately, the naïve and the foolhardy, of whom there is no dearth in this world, miss the point time and again. Fuddled with the ill-conceived notion that Science has the power to do and explain anything and everything on the face of the earth, they brashly dismiss the idea of God, forgetting the simple truth that science itself is nothing but Man's endeavour to understand God and his mysterious ways. Although, armed with the power of science Man has been able to carve out for Himself the most favourable niche on earth by subjugating or destroying all other life-forms and has also succeeded in protecting Himself to a great extent from the vagaries of nature. But still the catastrophes like earthquakes, cyclones, floods and droughts remain outside the manipulating power of humanity. Moreover, has science yet succeeded in building a single living cell?

"The crux of the problem lies in the unfortunate situation today where the atheists have become the self-appointed godfathers of the scientific community and these arrogant people, because of their invincible ignorance about life and the unique conditions that made it possible to evolve on this planet, have been systematically driving Mankind towards its own extinction by using their half-baked infantile knowledge of science in destroying our eco-system and natural habitat which took millions and millions of years to take shape. Isn't it then pretty amusing to hear Man speak about his future with such confidence and arrogance when even the mighty dinosaurs could become extinct after having roamed the globe for a time seventy times longer than Man has been around so far?

"Nevertheless, dazzled by the innumerable material benefits of science and the unforeseen comforts it has made available to man, he more often than not gets himself into thinking that he is the supreme intelligent being in the universe. But the moment he tries to unravel the mysteries surrounding the gigantic events unfolding in the skies every moment, he is faced with problems the solutions to which are perhaps beyond the cognizance of the human brain. Naturally, that is precisely the amusing situation when you wonder what is awareness and how your brain thinks what you wish to think. Perhaps you shall never find out the truth because in understanding your brain, the creation is trying to understand its Creator.

"Nothing, however, affects a man more drastically than a personal tragedy. It even metamorphoses the scientific man into the philosophical man. It reminds him of the limitations of his powers when dealing with the inevitable and the foreordained path of nature.

"The point is that the arguments in support of the existence of some supreme power are far too strong and overwhelming to be dismissed with the present level of man's knowledge and intelligence. True, God will not stop you from building or using an atom bomb or say, step in to save the world's poor from hunger, pain and injustice. But He has certainly given you a brain superior to that of all other animals and sophisticated enough to foresee and understand that the situations which apparently make you lose faith in Him are but the direct consequences of mankind's grave indifference and dispassion for the eternal forces of nature.

"Quiet contemplation can even turn the hardcore atheist into a believer. If you have the time and disposition to stand and watch a chick hatch, or a caterpillar withdraw from its cocoon and emerge a butterfly, or a bird build its nest, or a cat shifting its kittens to safety by the scuffs of their necks, you can no longer ignore the concept of God--the supreme driving force that ensures the harmonious coexistence of each one of the tremendous variety of life forms including the meekest and dumbest of nature's creatures.

"With the advancement of science and the break-neck pace of technological development, man today is in a position to look deeper and deeper into his own body as well as into the mysterious depths of the universe. Ironically, however, the nearer he gets towards understanding the complexities involved in either case, the further he finds himself from the truth and his ultimate goal! The ancient Hindu religious texts rightly say that while knowledge increases by arithmetic progression, ignorance simultaneously increases by geometric progression.

"Whereas this by no means should be construed as an argument to stifle the indomitable curiosity and inquisitiveness so inherent in man, it must though convince man to proceed towards enlightenment, both without forgetting his humble roots in nature and without a prejudiced mind that rejects the Supernatural--the mother of anything and everything natural.

"The great Indian Epics of Ramayana and Mahabharata and the ancient books of wisdom like *The Upanishads* and *The Puranas* have been stressing this approach in Man's quest for knowledge. Isn't it astonishing that scientists today are confirming the same old truths which the ancient religious scribes of the Hindus had written about nearly five thousand years ago? Don't you get the vivid descriptions of flying-chariots, sound-seeking and fire-spitting arrows in *The Ramayana* and that of the telescope in *The Mahabharata*? And in *The Mahabharata*, Sri Krishna, The Lord and Charioteer, tells Arjuna that there are millions and millions of solar systems in every hair of his body. Today, it is known that every atom is a miniature solar-system while astronomers say that there are numerous solar systems like our own in the Universe.

"You can hear God, you can feel God and you can even see God every time everywhere, once the understanding seeps into your consciousness that everything in this Universe has been created from nothing and shall ultimately dissolve into nothing, which is called 'Parambrahma'."

The shrill cry of a hungry child shattered the quiet and interrupted the discourse. It roused the passengers who began to move up and down the corridor to the toilet and that ended the peaceful ambiance of our profound discussion.

"Baba," I said, "you have taught me a great deal today; I would have been so happy if you were a teacher."

"I had been a Lecturer of Physics for twelve years," he said before a deep long yawn.

I looked at him now with great awe and veneration. "Indeed! Philosophy begins where Science ends," I mused.

# THE SNAGS

## Jerry Kalman

*Jerry Kalman co-authored* Internet Commerce Metrics and Models, *published by Prentice Hall PTR in 2001. He has written several short stories, most set in exotic locations throughout the American West. He has also written hundreds of articles for business, trade, and general interest publications.*

In the hard crusty sand, armed with a rusty metal rod he found on the shore, the old man prepared to write the memoirs he started countless times in countless other places. When he tried to write on the Pacific shore, the tide erased his thoughts as often as human interruptions disturbed him. This time he received inspiration from the cluster of dead trees that stood out in the shallow waters of the Salton Sea.

He paused to admire the buff-colored pristine beach and flat marshes behind him that vanished into fields of fresh green row-crops. "It's different here than at the noisy ocean," he told a lone white crane that strode through the water several yards offshore. "I can write and the waves leave me alone. The sand holds my words as long as I hold the thoughts. I can frame the argument that is my life for others more interested in it than I."

Society called him a derelict, a vagrant, a bum; but none of those terms bothered him anymore, nor did the rap sheet that spanned seventeen states for the same offense. Twenty-three years on the road hardened him to the vicissitudes of the language of the privileged. And on that hot March day he decided to settle for as long as anyone let him on the sandy beach that faced due west across the glassy-smooth waters.

He dragged the rusted piece of iron through the sand, but the broad tip made the letters and words too big and he tossed it aside. Then the old scribe used a small bone he found, which wore down to a nub after he scraped out a couple of paragraphs. He roamed the mile-long beach, tracked by the bored big white bird, his knapsack with the remainder of his belongings stashed at a culvert that drained fields into the Salton Sea.

"I need a pen, crane. Find me one and I'll help you forage."

Moments later he discovered a stiff bicycle spoke. "Thank you, crane. You *are* good luck. I owe you now." He returned to the place where he started the earlier screed, looked at what he wrote and erased the remnants of those earlier thoughts to begin again. Paused, ready to stroke the sand, his weathered hand held the spoke and he called out to the snags for an idea to start. The crane waited in the water and watched him struggle to rewrite the opening stanza of his life.

"Crane!" He called to the elegant white bird that gleamed in the mid-morning sun: "Do I start with the life wasted or the life found?"

The crane stood in contemplative silence and then sent its beak below the surface of the water to peck at an unseen food source.

"So, you tell me to look beyond the obvious. That's it, isn't it?" He stared at the bird and then looked to the closest of the several dead trees and watched as the shore-side branches filled with smaller water birds. At midday they always sat silent, and the old man took it as a cue to do his work in quiet, too.

He looked at the coarse sand where his sandaled foot brushed aside his prior work.

"I must wait for the words to come back. I've done this before. I can do it again." He sat cross-legged a few feet back from the water's edge to stare at the gnarled snags in the water. As the sun moved from south to west the reflections of the trees on the surface changed and he studied the shift in colors, too. He held his hands up and his fingers imitated patterns made by the twigs, his arms mirrored the main branches. By the time the sun moved high and west behind the trees the crane disappeared along with the other water birds.

"Hah," he said when he discovered the departures, "gave up on me, eh? You'll be back and my words in the sand will greet you!"

A new flock of birds ready to feed in the late afternoon descended on the isolated snags and started chattering. The noise disturbed his meditation and he threw a small stone into the water but it fell short of the nearest tree. The birds remained, unmoved by his request.

"Guess it's time to write again."

He rose from the beach, crusted sand stuck to his faded and torn black pants and bare legs. With spoke in hand he prepared for another session and this time the memories greeted him from the past and he wrote in the sand for more than an hour. He carved the words with care as his fluid motion carried him from left to right along the shore

297

for more than a hundred yards. Then he punctuated the idea and returned to indent and begin the next paragraph and the one after that in the same manner.

Bird delegations in the snags changed twice more before sunset and he worked on to craft word after word, the spoke an extension of his mind as it cut through the crust. Just as he finished the first chapter, dusk descended and he stepped back to the road that bordered his writing on the east and looked at the long string of words that flowed toward the levee at the far end of the beach.

Then the crane returned and the writer pulled a crust of bread from his pack and tossed it out to where the bird stood to make good on his promise. The white bird glanced at the bread floating on the water and moved away in search of something else.

"Ignore my morsel for the brine shrimp instead, will you? That's the best you're going to get from this old hack tonight. Ain't nothing else to share, other than companionship."

The diarist ambled down from the dirt road onto the beach and found a smooth spot, uncovered by his words, where he spread out a hunk of cardboard found alongside another long forgotten stretch of road. Then and only then he looked up to search for the stars.

"Too early, crane, for the stars just yet." He looked through the snags and watched the western glow change from yellow to orange and then deepen into indigo that darkened the silhouette of the trees. Stars appeared one at a time, and then blanketed the sky and he put potential comments for his memoirs aside until another day.

The crane found her mate at their nest and they settled in for the night, hidden from the old writer.

In the morning, the scene changed from dim gray at first light to black and white and then into Technicolor as dawn broadened. The crane emerged from her nest near the levee and flew over to check in on the author asleep on the sand. Out at the snags, a family of mergansers circled the trunks in search of breakfast; and a trio of skinny little avocets ran across his words, dotting i's and crossing t's with their footprints.

He awoke, ignored the empty growl in his stomach, and listened to the birds of the morning chatter as they ranged back and forth.

During the night a puff of wind blew some of the lighter sand off the surface and combined with the sleep to form a crust around his eyes, which the scribe wiped away to take stock of the new day. He stared at the unfinished memoir in front of him and the avocet tracks that ran through his thoughts, and he chuckled.

"Some improvements there. No doubt about it. Let me see what I can do to make it better."

He picked up the spoke and wrote with fervor as he forgot the morning hunger that dogged him when he drifted further from towns and villages. Another chapter unfolded and he set the spoke down and sat to admire his work from the roadside again. After several minutes of reflection, he looked out toward the snags and then at the sky and saw the Salton Sea was calm the fifty yards out to where the trees stood. No birds hovered above or in the branches; no water birds floated on the surface. They left him alone with his work. Not a ripple marred the integrity of the surface.

"Time for me to make my mark on the water."

He walked around two more chapters of work, reflected on his thoughts committed to the sand and waded out into the balmy water. By the time he reached the closest snags, the water reached his knees. He let the silt ooze up between his toes and he moved further out and the water found his waist when he reached the halfway point between the distant snags and those close to shore. He sat as deep as possible; but the buoyancy of the salty water pushed him back up toward the surface where he floated and watched for his friend the crane to return.

The old man tried to remain still and let the mirror form again, however, subtle ripples formed and he became the sole cause of the break in the surface tension. He floated like that for an hour; leathery skin, darker than the snags but no less firm, covered the sticks that formed his arms and legs. Even imperceptible motion continued to set off ripples that circled out away from him.

"No such luck. I've corrupted a placid place." He waded back to shore where he stood and waited for the glaze to reappear. Salty water dripped from his beard and long but thinning hair. Five minutes stretched to ten and the water smoothed once more. He stepped back off the wet sand at the edge of the Salton Sea and looked around. Still alone, without even the companionship of the crane, he returned to the roadway and let the remainder of the water drip from his pants as he studied the memoirs that faced him.

Refreshed from the swim, he said: "I'll write another chapter then go to town for some feed."

He walked over to the night-time resting spot and retrieved his gear, folded the cardboard along the crease lines and stashed all but his knapsack in the culvert south along the road. That done, he returned to the sandy manuscript and drew the spoke out of the sand and wrote for another hour, until the sun rose high overhead. He filled the beach with his life and wrote on from the roadway to the water's edge and down to the levee and back toward the culvert. When he put the last period on the last paragraph, the old writer tossed the spoke aside, into the weedy embankment, and scrambled back up to the road to stare at what he wrote in the sand.

Satisfied and without another thought he turned and trudged off down the road into the nearest town to forage in dumpsters behind the grocery store and fast food places. Passersby sneered in disdain, mindless that an author wrote his memoirs out at the snags along the beaches.

Down by the Salton Sea, the white crane lifted off to circle with grace above the beach. As she glided, she looked down and saw the words the old man wrote: "Call me Ishmael. Some years ago – never mind how long precisely – having little or no money in my purse, and nothing particular to interest me on shore, I thought I would sail about a little and see the …"

The crane never completed her read as she soared up into the sky and joined a flock of her kind in a nearby field. But then the old man did not complete his memoirs beside the Salton Sea that day, either. Later on, before he left town, the rains came and washed his pages away into the water and when he returned he found he had a choice: to start over once more or sail about on the land to find another watery place to write and leave his message for others to see.

# THERE WAS A MAN

## Frederic Rohner

*Second Prize – contest of March 2007*

*Frederic Rohner is a recent graduate of St. Mary's College of Maryland with a Bachelor's Degree in English. He is originally from Silver Spring but recently moved to Boonsboro. He works full time at Vegas Radio WTRI 1520 AM in Brunswick, Maryland.*

There was a man who returned from the war and looked at himself in the mirror. What he saw there was murder, mayhem, mindless violence. He saw the memories of what happened "over there," but they didn't stay "over there." They returned with him on the transport across the Atlantic Ocean. They followed him home. And these memories, these visions, assaulted him every night in his dreams, allowing him no rest.

*We pull over, "Spread out!" yells Sergeant Varne. Something is wrong.*

*It's quiet. Minutes ago this street was almost bustling, but now, quiet. Weird. A van pulls around the corner. It's shitty and old, just like all of the Iraqi cars. A white van with no markings except for dirt and grime turns slowly around the corner of the next block, about sixty meters from where we are. It straightens out coming toward us and the driver guns the engine, flooring the accelerator and directing the old shitbox directly toward our position. I can see his face. He's young, around my age, no more than twenty years old. And then the shooting begins.*

*I turn ninety degrees to my right and I can see barrels sticking out of windows. Why the fuck did we stop here? We're sitting ducks as insurgents shoot down at us with AK-47s; laying cover fire for the suicide bomber in the van to drive his payload directly into our convoy.*

*I try to yell out a warning, but there is no time, the attack is orchestrated perfectly, and we're caught off guard. The van strikes*

301

*our head vehicle and explodes. I watch it like it's in slow motion. The van hits the Hummer head on, the grill and engine block on the van crumple, the driver of the van cracks his head on the steering wheel just as the back of the van explodes into a ball of fire, sending shrapnel flying directly into our unit. The insurgents are still shooting at us as I feel myself being hurled into the street by the explosion. My ears begin to ring, and the last thing that I remember is the worst pain I've ever felt in my life. I look down and see a jagged piece of metal sticking out of my right side, just below my lungs.*

*And then darkness.*

The same dream every night, without any variation. When he slept he was afraid because he knew that the dream would come, and he knew that he couldn't change what happened. He had to relive the moment every night, in his sleep.

He woke up every morning, sweaty and cold from a night dominated by that one moment, that one dream that gave him little rest. The news was always on; he wanted to know what was happening to his fellow soldiers, the brothers he'd left behind to fight without him. He would look at the faces around him, at the bank, at the supermarket, at the gas station buying fuel sold to us by our enemies; the faces looked back at him but didn't really see him. They saw him as he saw his own face in the mirror, a reflection with nothing behind it.

But he hadn't always been this way. He was young once, with dreams and potential. He wanted to play baseball or, if that didn't work out, football. He was athletic, he was never the smartest kid in his class, but he also was never the slowest, either. Normal, average, ordinary, but that's not to say he couldn't have done anything he wanted to. His father had instilled in him the kind of work ethic that makes Amish mouths fall open in disbelief, which is why he mowed lawns, delivered papers, and bagged groceries to make extra money as a kid. "Industriousness is a virtue," that's what his father liked to say, "those that work harder get ahead, and the lazy ones are the ones who fall behind". So he worked hard and when he graduated from high school he could think of nothing better than to join the army and serve his country.

The drinking. When he went to Fort Bragg in North Carolina he was a child, eighteen years old. He had his first drink of alcohol with his brothers in the canteen on base. *A shot of whiskey and a bottle of beer kid. You're in the army now; it's time you started acting like it.* He loved the camaraderie, he loved hearing the stories that the officers told about past conflicts, past battles. He loved the way he felt in the canteen, exhausted from training hard for war, relaxing

302

with men that he would go to war with, men who would tell stories about him one day or men he would tell stories about. Drinking was an affirmation back then, he would drink and listen to the stories and imagine what war would be like. That was before he went "over there".

It was not as romantic as he had envisioned. There was carnage and death everywhere. The exaggerated stories told around bottles of Budweiser and shots of Jack Daniels did not prepare him for the reality that he experienced. Everyone was an enemy, women, kids, old folks; they were all suspects, monsters to be feared. And so he started drinking more, every night. Drinking helped him forget, he could get drunk and escape the terror and the danger, the fear of the job, get drunk and sleep without dreams. But that was "over there," here he could not drink enough to get rid of the dreams—not that he didn't try.

Every day was a fog, without direction. He did what seemed necessary: go to the bank, to the supermarket, to the V.A. office, talk to fellow soldiers, come home and drink alone.

The only real job he'd ever had was as a soldier. When he was younger he used to cut his neighbors' grass and shovel their driveways in winter, but he couldn't live off of that. Jobs would come and go. He worked in factories, in stockyards, driving around making deliveries, he even tried construction at one point, but they all ended the same way, he would get fired for fighting with his boss or his coworkers, he would disappear for hours at a time, or he just wouldn't show up at all. He was unfit for the job market, he'd heard it was called PTSD, post traumatic stress disorder. The vets from Korea at the V.A. office called it shell-shock, but it didn't matter what it was called, he was unhirable, and so he was unemployed.

He was forgotten by the very people he fought for, neglected by the ones who sent him "over there." He talked to a paper pusher at the V.A. office who very politely told him that he did not qualify for a disability pension, and they questioned whether he had actually seen any action in Iraq at all. When he told them that he was part of the Fourth Infantry Division, the division that led the fucking invasion of Baghdad, the paper pusher asked him to quiet down. When he took his shirt off to show the paper pusher the five inch long scar down his ribcage, he was asked to leave the paper pusher's office. Abandoned, he was left to fend for himself.

The eviction notice came two months later. He packed what hadn't already been sold into his Jeep and took one last look at his face in the mirror, one last look at the shell, at the man who had once been a boy with dreams, who had become a man with nothing but nightmares. A man with nothing.

He got fifty dollars for his war medals, mainly for the little amount of gold and silver within them. The pawnshop owner liked the gold star best and asked him to tell the story behind it. He politely told the owner he'd rather not tell that story, that it wasn't that good anyway, and asked where the nearest liquor store was. His dress uniform and his fatigues he sold to a collector he'd met at the V.A. office, an asshole named Anderson who liked to reenact the Civil War on weekends, who visited the V.A. office to hear stories from the vets and buy the uniforms they bled in for his collection. Anderson had American uniforms going back to the Revolutionary War and paid him $500 for the whole get up, including shoes and socks. He wondered if Anderson had a room full of mannequins wearing the uniforms, a room full of life sized G.I. Joes.

When he sold the last things that identified him as a soldier he was surprised at how much his stuff was worth to other people. He lived for a month off of that money. For a month he drank and slept, and sometimes he slept without dreaming, but the dream always returned in the end. He didn't think of himself as a soldier anymore because he no longer went to visit other vets at the V.A. office after that day he talked to the paper pusher; he didn't think of himself as a soldier because he no longer looked like a soldier without his uniform or fatigues.

And he drove around looking for menial jobs, handy-man jobs, field hand jobs and alcohol until his car broke down, and he decided he didn't care if it ever ran again. He walked after that, and he began begging for change and living on the street. Under overpasses, in alley ways, hidden back in wooded vacant lots, squatting in abandoned homes, sometimes in shelters run by the church. That was where he lived.

That's where he lives now, and that's where he'll die. The world goes on around him, and the war he fought continues. But he is forgotten; he no longer looks like a soldier because he sold his medals, fatigues, and dress uniform for booze. He looks like what he is: a shell, a ghost haunted by his own experiences and memories.

We walk past him and look away without making eye contact. We try not to see that he is even there at all, and he stares back at us because he doesn't see us either. When he first started living on the streets he was angry, all he could see in the faces of the people that walked past was money, clothes, cars, furniture, Starbucks, sex, houses, decadence, and materialism; the things that he fought and

304

others died for. Now he just sees ghosts, walking shades that he looks through and past, he sees nothing at all. America.

"Get a fucking job, you bum."

The Musician's Wings

Beth Mautz

*Beth Mautz graduated from Pensacola Christian College with a degree in Commercial Writing in 2005. Although she is now working as a legal secretary, she is still pursuing her goal of writing Christian novels.*

Sherry Michaels drew in a breath and let her voice resonate throughout the empty music room. Her voice, clear and melodious, echoed off the walls as she sang. She ambled toward the shiny black piano and halted beside it. As her voice caressed each note of "Ave Maria," her eyelids closed over her blue-gray eyes. She imagined herself singing to a crowded room. Her eyes remained closed even after she sang the last note.

"Wow, you have the voice of an angel."

Sherry gasped and pivoted to face the person who had intruded upon her singing in the high school music room. The young man standing in the open doorway was average height but his spiked black hair made him look tall. He had dark eyes that appeared huge in his pale face, and two silver loop earrings hung from his left ear. He wore jeans that had holes in the knees and a faded black t-shirt with a denim jacket over it.

"Sorry, I didn't mean to scare you. I was just passing by and heard your awesome voice," the young man said.

Sherry recognized him as Rocky Conlan, Clayville High School's rock band leader. She knew that he was in a couple of her classes, but she doubted that he had ever noticed her.

"With a voice like that, we'd dig it if you'd sing in our band." Rocky pointed at her emphatically. "I'm Rocky, leader of Rocky's Rockin' Band." He extended his hand to Sherry.

To shake Rocky's hand, Sherry had to turn completely around to face him. As she took his hand, she said, "I don't think you really want me in your band." She knew the instant he glimpsed the scar on the left side of her face because his dark eyes widened slightly. He averted his eyes away from her face a fraction of a second later, and he stepped back from her as soon as she released his hand.

He studied her for a few seconds. "Sure I do. I want you to sing in our band. You'd be a hit."

"I'm sorry, but I don't ever sing in front of people." Sherry shook her head, which caused her silvery blond hair to wave around her face. The afternoon sunlight streaming through the window caused her hair to shimmer. Sherry turned away from Rocky and went to gaze out the window. When Rocky spoke from right behind her, she started.

"Why don't you sing in front of people? Are you scared?"

"I just can't, and that's it. I see my mom's car. I have to go." She began to make her way to the door.

"Hey, you never told me your name."

"It's Sherry," she responded without stopping. As she exited the room, she heard Rocky call out again.

"Let me know if you change your mind."

The next morning at school, Sherry was spinning the lock combination on her dented gray locker when she saw Rocky coming toward her. She felt relieved that he could not see the left side of her face. Then she forced herself to turn and fully face him.

"Hello," Rocky muttered in his deep voice.

Sherry stifled the urge to turn her scarred face away from him when his eyes darted to the scar. Her eyes narrowed, and she nodded at him. Lifting his eyebrow, Rocky leaned his shoulder against the locker next to hers.

"Have you changed your mind yet?"

"I'm not going to change my mind. My answer's still no." Sherry turned back to her locker and opened it. "Why are you so interested in having me in your band?"

"'Cause you have a voice like an angel's, and I know you'd be great."

Sherry grabbed the books she needed and shut the locker door with a bang. "Even if I did sing for people, I'd never sing in a rock band." She glanced at him out of the corner of her eye. "It goes against everything I believe in."

Rocky shrugged his shoulder and moved away from the locker. "I wish you would."

Sherry just shook her head as he strolled away with his hands in his pockets. He did not seem like a bad guy, but he obviously needed moral guidance. As she walked to class, she could not forget about his offer. She loved music and never felt more content than when she was singing. There had been a time when she sang in the church choir, but that had been when she could hide her scar. With a shake of her head, she put her hand to the jagged, pink scar on her cheek. The scar stretched over her jaw line from her ear down to her chin. She blinked back the water in her eyes and marched toward geography class.

"Sherry, wait up. Are you okay?"

Sherry whirled toward the voice and let out a breath when she saw her friend Marianne. "I'm fine."

"You look like you're going to cry." Marianne peered at her through her silver-rimmed glasses.

"Well, I'm not." Sherry grabbed Marianne's arm and tugged her out of the path of a senior classman.

"What's wrong? You're acting kind of weird."

"I'm just having a bad day. That's all." Sherry glanced at her watch. "I've got to get to class, or I'm going to be late."

"Bye."

"Bye, Marianne."

Sherry managed to get seated in geography class a second before the bell rang. Because the teacher was writing on the board, Sherry had a minute to collect herself. As she scanned the other students' faces, her eyes connected with a pair of dark ones. Rocky smirked, and his left eyebrow rose. She turned her focus back to the teacher who began his lecture. Sherry could feel eyes on her during the entire class, and she was glad when it was finished.

Throughout the rest of her classes, Sherry forced herself to pay attention to the teachers and not think about Rocky or his offer. Although she had just about managed to forget about him, Rocky cornered her after school while she waited for her mom.

"Sherry, I'm glad I found you," Rocky said.

"Oh—hi, Rocky."

"I want you to come listen to our band." Rocky stuck his hands in his pockets before immediately pulling them out again.

"I really shouldn't."

"Come on. The least you can do is come listen to us. That's all I'm asking. There's nothing else for you to do while you wait."

308

Sherry opened her mouth to refuse, but the pleading expression on Rocky's face caused her to close her mouth. She wondered what it would hurt to listen to the band for a few minutes.

"Okay, I'll come, but just for a few minutes."

Those few minutes turned into ten as she listened to the band that included a drummer, a guitarist, Rocky, and a backup singer. She disliked the rock music, but she had to admit that Rocky had an incredible voice. When they finished their second song, Rocky jumped off the makeshift stage and came to stand beside Sherry.

"What'd you think?"

"Um, you guys sound—nice."

"You didn't like it." Rocky frowned.

I don't really like that type of music. I prefer classical and Gospel music.

"Oh."

"You definitely have talent," Sherry said softly. When Rocky's lips twitched with a small smile, Sherry could almost forget about his spiked hair and baggy clothes. "I have to go," she said breathlessly. Hoping her mom had arrived to take her home, she hurried away.

At home that night, she listened to her favorite singer, Maggie Pierce, while she did her homework. "Come in," she called when someone tapped on her door.

Her mom came and sat beside her on the bed. "How's the homework coming, dear?"

"I'm nearly done."

"Good, Bobby will be home from work in about ten minutes. Then we'll eat supper." She patted her back. "I got a call from Mrs. Taylor today. Her daughter is sick and won't be able to sing on Sunday. She wants you to sing a special."

"Mom! You know I can't sing in front of the whole church. You didn't say yes, did you?"

"Now, Sherry—"

"Did you?"

"No, of course not." Her mom squeezed Sherry's shoulder. "I have to go check on the chicken, but at least think about it."

Sherry suddenly wished she could hide in her room until morning.

The next morning at school, Sherry ran into Rocky in between classes. She immediately noticed that he wore newer clothes and the earrings were gone. He gave her a big grin and strolled on past.

Marianne who stood beside her glanced at Sherry with raised brows. "Do you know him?"

"He's been trying to get me to join his rock band."

Marianne snorted. "Why? You don't exactly look or act the part."

"I don't know. I guess he likes my voice. He heard me singing in the music room the other day." Sherry blew out a breath. "And Mrs. Taylor wants me to sing a solo in church on Sunday."

"What's wrong with that? You love to sing." Marianne removed her glasses and rubbed the bridge of her nose. "Why don't you want to do it?"

"I just can't. Let's talk about something else."

As they walked to class, Sherry managed to put Rocky and singing out of her mind until she saw him in algebra class. After the lesson started, Sherry received a note from him. It read, "I have something important to show you. Please meet me during lunch hour. Rocky."

Sherry inhaled deeply and crumpled the note. She would have to tell him that he had to leave her alone. She would meet him at lunch but only to tell him that this had to stop. When she arrived at the cafeteria for lunch, she searched the crowded room for him. The noise of about a hundred students nearly overwhelmed her. As she was about to sit at a nearly empty table, she spotted Rocky. He waved at her to follow him.

"I need to tell you something," Sherry said as Rocky opened his mouth.

"Okay, but let me go first." When Sherry nodded her head, Rocky continued. "I want to know something. Is it 'cause of your scar that you won't sing? Are you scared people will make fun of you?"

Sherry placed her hand over the scar. "What if it is? When people look at me, all they see is my scar. I don't want anybody's pity." Sherry removed her hand from her face. "I want—I don't want people to stare. I don't even know if I could sing in front of a lot of people."

Rocky did not laugh at her as she feared. "Yeah, I was scared out of my mind when my mom and I moved here three years ago. I had nightmares about coming to a new school." Rocky shoved his hand in his pocket and pulled something out in his clenched fist. "My parents got divorced a few years ago, and I don't see my dad very much 'cause he's in the military. But he wrote me a letter and sent me something once that really helped me." Rocky opened his fist to reveal a Navy pilot's pin with silver wings. "He told me that to get these wings he had to face his fears. It wasn't like he wasn't scared, but he focused on his dream instead of his fears. And he just did it." Rocky extended his hand toward her with the gleaming wings lying in his palm. "Whenever I've been in a scary situation, I have just held onto this and remembered what Dad said. Now I want you to have it."

While part of her told her she should stay away from Rocky and his ploys, she felt compelled to take the pin. Her hand stretched toward Rocky's hand, and he dropped it into her open palm.

"A voice like yours shouldn't be wasted on an empty room."

Sherry looked into Rocky's dark eyes. Suddenly an idea came to her. She lifted her head a little higher. "If you want to hear me sing, you'll have to come to church."

"What?"

"I can't sing in your band, but I'll sing at church if you come."

"I haven't been to church since—well, it's been a long time." Rocky tilted his head slightly. "You'll sing a solo in church if I promise to come?"

"Yes," Sherry responded, although her hands began to shake.

"It's a deal." Rocky stuck out his hand.

Sherry closed her fist more tightly around the pin and took Rocky's hand.

# PAYING A LAST HOMAGE TO COLERIDGE

## S. M. Spiers

*British author Stephanie Spiers is a retired journalist who usually specializes in crime fiction. She is a Trustee of the Creative Writing Charitable Trust, Rising Brook Writers.*
*www.risingbrookwriters.btik.com*

> In Xanadu did Kubla Khan
> A stately pleasure-dome decree
> Where Alph, the sacred river, ran
> Through caverns measureless to man
> Down to a sunless sea.
> So twice five miles of fertile ground
> With walls and towers were girdled round
> And there were gardens bright with sinuous rills,
> Where blossomed many an incense-bearing tree;
> And here were forests ancient as the hills,
> Enfolding sunny spots of greenery.
> > S. T. Coleridge
> > Kubla Khan: An Extract

"Through caverns measureless to man," from somewhere near, came the sound of that voice. The words flowing over her experienced as a warm glow, as her senses drifted backwards and forwards in and out of consciousness. A flood of affection emanating from the closeness of his warmth revived her again. Caroline's relaxed lids flickered, comforted: she wasn't dreaming. At peace, bluish lips smiled thinly in recognition. Michael was here: she could leave this Pleasure Dome now any time she wanted to.

In truth she remained only by sheer act of will: she'd been waiting for him to arrive. The spoken words began to clear, as that familiar deep brown voice softly intoned inches from her ear. It was Coleridge he was lilting.

Her favourite.

It would be, wouldn't it? He'd know that – at the last breath she'd want to hear Coleridge. Sharing their passion: part of their secret life. Secrets and confidences: only she knew the depth he concealed, the height of his intellect kept well hidden away from that all intrusive public eye of the camera lens.

The glitterati come and go, talking of Bobby Da Ni-rro, disconcerting how snatches of songs kept popping in and out of her thoughts when she was trying so desperately to focus on staying within the confines of the tiny world of that one special voice. The irony amused her. All those years in the 70s of just saying NO, and now here she was feeling little pain, free wheeling into the all consuming void on the crest of a high, compliments of a National Health Service drip.

"In a vision once I saw."

Caroline's eyes tried to focus, but, soon gave up the struggle: it was too hard a task. Her hand lay on his chest, although she didn't recall moving it there. He'd opened the shirt button and tucked the still fingers inside holding them against his flesh, where his breaking heart fluttered like a caged wing beating beneath the coolness of her bloodless palm.

The brushed cotton of the fabric felt warm against her cheek where, propped against the stacked pillows, Michael had climbed onto the high bed and snuggled the limp body up close against him, spreading her hair over his shoulder as he'd done so many times before, during their long years of growing up together.

Ah yes...tingling with the taste of a distant pang of want, in shades of vermillion, Caroline's mind flickered like the stills of a silent movie to recall the first time she'd ever laid eyes on a scrawny, disheveled youth, chain smoking and doing his best to play the hard-man. The leader of the work gang under the watchful, resentful gaze of his elder brother: Collum.

Collum McGann! She shouldn't have...she wished she hadn't...Regret flickered behind closed eyes, but, now was not the time to be wasted on omission and past ill judgement.

Are you going to Scarborough Fair? Parsley...They'd been playing that when...a vivid recollection of that first stolen time they'd lain together rolled over her.

Caroline sighed, as an echo of that wave of all consuming desire for Michael washed over and crashed against her shore. Etched memory of their bonding was enhanced, as breathing in deeply, she savoured the warm earthy smell of Michael's toil hardened body for probably the last time as he gently nestled her frame closer towards him: protecting her, keeping her limp and lifeless body safe in the crook of his arm.

"And on a dulcimer she played."

It seemed so long ago now. A life-time.

Could have played it better, she murmured, but strangely the sound didn't have the strength to carry past the thought. Ironic, now at the last, she couldn't say the one thing she had always wanted to say and never quite been able.

"And close your eyes with mortal dread." The voice was quavering. She caught the tremor, felt it deep inside the chest wall.

He knew.

Michael was so transparent, she recognised all his "tells," the way his mouth softened at the corners when she spoke, how the tone of his voice lowered when they talked, the way those dark darting eyes followed her every movement round the room. How they sparkled in the half light of a summer morning when they first awoke: it pained her that she couldn't see them now. No matter how hard she tried to see the light on his face for just one more time to carry with her, to be sustained on the journey by that one perfect memory, but no matter how hard she tried, the lids were refusing to open.

It would be soon now.

Yet she felt no fear at this parting.

He was with her. How could she fear, as his strength sustained her to ease this final passing? She'd lost the feeling in her legs: it had turned so cold. The impression of being in a room was becoming really faded at the edges now and still. Still: stillness settled upon her like a heavy weight. Time to let go. No need to tell him anything else was there?

He'd know.

The peripheries of the anti-ward closed in around them as the world retreated. The drone of the traffic three floors below, flashing by on the ring-road ceased its clamour. The wall clock silenced its ticking as Michael's tear-filled voice breathed the words that for years she had longed to hear into her hair, "For he on honey-dew hath fed, And drunk the milk of Paradise."

At ten past four the nurse came to take the half hour readings and found them, locked in that last embrace. The bearded Irishman still silently mouthing word perfect Coleridge to that cool, pale, lifeless cheek as the dying rays of a winter afternoon filtered into the side ward through the Venetian blinds casting long thin shadows across the bed.

Closing the door quietly the young woman in the crisp uniform caught sight of the junior registrar approaching.

"She's gone?" he asked. "Our celebrity's guest."

The blinking nurse nodded, picking up a pair of rubber gloves from a box on the nursing station counter: "And the Priest from St. Anne's has been – the mother's rang again but I didn't say." She paused, "not yet."

"Is he with her?"

"Oh yes. Never missed, been here for days."

The ward sister joined them as the three drew near to the circular glass window in the door of Room 16 – God's waiting room. "Look at them. Daft beggars. What a waste. All those years. The most recorded tempestuous relationship since Taylor and Burton so it said on the news. Their every fight splashed across day-time TV and just look at them."

The older woman suppressed the catch in her throat, not professional, was it? But, how could anyone not be caught up in the grief at the vibrant young woman's passing so before her time?

"Never understood it," said the young registrar who'd read modern classics in Mumbai in what now seemed like another lifetime. "How could two lovers not be able to talk to each other? Couldn't get it together, could they? Couldn't sort their life out."

"Oh, he told her he loved her right enough," said the sister pushing a strand of grey hair away from a tightly drawn mouth. "He just used an indirect route – he showed how much her he loved her in everything he ever built."

"Didn't he ever tell her then – you know, the three little words?" asked the young nurse, aware something momentous had happened and desperate to be included in this adult conversation.

The new doctor smiled, looking down for the first time into upturned sea-green eyes.

"If he didn't say them, everyone else knew he did. It can't be easy having your every intimate moment the subject of national debate. I'm glad I'm not a celebrity – even a minor one – couldn't take the pressure."

The sister eased open the door to intrude upon the man's last moments of privacy. At the sound of their entry the bereft TV hard-man enfolding the corpse of his beloved ever tighter to his chest, its radiance already fading into porcelain translucence, whispered almost inaudibly: "All thoughts, all passions, all delights."

# TWO WISHES FOR CHRISTMAS

## Philip Loyd

*Philip Loyd resides in Houston, Texas, and is the author of thirty-seven short stories. His work has appeared in eighty-three publications in seven countries, with one story even produced for radio in Australia. Included in his numerous awards is the Hemingway Center Short Story Prize.*

Three dollars and twenty-five cents. That was all? Jimmy remembered when gasoline wasn't even three bucks—and that was barely a year ago. But the snow was already falling fast, and between the frost on the windshield and the worn-out wipers, he couldn't see a thing. He remembered that the tires were balding and dangerously so. He needed to get off the road before it iced over completely, to the home he and his bride had made when they were still happy and in love, before the shouting had taken over, before she had withdrawn to her television and he to his computer—and that wasn't even a year ago. Three dollars and twenty-five cents? And the next day would be Christmas.

It was everywhere, on the Internet, on every weather website: low temperatures tonight would break all known records—blizzard conditions. Forecasts called for lows anywhere from ten degrees to five, to zero. One was even so bold as to predict temps below zero. That had never happened before. In fact, the last time it even snowed was fifty-eight years ago, and it had never snowed on Christmas. Last year it was eighty degrees, and humid. But it was already below freezing now, and Jimmy's fingers were brittle from having to pull over and pump gas—all because she had forgotten to fill the tank.

"Don't forget to let the water drip tonight," she had said, and even if she thought she was being helpful, to him she was nagging. Every word, every syllable that came out of her mouth was like scraping fingernails across a chalkboard. Hearing her voice only reminded him how everything about her pissed him off, and he blamed her for the empty tank, for the weather, and even for the price of gasoline. This was their first Christmas together as man and wife, and he was sure it would be their last.

They never talked anymore. She never spoke more than one sentence at a time outside of fighting, and always she was nagging..

*Don't forget to pay the cable bill; if you do they'll turn it off.*

*Don't forget to pay the electric bill; they'll cut us off if you're late.*

*Don't forget to have the car checked, the battery light keeps coming on.*

Forget? He didn't forget things. He never forgot anything. He wished he could forget he was married to her.

And what about the baby? What happened about the baby? It was something they never talked about anymore.

His little car came sliding onto the gravel driveway and, seemingly before it even stopped, he was out the door, up the stairs, and into the little old rental house. "You forgot to get gas, again," he shouted in passing, on the way to his office, which was really nothing more than the second bedroom with a computer in it. She never even looked up from the TV.

He rubbed his hands together, warming his fingers by the orange glow of the electric space heater. He blamed her for his cold fingers and for the furnace failing, and even for the landlord being in sunny Cancun for the holidays. He went online and checked prices again. Now he felt sure, he did get a great deal on her Christmas present. It wouldn't be delivered until around New Year's, but he could print a picture of it and give it to her in a card. He couldn't stand even the sight of her, but for some reason he still wanted to please her, to see her smile again, even if only once more.

What did he want from her? What was his Christmas wish? All he wanted was for them to be happy again, like they once were.

He then went to surfing the net, thinking how on his crappy old computer downloading took forever.

It might have been just a few minutes, or even a couple hours, when the door burst open and she was standing there saying, "You forgot to pay the cable bill."

He didn't respond; he was too busy minimizing his screen. Forgot to pay the cable bill? But that would mean that he was—yes, he was offline now. He had lost his internet connection.

"No, I did not," he said, "I paid it." But he didn't remember for sure whether he had, or not.

"Maybe you forgot, or maybe it's a problem," she said.

"Maybe if you quit ordering all those movies, it wouldn't be a problem."

317

"Or maybe if you spent more time at work and less time playing on your computer, there wouldn't be a problem," she said, spinning toward the living room.

"Playing? Is that what you think I do?" he said, fast on her heels. "I told you, I'm starting my own business. I'm not going to work at the nursery forever."

"Starting your own business?" she said. "What kind of business, pornography?"

"Those are spams."

"Really."

"They're pop-ups. I can't do anything about that."

"Maybe that's why you don't look at me any more."

"It's not my fault, it's just the Internet."

"You haven't touched me in months."

"It hasn't been months," he said, "maybe a couple weeks."

"The last time we made love was October seventh."

"It hasn't been that long, I'm sure," he said.

"It's been ever since, what happened about the baby," she said, even though she knew by mentioning the baby she had just ended the conversation. He just would not talk about it.

"Nag, nag, nag," he said, going back to his office. He sat back down at his computer, and with no Internet now, started playing minesweeper, spider solitaire, and other mindless games. The foul odor from cigarettes soon seeped from his office and throughout the house.

She popped a movie into the VCR, something old and black & white and taped from TV so the picture quality was awful, but it didn't matter; her TV was so small she could barely see the picture anyway. She looked at the Christmas tree, a sad little half-dead pine he brought home from the nursery. There was only *his* gift underneath; nothing for her. Things were bad between them, and if they didn't get better soon she feared she would be moving back in with her parents. But she wanted him to have his gift. Maybe he would smile again, even if only once more.

What did she want from him? What was her Christmas wish? All she wanted was for them to be happy, like they once were.

All at once the lights went out, the TV went black, and the orange glow from the space heaters faded faster than the sound of their humming coils could even go silent.

"You forgot to pay the electric bill" she shouted.

The entire house went pitch black. The only thing she could see was the glow of his cigarette as he came into the room.

"No, I did not," he said, "I paid it." But he didn't remember for sure whether he had, or not.

Without power there was no heat, and with nothing to beat it back the cold launched its assault into the leaky old house, starting beneath the door. The wind howled and banged against the windows, whistling through the cracks between the thin panes of glass and the peeling wood.

"And do you have to smoke in the house?" she said. "I thought you quit."

"I did, for six weeks; or did you forget?"

"It was five weeks."

"But you were just bound and determined to see me fail. You just kept turning the screws.

*"The bills are past due.*

*"Why are you only working half-shifts?*

*"The rent is late again.*

*"Maybe you should look for another job.*

"How could I win? If I quit my job, I couldn't pay the bills. If I kept my job, I couldn't get out from under. And you just kept needling me, nagging me, not a word of encouragement or even an *I know it's hard on you quitting smoking; I'm so proud of you quitting; you're doing the right thing for--"*

"The baby," she said.

"Nag, nag, nag," he said, and he went back into his office. Nothing to do in the dark, but at least he was away from her.

Without power, without heat, the crooked old house became cold like an ice box; and even though she wrapped herself in a nice, cushy blanket, she began to shiver.

Enough of this, she thought. Let him freeze in here. She snatched up the car keys from the kitchen table on her way out the door. At least in the car she could warm herself by the heater and listen to the radio.

He heard the door slam behind her, but she wasn't a door-slammer. It must have been the wind, he thought.

He went into the living room and sat down by the tree. The smell of dying pine brought back fond memories of Christmas past, before they were married, before all the fighting, and before what happened about the baby. He just didn't want to talk about it, and it seemed that's all she wanted to talk about. He wrapped himself up in the blanket and lit another cigarette. He'd rather freeze in here than be warm out there, with her.

It was almost too hot inside the car. Delly leaned her head against the window and the cold spot felt good against her warm forehead. She was thinking of days gone by and how happy they had once been, how happy they were always before they got married and even how great things were just after. Then the whole thing about the baby happened and she watched him come unraveled before her very eyes. If only he would talk to her, she was sure they could get past it. But he never would talk about it. All he ever did was call her a nag, then disappear into his office.

Suddenly the driver-side door flew open and Jimmy came barreling into the seat. The whole car shook and the air was so cold that all the heat was sucked out instantly. Delly shivered. The door closed and Jimmy shook the snow from his hair. All this happened in just one second.

"You forgot to take the car to the shop?" she said. "The battery light is still on."

"Probably just a short," he said. "I'm not worried about it; the radio still works." He turned up the radio, and at the same time the music faded out and the DJ faded in.

*Good Rockin' Christmas Eve out there to all you yuletide yodelers, this is Shiverin' St. Nicky Nick carrying you through mistletoe midnight and into the merry ol' morning with a reminder, before you take that last yawn by the yule log, don't forget to let your water faucets drip through the night cause it's gonna be unBEARably cold, with grisly low temps and polar-like conditions...*

"I think you forgot?" she said.

"I don't recall," he said.

"Well you had better check or else the pipes may freeze."

"I'm not going back out there," he said. "You go check if you're so concerned."

She just stared at him.

"No way I'm going back out in that cold for nothing, no-how." Staring at him.

"Say whatever you want," he said as he lit a cigarette, "but nothing and nobody is getting me back out there."

Yet before he could get even a second puff a sudden gust of air walloped its way through the little crack in the window he made, and with gale-like force blew the cigarette out of his hand and right into her lap. She started tossing and shrieking, slapping at the red cherry and smashing it into sparks that flew up and into her face, leaving black smudges and gray streaks all along her cheek and nose.

"I swear, Jimmy Dillingham Young," she said, clenching her jaw; and if there had been a backseat she would have climbed over and curled up in it. But Jimmy's little car was a two-seater, and there was nowhere to go; so she curled up anyway and crossed her arms and buried her head down deep.

Just then, the car began to hiccup. It choked and coughed like a wheezing old chain smoker, then spit and sputtered and breathed its last breath. It had run out of gas.

"You didn't get gas while you were out?" she said.

"Sure I did, but I only had a couple dollars on me, and it was freezing outside. I filled it up last week. You're the one who used it all going to your mother's."

It didn't matter. All the shouting in the world wasn't going to bring the car back again.

"But who cares?" said Jimmy. "The heater still works."

Delly put her hand to the vent. He was right. The air was still warm, comforting.

On the radio they were playing old-time Christmas classics, like *Grandma Got Run Over By a Reindeer*, and Cheech & Chong's *Santa Claus & His Old Lady*, and Delly remembered when she used to think they were funny. She thought back to sunny days, and that made her feel warm inside; so much so that she didn't even notice the air was now blowing cold. She shivered. Jimmy started playing with the thermostat. He tried starting the car. Neither did any good.

"At least we still have the radio," said Jimmy, and just as he did all the power was gone, as if it had been stolen away into the night. There was dead silence in the car.

"The battery light, you forgot to get it checked," she said.

"Nag, nag, nag," he said, and he turned to leave; but outside the wind was howling and beating against the window, pounding on the windshield and rattling the doors. He wasn't going anywhere.

That was it, he thought; that was all he could take. For months now he couldn't stand the sight of her, the sound of her, the thought of her. So many times he had come so close to telling her they were finished and that he was leaving, but never did. This time, with nowhere for him to run, he would finally end it for good.

"Who cares?" he shouted. "What the hell does it matter now?"

She was afraid, first of the wind and the cold, and now of him. They were but inches apart and he was shouting at the top of his lungs.

"What do you care anyway," he said, looking away; and now he was feeling sorry for himself. For a moment he forgot he was going to tell her they were finished.

"What does that mean?" she said, and as fast as his ire had turned to self-pity, her fear had turned to concern.

"Oh, you know," he said.

But she didn't.

"Everything, all of this started with the thing about the baby," he said.

There, he said it—finally. Now it was out.

"What do you mean?" she said.

"My smoking," he said. "The reason I quit. It was all about the baby."

"I thought you started again *because* of the baby."

"I started again because I couldn't handle the pressure any more. Where were you? I needed you."

"I, I didn't know it was that bad. I thought you started again because you wanted to."

"Of course I didn't want to. You have no idea how hard it was for me to quit. It was like the whole world was pressing down on me. I felt all alone. Where else could I to turn? That's why I started smoking again."

"What about you not wanting me, you know, as a woman?" she said. "Was that all about the baby, too?"

"Of course I wanted you," he said. "But if I did, if we did, well you know, the baby."

And there it was. There was the whole thing about what happened with the baby, or to be more precise, about what didn't happen about the baby. For you see, the whole thing about the baby was that there was no baby; there never was.

"Didn't you want to have a baby?"

"Of course I did," he said, "I still do, but I can't get past the situation."

"What situation?"

"Our situation. Look how we live; look *where* we live. Not only do we not have a nice home, we don't own a home at all, we rent." She could feel what he was feeling.

"We have no money saved. I couldn't even afford a decent Christmas tree."

She took hold of his hand.

"We don't even have the right kind of car, and I couldn't afford to get it fixed even if I wanted to, that's why I never took it to the shop."

She parted his hair.

"So this is what this was all about," she said, "all these months, you always at your computer, you not wanting to touch me because you were afraid we *would* make a baby. You were afraid you just weren't ready to be a daddy?"

He looked down. "Well, you were always watching TV, I figured you didn't want me anyway."

"Sweetheart," she said, "no one is really ever ready for a baby. All these things you're worried about, I think about them too. But you have to understand, you deal with the responsibility as it comes. It's not like the baby will just be here instantly, then in the next moment off to school, then grown. It all happens very slowly. There will be plenty of time to deal with the responsibilities. Shoot, when my mother became pregnant with me my parents were living with my grandparents, and they didn't even have a car. You'll see. It's like swimming. You just have to jump in."

"Hell," he said, "I can't even afford to keep the car running. Now we may freeze to death."

Delly climbed over onto his lap. No amount of talk in the world was going to make him feel like a man again. "No one is going to freeze tonight," she said.

And then, right there in the car, they were as man and wife for the first time in a long time. Afterward, she remembered it was exactly this same way the very first time they were together, and in the very same place. She smiled her loving smile, a look he had not seen in far too long. He was so in love with her. The thought of them ever being apart was just unbearable. His feelings from earlier, from the past few months, might as well have never been at all.

There was a warmth and a glow about Delly, like she was on fire and the flames flickered all around her; but when Jimmy looked past her he realized she wasn't the one on fire—it was the house.

Not even half an hour ago he would have torn out in a panic, running all around the raging inferno frantically trying windows while dodging falling timbers in a mad scramble, desperate to salvage anything he could (his computer), and quite possibly even risking his life. He might have even made a frenzied dash to the neighbors, beating hysterically on their door screaming "Call 911, call 911."

Instead he stood calmly by the car, holding onto the woman he loved, content. The flames were welcomed and warm.

"I thought you had just lost interest in me," she said.

"Why would you think that?"

"Well, I thought that's why you spent all your time at the computer, you know, downloading."

"No download could ever compare with you," he said.

She pulled him tight.

"Funny thing is," he said, "I thought you didn't want to have anything to do with me either."

"What on earth would make you think that?" she said.

"All you ever did any more was watch TV."

"Oh you silly man," she said, "that was just to dull my brain so I wouldn't think how much I missed you, how much I missed us. I could care less about TV."

She giggled.

"What's so funny?" he said.

"Oh, just your Christmas present."

"Why, was it marshmallows?"

"It may be now," she said, "but it *was* a new computer."

He laughed.

"What's so funny?" she said.

"Well, that's about as good as my gift for you."

"You got me something?"

"A new television, a 37-inch, flat-screen LCD TV with built in DVD."

He laughed again.

"What?" she said.

"I ordered it on the Internet. I was just thinking, they're going to have a hard time delivering it now."

They both found humor in this.

He looked at his watch; and just as he did the big hand joined the little hand straight up: midnight.

"Merry Christmas," he said.

"Merry Christmas," she said.

And just then she noticed the water faucet outside was dripping. He had not forgotten after all.

In the glove box of the car were two receipts—she would later find—one for the cable and one for the power: both marked PAID. To think that someone from the electric company had actually come out in this weather—and on Christmas Eve—to shut off their power; well, her brain must have been lost in the blizzard, or taken holiday as well.

He pulled a cigarette from his shirt pocket and began lighting up, and just as he did she said, "I wonder what started the fire?"

He stopped short, waiting for her to say *did you forget to put out your cigarette?* But she didn't say a thing. He looked at her and they both smiled. He heaved his cigarette—the whole pack—into the flames.

What would happen next? It didn't matter to him.

What did matter to him was that his Christmas wish had come true. And what mattered to her was that her Christmas wish had come true. Two wishes for Christmas; two wishes come true.

But in fact, that wasn't entirely accurate, for his wish and hers were the same, and technically speaking, just one wish. So how did *two* wishes come true?

Though long forgotten now, when Jimmy was just six years old, at 11:58 PM on December 24, 1991, he was looking out his window into the sky when across it gleamed a shooting star. He thought it was Santa, so he closed his eyes and made a wish. He wished for a white Christmas. He had never before seen snow, and wondered what miracles it might bring.

What other miracles might this Christmas bring? Maybe he would get that long-awaited call and in just a few weeks toss the game-winning touchdown on Super Bowl Sunday. Maybe by the morning light he would find that his car had magically changed from a pumpkin to a Porsche, or discover suddenly that he was orbiting the earth, floating weightlessly through outer space as all the world watched. Maybe he would be faster than a speeding bullet, more powerful than a locomotive. Maybe he would even be able to leap tall buildings in a single bound. Why not? Anything was possible. After all, today was Christmas.

# THE REUNION

### Jeanette Hollman

*Jeanette Hollman is a wife of forty-one years, a mother, and a grandmother. She has been editor of a college newspaper and reporter for her local paper. She now writes short fiction.*

Angie paced back and forth from the window to the door. Was that a car door she heard? It could be a taxi, she told herself. She was only vaguely aware that Jo Anne was talking to her.

"Angie, come sit down and watch TV. You'll wear a hole in the rug if you keep pacing like that," Jo Anne was saying.

"Oh, Jo, I just can't sit still," Angie said as she peered out the window. "Did you hear a car? I thought maybe I saw some headlights. Oh...I wish the house wasn't set so far back from the street. I can't see anything from here."

"Angie, you don't even know if he's coming home today," Jo Anne said. "You need to relax and quit worrying."

Maybe she was being silly to worry so much, Angie thought, but she didn't know what to think. The last letter she had written to her husband, Joe, had been returned unopened. That was over a week ago and still no word from him.

Joe had been stationed aboard an LST based in Yokosuka, Japan for the last eighteen months. His ship had traveled back and forth to Viet Nam, Okinawa, and the Philippines. They were out at sea a vast majority of the time so mail pickup and delivery were often erratic. Sometimes they'd receive three or four letters at a time, but her letters had never been returned before.

Joe was due to be discharged from active duty at the end of the month. In his last letter, he had only hinted that he might get an early leave, and that they could be in each other's arms by the fifth. Well, today was the fifth, but she hadn't heard anything more from him. If he wasn't on his ship anymore, where was he? Why hadn't she heard from him?

326

Could he already be on his way home? Why would he not have called to let her know he was coming? She had received phone calls from him before when his ship was in port. Was something wrong? The anxiety was overwhelming.

She had written him that she wanted to fly to California to meet him, but that was the letter that had been returned. So, she just had to wait until she heard from him before she could make any plans.

Jo Anne's voice interrupted her thoughts again. "There is still some pizza left. Why don't you try eating something? I'll bet you haven't eaten anything all day."

The thought of food right then made her stomach queasy. She had been tied up in knots all day at work, and couldn't concentrate-- worried sick that something bad had happened. Every time the phone rang at work, her heart jumped and pounded so fast she thought everyone could hear it. She tried typing, but her fingers were all thumbs and she made so many mistakes that the girls decided she should file papers instead.

Her younger sister, Jo Anne, had decided to stay with her instead of going to a movie with her boyfriend. Even though Angie was wrapped up in her own thoughts, she appreciated having Jo Anne there to help her take care of her eighteen-month-old daughter, Carrie. Thank goodness, Carrie was sound asleep already.

She and Joe had only been married eight months when he left for overseas. They had met in September and were married in February, on Valentine's Day. Joe told her he fell in love with her the first night they met. She liked believing that he did, even though she didn't believe in love at first sight.

Her parents had been against them getting married before Joe's tour of duty, but when Angie got pregnant, they decided to elope. It had been a wonderful eight months. They spent as much time together as possible. They were so much in love and life was beautiful.

Angie went into labor while Joe was home on a month leave between basic training and his overseas tour. Joe was there when their baby daughter was born. Joe was so happy to be a daddy. He loved children and all his letters were about how he missed her and their beautiful Carrie.

Suddenly, the phone rang. "Angie, honey. It's Joe," the voice on the other end said.

"Oh, Joe!" she cried, as her heart skipped a beat. "Where are you? I've been so worried! My last letter was returned."

"I'm here in St. Louis--at the airport. I wanted to surprise you. I been in California waiting for my discharge. I couldn't call before then, and after I got my papers, I was lucky to grab the first flight to St. Louis. I just wanted to get home to you and Carrie. I miss you both so much."

"Oh, my God! I miss you so much too. I can't believe you are really home. I'll come pick you up. Meet me in front of the coffee shop in twenty minutes."

Putting down the receiver, she grabbed her purse and car keys and headed for the door. She turned her head back and saw Jo Anne waving for her to go ahead. Carrie was in good hands and Joe would see her when they got home.

Pulling onto the highway, her thoughts turned to the last time she had been to the airport-- the day Joe left for California before flying on to Japan to meet up with his ship. It was her 20$^{th}$ birthday. Joe had hated like hell to leave her on her birthday, but when the Navy calls, you go—birthday or no birthday.

She pictured Joe as he had looked that day in his white navy uniform, his dark curly hair and clean-shaven face. Angie had fantasized about their reunion a hundred times. They would spot one another and simultaneously start running towards each other (in slow motion, of course, like all the great movie love scenes). Their song, "Unchained Melody" by the Righteous Brothers, would be playing in the background. As they embraced and their lips met, she would again smell the familiar scent of English Leather cologne. Everything would be just like it was before he left.

She had waited so long for this day; she could hardly believe that in less than twenty minutes her fantasy would be real. And yet she couldn't help wondering if things really would be the same.

How much had they each changed in the last eighteen months? Physically, she was the same, except her dull brunette hair was now a sexy strawberry blonde. Would he like her new hair color or want her to change it back? From the last picture he had sent her, she could tell that he had lost some weight. He was also sporting a beard. She tried to imagine what it would be like kissing Joe with a beard. She had never kissed anyone with a beard before and the thought made her nose itch.

Emotionally, Angie felt she had matured a lot in the eighteen months they had been apart. Motherhood had changed her. Instead of someone taking care of her, she was now responsible for this tiny wonder she had given birth to. She loved her daughter and wanted to be the best mom she could.

At first, she had moved back with her parents who were very supportive and helpful with Carrie. Her mom took care of Carrie during the day, but Angie did all the mothering in the evening and on weekends. She took a typing class and got a good job at a bank. Eventually she was able to put Carrie in a home day care and rented a small cottage. She learned to handle the finances, something she was not good at before. With Joe's monthly allotment checks, she even opened a savings account and had saved enough for a small down payment on a house. She hadn't told Joe about the savings. She wanted it to be a surprise. In their letters, they each had written about someday owning their own home. She hoped Joe would be pleased and not feel like a failure that she saved the money and not him. Joe liked taking care of her. Had she become too independent, she wondered?

Angie thought she knew Joe like a book when they married, but after only one month, she realized there was still a lot to learn about her husband. On their first month anniversary, they were at a dinner dance in the Starlight Ballroom of the Chase Hotel. The band had taken a break and they were sitting in the bay window overlooking the city. It was a foggy, rainy night and the visibility was poor. Joe started talking about the farm of some family friends where he had spent his summers as a boy. He went on and on about how clean and fresh the air was on the farm, and how much he loved working with the earth, planting and harvesting, and working with the animals. The way he talked about the farm, and the look on his face, it was as if he was saying he wanted to become a farmer and move to the country. She had never been on a farm and being a farmer's wife was something that she had never considered before. She was a city girl and only knew city life.

The whole idea of living on a farm scared her. She excused herself, grabbed her best friend, Pam, and rushed to the ladies room where she sat down and cried.

"Oh, Pam," she blubbered through her tears, "how can I make him happy? I've never been on a farm in my entire life, and I don't think I could ever be a farmer's wife." She tried to picture herself slopping hogs and pitching hay. When she looked in the mirror at her elegant blue chiffon dress and fancy hair-do, she cried even more.

On the way home that evening they both were very quite. When they got into bed, Joe asked her what was wrong. As she talked, he smiled and told her that it was only a dream he had as a youngster, and that if she wouldn't be happy, then it wasn't for him. He just wanted them both to be happy. Would Joe want his dream of living on a farm again, she wondered? Were they both so different now that they wouldn't still be compatible?

She knew from Joe's letters that traveling to the different countries and being so far from home had also changed him; she just didn't know how much. She had heard that many of the Viet Nam veterans who made it home had emotional scars. Being aboard ship, she wondered how much of the war Joe had actually been exposed to. In his letters he had written about his work on the ship and the ports they had docked at, but not much about the war.

As she lit a cigarette, she wondered if he still smoked. If he had quit, would he expect her to? What would it be like being together again? Had their love for one another somehow changed? Did Joe still love her; want her? Had he had any lovers; would he wonder about her? Angie was sure that she still loved Joe. In fact, somehow, she felt even closer to him now than when they were first married. His letters had kept the flame burning in her heart. She had read them over and over until the ink was almost worn off from her handling them. Did her letters do the same for him?

As she turned onto the ramp leading to the airport, her throat tightened. She was so anxious, she could hardly breathe. She pulled into a parking spot inside the airport garage. Almost tripping as she ran, she made her way to the coffee shop. Joe was running towards her. As their lips touched, the whiskers on his beard tickled her nose. Then, she smelled the familiar scent of English Leather cologne. She even thought she heard their song, "Unchained Melody," coming from the coffee shop jukebox. That's when she knew that nothing really important had changed. Her Joe was home and nothing else mattered.

# VALENTINE'S DAY

## Philip Loyd

*Philip Loyd resides in Houston, Texas, and is the author of thirty-seven short stories. His work has appeared in eighty-three publications in seven countries, with one story even produced for radio in Australia. Included in his numerous awards is the Hemingway Center Short Story Prize.*

With a name like Billy Valentine...well, it just goes without saying that a lot would be expected of him on February fourteenth. It's not that anyone ever demanded much, he just assumed such--with his first love; with his high school sweetie; and now with his wife. He just couldn't do like anybody might. With a name like Valentine, he had to do more.

It sure hadn't done anything for him, though. He had broken his piggy bank for Betsy, his first love, and shown her the night of her life: limousine, fine French cuisine, and a night on the town--as nights on the town go for a fourteen-year-old. The limo driver, he thought, tipped his hat sort of funny, and his waiter must have thought him a fledgling sap, what with the size of the tip and all. A swing by the arcade and he was left with only pennies. But he was in love. And with a name like Valentine...well, he was just a natural born romantic.

Yet, their relationship didn't last a week after that. What had he done wrong? He wholeheartedly believed he just hadn't done enough.

Jamie, his high school sweetie for the better part of two years, was the one--he believed--the girl he was going to marry. He thought of it constantly; she talked about it likewise. On February fourteenth he emptied his savings account--money he had set aside for their future, and bought her the most exquisite necklace he had ever seen--beautiful in reverie, stunning in reality as it hung sparkling beneath the light of her smile. She wept and threw her arms around him, whispering, "I love you." This was it, he was sure. This was forever.

But that didn't last either. She asked him if he wanted the necklace back, but of course he didn't. What was the point, anyway?

And now Allyson, his wife. They had been married but six months, as of last Tuesday. They had known one another only three months before that. So this was their very first day of hearts, although February fourteenth was still actually a day away. His mind had been searching for weeks, and though she hadn't directly told him what she wanted, he knew a lot was expected of him.

"Oh, you know what I want," she said, her arms wrapped around him inside the open door.

"No, I don't," he said, looking down into her big, brown eyes, searching for any inkling of confirmation.

"Yes, you do," she said, raising on her tiptoes and kissing him sweetly on the lips. "Of course you do."

He thought he knew; he was pretty sure he did. He had known for the past couple weeks, dozens of days and nights on the lonely road in a thundering, diesel-spewing truck. Across South Louisiana, into Texas and halfway to the Rio Grande, then up to the Oklahoma border, all the way down the Red River through Shreveport, across the Mississippi River into Natchez and back down home again...all for several hours of sleep and a few fleeting moments with her. Then back on the road again, just like tonight. But this would be his last run. After this go round, he would have the money he needed.

"Please, sweetheart," she said, kissing him good-bye, "please be careful."

"I will. I promise," he said.

"And promise me something else," she said, holding him tight.

"Anything."

"Promise me you won't do this anymore. I know we need the money, but it just isn't worth it. We'll make do. We'll get by somehow. I've got my job. It's just that--"

"Yes sweetie--yes," he said, pulling her close, holding her tight. "I promise."

He could see her beneath the porch light as he motored away in the fog.

He felt bad about leaving, and lying (telling her they were way over their heads in debt, yet not telling her the real reason why); but he didn't feel guilty. He was doing it for her. It might hurt now, but it was all for the best. He had wanted to hear her say it, but even so he knew exactly what she wanted for Valentine's Day. That's why he had been on the road so long; that's what kept him going through the lonesome days and nights: the thought of her face as she opened her present. Oh, what a very special Valentine's Day this would be.

He had begun saving just after their wedding, putting a little away here and there, but not quite sure for what. He just knew he had to get her something, all to make up for the trashy looking trailer that was the best he could provide, and the too brief consummation that was more like a conjugal visit than a honeymoon. Then, several weeks ago, it came to him. He was dawdling in the hall by their bedroom door, something he didn't ordinarily do, when he heard her talking on the phone. She was talking to her friend, Amanda.

"A diamond ring," she said loudly, "that's just the most romantic thing. I sure would love that."

He got himself a beer and walked outside. How ashamed he felt. The ring he gave her when he asked her to marry him, well, he certainly couldn't afford a diamond. Even with the money he had put aside, he couldn't now. So he decided then and there, he would do whatever it took to get it for her. If a diamond ring was what she wanted, then by God a diamond ring was what she would get. She would have it even if it killed him. She deserved it, and more. Why she had ever married a hick like himself, he would never know.

As he drove north from San Antonio, with the sun just now peeking over the eastern horizon, he thought about her present: the stunning, sparkling diamond ring he had hocked his every spare moment for. Having stopped for a greasy bite to eat somewhere, some sleepy town he couldn't even pronounce, he carefully opened its box and held the gem up against the light. How exquisite it was in his hand, but, oh, how much more so it would be on her finger. He stretched his legs as his head fell back into daydreaming. He could just see her now, all glowing and pretty in a snow-white sun dress with a soft pink carnation tucked behind her ear, her curly, brown hair bouncing upon her shoulders against a clear blue sky. There she was, splendor in the grass with the wind catching one side of her dress and blowing it against her slender figure, the other side whisking playfully in the breeze. All her friends and the ladies of the town spoke of and admired her. She was the center of attention and envy, barefoot amidst the daisies and daffodils, staring at him and blushing all the while. She deserved that, and so much more.

He snapped back to reality when his waitress asked him if he wanted any more coffee. He just didn't have the time. So he dropped a five-dollar bill next to his untouched plate and shoved the ring box in his pocket on his way out the door. His next stop: Gainesville, Texas, just a few miles from the Oklahoma border.

Just west of Shreveport, with the sun having only dipped over the western horizon behind him, he thought of her present again. Every time he had asked her what she wanted, she only smiled knowingly and looked away for a moment, saying "Oh, quit fooling, you know what I want." Then she would hug him and bury her head in his chest.

At first, he didn't know what she meant; but after thinking on it, he was sure he did. Why else would she have so thoughtlessly left the door open, and spoken so loud? She was neither thoughtless nor loud. And she never talked about things like that, material items--not even to him. She certainly wouldn't have told Amanda Blake, the movingest mouth in town. Allyson would have considered that tacky. So why would she have done it? Only one reason, he reassured himself as he crossed over the Mississippi River Bridge into Natchez. She wanted him to hear, and he had.

He could just hear Amanda's big mouth gossiping on and on about how cheap Allyson's husband was, and how she could never understand her marrying such a rube, not when she could have had any man in town. Allyson would be a laughingstock, and that, he could not allow.

But now, as he drew nearer to home with midnight approaching--nearly twenty-four hours straight on the road--he didn't feel so ashamed. Now, he felt regal. Now his wife could walk through the town with her head held high and be proud of the man she married. Now she wouldn't have to keep her hands in her pockets because of the humiliation on her finger, of what her husband could not provide. He reached into his pocket and ran his fingertips along the smooth box, thinking he had never known felt to feel so soft. Now, she would be proud of him. Now everyone would know that her husband was no hayseed.

As he eased off the highway and coasted down the dirt road--with his trailer just now in view--he pictured her face when he slipped the ring on her finger. She would cry, there was no doubt about that. She always cried when she was happy. He could already feel her heart beating upon his chest. But there was nothing like the real thing, and he readied himself as he came to a slow stop in front of his trailer.

He switched off the key and put on the parking brake, then took the ring box from his pocket, looking out the window and seeing her standing on the porch, waving. Oh how happy she was going to be. He opened the box--just one more peek. Still staring at her, he smiled, then looked down. "What the--" he uttered. The ring was missing. He searched his pockets, then the glove box, then the cab floor and between the crack in the seat. He glanced out the window and could see Allyson looking quite confused. Then, she began walking toward him.

He jumped out the door and signaled for her to stop. She did.

"Just a sec', sweetie," he said as calmly as he could. She mistook his panic for enthusiasm and back-stepped toward the trailer.

He searched again, everywhere, but it was gone. It just wasn't there. He thought hopelessly of where it could be, but had been on the road so long and was so very tired. The important thing, he knew, was where it wasn't.

With a sigh of surrender he closed the cab door, leaving the box on the floor. Then, he walked slowly up the shell driveway toward her, defeat scribbled all over his face.

But hers was aglow, until she saw his. "Sweetheart," she said, concerned, "you look so tired."

"I am," he said, and he fell into her arms.

He just couldn't let her go; he couldn't bring himself to look her in the eye. Then he felt her heart beating upon his chest, and a warm tear drop from her cheek to his. Now, he could look.

"What's wrong," he said, forgetting his troubles.

"Oh, nothing," she said, drying her eyes, "it's just that, that I'm so happy."

"Huh?" he said, bewildered.

"I'm just so happy for my present, my Valentine."

He still didn't understand.

"Thank you," she said, kissing him sweet, "thank you for giving me exactly what I wanted."

For a moment he thought she was being sarcastic, but she was never that way. "I don't understand," he said, and he didn't.

"Don't be coy," she said. "I know you know. You always know exactly what to give me."

"Give you?"

"Yes, silly· you. You're my Valentine."

He stood stunned. How could he have been so blind? "I love you," he said, and that's all he wanted to say.

"I love you," she said, and they stood gazing into one another's eyes, each knowing.

"Come on," she said, taking him by the hand. "Let's go inside and celebrate proper."

He smiled. What had upset him so, he didn't recall.

Beneath the cover of night, and the warmth of their quilt, Allyson held his hand, saying "You know, what we have together is wonderful. Amanda--you know Amanda Blake--well, she's been after her husband to get her a diamond ring; and when I say *after*, I mean *AFTER*. She's practically threatened to leave him if she doesn't get one by today. Poor guy. He's probably been working himself to death, all for some ridiculous ring. I mean, what material object could be that important? I feel sorry for them. That's not love. They can't be happy. If only they had what we have. Sure, maybe we're broke, but at least we have each other. That's why I married you, you know, because I know that you'll always be there for me. That's all I've ever wanted."

In the dark, Billy smiled. Allyson rolled over and he could feel her heart beating upon his chest. He looked toward the door and saw that it was open. It was just open, that's all. What they had was love. What they had was happiness. This was truly Billy Valentine's day.